New Sunday and Holy Day Liturgies

Year A

Revised & Expanded

Flor McCarthy

DOMINICAN PUBLICATIONS

Published (2013) by
Dominican Publications
42 Parnell Square
Dublin 1

ISBN 978-1-905604-19-7

British Library Cataloguing in Publications Data
A cataloguing record for this book is available from the British Library.

Origination by
Dominican Publications

Cover design by
Bill Bolger and Susan Waine

Reprinted(June 2016, August 2019) by
SPRINT-print, Rathcoole, Co. Dublin

New Sunday and Holy Day Liturgies
Year A

Revised and expanded edition

Contents

Introduction

This new revision of *New Sunday & Holy Day Liturgies* contains a considerable amount of new material. For instance, there are several new homilies. Where I have retained the old ones, I have improved them. Apart from the work done on the homilies, there are two major improvements.

The first of these is a better Scripture Note. Unless we understand the message of the Scriptures, we really have no right to be preaching. A lot of work has gone into the preparation of these Notes. While keeping them as brief as possible, I have tried to ensure that they convey the essence of the readings.

The second major improvement concerns parts of the Mass such as the Introduction, the Confiteor, the Prayer of the Faithful. I have tried to relate these to the particular feast (or Sunday) that is being celebrated. The aim of these suggestions is to capture the 'flavour' of that feast, and to convey something of its meaning and spirit. I believe they contain a good mix of comfort, inspiration, and challenge.

These 'inputs' shave been scripted very carefully. In preparing them I have drawn especially on ideas that occur in the Scripture Readings of the day. But I have also drawn on related ideas found elsewhere in the Scriptures, particularly in the New Testament.

For many years when I sat down to prepare a Sunday liturgy my only concern was the homily. But, gradually, I came to realise that there is more to a good liturgy than a homily. Every part of a liturgy should speak.

Flor McCarthy

Season of Advent

Stay awake that you may be ready

Praying with the Word of God today

INTRODUCTION AND CONFITEOR

The liturgical year begins with the season of Advent. The chief characteristic of Advent is joyful expectation.

We are waiting for the final coming of Christ. And we are waiting for his coming at the time of death.

Since both times are hidden from us, we should maintain a state of watchfulness so that we are ready to meet the Lord at any moment. [Pause]

Lord Jesus, you keep us watchful in prayer. Lord, have mercy.

You keep us active in good works. Christ, have mercy.

You keep us true to your teaching. Lord, have mercy.

PRAYER OF THE FAITHFUL

Celebrant: Let us now bring our needs before God, who calls us out of darkness into the wonderful light of his Son.

Response: Lord, help us walk in your light.

Reader(s): For Christians: that they may be watchful and faithful disciples of Christ. [Pause] Let us pray to the Lord.

For world leaders: that in the midst of conflict and division, God may turn their minds to thoughts of peace. [Pause] Let us pray to the Lord.

For grace that the money being spent on weapons of war may be spent instead on the relief of poverty and hunger. [Pause] Let us pray to the Lord.

For all gathered here: that we may be strong in faith and serene in hope. [Pause] Let us pray to the Lord.

For all the dead: that the Lord may free them from the shadows of death and gladden them with the light of his face. [Pause] Let us pray to the Lord.

For our own special needs. [Longer pause] Let us pray to the Lord.

Celebrant: Heavenly Father, may your Son at his coming strengthen us, so that we may shun the works of darkness, and walk in the light of truth and goodness. We make this prayer through the same Christ our Lord.

OUR FATHER

We are waiting in hope for the final coming of God's kingdom. Let us pray for the coming of the kingdom as Jesus taught us.

SIGN OF PEACE

Isaiah said, 'They will hammer their swords into ploughshares, and their spears into sickles. There will be no more war or training for war.'

Lord, grant that the world may put away the weapons of war, so that all of God's children may enjoy the peace and unity of your kingdom where you live for ever and ever.

PRAYER/REFLECTION

Isaiah invites us to go up to the mountain of the Lord.
But who will climb the mountain of the Lord?
Who will stand in his holy place?
'Those who walk without fault and who act with justice.
Those with clean hands and pure heart,
who desire not worthless things,
but whose delight is in the law of the Lord' (Ps 15. Ps 24).
Lord, send forth your light and your truth;
let these be our guide.
Let them bring us to your holy mountain,
to the place where you dwell.

FINAL BLESSING

May the message of Christ, in all its richness, find a home in you.

May the Lord, who is faithful, strengthen and guard you from the evil one.

May the Lord confirm your hearts in holiness so that you may be blameless in his sight.

Sharing the Word of God today

SCRIPTURE NOTE

Advent is divided into two parts. The first part, which runs from the beginning until December 16, focuses on the final coming of Christ. The second part, which runs from December 17 to December 24, focuses on the first coming of Christ at Bethlehem.

The liturgy turns to the passages in Scripture that speak of the two comings of Christ. The Old Testament readings centre on the messianic hope of Israel as it takes shape and grows. The Gospel readings focus on Jesus in whom the messianic prophecies are fulfilled, and on his forerunner, John the Baptist.

First Reading (Is 2:1-5). All of the First Readings of the Advent Sunday Masses for Year A are taken from Isaiah, the greatest of the messianic prophets.

Today's passage contains a vision of a world at peace under God. The most compelling image here is of nations turning their weapons of war (swords and spears) into farm implements (ploughshares and sickles).

But this can happen only when all nations come to the mountain of the Lord (Mount Zion).

It is Israel's task to focus attention on Yahweh, the merciful God who desires the unity of the nations. Hence, the reading ends with a call to Israel to 'walk in the light of the Lord'. It also makes clear that the messianic blessings are meant, not just for Israel, but also for all nations.

Second Reading (Rom 13:11-14). The theme is that of the Second Coming, which the first Christians believed was imminent. Paul urges the Romans to turn away from the darkness of evil, and to walk in the light of Christ. The reading thus continues the theme of walking in the light of the Lord of the First Reading.

Gospel (Mt 24:37-44) The Gospel is a brief extract form Jesus' discourse concerning the Parousia. The emphasis is on readiness. Since the exact time of the Lord's coming is not known, the disciples are urged to be ready to greet him at any time. The phrases 'stay awake' and 'stand ready' convey a sense of urgency.

Let us walk in the light of the Lord

The theme of light figures prominently in today's readings. Isaiah urges us to 'walk in the light of the Lord.' And St Paul urges us to turn away from darkness and live in the light. But what in practice does this entail?

There was a wise and learned rabbi. One day he turned to his pupils and asked the following question: 'How can you tell when the night is passed and the day is on its way back again?'

One said, 'When you see an animal in the distance, and you can tell whether it is a sheep or a goat.'

Another said, 'When you see a tree in the distance, and you can tell whether it is a fig tree or a peach tree.'

Yet another said, 'When you can see a person in the distance, and you can tell whether it is a friend or an enemy.'

There were a number of other answers. But the rabbi was not impressed. Then his pupils pleaded with him to tell them his answer. And he replied as follows: 'It is when you can look at the face of any human being, and see there the face of a brother or sister, because if you cannot do this, then no matter what time it is, for you it is still night.'

We are a people on whom the light of Christ has shone and still shines. We must, therefore, strive to walk in the light – the light of truth and life, the light of holiness and grace, the light of justice, love and peace.

Nevertheless, darkness still has power over us. Darkness can take many forms. Any kind of hatred, enmity, lack of forgiveness, lack of reconciliation, injustice done to another, immoral behaviour – all of these are forms of darkness. A little reflection will help us to identify what form or forms the darkness takes for us.

It takes courage to recognise the darkness in our lives. There is no joy in living in darkness. Quite the opposite. But with God's grace we can free ourselves from the darkness, and experience the joy of walking in the light of truth and goodness.

Let us listen again to the words of Scripture. 'Come, let us walk in the light of the Lord' (First Reading). 'The night is almost over ... Let us give up the works of darkness' (Second Reading). Advent is a wonderful opportunity to respond to these words.

The shortest journey to the light is by doing good. We must try to ensure that the light of truth and justice shines in our words and deeds.

The most precious light of all is the light of love. Without that light the world would be a very dark place. Love lights up everything. It brings hope to a world darkened by selfishness, indifference, and hatred.

The image of God is at its best and brightest in us when we love. People who love shed light around them. They are like a lamp alight and shining. Those who live in the light have nothing to fear from the Lord's coming. Quite the contrary. They ought to welcome it.

Isaiah's dream

Alan Paton was a South African writer. Among the books he wrote was the haunting story, *Cry the Beloved Country,* which so poignantly described the situation in South Africa under apartheid. Paton had a dream. He dreamt of a new day for his beloved South Africa, a day in which there would be justice and equality for all.

For this reason he entered politics, and fought to end the iniquitous system of apartheid. For decades he followed his dream, and worked courageously to make it a reality. It was a dream that many said would never be realised. Yet it was realised. Unfortunately Paton didn't live to see it. He died just before the dawn.

The prophet Isaiah had an even bolder dream than Paton's. He had a dream of universal peace. He dreamt of a world where there would be justice between the nations, an end to war, and the prosperity that would follow when people turned their energies to cultivating the earth instead of making war (First Reading).

Every gun that is made, every warship launched, every rocket fired signifies, in the final sense, a theft from those who hunger and are not fed, those who are cold and are not clothed.

Isaiah's vision was a splendid one. Some believed that it would be realised at the first coming of Christ. Others believe that it will be realised only at his Second Coming. Still others dismiss the dream as mere daydreaming.

Isaiah's dream of universal peace is not mere daydreaming. This is the kind of world we long for. And this is what is promised. This is the 'mountain' towards which we, Christians, spend our lives travelling in hope.

Christians believe that this new world – the kingdom of God – was inaugurated by Jesus. He showed us how to bring about true justice by his preference for the poor; and how to bring about true peace by his teaching on forgiveness and reconciliation with everyone, including one's enemies.

Sadly, far from being a force of reconciliation, religion has sometimes fuelled the flames of conflict. Nevertheless, religion has a great capacity to break down barriers. Of all the things that draw people together, worship alone has the power to turn them into a loving family.

Peace is a core value of the kingdom. Each of us can play a part in the breaking down of barriers and in the making of peace. The first requirement is that we be at peace with one another. Peace is more than an absence of conflict. It is living together as friends.

Reconciliation is another core value of the kingdom. The work of reconciliation begins with a simple gesture. It demands that those who do not normally speak to one another should begin to do so. Practising any kind of apartheid, keeping one's distance, only exacerbates differences.

The new world cannot be achieved without God. But neither can it be achieved without us. Our task as Christians is to keep the vision alive, and to pursue it. Isaiah's vision is both a promise and a challenge. We are the instruments through which God brings it about. We already have in part what we hope for. Already the first fruits of the kingdom are among us.

Story

Martin Luther King was a major figure in the US Civil Rights Movement. His speech, 'I have a dream', was delivered to a quarter of a million supporters on the steps of the Lincoln Memorial in Washington DC in 1963.

In that speech King said: 'I have a dream that one day this nation will rise and live out the true meaning of its creed: We hold these truths to be self-evident that all men are created equal. I have a dream that my four little children will one day live in a nation where they will not be judged by the colour of their skin but by the content of their character. I have a dream today.'

It was a dangerous dream. The pursuit of that dream cost King his life. (He was assassinated in Memphis, Tennessee, on April 4, 1968).

But the dream came true.

Every Christian should have a passion for a just world. Every Christian should have a hunger for a world in which the divine beauty of all God's children will be apparent, and the world will be healed of its disfigurement.

A wake-up call

Today's liturgy addresses a wake-up call to us. St Paul tells us that we must wake up *now* (Second Reading). The Gospel goes even further; it tells us to *stay awake*. But there is more at stake here than just being awake. We could be awake and yet be only half alive, because we have no awareness, no understanding, and no vision.

Each day summons us to awake from sleep. Sometimes we can't wait for the morning to come. We wake up in joyful anticipation. We feel good to be alive. We are thankful to God for the gift of a new day. It gives us a chance to carry on some task we have started, or to begin something we have been postponing, or to repair some damage or neglect in our lives.

Other times we are apathetic about waking up. We greet the new day without enthusiasm. Life may be monotonous or empty for us. Perhaps we are unemployed or retired, and there is nothing to look forward to.

And most of us know or have known days, hopefully not too many, when we dread the approach of morning. We wake up fearfully, and get up reluctantly. Life is dark and burdensome. Perhaps we are old or sickly or alone.

How we greet each morning is very important. If we greet the day with joy and thankfulness, we will bring energy and enthusiasm to its tasks. But if we greet the day with apathy or dread, we will face its tasks in a half-hearted manner, which means we are going into the day with a very severe handicap.

No one has a perfect life. All of us have to face difficulties. It is what we make of these difficulties that matters. Difficulties can be challenges. If we don't like something we should try to change it. If we can't change it, then we should try to change the way we think about it. Complaining won't do us any good. Circumstances are beyond our control but our conduct is in our own power.

Advent issues a spiritual wake-up call to us, and has an awakening power. Spirituality is about waking up. Unless we are spiritually awake we are only half living. To be awake spiritually means to be open and receptive, vigilant and active. To be spiritually awake means to be attentive to God and to others.

We have two choices: we can be a *watcher* or a *sleeper*. It is easy to be a sleeper. But sleepers waste their lives. It's harder but infinitely more rewarding to be a watcher. To watch means to be awake, to be alert, to be concerned, to be active, to be interested, to care. In a word, to be a watcher is to be responsible. Jesus wants us to be *watchers*.

This is the first Sunday of a new liturgical year. Another year has come and gone. Time is passing. We must seize the day. We shall pass through this world but once. Therefore, any good that we can do, to any human being, let us do it now; let us not defer it or neglect it; for we shall not pass this way again. We have nothing to fear and everything to gain from answering Advent's wake-up call.

Story

It may take a shock or at least a jolt of some kind to wake us up.

Bishop Samuel Ruiz served in Mexico, and almost 80% of the population of his diocese was indigenous. He became known as the 'defender of the Indians'. But it wasn't always like that. In a talk given in Westminster Cathedral in Lent, 1996, he said:

'For twenty years I was like a sleeping fish. I had my eyes open but saw nothing. I was just proud to be in a diocese where the churches were full. Then one day I saw an Indian tied to a tree and being whipped by his boss because he had refused to work an extra eight hours.'

That incident opened the bishop's eyes and he began to look. What he saw being done to his people spurred him into action. He got involved in negotiations between the Zapatista rebels and the Mexican government.

It is not enough to be physically awake. We need to be awake socially, morally and spiritually. For Christians the worst kind of sleep is that of indifference.

SECOND SUNDAY OF ADVENT
Prepare a way for the Lord

Praying with the Word of God today

INTRODUCTION AND CONFITEOR

In today's liturgy we hear again the lonely voice of John the Baptist: 'Prepare a way for the Lord, make his paths straight.'

It is not God's way that needs to be straightened out but our ways. God's way is straight. But our ways are not always straight. Let us reflect for a moment on the fact that we haven't always walked in God's way. [Pause]

Lord Jesus, you guide the humble in the right path. Lord, have mercy.

You smooth the way for the upright. Christ, have mercy.

You seek out and save the lost. Lord, have mercy.

PRAYER OF THE FAITHFUL

Celebrant: Let us pray for the coming of a new age of justice and peace for all peoples.

Response: Lord, you save the poor and the needy.

Reader(s): For the followers of Christ: that their lives may bear witness to the values of the Gospel. [Pause] Let us pray to the Lord.

For world leaders: that through goodwill and co-operation they may strive to put an end to war and oppression. [Pause] Let us pray to the Lord.

For those who have lost their way in life: that God may guide them into the right path. [Pause] Let us pray to the Lord.

For the members of this community: that we may be steadfast in faith, joyful in hope, and untiring in love. [Pause] Let us pray to the Lord.

For our deceased relatives and friends, and for all the faithful departed: that God may lead them to the green pastures of eternal life. [Pause] Let us pray to the Lord.

For our own special needs. [Longer pause] Let us pray to the Lord.

Celebrant: Almighty and ever-loving God, take the blindness from our eyes, the weakness from our wills, and the hardness from our hearts, so that we may know the happiness of those who walk in your way. We ask this through Christ our Lord.

OUR FATHER

Jesus is the way that leads to the Father. Let us pray to our heavenly Father as he taught us.

SIGN OF PEACE

Isaiah said, 'In those days, the wolf will live with the lamb, calf and lion cub will feed together. They will do no hurt, no harm, on all my holy mountain, for the country will be filled with the knowledge of the Lord.'

Lord, look not on our sins but on the faith of your Church, and grant that all of God's children may enjoy the peace and unity of your kingdom where you live for ever and ever.

PRAYER/REFLECTION

The voice of John the Baptist was a lonely voice.
There are many lonely voices in our world,
coming not only from the prophets,
but also from the victims of injustice and neglect.
Lord, help us to listen to these voices.
Above all, help us to listen to *your* voice,
whispering to us in the wilderness of our hearts,
telling us that we are loved by you,
and that we are to love one another.

FINAL BLESSING

May you know the happiness of those who walk in God's way.

May the Lord turn the darkness before you into light, and rough places into level ground.

And may you never doubt but that God will fulfil the promises he has made to us in Christ.

Sharing the Word of God today

SCRIPTURE NOTE

First Reading (Is 11:1-10). The reign of David was the high point in the history of Israel. But his successors failed wretchedly. Still, the hope remained that a future king would succeed where his predecessors failed.

Here Isaiah foretells that even though the family tree of Jesse (David's father) has been reduced to a mere stump, nevertheless from that stump a new shoot (a new king) will spring. He goes on to sketch a portrait of the true king.

He will be filled with the Spirit of Yahweh and endowed with all the virtues of his ancestors: the wisdom and understanding of Solomon, the prudence and might of David, the knowledge and fear of the Lord of the patriarchs and prophets. Thus endowed, he will judge fairly and be the champion of the poor.

Furthermore, he will restore paradisal peace. The images used here have become proverbial: prey and predator feeding and sleeping in harmony; a child keeping an adder as a pet.

Second Reading (Rom 15:4-9). Paul sees Jesus as the one through whom God fulfilled his promises. He highlights the value of hope. The scriptures show that those who hope refuse to give up. By urging us to treat others in the same friendly way Christ has treated us, the reading continues the theme of peace and harmony of the First Reading.

Gospel (Mt 3:1-12). Matthew portrays Jesus as the one who fulfils the Old Testament promises. Here he introduces us to John the Baptist and his mission. He has John preaching in the wilderness as Isaiah had foretold, and baptising with water in anticipation of the one who would baptise with the Holy Spirit.

He tells us that John wore a garment made of camel hair with a leather belt round his waist, and his food was locusts and wild honey. Why these details about his clothes and diet? Because this is how Elijah was clothed (2 Kgs 1:8). Thus Matthew is telling us that John is that 'Elijah' who was to come.

John begins with the urgent call: 'Repent, for the Kingdom of Heaven is close at hand.' For John, the Messiah would be an uncompromising judge. He issued a particularly grim warning to the Pharisees and Sadducees, who were to unite in common opposition to Jesus.

Vision of a new world

The astronauts were the first human beings to see the earth from space. As they gazed down on the earth from space, they realised as never before that we are one family, with spaceship Earth as our common home. One of them said later: 'The first day in space, we all pointed to our own countries. The second day, we pointed to our continents. By the third day, we were aware of only one Earth.'

The prophets had the same kind of high and wide vision. Isaiah dreamt of a world in which the wolf would lie down with the lamb. A world in which those who were furthest apart from each other would be united in friendship.

But how real is this vision? When one reads a history book, or even just the daily newspaper, at times one is ashamed to be human. What is human history if not wars, wars, and more wars? The world is drenched in blood.

As for the wolf and the lamb living together, often two neighbours, or even two members of the same family, have a falling out and refuse to talk to one another. Should not all hope be abandoned? Is not this great vision of peace and harmony among all peoples just a utopian fairy tale?

The prophets lived in the real world, and were just as dismayed by its horrors and injustices as we are. Yet, through faith in God, they continued to dream of a new world, a world free from injustice and war.

And the prophets weren't idle dreamers. They were people with a vision. They were people with hope. They were people who were fiercely committed. They held a bright vision up before us, a vision unrealisable to humans alone, but realisable with the help of God.

Isaiah's vision lives on in our midst as a task for today and a promise for tomorrow. This vision nurtures our souls and our hearts. It offers us hope when we are tempted to despair, and courage when we are tempted to give up.

Isaiah's vision corresponds to the deepest longings of the human heart, and points to God's ultimate goal for humanity. It's a blueprint of what can be achieved by the grace of God, given so lavishly in Christ.

The marvellous vision of the peaceable kingdom is not an escapist dream. Jesus had a word for the new world. He called it the 'kingdom of God.' It was to establish this kingdom that he came on earth. He inaugurated it. And he now wants his followers to dedicate themselves to the building of that kingdom.

We must keep the vision before us and try to live it out, right where we are. Far from encouraging us to escape from real life, this beautiful vision summons us to get involved. Even though it is a struggle we will never win completely, the struggle is good for us. It awakens everything that is best and precious within us.

Every time we forgive a neighbour, every time we make a child smile, every time we show compassion to a suffering person, take care of animals, prevent pollution, and work for peace and justice among peoples and nations, we are helping the vision to become a reality.

Advent hope

Isaiah was the greatest of the messianic prophets. One of the images he uses to describe the messianic age is that of a lamb lying down with a wolf and having nothing to fear. It is a picture of a time of universal peace – the strong would no longer prey on the weak, or the cunning on the innocent.

Advent is a time of hope and promise. If things and people were perfect, hope would not be needed. Hope is required precisely because we live in an imperfect world.

Hope it a vital part of life. We spend a great deal of our lives longing, waiting, hoping for one thing or another. It is impossible to live when one is completely without hope. Hope is to the spirit what bread is to the body.

Hope doesn't mean sitting back waiting for things to happen. Hope spurs us into action. It is precisely because we have hope that we work so hard. We believe our efforts are worthwhile, and that they do make a difference. Our strength, our commitment, depends to a great extent on the degree and quality of our hope. If we had no hope we would give up.

Cynicism is the enemy of hope. Many refuse to accept hope into their hearts. They say: 'It's no good. Things will never change.' Cynicism comes easy. It requires nothing from us – no trust, no effort, no love.

Hope is not the same thing as optimism. Optimism is the expectation that things will get better, whatever the situation. Hope is the trust that God will fulfil the promises he has made to us (Second Reading), but in his time and in his way.

All great leaders were people of hope. They felt no need to know what the future would look like. They just tried to do what was right in the present, and trusted that God would take care of the future. It was enough for them to know that God is a faithful God.

It is the task of Christians to keep hope alive, and to set an example. However, we must not depend on results, but only on the rightness and truth of the work itself.

Our hope rests in God. St Paul says that scripture shows that people who didn't give up were helped by God (Second Reading). We invest our hopes in flawed human leaders. So why not in God? God has given us his word in Christ. That word is the basis of our hope. And that hope is an anchor of our lives.

What the world needs is new people. Hence, the relevance of John the Baptist's call to repentance. To repent means to change our understanding of what is important in life, and to change our lives accordingly.

But what can we do? St Paul brings it down to everyday realities. He says, 'Treat each other in the same friendly way that Christ has treated you.' If we did as Paul suggests, we would make the world, or at least the corner of it we inhabit, a more hopeful place.

This world will never fulfil our deepest hopes. Only God can do that. Meanwhile, we live in a place called hope. This enables us to keep one foot in the world as it is, and the other in the world as it should be.

John the Baptist and his message

John the Baptist is at the centre of today's liturgy. John was the last and greatest of the long line of prophets who prepared the people for the coming of the Messiah.

The Jews believed that Elijah would return to herald the coming of the Messiah. This belief was based on a literal interpretation of a prophecy of Malachi (3: 23-24). John *was* that 'Elijah'. The account of his clothing (see Gospel) is almost an exact echo of the account of Elijah's clothing in 2 Kings 1:8. Like Elijah, John was an outsider, living in the desert. And, imbued with the spirit and power of Elijah, he brought many Israelites back to God.

However, John's idea of the Messiah was that of a stern, uncompromising judge, who would execute a fiery judgement on sinners. He issued a particularly grim warning to the Pharisees and Sadducees, who were to unite in common opposition to Jesus.

He said, 'Already the axe is laid to the roots of the trees, so that any tree which fails to produce good fruit will be cut down and thrown on the fire.' This is a terrifying image.

John preached a messiah in his own image. Jesus' idea of the Messiah was radically different from that of John. For Jesus, the Messiah would be a saviour. For John, the Messiah would be an uncompromising judge.

But we must remember that, like the first Elijah, John was an Old Testament man. His preaching of repentance resumed the cry of the great Old Testament prophets. Still, there are many things we can learn from him.

We should heed his call to repentance. The repentance he called for was not the weak 'feeling sorry' for our sins, much less did it consist of sterile regrets about what has happened. It was nothing less than a radical change of heart.

We can learn from his commitment to the task God gave him, namely, that of preparing the way for Jesus. He devoted himself heart and soul to that task. No half-heartedness for him.

We can learn from the kind of life he lived. His was not a life of self-indulgence. It was a life of self-discipline and self-sacrifice. This made him a credible witness for Jesus.

We can learn from his humility. He didn't seek to be the star of the show. He was content to be in a supporting role. He recognised that Jesus was more important than he was. He declared, 'I am not fit to undo the strap of his sandals' (Jn 1:27).

We can learn from his generosity of spirit. He was inviting people to a feast, knowing that he himself would not sit at the table. That takes greatness.

And finally we can learn from his courage. He confronted Herod for unlawfully taking his brother's wife, and paid the price, dying a martyr's death.

THIRD SUNDAY OF ADVENT
Courage! The Lord is coming to save you

Praying with the Word of God today

INTRODUCTION AND CONFITEOR

In today's First Reading the prophet Isaiah says to us, 'Courage! Do not be afraid. God is coming to save you.' And in the Gospel we see Jesus, our Saviour, at work, enabling the blind to see, the deaf to hear, and the lame to walk.

In this Eucharist we encounter the same compassionate Jesus. Let us not be afraid to let him see our wounds and handicaps. [Pause]

Lord Jesus, you take the blindness from our eyes. Lord, have mercy.

You take the darkness from our minds. Christ, have mercy.

You take the hardness from our hearts. Lord, have mercy.

PRAYER OF THE FAITHFUL

Celebrant: God is faithful to his word and true to his promises. With confidence, then, let us bring our needs before him.

Response: Come, Lord, and save us.

Reader(s): For the pope and the bishops: that they may be strong, loving and wise in their leadership of the Church. [Pause] Let us pray to the Lord.

For those who hold public office: that they may carry out their responsibilities faithfully and well. [Pause] Let us pray to the Lord.

For those who are working for the relief of suffering in others: that they may know comfort themselves. [Pause] Let us pray to the Lord.

For prisoners: that they may not lose hope. [Pause] Let us pray to the Lord.

For this community: that God may strengthen our faith so that we do not lose heart in times of difficulty. [Pause] Let us pray to the Lord.

For our own special needs. [Longer pause] Let us pray to the Lord.

Celebrant: God of love and mercy, take pity on our weakness. May the coming of your Son confirm our faith, strengthen our hope, and deepen our love. We ask this through Christ our Lord.

OUR FATHER

God is the source of our strength and our hope. Let us pray with confidence to the Father in the words our Saviour gave us.

PRAYER/REFLECTION

John the Baptist was no reed swaying in the wind.
A reed swaying in the wind is a symbol
of the person who is easily influenced,
and who has no convictions of his/her own.
Still, we can learn something from the humble reed.
The fact that it is able to bend
means that the greatest storm cannot uproot it.
Lord, teach us that there is strength
in weakness and suppleness,
and give us the wisdom to know
when to bend and when to stand firm.

FINAL BLESSING

May you be brave in times of trial.

May you never lose faith in God's love for you.

And may you be good witnesses for the Gospel by the love and joy you radiate.

Sharing the Word of God today

SCRIPTURE NOTE

First Reading (Is 35:1-6.10). This contains a message of hope for God's people in exile. The prophet assures them that God himself is coming to their rescue and will lead them back to Zion. He uses the image of the desert, made fertile by rain, to portray the confident hope that God would restore his people, crushed by misfortune. Their most crippling disabilities – blindness, deafness, and lameness – will be relieved when God sends salvation to his people.

Second Reading (Jam 5:7-10). St James is talking about the second coming of Jesus. He urges the kind of patience and hope farmers show in waiting for the harvest, and which the prophets of old showed as they waited for the promises to be fulfilled.

Gospel (Mt 11:2-11). John the Baptist's image of the Messiah was that of a stern judge who would execute a fiery judgment. But Jesus did not fit this image. This may account for John's doubts about him. Jesus dispelled John's doubts by showing that he was doing precisely the kind of things that had been predicted for the messianic times (by prophets such as Isaiah). Once again, Matthew presents Jesus as the one who fulfils the messianic prophecies.

Jesus goes on to praise John, declaring him to be a true prophet. He is more than a prophet: he glimpsed the age of fulfilment. As the forerunner of the Messiah, he was in a very privileged position. Yet he himself did not belong to the kingdom. Jesus says that 'the least in the kingdom is greater (more privileged) than he'. Far from diminishing John's role in God's plan of salvation, this increases his heroism in that he prepared the way for a kingdom that he himself would never enter (on earth).

Blessed is the one who does not lose faith in me

All three readings of today's Mass contain comforting words. In the First Reading Isaiah says: 'Courage! Do not be afraid ... God is coming to save you.' In the Second Reading St James says: 'Be patient! Do not lose heart.' And in the Gospel we have the lovely words of Jesus to his cousin, John: 'Happy the person who does not lose faith in me'. These words are now addressed to us. And we should drink them in, because at times we too can find ourselves in dark situations.

1. John the Baptist was a God-fearing man, yet he ended up in a dungeon under sentence of death. We can do our best, but bad things can happen to us. We feel let down by God. We doubt his love for us, and perhaps even his existence. At times like these we should take courage from the words of Jesus: 'Blessed is the one who does not lose faith in me.'

2. We might be going along nicely but then a 'storm' suddenly hits us: unemployment, a serious illness, a tragedy in the family. These kinds of things shatter our faith in the right order of things and even in God. At times like these we should take heart from the words of Isaiah: 'Courage! Do not be afraid.'

3. We all want a lasting peace in the world. Some people are working to bring that peace about. These have every reason to grow weary and give up, because of the apparent lack of progress. Peacemakers should take heart from the words of St James: 'Be patient! Do not lose heart.'

4. Death constitutes the severest test of all for our faith. We live our lives in the shadow of death. All of us, but especially those who have recently

lost a loved one, should take comfort from the words of Jesus: 'Blessed is the one who does not lose faith in me.'

5. Alcoholism and drug addiction are terrible afflictions. They cause misery to the sufferers and their families. The alcoholic and the addict need to seek help. It takes courage to admit one's need and ask for help. May the words of Isaiah encourage such people to seek help: 'Courage! Do not be afraid.'

6. At times we are bewildered by some of the things that are happening in our world: tragedies, wars, famines, genocide ... We feel numbed and powerless, and we wonder where God is, and why he doesn't intervene. In the midst of our bewilderment we should find hope the words of Jesus: 'Blessed is the one who does not lose faith in me.'

7. Some parents have experienced the pain of seeing their children give up the practice of the faith, in spite of having given them good example. These parents should take courage from the words of St James: 'Be patient! Do not lose heart.'

8. Thousands of men and women, many of them young and poor, are locked up in our jails. Many of them have very little hope for their futures. May all prisoners find hope in the words of Jesus: 'Blessed is the one who does not lose faith in me.'

Each of us knows the kind of situations that cause us to be fearful. We can't stop ourselves from feeling afraid. But we must not allow our fears to cripple us. Courage is not never feeling afraid; it is feeling afraid and going on in spite of it.

Faith is a fragile thing. We mustn't be surprised when doubts arise within us. God will understand our doubts in a world like this. But blessed are we if we do not lose faith in Jesus. And twice blessed are we if, like Jesus, we are able to show forth our faith in deeds of love and mercy.

Are you the one?

John the Baptist had spent his life preparing the way for Jesus. But now, locked up in a dark dungeon with the threat of death hanging over him, it seems that he was having doubts about Jesus. What could have brought this about?

John's idea of the Messiah was radically different from that of Jesus. For John, the Messiah would be a stern, uncompromising judge, who would execute a fiery judgement on sinners. But Jesus didn't fit this image. Jesus made it clear that he had come, not to condemn sinners, but to save them.

John preached bad news; Jesus preached good news. John prophesied the judgement of God; Jesus prophesied the salvation of God.

Moreover, their approaches were very different. John was an ascetic, who lived apart from the people. Jesus mixed with the people, eating and drinking with sinners. John was severe. Jesus was radiantly friendly.

All of this may have accounted for John's doubts about Jesus. Now that his life was ending, he wanted to know for sure if Jesus was the Messiah or not. Because if Jesus was not the Messiah, it would mean that he had wasted his life and misled the people. So he sent two of his disciples to question Jesus.

When the two asked Jesus, 'Are you the one who is to come?' Jesus might have replied with a straightforward, 'Yes, I am', and left it at that. But he didn't. Instead of trying to convince John's messengers with words, he pointed to the works he was doing: 'the blind see, the lame walk, lepers are made clean, and the good news is preached to the poor.' These were exactly the kind of things that had been predicted for the messianic times by prophets such as Isaiah (First Reading). In other words, Jesus is the one who fulfils the messianic prophecies.

There is well-known saying: Actions speak louder than words. Jesus was quite happy to let his deeds speak for him. And they did so, eloquently.

If someone were to ask us: Are you a disciple of Jesus? We would probably reply: 'Yes, I am.' But would there be enough evidence in our lives to bear this out?

John's situation was a grim one – locked up in a dungeon with the threat of death hanging over him. Jesus knew that he needed comforting and reassurance. So he sent a special message to him: 'Blessed is the one who does not lose faith in me.'

These beautiful words are now spoken to us. Blessed are we if we do not lose faith in Jesus. And twice blessed are we if we show forth our faith in deeds of love and mercy. People will encounter Jesus in us. Where can Jesus be found today? If he is to be found at all, it will be in us his disciples.

Story

Once a group of salesmen were attending a convention. They had assured their families that they would be home in time for dinner. But the meeting ran late so they had to run for the train. Tickets in hand, they dashed along the platform. One of them knocked over a table supporting a basket of apples. But neither he nor any of his companions stopped to help the young boy who manned the apple stand.

All reached the train and boarded it with a sigh of relief. But then one of them felt a twinge of compassion for the boy whose apple stand had been overturned. Saying good-bye to his companions, he returned to the scene of the accident. He was glad he did so. He discovered that the boy was blind.

The salesman began to gather up the apples. As he did so he noticed that some of them were bruised. He took out his wallet and handing the boy some money he said, 'Here, take this for the damage we did. I hope we didn't spoil your day.' As he started to walk away, the bewildered boy called after him, 'Are you Jesus?'

Are you Jesus? In a sense, he was. Because he acted like Jesus. Where can Jesus be found today? He will be found in us his disciples, if we show forth our faith in deeds of love and mercy.

The witness of John

John the Baptist was the last and greatest of the long line of prophets who prepared the way for the coming of the Messiah. One thing we require from prophets is that they live what they preach. When there is a wide gap between the message the prophet is preaching and the kind of life he is living, a serious shadow is cast over the authenticity of the message.

John was exemplary in this regard. He was a living example of what he preached. No wonder people flocked to see and hear him. In today's Gospel Jesus himself testifies to the greatness of John.

Firstly, he paid tribute to the kind of person John was. John was no reed swaying in the wind. A reed swaying in the wind is a symbol of the person who is easily influenced, and who has no convictions of his own. John was not like that. He was his own man – a strong personality and a man of principle.

Secondly, Jesus paid tribute to John's lifestyle. His lifestyle was that of an ascetic. He didn't go in for a life of ease and comfort. He lived, not in a palace, but in the desert – a place of sand, thorn bushes, heat, cold, hunger, thirst, and loneliness.

Nor did he go in for soft and expensive clothes. He wore a garment made of camel hair. Nor did he eat rich and expensive food. His food was the scant food of the desert – locusts and wild honey.

Thirdly, Jesus stressed the greatness of the role John played. John was a prophet, but more than that. He was the messenger sent by God to prepare the way for the Messiah. He devoted himself totally to that mission. And when his task was done, he moved aside to make way for Jesus.

Yet, for all his greatness, John missed out of the greatest thing of all. He did not see the coming of the kingdom of God. This increases his heroism in that he prepared the way for a kingdom that he himself would never enter (on earth). Those who did were more blessed and more privileged than he.

We have the joy of belonging to the kingdom of God. We must ask the Lord to help us to live in such a way that the blessings of the kingdom will be evident in our lives.

Story

The great astronomer, Galileo, was born near Florence, in the year 1564. He confirmed what Copernicus had said, namely, that it is the earth that goes round the sun, and not vice versa. His discoveries greatly enlarged our knowledge of the universe. Yet he spent his last years in darkness.

When summoned before the Inquisition he wrote: 'Alas, poor Galileo, your devoted servant, has been for a month totally and incurably blind; so that this heaven, this earth, this universe, which by my observations and demonstrations, I have enlarged a thousand fold beyond their previous limits, are now shrivelled for me into such a narrow compass as is filled by my own bodily sensations.'

Galileo reminds us of John the Baptist. Like Galileo, John the Baptist ushered in a new age – the age of Jesus. And like Galileo, he died in darkness. Both paid a high price in bringing the light to us.

We should draw inspiration from both, but more especially from John. He is a wonderful example of unselfish love. But it is in Jesus that our hope lies. He is the one who gives meaning to all our work and suffering, to our living and dying.

FOURTH SUNDAY OF ADVENT
Let the Lord enter

Praying with the Word of God today

INTRODUCTION AND CONFITEOR

We are on the edge of Christmas. We must use the little time that is left to prepare ourselves to celebrate this lovely feast worthily.

Let us begin by calling to mind our sins and our need of God's salvation. [Pause]

Lord Jesus, you come to us in an outrush of goodness and a downpour of light. Lord, have mercy.

You come to enable us to live in holiness and justice all the days of our lives. Christ, have mercy.

You come to guide our feet into the way of peace. Lord, have mercy.

PRAYER OF THE FAITHFUL

Celebrant: God sent his Son into the world, not to condemn the world, but to save it. Let us bring our needs before him with confidence.

Response: Come, Lord Jesus.

Reader(s): For Christians: that free from fear, they may serve God in holiness and uprightness all the days of their lives. [Pause] Let us pray to the Lord.

For the Church: that through its deeds, the compassion of Christ may be seen and felt in the world. [Pause] Let us pray to the Lord.

For all rulers: that Christ, the Prince of peace, may guide their feet into the way of peace. [Pause] Let us pray to the Lord.

For those for whom Christmas will be tinged with sadness: that God may visit them with his comfort. [Pause] Let us pray to the Lord.

For our families: that Christmas may find them united in peace and love. [Pause] Let us pray to the Lord.

For this community: that through the grace of his coming, the Lord may keep us strong in faith, joyful in hope, and untiring in love. [Pause] Let us pray to the Lord.

For the dead, whose absence is felt intensely at Christmas: that Christ may lead them into the joyful vision of his glory. [Pause] Let us pray to the Lord.

For our own special needs. [Longer pause] Let us pray to the Lord.

Celebrant: God of love and mercy, fill our hearts with your love as we prepare to celebrate the birth of your Son. Give us the grace to overcome our fears, and keep us joyful in your service. We ask this through Christ our Lord.

OUR FATHER

Let us pray to our heavenly Father as Jesus our Saviour and Brother has taught us.

PRAYER/REFLECTION

Some people find Christmas Day a lonely day.
If that should happen to us, let us not be alarmed.
Loneliness can be a grace.
A sense of something missing
is God's way of calling us into greater intimacy with himself.
In the end, only God can satisfy the longings of our hearts.
Lord Jesus, help us to welcome you into our hearts this Christmas,
because without you our hearts will always be empty.

FINAL BLESSING

Through the grace of his coming, may the Lord dispel your fears.
May he banish your sorrows.
And may he illuminate your hearts with his love.

Sharing the Word of God today

SCRIPTURE NOTE

First Reading (Is 7:10-14). Here the prophet is counselling king Ahaz at a moment when the dynasty of David was in jeopardy. The king refuses a sign from God. He has no confidence in the help of Yahweh, and has already made up his mind to seek the help of Assyria. But he will have a sign whether he wills it or not. The queen is, at this moment of crisis, pregnant with the one who will continue the threatened line.

Second Reading (Rom 1:1-7). In these opening lines of his Letter to the Romans, Paul designates himself 'servant' and 'apostle', called by God to preach the Good News that God's ancient promises have been fulfilled in Jesus Christ. He stresses the twofold identity of Jesus. Through human origin Jesus is son of David; through his resurrection from the dead he is Son of God.

Gospel (Mt 1:18-25). Matthew seized on Isaiah's prophecy and refers it to Jesus. Born of a virgin, he will embody God's promise to be with us, and continue David's line for ever. The Gospel stresses the twofold identity of Jesus. He is the son of David because Joseph, his legal father, was descended from the line of David. But he is more than that. He is also the Son of God.

All three readings deal with the identity of 'the One who was to come'. The identity of the child was vaguely glimpsed in the Old Testament. The New Testament reveals the true identity of this special Child (Jesus).

Twofold identity of Jesus

There is a danger that Christmas becomes something that concerns only the children. While it's true that a child (the Christ Child) is at the centre of Christmas, Christmas concerns us all.

The prophet Isaiah talked about the coming of a very special child (First Reading). But there is no reason to believe that he knew just how special that child would be. Every king of David's line was an embodiment of God's promise to be 'with us'. But Christians believe that Isaiah's prophecy only found its complete fulfilment in Jesus.

The Second Reading and the Gospel reveal to us the true identity of this special Child (Jesus). No prophecy is fully understood until after its fulfilment.

Both St Paul and St Matthew make it clear that, in the first place, Jesus was the *Son of David*. This was so because Joseph, his legal father, was descended from the line of David. David is one of the greatest figures in the Old Testament. He succeeded Saul as king of Israel. It was he who united the scattered tribes and formed them into a nation. Even though he sinned, he repented. Another sign of his greatness is the fact that he forgave his enemies. Many times in the Gospel Jesus is called 'Son of David'.

To say that Jesus came from the line of David was already a great thing. But he is more than that. He has another, and infinitely greater, identity. He is 'Emmanuel', which means 'God is with us.' He is not just the Son of David but also the *Son of God*. Therefore, he is able to save his people from their sins.

The second identity of Jesus was something that was only gradually revealed and gradually understood. In fact, it was only after he had been raised from the dead that he was accepted as 'the Lord' (see Second Reading). He himself said this identity could not be recognised unless it was revealed by the Father. It is a matter of faith, which is a gift of God.

Jesus has a twofold identity. He is Son of David *and* Son of God. But we too have a twofold identity. As children of our parents we are human beings, which means we have a human dignity. That in itself is a great thing. But Jesus has made us children of God (Jn 1:12). This means we also have a divine dignity. However, our divine dignity, like that of Jesus, is a matter of faith.

Christmas is a wonderful time. It recalls the greatest event in history, namely, the incarnation, when God's Son came down on earth to confer on us the dignity of children of God. It is not true that Christmas is just about children. It is about us all. We may consider ourselves very ordinary. But nobody is ordinary any longer, not since Christ came on earth.

The world today is in danger of drowning in bad news. It is crying out for good news. But the best news of all is the news brought by the angels to the shepherds: 'Behold I bring you good news of a great joy for all the people. This day a Saviour is born to you. He is Christ the Lord.' We should open our hearts to receive the good news.

Joseph: a just man

When the birth of a child is imminent, the focus naturally shifts to the mother. But surprisingly in today's Gospel the focus is not on Mary, but on Joseph.

St Matthew's infancy narrative is centred on Joseph. The annunciation is made, not to Mary, but to Joseph. In his genealogy of Jesus, Matthew tells us that Jesus is 'son of David'. He is 'son of David' through Joseph, who was descended from the line of David.

But how could that be if Joseph was not his physical father? Because by naming the child, Joseph became his legal father.

Even though he was not the physical father of Jesus, but only the legal father, nevertheless, he was a father to Jesus, and Jesus was a son to him. Later Jesus was known simply as 'the son of the carpenter' (Mt 13:55).

What kind of person was Joseph? Today's Gospel refers to him as a 'just' man. The Hebrew Bible doesn't use the word 'saint' to describe someone who is holy. It uses the word 'just' (or 'righteous'). It applies this term to someone for whom duty is everything – someone who makes the Law of God the guiding rule of his/her life. By referring to Joseph as a 'just' man, the Bible goes right to the core of who and what he was.

Joseph was a man of action rather than words. Through these opening chapters of Matthew's Gospel he never says a word. It is in his actions that we see his love for the Christ Child and for Mary. St John says that love is not a matter of words or speech but of truth and action (I Jn 3:18). This could be a summary description of Joseph.

In today's Gospel we see his sensitivity and unselfishness in the way he handled the difficult situation in which he found himself. His wife, Mary, was with child, even though they had not lived together yet. He didn't think of himself and his own honour. He thought of Mary and her honour. He made up his mind to do the right thing, even if it proved costly for himself. By taking Mary to his home he saved her from becoming a social outcast.

Joseph was always there – in a supporting role, playing second fiddle to Mary. Humble and God-fearing, you won't find him complaining. He just got on with it. He steered the holy family through the rough times – doing his best, providing for his family. He is typical of many fathers.

Joseph doesn't get the credit he deserves. But that's how it often is with the real saints – they are hidden, and therefore go unnoticed. But that doesn't mean they have no effect on the world. There are on earth those whose integrity, kindness, and generosity make up for the greed and self-ishness of others. In a dark age they maintain a candle light of humanity and so guarantee that darkness doesn't have the last say.

A child is not likely to find a father in God unless he finds something of God in his father. Jesus spoke about God as a father. His human experience of a father would have come in great part from Joseph.

Joseph is a model for parents, and especially for fathers. But he is also a model for all of us. He shows us how to walk blamelessly in the sight of God.

Celebrating Christmas

How should we celebrate Christmas? Two extremes should be avoided. The first is to regard Christmas as a purely religious feast to be celebrated only in church. The other extreme is to see Christmas as a purely secular event without any spiritual meaning.

In reality, our celebration of Christmas has many layers. (Anthony Philpot identifies four layers. See *The Tablet*, Dec 1998).

The top layer is the consumer Christmas: insistent Christmas carols, reindeer and Santa Claus, and the aggressive merchandising of all kinds of goods. It encourages acquisitiveness among children, and creates anxiety about overspending and fatigue among adults. It is a Christmas with a hollow core. To eliminate the religious aspect of Christmas is to remove the heart and soul of Christmas.

Next comes the Charles Dickens layer – cards depicting snowy scenes, roaring fires, turkey and ham, plum pudding and mince pies. It is the Christmas of the family get-together, of goodwill to all, of philanthropy and expansiveness. These values have a lot to be said for them. Most people have a shot at this version of Christmas. But in the absence of faith what does it amount to? A little uplift. A few pious phrases. A few gifts given and received. And then everything goes on as before.

The third level is that of the crib, which depicts for us what Christmas is all about. This is the layer of the school Nativity play, which re-enacts the Christmas story, and which for all its simplicity can be deeply moving.

The fourth and deepest layer is the spiritual one. It is the story of how in Israel 2000 years ago a baby was born. In the person of this baby, God's Son took our nature upon himself and entered our world in weakness and in love. He came to remind us that we are God's children and have an eternal destiny.

There is a tendency to dismiss, or even condemn, the first three layers, and to see the spiritual layer as the only true one. This is based on the supposition that the spiritual and the material are opposed to one another.

There can be no such thing as a purely spiritual Christmas. Christianity includes matter as well as spirit. What we have to do is find a connection between the secular marketplace and the spiritual content of the feast. Much of the buying and selling that occurs at Christmas fosters gift-giving, good works, joy, and the affirmation of family ties.

We tend to make a clear division between the sacred and the secular. But you won't find that in Christmas. At Christmas these are so interwoven that they seem to be one and the same thing. The Christmas story (as related in the Gospel) is set, not in a church or temple or synagogue, but in the everyday world.

The birth of Jesus in a crowded Bethlehem is a reminder to the secularists among us that God cannot be kept out. And to the religious among us it is a reminder to avoid any notion of confining God within our institutions, because God cannot be kept in either.

Christmastide

Praying with the Word of God today

INTRODUCTION AND CONFITEOR

Christmas means the coming of God's light into the darkness of our world. This night is made radiant by the light of Christ.

Let us call to mind the darkness that overshadows our world, and the darkness in which we ourselves sometimes walk. [Pause]

Lord Jesus, your light shines in the dark, and no darkness can overpower it. Lord, have mercy.

You grant that those who follow you will never walk in darkness but will always have the light of life. Christ, have mercy.

To all who accept you, you give the power to become children of God. Lord, have mercy.

PRAYER OF THE FAITHFUL

Celebrant: With Christ's light shining on us this night (day), let us pray to God for our own needs, the needs of the Church, and of the world.

Response: Lord, let your light shine upon us.

Reader(s): For Christians: that they may be a source of light to a darkened world. [Pause] Let us pray to the Lord.

For all rulers: that Christ, the light of the world, may show them the path to peace. [Pause] Let us pray to the Lord.

For the sick and the lonely: that Christ, who shared our humanity, may renew their strength and rekindle their hope. [Pause] Let us pray to the Lord.

For prisoners: that Christ's light may shine into their darkness. [Pause] Let us pray to the Lord.

For those who grieve the loss of a loved one: that the light of God's consolation may shine on them. [Pause] Let us pray to the Lord.

For those who are away from home this Christmas: that they may know they are not forgotten. [Pause] Let us pray to the Lord.

For our loved ones who have died, and whose absence is felt intensely at Christmas: that Christ may bring them into that light that no darkness can quench. [Pause] Let us pray to the Lord.

For our own special needs this Christmas. [Longer pause] Lord, hear our prayer.

Celebrant: God of love and mercy, may the coming of your Son scatter the darkness of the world, and make it radiant with his light. May we follow him faithfully, and come to the light that shines for ever. We ask this through the same Christ our Lord.

OUR FATHER

God has called us out of darkness into the wonderful light of his Son. Let us pray to our heavenly Father as children of the light.

SIGN OF PEACE

Lord Jesus Christ, when the angel appeared to the shepherds to announce your birth, the glory of God shone round them.

Grant that the light of God's glory may shine on us tonight, so that we may enjoy the peace and unity of your kingdom where you live for ever and ever.

PRAYER/REFLECTION

Christ is the Light of the world.
His light was not lit once in Bethlehem and then extinguished.
It continues to shine for all who believe in him.
It is a persistent and defiant light
that no darkness can overpower.
Lord, may the radiance of your glory light up our lives,
and bring us safely through the shadows of this world
to our homeland of everlasting light.

FINAL BLESSING

May the coming of God's Son scatter the darkness of the world, and make it radiant with his light.

May you taste the joy the shepherds experienced when the light of God's glory shone round them on that first Christmas night.

May you follow Christ's light faithfully on earth, and come to the light that shines for ever in heaven.

CHRISTMAS DAY MASS
Today a Saviour is born to us

Praying with the Word of God today

INTRODUCTION AND CONFITEOR

'Behold, I bring you news of great joy. Today a Saviour has been born to you; he is Christ the Lord.' This is the message that was given by angels to the shepherds.

Today this marvellous message is announced to us. Let us open our hearts to receive the 'great joy'. [Pause] Christ is the 'great joy'.

Lord Jesus, you reveal to us the mystery of the God's unconditional love for us. Lord, have mercy.

You reveal to us the mystery of our dignity as children of God. Christ, have mercy.

You reveal to us the splendour of our eternal destiny. Lord, have mercy.

PRAYER OF THE FAITHFUL

Celebrant: God sent his Son into the world, not to condemn the world, but to save it. Let us pray to God with confidence for our needs, the needs of the Church, and of the world.

Response: Lord, let your salvation reach to the ends of the earth.

Reader(s): For Christians: that Christ may fill their hearts with joy and make them heralds of his Gospel. [Pause] Let us pray to the Lord.

For all rulers: that Christ, the Prince of peace, may guide their feet into the way of peace. [Pause] Let us pray to the Lord.

For the sick and the lonely: that Christ, who shared our humanity, may enflame their hearts with his love. [Pause] Let us pray to the Lord.

For our families: that Christmas may find them united in peace and love. [Pause] Let us pray to the Lord.

For those who are away from home this Christmas: that they may know they are not forgotten. [Pause] Let us pray to the Lord.

For the dead, whose absence is felt intensely at Christmas: that Christ may lead them into the joyful vision of his presence. [Pause] Let us pray to the Lord.

For our own special needs this Christmas day. [Longer pause] Let us pray to the Lord.

Celebrant: God of love and mercy, may the coming of your Son among us confirm our faith in your love for us, and deepen our love for you and for one another. We ask this through Christ our Lord.

OUR FATHER

God loved the world so much that he gave his only Son, so that everyone who believes in him may have eternal life. Let us pray to the God of love as Jesus taught us.

SIGN OF PEACE

Lord Jesus Christ, at your birth the angels sang: 'Glory to God in the highest, and peace to his people on earth.'

Grant that we, who have heard the message of the angels, may enjoy the peace and unity of your kingdom where you live for ever and ever.

REFLECTION

In our times Christmas has become very commercialised.
However, this mustn't blind us to the true meaning of Christmas.
When thick smoke rises up, catches in your throat,
and brings tears to your eyes, it is because a fire has been lit.
At the coming of Christ, a fire was lit on our earth,
a fire that will never die.
At this fire we experience the warmth of God's love,
and the glow of human fellowship.
Let us not be afraid to come in out of the cold
and warm ourselves at this fire.

FINAL BLESSING

May the Lord fill your hearts with wonder and joy as he filled the hearts of the lowly shepherds.

Like the shepherds, may you go back to your homes, glorifying and praising God for his goodness to us.

And may the peace of Christ reign in your hearts and in your homes.

Sharing the Word of God today

SCRIPTURE NOTE

VIGIL MASS

First Reading (Is 62:1-5). This reading contains a message of hope for God's people at one of the lowest moments in their history. Jerusalem lay in ruins. The city's plight reflected that of the nation as a whole. Israel, once God's bride, was now like a widow bereft of children. However, her husband, God, has not forgotten her. There will be a new wedding feast, and God and his people will be like newlyweds again. The prophecy of Isaiah was fulfilled in Jesus.

Second Reading (Acts 13:16-17.22-25). This is part of a sermon given by Paul to Jewish listeners. He gives a brief summary of their history, from their call by God, to their liberation from Egypt, to the kingship of David. This was the era of promise. But now the promise is fulfilled in a descendant of David – Jesus. He is the Saviour whose coming was heralded by John the Baptist.

Gospel (Mt 1:18-25). Here we have Matthew's account of the annunciation of the birth of Jesus. The annunciation is made, not to Mary, but to Joseph. (Matthew's infancy narrative is centred on Joseph.)

In his genealogy of Jesus, Matthew has told us that Jesus is 'son of David'. He is 'son of David' through Joseph, who was descended from the line of David. But how could that be if Joseph was not his physical father? Because by naming the child, Joseph became his legal father. Matthew sees the annunciation of the birth of Jesus as the fulfilment of the prophecy of Isaiah 7:14. Born of a virgin, Jesus will embody God's promise to be with us, and continue David's line for ever.

MIDNIGHT MASS

First Reading (Is 9:1-7). This is a prophecy about the coming of a Saviour-child, who will rescue his people from the darkness of oppression. The child who is to be born will be the complete ruler and will inaugurate a reign of justice and peace. Christians see the prophecy as fulfilled in Jesus, the 'Prince of Peace' and the 'Light of the world.'

Second Reading (Tit 2:11 – 14). Even as we recall the first coming of Christ in Bethlehem, we are still waiting for his second coming at the end of time. St Paul tells us how to should live in the meantime.

Gospel (Lk 2:1-14). Luke's account of the birth of Jesus forms the Gospel for the first two Masses of Christmas.

The story reflects the faith of the post-resurrection Church. The same titles that Peter attributes to the risen Jesus, 'Lord and Messiah' (Acts 2:36), are now applied to the newborn child by the angel: he is 'Christ the Lord'. Luke's chief concern is theological. Every detail in the story serves this purpose. This is not to say that there is no historical basis for what he recounts.

The birth of a child appears to us to be a very private and family event. But St Luke does not think that way about the nativity. He sets the birth of Jesus in the context of the Roman Empire, thus giving it a cosmic significance. His mission is to bring peace to the ends of the earth.

Unwittingly, Augustus becomes an instrument of God by ensuring that Jesus (the Messiah) was born in the town of David. His rejection at the inn anticipates his rejection by the Jewish people as a whole. Mary is shown to be a caring mother, wrapping the child in swaddling clothes and laying him in a manger-cradle. Her loving care reflects God's care.

Since Jesus was born in poverty, it is fitting that the news of his birth was first announced to simple shepherds. This also reflects Luke's concern for the poor and the lowly.

DAWN MASS

First Reading (Is 62:11-12). The context here is the joyful return of the exiles from Babylon. Jerusalem will no longer be a forsaken city; the Lord will redeem its people. The joy of the exiles returning from Babylon is a foretaste of the joy Christians experience at the birth of Jesus.

Second Reading (Tit 3:4-7). Without any merit on our part, God has lavished his love on us. Freely he sent his Son to cleanse and renew us, and make us heirs to eternal life. Our response to God's gift must be one of humble thankfulness and acceptance.

Gospel (Lk 2:15-20). This is a continuation of the Gospel of Midnight Mass. Having received the good news of Jesus' birth, the shepherds go to Bethlehem to see for themselves what has come to pass. Having seen, they go back to their flocks 'glorifying and praising God.' The shepherds are the forerunners of future believers. Their joy anticipates the blessings that will come to those who accept Jesus as the Saviour sent by God.

Mary herself lives in the darkness of faith, puzzling over the meaning of all that has happened. She is pictured here as a loving and capable mother, and as a reflective woman.

Day Mass

First Reading (Is 52:7-10). This is a hymn of exultation at the return of the exiles from Babylon. A messenger runs ahead of them along the mountain ridges to announce the good news of salvation and peace. Watchmen on the ruined walls of Jerusalem take up the joyful message and relay it to the city. The reading ends with a note of universality: all the ends of the earth will see the salvation of God. At Christmas we should rejoice at the good news of our salvation in Christ.

Second Reading (Heb 1:1-6). The whole history of God's dealings with his people in the past was a preparation for the coming of his Son at a particular moment in history. In Old Testament times God spoke to his people through the prophets, but only in a fragmentary way. Now God speaks through his Son. His Son is the reflection of his glory and bears the very stamp of his nature. We have something better than the shepherds had (the word of an angel); we have the word of God's own Son.

Gospel (Jn 1:1-18). This is the prologue to John's Gospel, a text that brings out the full identity of the child born in Bethlehem. Here John introduces the main themes that will be developed in his Gospel – life, light, darkness, truth, witness, glory, and the world. It cannot be fully understood until the Gospel as a whole has been read.

Through a summary of history, the prologue shows that from the dawn of creation God has been with humans, and in spite of darkness and ignorance, has invited them to knowledge of and intimacy with himself. But in Jesus something infinitely better is offered to us.

According to John, the Son descends from heaven to our level, and ascends back to heaven bringing us up with him to the divine level. The prologue describes the Son in heaven and the descent; the Gospel describes the Son walking among us and his final elevation and return to the Father.

The first part (vv. 1-11) presents the Son as the Word. Eternally present with God, the Word brings life and light to the world. Sadly, the world, and even his own people, rejected him. This negative response is something that recurs throughout John's Gospel.

The second part (vv. 12-18) indicates a more positive response. The Word becomes one of us and lives among us. To those who accept him he gives the power to become children of God.

Christmas: feast of the heart

I once asked a class of school children if they thought Christmas made people more selfish or more generous? Every single one of them said it made people more generous. I believe they got it right.

In his autobiography, *An Only Child,* the Irish writer, Frank O'Connor, tells how one Christmas Santa Claus brought him a toy engine. On Christmas afternoon his mother took him to visit the local convent where she had gone to school. As the engine was the only present he had received, he took it with him to show it to the nuns.

While he was in the convent one of the nuns brought him to visit the crib in the chapel. As he looked into the crib he noticed something that upset him very much. What upset him was the fact that the Child Jesus was lying there in the manger without a single present.

He knew exactly how that child felt – the utter despondency of realising that he had been forgotten. Turning to the nun, he asked, 'How come the Holy Child hasn't got any toys?'

'His mother was too poor to afford them,' the nun replied.

That settled it. His mother was poor too, but at Christmas she had always managed to buy him something, even if it was only a box of crayons.

Taking the toy engine, he climbed into the crib, and placed it in the outstretched arms of the Child. And he showed him how to wind it as well, because a little baby would not be clever enough to know a thing like that.

In that instant Frank O'Connor grew from being a child concerned with his own feelings and inclinations, to a young man capable of noticing and responding to the needs of others.

This story shows us the power of Christmas. The power of Christmas consists in its ability to move the human heart like nothing else. Charles Dickens said, 'Christmas is the one time in the long calendar of the year when people freely open their shut-in hearts to one another.'

Christmas was born out of love and carries on out of love. It was God who began it, when he made a gift to us of his most precious possession – his only Son.

Christmas is a feast of the heart. It reveals to us what the heart of God is like. And it reveals to us what our hearts are capable of. The human heart is a great repository of compassion.

To close our heart is to begin to die. To open our heart is to begin to live. And the extent to which we open our heart is the extent to which we will experience the great joy the angels announced to the shepherds: 'Behold, I bring you news of a great joy; today a saviour is born to you in Bethlehem.'

Joy is the fruit of love. Joy is an over-flowing heart. So, if we want to taste the 'great joy' what we have to do is open our hearts to receive the gift of God, and then open our hearts to one another. The Lord made himself poor and needy in order to make us strong and generous.

The light of Christ

We celebrate Christmas at the darkest time of the year. It's a time when we appreciate the value of light. Christmas is a pool of light in the inky darkness of winter.

The Christmas liturgy is filled with references to light. For instance, the First Reading of Midnight Mass contains these wonderful words: 'The people that lived in darkness have seen a great light; on those who live in a land of deep shadow a light has shone.' Light is used here as a symbol of liberation and salvation.

Mother Teresa told of how one day in Melbourne, Australia, she visited a poor man whom nobody knew existed. He was living in a basement room that was in a terrible state of neglect. There was no light in the room, and he rarely opened the curtains. He didn't seem to have a friend in the world.

She started to clean and tidy the room. At first he protested, saying, 'Leave it alone. It's all right as it is.' But she went ahead anyway. As she cleaned, she chatted with him. Under a pile of rubbish she found an oil lamp covered with dust. She cleaned it and discovered that it was a beautiful lamp. And she said to him, 'You've got a beautiful lamp here. How come you never light it?'

'Why should I light it?' he replied. 'No one ever comes to see me.'

'Will you promise to light it if one of my sisters comes to see you?'

'Yes,' he replied. 'If I hear a human voice I'll light the lamp.'

Two of Mother Teresa's Sisters began to visit him on a regular basis. Slowly, things began to improve for him. Every time the sisters came to visit him he had the lamp lighting. Then one day he said to them, 'Sisters, I'll be able to manage on my own from now on. But do me a favour. Tell that first sister who came to see me this. Tell her that the light she lit in my life is still burning.'

All of us have experienced darkness in our personal lives – disappointment, failure, sorrow, grief, broken dreams. Moreover, we live in a world darkened by greed, violence, and tragedy.

But Christ lit a lamp in our world. He fulfilled the beautiful prophecy of Isaiah: 'The people that lived in darkness have seen a great light; on those who live in a land of deep shadow a light has shone.' Christ is that great light.

He shed light through his teaching. But it was especially through his deeds that his luminous goodness manifested itself. Countless people came to him in darkness and went away bathed in light.

His light was not lit once in Bethlehem and then extinguished. It continues to shine on all who believe in him. It is a persistent and defiant light that no darkness can overpower.

Christ's light shines on us tonight (today). Therefore, we need not be afraid of the darkness of the world, because Christ is the light of the world. At baptism the lamp of Christ's love was lit in our lives. However, we might keep the lamp all our lives without realising that its light is extinguished. If that should have happened, Christmas is the ideal time to relight it.

The lamp of Christ's love burns in this world only with the oil of our lives. Christmas provides us with a marvellous opportunity to make the small corner of the world we inhabit a brighter place.

And the extent to which we do this, is the extent to which we will experience the *great joy* the shepherds experienced when the light of God's glory shone around them that first Christmas night.

Connecting with God

Every year when the time comes to send out my Christmas cards, I get out my address book. Invariably I come across a name, and exclaim, 'Gosh! I haven't heard from him/her for ages.' I'm faced with a decision: will I or won't I send a card?

Most of us have someone like that in our lives, someone with whom we communicate only now and again. At one time we may have been very close. But, for one reason or another, a distance grew between us, and we got disconnected. Now we have reached the sorry stage where we are communicating only through a card at Christmas.

It shows that a relationship suffers from neglect just as surely as a garden does. And a relationship such as I described is not a nourishing one. In truth, it has no real impact on our life.

We can get disconnected from God too. We may have been very connected with God as children, but over the years we got disconnected from God. It's not necessarily that we stop believing in God. It's just that we stop communicating with God. And to stop communicating with God is effectively to have no relationship with God.

When we allow ourselves to get disconnected from God, an enormous loss occurs. Life is unintelligible without God. The author, Salman Rushdie, said, 'When I was young, I was religious in an unthinking way. Now I am not, but I am conscious of a space where God was.' And Pascal said, 'What a melancholy thing it is to be without God.'

A close and loving relationship with God is at the core of the Christian faith. Here is where Christmas comes to our aid. By bringing us back to our childhood, Christmas can put us back in touch with God. It's easy to connect with God at Christmas because God seems very close to us and very loving towards us at this time: 'The Word [God's Son] was made flesh and dwelt among us.'

On that first Christmas night the lowly shepherds discovered that the world might have forgotten them, but God had not forgotten them. 'Today a saviour has been born *for you.*' For them? Yes, for them. Their lowly lives were illuminated by a sense of God's closeness to them, and love for them.

If we open ourselves to the mystery of Christmas, we too will feel touched by the Divine presence. An inner peace springs from being connected with God, who is love.

But an occasional gesture, even a big one, will not sustain a meaningful relationship. It is the little gestures that sustain a relationship. This is why we need religious practice. Religious practice nourishes faith, and sustains that relationship with God we all need.

In his Gospel St John says, 'To all who accept him he gave power to become children of God.' We are not grains of sand or specks of dust. We are God's precious sons and daughters, and heirs to the kingdom of heaven.

And Christmas also provides us with an opportunity to reconnect ourselves with other people, especially our families. This too will bring us peace.

The incarnation: a mystery of love

Once there was a little boy who was given the gift of a tin soldier for Christmas. For a while it made him happy. But then he thought that it would be fun if the soldier came to life. Suppose he could really bring him to life. Imagine turning a tin soldier into a real little person. It would involve turning the tin into flesh.

But then the boy wondered how the tin soldier would take to such a radical change. Suppose the tin soldier didn't like it? Suppose he didn't like the idea of becoming flesh, because to become flesh would leave him open to all kinds of hurt, and of course to the greatest hurt of all – death. No, the boy didn't think the tin soldier would want that. He would think you were killing him, and would do everything to prevent it.

Yet Christians believe that this is what happened in the Incarnation. Jesus, the Son of God, became flesh like us. Not only that. He became a baby, and before that, a foetus inside a woman's body. He accepted the humble road that begins in infancy. He became poor, weak, little, and gave himself into the hand of history, trusting only in the heavenly Father.

There you have the Incarnation. The Incarnation means that the indescribable mystery that we call God can be found in someone entirely like you and me. God entered our world on our terms. Here was no safe remoteness. Here was closeness. Here was involvement at the deepest level. In the immortal words of St John: 'The Word [God's Son] was made flesh and lived among us.' Now we have a God who understands us when we speak to him about our pain.

In the Hindu tradition, Krishna and Rama are regarded as incarnations of God. But they are not described as having suffered and died. God does not really become man. He only *appears* in human form. Behind this earthly appearance, he remains purely divine and unaffected by the joys and sorrows of human life. But Christians believe that in the incarnation God made himself present to us in the life of one who walked on this earth. In the Incarnation we recognise God's love for us.

God's Son came not in power but in weakness and vulnerability: 'They wrapped the baby in swaddling clothes, and laid him in a manger.' Yet, though he came among us weak and empty-handed, he brought us priceless and everlasting gifts.

By clothing himself in our fragile, mortal humanity, he has shown us that there is nothing fundamentally wrong with that humanity. In that humanity he lived, suffered, and died. And by rising from the dead, he clothed our mortal humanity with immortality.

We are not specks of dust, but sons and daughters of the heavenly Father destined for eternal glory. Though we are made of flesh, we have a divine dignity. But we carry this priceless treasure in a vessel of clay.

As we look at Jesus today, we thank him for joining us where we are, for becoming one of us, for becoming one with us. He does so in order to raise us up. He humbled himself to share in our humanity so that we might share in his divinity. This is the 'great joy' announced to the shepherds. Let us open our hearts to receive the 'great joy'.

Story

The mystery of the incarnation is the central mystery within Christianity. Why would God want to take on human flesh? Why would an infinite power want to limit itself within the confines of history and a human body?

There is a story about a four-year-old child who awoke one night frightened, convinced that in the darkness around her there were all kinds of spooks and monsters. She ran to her parents' bedroom. Her mother calmed her down, and taking her by the hand, led her back to her own room.

There she put on a light and reassured her with these words, 'You needn't be afraid. You are not alone here. God is in the room with you.' At this the child replied, 'I know God is here, but I need someone in this room that I can touch.'

In essence the story gives us the reason for the incarnation, as well as an excellent definition of it. In the incarnation God took on human flesh. Jesus walked the roads of Palestine. He could be seen, touched, and heard.

The incarnation constitutes the very heart of the Christian faith. It is a mystery of love. No wonder Christmas is such an important feast. In Jesus we see our God made visible, and so are caught up in love of the God we cannot see.

FEAST OF THE HOLY FAMILY

Praying with the Word of God today

INTRODUCTION AND CONFITEOR

On this feast, the focus is on the Holy Family. But it also gives us an opportunity to think of our own families. There is no such thing as the perfect family. Even the Holy Family knew tensions, misunderstandings, and sorrow.

To some extent all of our families are wounded by sin. Let us turn to God for forgiveness and healing. [Pause]

Lord Jesus, you reconcile us to one another and to the Father. Lord, have mercy.

You heal the wounds of sin and division. Christ, have mercy.

You intercede for us with the Father. Lord, have mercy.

PRAYER OF THE FAITHFUL

Celebrant: Let us now bring our prayers before God from whom every family in heaven and on earth takes its name.

Response: Lord, hear our prayer.

Reader(s): For the Christian community: that it may set an example of unity and peace for a world wounded by conflict and division. [Pause] Let us pray to the Lord.

For the human family: that all the different races may realise that they form one family under God. [Pause] Let us pray to the Lord.

For our leaders and legislators: that they may protect the family as the most important unit in society. [Pause] Let us pray to the Lord.

For families in hardship: that they may find support. [Pause] Let us pray to the Lord.

For the deceased members of our families: that they may enjoy the peace of God's eternal home. [Pause] Let us pray to the Lord.

For the particular needs of our own family. [Longer pause] Let us pray to the Lord.

Celebrant: O God, you are the Father of every family. Against you no door can be shut. Convert our homes into fit dwelling places for your Son, who lives and reigns with you and the Holy Spirit, one God, for ever and ever.

OUR FATHER

God has brought together in a single family people of every nation, culture, and language. Let us pray to our heavenly Father as Jesus, our Saviour and Brother, has taught us.

SIGN OF PEACE

Lord Jesus Christ, at your birth the angels sang: 'Glory to God in the highest, and peace to his people on earth.'

Grant that we who have heard the message of the angels may enjoy the peace and unity of your kingdom where you live for ever and ever.

REFLECTION

Of all the influences upon us,
the family is the greatest.
Every family is a small community.
The virtues that build and foster community are:
kindness, gentleness, humility, patience,
mutual forgiveness, and love.
These are not easy virtues to practise.
But when practised with consistency,
the rewards are great in terms of peace
and harmony in the home.

FINAL BLESSING

May the message of Christ, in all its richness, find a home with you.

May you bear with one another in complete selflessness, gentleness and patience.

And may the peace of Christ reign in your hearts and in your homes.

Sharing the Word of God today

SCRIPTURE NOTE

First Reading (Sir 3:2-6.12-14). This is a brief commentary on the commandment: Honour your father and your mother. Too often we think of this commandment merely in terms of obedience on the part of younger children. This reading stresses the obligation of grown children to care for their aged parents.

Second Reading (Col 3:12-21). This beautiful passage describes the atmosphere that should reign in a Christian community and in a Christian household. The virtues mentioned in v. 12 are designed to build and foster community. Love is singled out as the most important one of all.

The demand that wives be subject to their husbands reflects the outlook of another age and of another culture. The first part of the reading, rather than its close, truly depicts the atmosphere of the Christian family.

Gospel (Mt 2:13-15.19-23). The Gospel story is coloured by the story of Moses in Egypt. Just as Moses had to be rescued from Pharoah, Jesus had to be rescued from Herod. The story also contains echoes of the Exodus. Matthew sees Jesus as reliving the history of his people.

Even though the evangelist's intentions are theological, he does cast the Holy Family as displaced persons and homeless refugees.

Reflecting on the Scripture readings

(This is a brief commentary on the Scripture readings for today's feast, and points to their relevance for family life today.)

First Reading. This is a commentary on the fourth commandment: 'Honour your father and your mother.' Too often we think of this commandment solely in terms of the obligation of younger children to obey their parents. That is part of it. But there is another part of it: the obligation of grown children to ensure that their aged parents are able to live out their final years in comfort and dignity. It is this second element that is the focus of the reading.

This has great relevance today. Because of the pace of modern life, the elderly tend to be pushed to the margins. In our strength, it is easy to forget those who are weak and perhaps a little senile. Under God, we owe everything to our parents. The author of Ecclesiasticus asserts that kindness to parents is especially pleasing to God, who accepts it as atonement for sin.

Second Reading. Fraternal love is the hallmark of a Christian community. This love begins in the home. Every family is a small community. St Paul talks about the harmonious atmosphere that should reign in a Christian household. Harmony in the family depends not just on the obedience of the children, but also on harmonious relations among all its members. The parents should set an example by the love they show one another. That love is the best gift they can give their children. Education is important. But what a child sees at home is what matters most.

This harmony can be achieved only by the practice of virtues such as kindness, humility, gentleness, patience, mutual forgiveness, and above all, love. All of these virtues refer to interpersonal relationships, and build and foster community. They are not easy virtues to practise. But when they are practised with consistency, the rewards are great in terms of peace and harmony in the home.

Gospel. In the Gospel we see exemplified the primary obligation of parents, which is to love and care for their children. Here we see what Mary and Joseph did in order to ensure the safety of the Child Jesus. As soon as they learned that his life was in danger, they uprooted themselves and went into exile.

There is a tendency to see life for the holy family as all sweetness and light. This was far from being the case. Matthew casts the Holy Family as homeless refugees. As refugees, they shared the fate of the many uprooted and dispossessed families in our world today. But because of their deep faith in God, and love for one another, they stayed together and came through it.

When the danger passed, they uprooted themselves again and returned to their native country, settling in Nazareth. Nazareth became the place of family life, of prayer, work, and silent virtues, practised with no witnesses other than God, and their friends and neighbours. Nazareth was the place where Jesus lived thirty years of his short life, and is where many people live their entire lives. There Mary and Joseph provided the kind of atmosphere in which he was able to grow 'in wisdom and in favour with God and people' (Lk 2:52).

The family is a fragile entity. Family life requires a lot discipline to make it work. The family is built on bonds of commitment, fidelity, and self-sacrifice. Many parents today make enormous sacrifices for their children. All such parents can draw inspiration from the example of Mary and Joseph.

The role of the family

A tree planted in an exposed place is very vulnerable. It is at the mercy of every wind that blows. If it survives at all, it will be in a twisted and stunted form. If you want a tree to grow to its full potential, you must plant it in a more sheltered place. And not on its own, but with some other trees.

It is vital to get the space between the trees right. They must be close enough to be able to provide shelter and protection for one another. But not so close as to stifle one another. Each must have room to grow to its full potential. This is a great challenge: how to achieve closeness without stifling or dominating one another.

It is not good for a tree to be alone. And it is not good for us human beings to be alone. Alone we are at mercy of cold winds of anguish and loneliness. We need ties of love and friendship with other human beings in order to become what God intended us to be.

This is where the family comes in. In the family we have close ties with people who accept us for what we are. We have people to whom we are special, and who are special to us. We have a clear and unmistakable identity. We have a sense of belonging.

There are two things people suffer from in families or communities. One is the feeling of suffocation, of not being allowed to be oneself. The other is the opposite – a feeling of loneliness, of not really being together.

In the ideal family there is both closeness and space. The closeness means members are able to provide mutual support. The space ensures that they do not stifle one another.

Harmony in the family is achieved by the practice of virtues such as kindness, humility, gentleness, patience, and mutual forgiveness. These are not easy virtues to practise. But when practised with consistency, the rewards are great in terms of peace and harmony in the home.

No family is perfect, but no better place for raising children has been devised. It was by living in a small community of love with Mary and Joseph at Nazareth that Jesus grew in wisdom and in favour with God and people.

'Like the tree that puts roots deep into the clay, each of us needs the anchor of belonging to bend with the storms and continue towards the light' (John O'Donohue).

Parents and children

The First Reading is a commentary on the fourth commandment: 'Honour your father and your mother.' Unfortunately, this commandment tends to be seen in a very narrow way. There are three essential elements in it.

First of all, there is the primary obligation of parents to love and care for their children. We see a beautiful example of this in today's Gospel. There we see what Mary and Joseph did in order to ensure the safety of the Child Jesus. As soon as they learned that his life was in danger, they uprooted themselves and went into exile.

And when the danger passed, they uprooted themselves again, returned to their native country, and settled in Nazareth. In their home in Nazareth they provided the kind of environment in which Jesus was able to grow 'in wisdom, in stature, and in favour with God and with people' (Lk 2:52).

Secondly, there is the obligation of children to obey their parents. At Nazareth Jesus was subject to Mary and Joseph. Mary was a woman of faith, who loved God with all her heart and soul. Joseph is described in the Gospel as being a 'just' man, that is, a man who made the Law of God the guiding rule of his life. It was these two dear people who nurtured Jesus.

At Nazareth Jesus was able to grow quietly in the shadows. Those first thirty years were of crucial importance to him. During those years he was growing, maturing, and ripening. Of all the influences upon us, the family is by far the most powerful. Its effects stay with us for a lifetime.

Thirdly, there is the obligation of grown children to ensure that their aged parents are able to live out their final years in comfort and dignity. It is this element that is the focus of today's First Reading.

This has particular relevance for our times when the elderly tend to be pushed to the margins. In our strength, it is easy to forget those who are weak and perhaps a little senile. There is a saying: 'One mother can take care of ten children, but ten children can't take care of one mother.' Under God, we owe everything to our parents. The author of Ecclesiasticus asserts that kindness to parents is especially pleasing to God, who accepts it as atonement for sin.

Here again the Holy Family serves as a model. As Jesus was dying on the cross he thought of his mother, and entrusted her to the care of his disciple, John. (According to tradition Joseph had already died).

Caring for one's own kin can be difficult. Nobody is more demanding than one's own. Nevertheless, our first and holiest duty is kindness towards our own kin. God is served when we give them a cup of water in his name.

Story

There is a saying: 'One mother can take care of ten children, but ten children can't take care of one mother.' But it's not always that simple, as the following story illustrates.

Once there was a mother bird that had a young fledgling that she loved very much. Then the time came to migrate. Knowing that her fledgling was too young to fly so far, she took it on her back.

And so they began the journey south. At first the flight was relatively easy. But as time went by, the fledgling began to feel heavier, and the mother began to get tired. Nevertheless, she kept on going.

One day while they were resting, the mother turned to her fledgling and said, 'My child, tell me the truth. When I get old and won't have the strength to fly south over the great ocean, will you take me on your back and fly me across?'

'Mother, I can't promise you that,' her fledgling answered.

'And why not?' asked the mother.

'Because I may be busy flying my own children on my back, just as you are doing for me now.'

In cases like this, it's hard to avoid blame and guilt. While the mother's request was understandable, it was a little selfish. One must do what one can to care for one's elderly parents. Our first and holiest duty is kindness towards our own kin. But maybe caring for one's own children is the best way of repaying our parents for caring for us.

SECOND SUNDAY AFTER CHRISTMAS
He dwells among us

Praying with the Word of God today

INTRODUCTION AND CONFITEOR

In the prologue to his Gospel, St John says, 'The Word [God's Son] became flesh and dwelt among us.' Our religion is founded on this great mystery.

As we gather to celebrate the Eucharist, let us call to mind our sins, confident that he who shared our humanity will help us to rise above them. [Pause]

Lord Jesus, you are the light that enlightens all people. Lord, have mercy.

To all who accept you, you give power to become children of God. Christ, have mercy.

You share with us the riches that are yours as the only Son of the Father. Lord, have mercy.

PRAYER OF THE FAITHFUL

Celebrant: Let us pray to Christ our Brother, who assumed our human nature and showed us what we can become.

Response: Lord, hear our prayer.

Reader(s): For the shepherds of the Church: that they may be faithful and compassionate ministers of the Gospel. [Pause] Let us pray to the Lord.

For government leaders: that God may bless them with the gifts of wisdom and integrity. [Pause] Let us pray to the Lord.

For the sick, the lonely, and the dispirited: that Christ, who shared our humanity, may renew their hope. [Pause] Let us pray to the Lord.

For all gathered here: that we may be conscious of the great dignity that we enjoy, and the great destiny that is ours, as children of God. [Pause] Let us pray to the Lord.

For all the dead: that the Lord may free them from the shadows of death and gladden them with the light of his face. [Pause] Let us pray to the Lord.

For our own special needs. [Longer pause] Let us pray to the Lord.

Celebrant: Father, your Son came down from heaven to share our earthly lives. May we come to share his glory in heaven, where he lives and reigns with you and the Holy Spirit, one God, for ever and ever.

OUR FATHER

Jesus is the image of the unseen God. To see him is to see the Father. Let us pray to our heavenly Father as he taught us.

REFLECTION

When God's Son came on earth,
he came dressed in the cloak
of our weak and mortal humanity:
'They wrapped the baby in swaddling clothes,
and laid him in a manger.'
Like an acorn that falls to earth, silently and unheralded,
in a remote corner of the forest,
and which grows into a great oak tree,
so from these lowly origins Jesus grew up
to show us the greatness of our humanity.

FINAL BLESSING

May the Lord bless you with every spiritual blessing.
May he keep you holy and blameless in his sight.
May he enlighten your minds so that you may grasp the greatness of the glory that is promised you.

Sharing the Word of God today

SCRIPTURE NOTE

First Reading (Sir 24:1-2.8-12). This is a poem in praise of divine wisdom, a wisdom that has made her dwelling among God's people. Sirach identifies wisdom with the Law because it is a practical guide to living according to God's will. This emphasis on divine wisdom prepares us for the Gospel. There John tells us that the 'word' (or wisdom) of God became incarnate in Jesus.

Second Reading (Eph 1:3-6.15-18). In the first part (vv. 3-6) Paul introduces the theme of God's plan of salvation, a plan centred in Christ and realised through him. This reinforces the gratuitous nature of our salvation.

The second part (vv. 15-18) is a prayer of thanks for the faith and love of the Ephesians, and also a prayer of intercession that they may really grasp the greatness of the hope that is held out to them.

Gospel (Jn 1:1-18). For the third Mass of Christmas the prologue of John's Gospel is used. This brings out the full identity of the child born in Bethlehem. Here John reaches back even before creation and identifies the newborn child as the Word of God, who brings life and light to the world. To those who accept him he gives the power to become children of God. (For a fuller note on John's prologue, see Christmas, p. 38.)

He lived among us

In an audience Pope Paul VI told how one day, when he was Archbishop of

Milan, he went out on parish visitation. During the course of the visitation, he found an old woman living on her own.

'How are you?' he asked her.

'Not bad,' she answered. 'I have enough food, and I'm not suffering from the cold.'

'You must be reasonably happy then?' he said.

'No, I'm not', she said as she started to cry. 'You see, my son and daughter-in-law never come to see me. I'm dying of loneliness.'

Afterwards he was haunted by the phrase 'I'm dying of loneliness'. And the Pope concluded: 'Food and warmth are not enough in themselves. People need something more. They need our presence, our time, and our love. They need to be touched, to be reassured that they are not forgotten.'

This is a simple yet profound truth. There is nothing as important as *presence* to those we love. Gifts, letters and phone calls are good, but they cannot take the place of presence. Presence brings comfort. Presence brings peace. Time is the best gift we can offer to another person, time just to sit and share.

In today's liturgy we celebrate God's presence with his people. In the immortal words of St John: 'The Word [that is, God's Son] was made flesh, and lived among us.' In Jesus, God is truly present among us. Before starting his public ministry Jesus proved his love by simple presence among the people. He didn't drop in, say 'hello', and disappear again. He came and lived among the people.

In Jesus, God has drawn near to us in person. He has become one of us. This is no loving 'from a distance'. This is loving at close quarters. It shows us how close God is to us, and how close we can be to God in the midst of our sometimes painful and sometimes joyful lives.

When people allow themselves to get disconnect from God an enormous loss occurs, and a huge vacuum results. Life is unintelligible without God. On the other hand, a sense of God's presence with us, and of his love for us, is the only riches worth having. This is the special gift of Christmas. We feel that God is very close to us and very loving towards us.

We also must try to be present to one another, especially to those we love. By being present, we make God's presence real for people.

The Word was made flesh

Words are very important. They can give insight and understanding. They can give comfort and hope. They can take away fear and bring peace. In short, words can be messengers of love.

Nevertheless, words are a poor substitute for deeds. Deeds make words redundant. One small deed can be worth a thousand words.

Antoine de Saint-Exupery, author of *The Little Prince*, was a pioneer airman. His name is synonymous with the golden age of aviation when pilots flew through desert sandstorms and over high mountain ranges in open cockpits carrying mail. By the time the Second World War broke out he had become a famous writer as well.

Saint-Exupery had a great love for his native country, France, which was occupied by Germany. Determined to help his country in its hour of need, he volunteered for active service. However, believing that he was more valuable to his country as a writer than a flier, his friends secured a safe job for him – doing government research. The idea of being a detached witness filled him with horror. He refused to take the job, insisting that he be allowed to fly combat missions.

'But what about your writing?' they said.

'If I did not resist with my life, I would not be able to write,' he replied. Then he added, 'The word must become flesh.'

Eventually a compromise was reached. He was allowed to fly reconnaissance missions. It was during one such mission in 1944 that he disappeared without a trace. His small plane is believed to have been shot down over the sea by a German fighter.

We can only marvel at Saint-Exupery's courage and spirit of self-sacrifice. But what exactly did he mean when he said, 'The word must become flesh.' Words are abstractions. They have to be made concrete. You could talk forever to a starving person about food. But if you really care about him you must one day put a loaf of bread in his hand. That day your word becomes flesh.

Saint-Exupery could have written volumes about patriotism, but what he did spoke louder than anything he might have written. His example helps us to understand today's Gospel. In that Gospel St John calls Jesus the 'Word' of God. In his love for us, God spoke many words to us through creation, and through the prophets. But finally the Word became flesh, in the person of his Son. This is the ultimate proof of God's love.

Jesus was not passing through like a tourist. No, he pitched his tent among us. He became one of us. He joined the human family and lived among us. He knows what it is like to be human, what makes us weep, what makes us fall and stumble and somehow rise and go on again. He assumed our nature, made of the same fragile, perishable material as ours, in order to show us the greatness of our humanity, to show us what it is capable of.

In Jesus, God is present to us in a way that we can relate to, for Jesus in like us in all things but sin. He is a brother to us. He has made us children of God. From his fullness we have all received. In us too the words of Jesus can and must become flesh.

Receiving from his fullness

One day a man and his wife went to an art gallery to see an exhibition of paintings by a promising young artist. On the way into the exhibition they passed a beggar sitting on the steps of the building. The wife gave him a little money, but the husband scolded her, saying, 'I never give anything to his kind, because they only go off and drink it.'

Inside, the husband admired several of the paintings, but one in particular caught his eye. It was a painting of a beggarman. 'It's so realistic,' he exclaimed enthusiastically to his wife. 'Look at the patches on the beggar's coat. See the dirt on his hands, the sadness in his eyes, and the indifference of the passers-by. It's wonderful.' He bought it for a tidy sum of money.

As they made their way out of the museum the beggarman was still sitting there, only this time the husband didn't even see him, so excited was he because of the painting he had bought.

That man was a wealthy man. From his 'fullness' he might have enriched the beggarman. At the very least he could have spoken to him. That simple gesture might have given him back a little confidence in himself.

But he refused to have anything to do with him. He refused on the pretext that if he fed him, he might feed his vices too. If God used the same logic in dealing with us, where would we be?

In today's Gospel St John says of Jesus, 'He lived among us … full of grace and truth … And from his fullness all of us have received.'

'From his fullness we have all receive.' Jesus was like an overflowing fountain. From him God's love and forgiveness flow down like a stream to people.

From Jesus we receive mercy, compassion, love, truth and life. But the aim is not to make us dependent, but to bring us to life so that we in our turn can bring life to others. He yearns to liberate the deepest energies within us. He came to make us rich in the sight of God.

As people who have been enriched by Christ, we must share with others. The greatest good we can do for other people is not to give them of our own wealth, but to show them their own.

EPIPHANY OF THE LORD
Christ the light of the nations

Praying with the Word of God today

INTRODUCTION AND CONFITEOR

The theme of light dominates the feast of the Epiphany. Guided by the light of a star, the Magi came to Bethlehem to honour the Christ-child.

Guided by the light of faith, we are journeying towards the heavenly Bethlehem, where we hope to see Christ in glory.

Let us ask the Lord to strengthen our faith and deepen our trust in his love. [Pause]

Lord Jesus, you are the light the world. Lord, have mercy.

You grant that those who follow you will never walk in darkness but will always have the light of life. Christ, have mercy.

You lead us through the darkness of this world to the radiant glory of your kingdom. Lord, have mercy.

PRAYER OF THE FAITHFUL

Celebrant: Today Jesus is revealed as the light of all peoples. Let us pray that his light may reach the ends of the earth.

Response: Lord, hear our prayer.

Reader(s): For the Church: that it may strive to make Christ known to all nations. [Pause] Let us pray to the Lord.

For the human family: that Christ may be a beacon of hope for all the peoples of the world. [Pause] Let us pray to the Lord.

For those for whom the star of faith has disappeared: that the light of the Holy Spirit may show them the way to salvation. [Pause] Let us pray to the Lord.

For all gathered here: that we may shed light into the path of others by the way we live. [Pause] Let us pray to the Lord.

For all the faithful departed, especially our relatives and friends: that the light of God's glory may shine on them. [Pause] Let us pray to the Lord.

For our own special needs. [Longer pause] Let us pray to the Lord.

Celebrant: Almighty and eternal God, today you revealed your Son as the light of all peoples. May we follow him faithfully, and come to the light that shines for ever. We ask this through the same Christ our Lord.

OUR FATHER

We are no longer strangers or aliens; we are part of God's family. Let us pray to our heavenly Father as Jesus our Saviour has taught us.

SIGN OF PEACE

Lord Jesus Christ, the Magi recognised you as the Saviour of the world and the light of all peoples. May we recognise you in the bread of the Eucharist, and receive you with love, so that we may enjoy the peace and unity of your kingdom where you live and reign for ever and ever.

Jesus is truly the light of the world.
His words have echoed down the centuries,
bringing light to those in darkness
and hope to those in despair.
And for two millennia his compassionate deeds
have illuminated the world.
Lord, keep us strong in faith,
fill our hearts with your love,
and bring us to the glory you promise.

FINAL BLESSING

May your earthly journey be illuminated by the light of a steadfast faith.

May your blameless lives cause you to shine like stars amidst the darkness of the world.

And when your earthly pilgrimage is over, may Christ welcome you into his heavenly kingdom.

Sharing the Word of God today

SCRIPTURE NOTE

First Reading (Is 60:1-6). The exiles returned to Jerusalem to find the city in ruins. Here the prophet cheers them with a vision of a restored city that will become a beacon of light for all the nations. The nations will come from afar to pay tribute to and worship the Lord in Jerusalem. Though addressed to Israel as God's chosen people, the prophecy will be fulfilled in Christ ('the light of the world'), and in the new Israel, the Church.

Second Reading (Eph 3:2-3.5-6). This reading expresses the theological meaning of today's feast: God invites Jew and Gentile to share on an equal footing the benefits of the salvation brought by Christ. This is the mystery, hidden in the past, now revealed in Christ.

It is difficult for us to appreciate the sense of shock that the Jews felt at the fact that the pagans were to be accepted into the Church on equal terms with themselves. This is the aspect that is highlighted in the reading.

Gospel (Mt 2:1-12). For Matthew, the story of the Magi becomes an anticipation of the fate of the good news of salvation, a fate that he knew in the aftermath of the resurrection.

God revealed himself to the Jews through the Scriptures, and to the Gentiles through nature. Hence, Matthew shows the Magi (who were Gentiles) receiving a revelation through astrology. The story highlights the paradox: the Jews who have the Scriptures reject Jesus, while Gentiles come and, with the help of the Scriptures, find and adore him.

There is nothing to be gained by speculating where the Magi came from and what exactly the star was. The star was merely the means by which a great mystery was revealed – the revelation of Christ as the Saviour of the Gentiles too.

The theme of light dominates the feast of the Epiphany as it does the feast of Christmas.

Journeying by the light of faith

The journey of the Magi was bold, courageous, and imaginative. Yet to many it must have appeared foolish, even a little crazy. It can't have been an easy journey. No doubt they encountered many difficulties, and knew moments of doubt and danger. Yet, in spite of difficulties, doubts and dangers they persevered in their quest, and were rewarded when they finally found the Christ-Child.

Though the light of a star guided them, they did not know where the star would lead them. Hence, their journey was very much a journey of faith. And even when they saw the Child, they still had to make an act of faith. Seeing is not necessarily believing.

The journey of the Magi symbolises our journey of faith, and it can serve as a model for that journey. Just as the Magi were guided by the light of a star, so we are guided by the light of faith.

Their journey was one of searching and questioning, of fear and hope, of pain and joy. The faith journey contains all of these elements. It's not an easy journey. Like the Magi we can expect to encounter difficulties, and to experience doubts. To those with no faith it may appear a little crazy. We can draw inspiration from the courage and perseverance of the Magi.

Another thing we can learn from the Magi – they didn't travel alone. They travelled in a little community of three, three believers. In this way they supported one another. We must not try to make the journey of faith alone. We travel with our brothers and sisters in the Christian community, and so are able to support one another.

However, we have one great advantage over the Magi. At the start of their journey they knew nothing about Christ. We already know Christ, and have encountered him in faith. Nevertheless, the fact that we haven't seen him face to face means we haven't yet arrived at our final destination.

And the fact that we have faith doesn't mean we know all the answers. In that sense, we are still searching, still journeying. The journey of faith is the journey of a lifetime, and in a sense we never arrive in this life. The goal of our journey is to arrive at the heavenly Bethlehem, and to see Christ in glory.

A revolutionary feast

I've listened to learned discussions (on radio and television) about the star that led the Magi to Christ – what exactly it was, when it appeared, and so on. But these are the wrong questions. To put the emphasis on the star is to run the risk of missing the meaning of the story. The star was only the means by which a great mystery was revealed.

The word 'epiphany' means a manifestation or revelation. Literally it means a 'drawing back of the veil'. On this day the veil is drawn back on a great mystery, namely, that Christ is the Saviour not only of the Jews but also of the Gentiles. Christ is now the Saviour of the whole human race.

The Messiah who was revealed in Bethlehem to the lowly shepherds is now revealed to three kings (Magi). The shepherds represent those who are near – the insiders (the Jews); the Magi represent those far away – the outsiders (the Gentiles). Thus Christ is shown to be the light of people of every time and place. This is the theological meaning of the feast.

In the Old Testament the Jews are portrayed as God's chosen people. But this was interpreted in a way that involved second-class status for all other peoples. This feast shows that election by God is not a privilege for some but a hope for all.

This is a revolutionary feast. It does for the idea of salvation what Copernicus did for astronomy. It puts an end to every kind of exclusivism. It declares that the kingdom of God is an inclusive place. God invites all, Jew and Gentile, to share on an equal footing the benefits of the salvation won by Christ. (See the Second Reading in particular).

Jesus own mission was restricted to his own people. But he did reached out to Samaritans, foreigners, and all kinds of social outcasts. And in his final commissioning of the apostles he said, 'Go out into the whole world and make disciples of all nations.'

This great and wonderful truth was revealed in embryo when the Magi, three Gentiles, came to honour Christ as their Saviour. The Magi are the first fruits of the Gentile world coming to share in the messianic blessings.

This is a joyful feast. This is an inclusive feast. We who were once outsiders are now insiders. We who were once aliens are now part of God's family.

But it is also a challenging feast. It challenges us to open our minds, our imaginations, and above all our hearts. It is God's will that all people should be saved and come to the knowledge of the truth.

The blessedness of those who believe

The Jews were very privileged. God revealed himself to them in a very special way, namely, through the Scriptures. The Gentiles didn't have the Scriptures. It was through nature that God revealed himself to them, and so Matthew shows the Magi (who were Gentiles) receiving a revelation through astrology.

This was an imperfect revelation, for while it told them of the birth of the 'King of the Jews', it did not tell them where they could find him. The ultimate secret of his whereabouts was locked in the special revelation of God to Israel, namely, in the Scriptures.

But Matthew contrasts the faith of these pagan visitors and the unbelief of the Jewish leaders (civil and religious). The pagans have answered the call to faith in Christ, whereas the chosen people have for the most part rejected it. Matthew highlights the paradox: those who have the Scriptures reject Jesus, while Gentiles come, and with the help of the very same Scriptures, find and adore him.

In this story we see the two main responses to Jesus: acceptance and rejection. Here we have the essential Gospel story in miniature. The story of the Magi and the star becomes for Matthew the anticipation of the fate of the good news of salvation, a fate that he knew in the aftermath of the resurrection.

The essence of the good news is this: God made himself present to us in the life of one who walked on this earth, so truly present that this one, Jesus, was his Son. This revelation was an offence and contradiction to some, but salvation to those who had eyes to see and hearts to believe. The Magi are the forerunners of all those who would come to worship the risen Jesus proclaimed by the apostles.

The story shows us the great benefits of faith. Herod and many in Jerusalem are troubled because of their unbelief. Their fear contrasts with the great joy the Magi felt as they followed the star on the road to Bethlehem. Their joy is the fruit of their faith.

The theme of the happiness of those who believe runs right through the Gospel. You could say that the central theme of the Gospel is the blessedness of those who believe. All of Jesus' preaching had as its aim to elicit faith in people.

However, it is not simply a matter of believing, but of living according to that belief. It is a question of taking risks and making sacrifices because of it (as the Magi did).

The Magi are models of faith. Countless people have followed their footsteps and come to Christ. We count ourselves among those fortunate people. May the fruits of our faith be evident in the hope and joy we radiate.

BAPTISM OF THE LORD

Praying with the Word of God today

INTRODUCTION AND CONFITEOR

Today we celebrate the baptism of Jesus. In celebrating Jesus' baptism, we are celebrating our own baptism too, and renewing its grace within us.

We know that we have not yet fully lived the life of a Christian. Let us call to mind our failures, and ask the Lord's forgiveness. [Pause]

Lord Jesus, in baptism you made us children of the Father and heirs to eternal life. Lord, have mercy.

In baptism you made us your disciples and witnesses for you before the world. Christ, have mercy.

In baptism you made us members of the Christian community, a community dedicated to preaching and living the Gospel. Lord, have mercy.

PRAYER OF THE FAITHFUL

Celebrant: Let us pray that with the help of the Holy Spirit, we may model our lives on that of Jesus, the beloved Son.

Response: Lord, bless your people with peace.

Reader(s): For all the baptised: that they may live out their calling to be other Christs in the world. [Pause] Let us pray to the Lord.

For all in public office: that God may watch over them, so that people everywhere may enjoy religious freedom, security and peace. [Pause] Let us pray to the Lord.

For those who have strayed from the Christian community: that they may find their way back to the flock Christ nourishes. [Pause] Let us pray to the Lord.

For the members of this congregation: that our lives may bear witness to the faith we professed at our baptism. [Pause] Let us pray to the Lord.

For our deceased relatives and friends, who were marked with the sign of Christ's cross in baptism: may they now share his glory in heaven. [Pause] Let us pray to the Lord.

For our own special needs. [Longer pause] Let us pray to the Lord.

Celebrant: Heavenly Father, at his baptism, you revealed Jesus as your beloved Son, you anointed him with the Holy Spirit, and sent him to bring to the poor the good news of salvation. Grant that we may be envoys of his love and peace to the world. We ask this through the same Christ our Lord.

CREED

Before: A profession of faith is an essential part of the rite of Baptism.

This is a longer version of what we professed in Baptism.

After: And, as we say when celebrating Baptism, 'This is our faith. This is the faith of the Church. We are proud to profess it, in Christ Jesus our Lord.'

OUR FATHER

There is one faith, one baptism, and one God who is Father of all. In fellowship with all the baptised, let us pray to our heavenly Father in the words our Saviour gave us.

REFLECTION

To be baptised is to be christened,
that is, to be made like Christ.
But this doesn't happen automatically.
We have to grow into it.
Towards the end of his life a saint was asked
if he was a Christian, and he replied, 'not yet'.
Baptism is like the planting of a seed.
It will take a lifetime for this seed to grow and ripen.

FINAL BLESSING

May you go on growing in the knowledge and love of our Lord and Saviour Jesus Christ.

May the Lord confirm your hearts in holiness so that you may be blameless in his sight.

May you remain firm in the hope we profess because the One who made the promise is faithful.

Sharing the Word of God today

SCRIPTURE NOTE

First Reading (Is 42:1-4.6-7). This passage is from the first of the four Servant Songs of Second Isaiah. Though the identity of the Servant remains a mystery, the early Christians saw the 'servant songs' as being perfectly fulfilled in Jesus. This reading is chosen for today because the words spoken by the heavenly voice at the baptism of Jesus (Gospel reading) are taken almost verbatim from Isaiah 42:1.

Second Reading (Acts 10:34-38). The conversion of Cornelius (a Gentile) was a significant milestone in the transmission of the Good News and the formation of the people of the Church. In his sermon on that occasion Peter declares that God has no favourites: God would grant salvation to all people in Christ. For today's feast the relevant passage is the description of Jesus' baptism: an anointing with the Holy Spirit and with power.

Gospel (Mt 3:13-17). The story of Jesus' baptism is an epiphany story: Jesus is revealed as the Father's beloved Son, and given power for the mission he was about to begin. This is Matthew's main emphasis.

John's baptism was a baptism of repentance for the forgiveness of sins (Mk 1:4). The fact that Jesus should undergo such a baptism was a source of embarrassment for the early Christians. Why did he undergo it? To give an example of humility, to show solidarity with sinners, and to inaugurate his mission to sinners.

The greatness of Baptism

Once Pope Paul VI was asked what was the greatest day in his life. Everyone expected him to say, 'It was the day I was made pope.' But without a moment's hesitation he replied, 'It was day I was baptised.'

He rightly put Baptism above ordination to priesthood and elevation to the papacy. But over the years the primacy of Baptism got obscured. Ordination to the priesthood was put above it. The result was that a gulf opened up between clergy and laity. This was bad for both. It was bad for the clergy – it removed them from ordinary people and put them on a pedestal. And it was bad for the laity – it reduced them to second-class members of the Church.

From spiritual point of view, Baptism is the greatest thing that can happen to us. The ceremony of Baptism is beautiful, and rich in symbolism.

1. In Baptism we were formally given a name and welcomed into the family of God's people.

2. In Baptism we were signed with the sign of the cross – the mark of Christ's love for us.

3. Water was poured over us. Water is a symbol of cleansing –in Baptism we were cleansed of sin. But water is especially a symbol of life – in Baptism we were given a share in the life of God.

4. Our bodies were anointed with holy oil – not once but twice. The bodies of athletes were smeared with oil to give them strength to compete. Our bodies were anointed with holy oil for the struggle against evil. Kings, prophets and priests were anointed with oil and thus marked out as God's ministers to the community. We were anointed with the oil of chrism so that we may be Christ's ministers and witnesses to the world.

5. Our body was covered with a white garment, the outward sign of our Christian dignity. The pall, which is used at funerals, is a reminder of the white garment of Baptism.

6. We were given lighted candle to signify that God was calling us out of darkness into the wonderful light of his Son.

7. What happened at Jesus' baptism happened at our baptism too.

God said to each of us: 'You are my beloved son,' or 'You are my beloved daughter.' And the Holy Spirit was given to us to enable us to live the life of a Christian and to participate in the work of Jesus.

There are many vocations in the Church. Of all these vocations the most important one is the one we received at Baptism – the vocation to be a disciple of Jesus.

We have other sacraments to help us. We have Confirmation to strengthen us. We have Penance to help us when we fail. We have the Eucharist to nourish us. We have the Sacrament of the Sick when we get ill.

At the entrance to every Catholic Church you will find a holy water font. Why? So that we can bless ourselves with that water as we enter. By so doing we are reminding ourselves of our baptism, and committing ourselves to live up to it. To live one's baptism means to live as a disciple of Jesus.

Identifying with sinners

When leprosy broke out among the people of the Hawaiian Islands in the middle of the nineteenth century, the authorities responded by establishing a leper colony on the remote island of Molokai. The victims were snatched by force from their families and sent to this island to perish.

Moved by their terrible plight, a young Belgian priest, Damien De Veuster, asked to be allowed to minister to them. He realised that if he was to do this effectively he would have to go and live among them.

Having got permission, he went to Molokai. At first, he tried to minister to them while maintaining a certain distance. But he soon realised that he had to live among them in order to gain their trust. As a result he contracted leprosy himself.

The reaction of the lepers was immediate and whole-hearted. They embraced him and took him to their hearts. He was now one of them. There was no point anymore in keeping his distance. The lepers now had someone who could talk with authority about leprosy, and about the rejection and public shame that went with it.

The baptism of Jesus was a source of embarrassment to the early Christians. Even John the Baptist himself found it incongruous, and, as we saw in the Gospel, tried to prevent it. Why was this? It was because John's baptism was a summons to repentance, and therefore was for sinners. Now of one thing the early Christians were certain – Jesus was no sinner. He did not stand in need of repentance. So what relevance could John's baptism have for him, and why did he submit himself to it?

It was a symbolic act. He wanted to show solidarity with the people he had come to help. For this reason it was important that he was baptised, and baptised publicly. In this way he was identifying with sinners. When he stepped into the waters of the Jordan he was in effect saying to them, 'I'm on your side.'

In the words of the letter to the Hebrews: 'It was essential that he should in this way become completely like his brothers so that he could be a compassionate and trustworthy high priest of God's religion, able to atone for human sins' (2:17).

On the day of his baptism, Jesus joined the ranks of sinners. The Father approved of what he was doing, and set his seal on it by sending the Holy Spirit to anoint him with the oil of compassion for his mission.

What Jesus did that day at the Jordan, was to serve as a model for his public ministry. He didn't put himself above the sinners he came to save. Just as Fr Damian placed himself among the lepers, Jesus placed himself among sinners. He befriended them. So much so that he was accused of being a sinner, and was treated as a sinner.

Though completely sinless, Jesus took our sinful condition on himself. He placed himself beside us as an older Brother. He reveals to us that we are God's precious children. He wants to leads us out from our wretched condition of sin and death. He wants us to live in the glorious freedom of the children of God.

In this way he shows his love for us. And he also shows us what we have to do if we want to help those who are down and excluded.

The call to service

Nelson Mandela was instrumental in ending apartheid and bringing about a multi-racial society in South Africa. Mandela belongs to the Xhosa people, and grew up in the Transkei. How did he come to play such a crucial role in the history of his country?

In his autobiography, *Long Walk to Freedom,* he tells us that all the currents of his life were taking him away from the Transkei. Yet he had no epiphany, no singular revelation. He says, 'a steady accumulation of insights helped me to see that my duty was to the people as a whole, not just to a particular section of it. The memory of a thousand indignities awakened in me a desire to fight the system that imprisoned my people. There was no particular day on which I said, From now on I will devote myself to the liberation of my people; instead I simply found myself doing so, and could not do otherwise.'

Jesus spent the first 30 years of his life at Nazareth. There is a tendency to regard those years as a waste of valuable time. Nothing could be further from the truth. Those years were of crucial importance to him.

What was he doing during those years? He was growing, maturing, and ripening in the shadows. There were no pressures, no burden of expectations. The main influences in his life would have been home, school, and synagogue.

But all the currents of his life were taking away from Nazareth. During those years the call to the service of his brothers and sisters in the wider community had been sounding inside him.

Why did he wait so long to begin his public ministry? The simple answer is: he wasn't ready. Jesus was a spiritual teacher. Spirituality has to be lived before it can be taught effectively.

His baptism was crucial. That was the moment when he committed himself irrevocably to the work God has sent him into the world to do. At his baptism the words were heard: 'This is my Son, the Beloved; my favour rests on him.' These words set the seal of divine approval on the mission he was about to begin – the mission to bring sinners back to God. He also received power from on high for that mission. This is signified by the descent of the Holy Spirit.

The day he was baptised, he didn't suddenly become a different person. 'No single event can awaken in us a stranger completely unknown to us' (Antoine de Saint Exupery). On that day he begin to reap the harvest from what had been growing within him.

There is an important lesson for us in all of this. We must not write off any part of our lives as useless, or any experience as a waste. Everything gives us an opportunity to grow as human beings and children of God.

The baptism of Jesus reminds us of our own baptism, and provides us with an opportunity to commit ourselves once again to the Christian life. Through our baptism Jesus leads us out from sin and death and enables us to live in the glorious freedom of the children of God. And through our baptism we are called to the service of our brothers and sisters.

Lent

Praying with the Word of God today

INTRODUCTION AND CONFITEOR

On the First Sunday of Lent, the liturgy puts before us the tempting of Jesus. Because Jesus shared our humanity, he was tempted in every way that we are, yet was without sin.

Let us reflect for a moment on our struggles with temptation. [Pause]

There is nothing we cannot master with the help of the One who strengthens us.

Lord Jesus, through this holy season you give us strength to purify our hearts and control our desires. Lord, have mercy.

You give us a spirit of loving reverence for you, and of willing service of our neighbour. Christ, have mercy.

You teach us how to live in this passing world with our hearts set on the world that will never end. Lord, have mercy.

PRAYER OF THE FAITHFUL

Celebrant: Jesus was tempted in every way that we are, yet was without sin. Let us with confidence approach him in our many needs.

Response: Have mercy on us, O God, in your kindness.

Reader(s): For Christians: that the grace of this holy season may help them to deepen their commitment to Christ. [Pause] Let us pray to the Lord.

For the Church: that it may nourish its members with the bread of God's word. [Pause] Let us pray to the Lord.

For those who hold public office: that they may serve the community faithfully and generously. [Pause] Let us pray to the Lord.

For those who have fallen to temptation: that they may have the strength to get up again. [Pause] Let us pray to the Lord.

For the members of this community: that we may not be discouraged by our weakness or demoralised by our failures. [Pause] Let us pray to the Lord.

For our deceased relatives and friends: that the Lord may gladden them with the light of his face. [Pause] Let us pray to the Lord.

For our own special needs. [Longer pause] Let us pray to the Lord.

Celebrant: God of mercy, your Son became like us in all things but sin. Keep us true to his teaching, and grant that we may demonstrate our love for him by a loving service of our brothers and sisters. We ask this through the same Christ our Lord.

In all his trials Jesus had recourse to the Father in prayer. Let us pray to our heavenly Father as he taught us.

PRAYER/REFLECTION

Lent is the Church's 'holy spring'.
It is a time of self-denial.
But it is also a time of joy,
because we are preparing for Easter.
Lord, help us to let go of old habits of sin,
and clothe us in newness of life,
so that when Easter comes,
we will feel young again in our discipleship.

FINAL BLESSING

May the Lord help you to resist evil and conquer it with good.

May you stay firm in the faith and be strong in time of trial.

May you be filled with a joyful trust in God, and never tire of doing what is right.

Sharing the Word of God today

SCRIPTURE NOTE

First Reading (Gen 2:7-9; 3:1-7). The first section of the reading deals with the creation of Adam and Eve. Though made of dust, man and woman are the pride of God's creation. Enlivened by his breath, God has destined them for happiness – they live in an idyllic garden.

The second section deals with the tempting and fall of Adam and Eve. It illustrates the psychology of temptation. The cunning serpent succeeds in portraying God as unreasonable and jealous. After that, the fall is inevitable.

The source of all evil, the writer suggests, is man's foolish striving to be independent of God. Only by accepting their status as favoured creatures of a loving, caring creator, can man and woman find fulfilment.

The result of their disobedience is that there is in human beings a sinful tendency which goes beyond personal sins we may commit. This basic tendency towards evil is part of the corruption that human beings introduced into the world, not an endowment of God.

The story of the tempting of Adam and Eve prepares us to hear the tempting of Jesus in the Gospel.

Second Reading (Rom 5:12-19). Paul portrays Jesus as the new Adam, who by his obedience to God restores for us the gifts lost by the disobedience of the first Adam.

Gospel (Mt 4:1-11). The story of the temptations of Jesus is a highly contrived story. First of all, it looks to the past. Matthew sees Jesus as reliving the history of his people. He goes into the desert for forty days and forty nights. This recalls the forty years the people spent in the desert, a period in which they were tempted but also enjoyed a special closeness to God. Jesus shares in the temptations of his people. But whereas they were found wanting, he remains faithful to God.

The first temptation is the same as that which confronted the Israelites: to doubt the power of God to provide for him. The second temptation is to turn his trust in God into crass presumption: if God cares for you, then you will come to no harm no matter what you do. The third temptation is to commit the sin of Israel of old, idolatry.

But the story also looks to the future. Jesus has come to inaugurate the kingdom of God. The story condenses into a single expression the struggle he endured at every step to be faithful to that mission. The temptations illustrate the ways in which the proclamation of the kingdom might have been distorted, so that it would have become a kingdom according to the standards of this world.

The temptations are prognostic of eventual victory, for after Jesus has demonstrated that he is the Son of God who completely serves God's will, the devil departs and angels wait on him.

The tempting of Jesus

The story of the tempting of Jesus is clearly a highly contrived story, which means we don't have to take it literally. But that Jesus was tempted there can be no doubt. The Letter to the Hebrews says that he was tempted 'in every way that we are, but was without sin' (4:15).

But what did his temptations consist in? The temptations came immediately after his Baptism. Having heard the voice of the Father calling him to bring the Good News of salvation to his brothers and sisters, he went into the desert to reflect on the nature of that mission and to prepare himself for it. The temptations were an attempt by the devil to distort that mission.

Take the first temptation. When the devil said to him, 'If you are the Son of God, command these stones and they will turn into bread,' Jesus responded by saying, 'A human being does not live on bread alone, but on every word that comes from the mouth of God.'

This doesn't mean that Jesus wasn't concerned about hunger. He was, and in the course of his ministry he did provide bread for hungry people. However, he was well aware that while food is the first necessity of life, it is only the beginning. We eat in order to live, not the other way round.

He didn't come to provide ordinary bread. That we can provide for ourselves. He came to provide another kind of food – the food that only God can give us. His chief task was to nourish the minds and hearts of people with the bread of God's word.

Take the second temptation – to throw himself off the Temple. This was the temptation to do something spectacular in order to get people to believe in him. A stunt like that would have made him the talk of Jerusalem. But sensationalism redounds to one's own glory, rather than to the glory of God.

Throughout his public ministry, he refused to give the people this kind of sign, even when pressed to do so. To give in to this kind of demand would be to cheapen faith. Faith is not magic. Faith is trust in God. But trust in God must not be turned into crass presumption by putting God to the test.

In the third temptation, the devil showed him all the kingdoms of the world, and said, 'All these I will give you, if you fall at my feet and worship me.' This was the most fundamental temptation of all – the temptation to idolatry. But Jesus would not repeat the sin of the Israelites of old by worshipping false gods.

The temptations were attacks on all that was fundamental to his mission. Besides, they were no once-off affairs. They continued through his ministry as Satan sought to undermine his mission. It is not surprising then that he shunned publicity, tried to impose silence about his miracles, and stead-fastly refused to give that sign from heaven that his adversaries demanded.

The temptations of Jesus represent the major temptations of the Church as a whole, and of each of us who are its members: the temptation to live by bread alone; the temptation to look for signs and wonders rather than trying to live by faith; and the temptation to worship false gods.

All those who are struggling to live a good life can take heart from the example of Jesus. Resisting temptation was not easy for him; nor will it be for us. But in Jesus we have a brother who knows what we are up against. He forgives us when we fall and enables us to start again. He enables us to obey God's word, to trust in God, and to worship God alone.

The purpose of penance

We have just begun Lent. When we think of Lent we think of penance. Most Christians undertake some penance for Lent. This is a good and worthwhile practice. However, penance is not an end in itself.

There was a very earnest young man who wanted to become a rabbi. He went to see an elderly rabbi for advice. It was winter time. The rabbi stood at the window looking out into the yard while the rabbinical candidate gave him a glowing account of his piety and austere lifestyle.

The young man said, 'I always dress in spotless white like the sages of old. I never drink any alcoholic beverages; only water ever passes my lips.

I perform numerous penances. For instance, I always carry sharp-edged nails inside my shoes to mortify myself. Even in the coldest weather, I lie naked in the snow to punish my flesh. And to complete my penance, I take a dozen lashes every day on my bare back.'

As the young man spoke, a stable boy led a white horse into the yard and took him to the water trough. The horse drank his fill of water, and having done so, rolled in the snow, as horses sometimes do.

'Just look!' cried the rabbi. 'That animal, too, is dressed in white. It also drinks nothing but water, has nails in its shoes and rolls naked in the snow. Also, rest assured, it gets its daily ration of lashes on the rump from its master. Now, I ask you, is it a saint, or is it a horse?'

The point the rabbi was making was that penance is not an end in itself. What is the purpose of penance? Penance is not meant to undo the past – the past is done. Nor is it meant to persuade God to erase our sins and forgo the punishment we deserve for them.

The first thing we are doing when we undertake penance is acknowledging that we are sinners. The second thing we are doing is expressing the desire to change our lives. The whole object of penance is to reform a sinful way of life.

Penance is an exercise in saying 'no' to ourselves. Its purpose is to acquaint us with our better side, and to convince ourselves that we can do better. It signifies that we want to reform our lives. It means taking a step in the right direction.

When people prune a fruit tree, they are not doing it to punish the tree, but to enable it to produce more and better fruit. So our penances have as their goal to lead us to a new and better life.

It is a lot easier to undertake penances, even severe ones, than to change a sinful attitude or eradicate a sinful habit. For our penance to bear fruit it must result in a sincere effort to change our lives.

Lent provides us with a window of opportunity to look at ourselves to see how we can become better followers of Christ. The example of the sinless Jesus battling with Satan should act as a spur to us. He triumphed over Satan through prayer, fasting, and obedience to the word of God. He will help us to be victorious in our struggles with sin and evil.

Longing for a lost Paradise

The story of the fall of Adam and Eve is a sophisticated story. The question to ask is not 'Is it true?' (Did it really happen?), but 'What does it mean?' The story is concerned with the concept of sin and its origins.

The story tells us that human beings were created by God. Furthermore, they were created good, and not evil. God gave them the freedom to choose.

In so doing God made it possible for them to be moral, that is, to freely choose to do what is right. Without the freedom to choose, they would be no better than the animals that live not by choice but by instinct.

All our achievements, all our discoveries, all our wars, all the heights to which we have risen, and the depths to which we have sunk, have been about using or abusing the freedom of choice which God gave us.

Unfortunately Adam and Eve abused their freedom. They chose to say 'no' to God. Thus sin was introduced into the world. The essence of sin is disobedience to God.

Jesus is the new Adam. By his obedience to God he restores for us the gifts lost by the disobedience of the first Adam. In the desert he was faced with the same choice that Adam and Eve faced: to do his own will or to do the will of God. Unlike Adam and Eve, he chose to do God's will rather than his own.

We may think that it was easy for Jesus. It wasn't easy for him. He triumphed over Satan through prayer, fasting, and obedience to the word of God.

Like Adam and Eve, we are constantly drawn to forbidden fruit. Every day we are faced with choices: to do good or to do evil. It is clear that we have in us a strain of self-centredness and shortsightedness that causes us to make the wrong choices.

When we make wrong choices, we tend to blame others. We live in a culture in which blame has become an industry. But this is nothing new. Adam blamed Eve; Eve blamed the serpent. (And the serpent hadn't a leg to stand on).

Adam and Eve lost their original innocence. So did we: we lost our childhood innocence. But we can regain it. No matter how old we may be, Jesus makes it possible for us to be reborn in innocence of character.

This recovered innocence is different from the first. The first is harmless through weakness; the second is innocent through virtue. The first is incapable of sin; the second is unwilling to sin.

The fact that Jesus won an important victory in the desert didn't mean the war was over. There would be other attacks. Every choice in life must be remade perhaps many times. However, every right choice makes the next right choice easier. If we do the right thing often enough, eventually it becomes second nature to us.

Story

A priest who spent several years as a school chaplain tells the following story.

Late one night one of his past pupils, now a young man, came to see him. He had a sad and murky story to tell. After leaving school he entered the world of work. There, unfortunately, he got involved in crime.

He told the priest that he now wanted to get out of it. Then he made a most unusual request. He said, 'Father, make me the boy I was when I was fifteen.'

The boy's earnest request moved the priest deeply. The young man knew that he had tarnished himself. Now he felt a longing for the unstained innocence of his boyhood. Just as Adam and Eve lost their original innocence, so that young man had lost his childhood innocence. But the priest could see that within the young man the boy who made his First Holy Communion still survived.

There is in every human heart a longing for the lost Eden. When the Lord says to us, 'Unless you become like little children you will not enter the kingdom of heaven,' he is recalling us to our lost childhood. No matter how old we may be, he makes it possible for us to be reborn in innocence of character.

SECOND SUNDAY OF LENT
It is good for us to be here

Praying with the Word of God today

INTRODUCTION AND CONFITEOR

On Mount Tabor the apostles got a glimpse of the glory that belonged to Jesus as the Son of God. So wonderful was this that Peter exclaimed, 'Lord, it is good for us to be here.'

And surely it is good for us to be here this morning (evening), because here we get a glimpse of *our* glory, for we too are children of God and heirs to eternal life. Let us reflect on this for a moment. [Pause]

Lord Jesus, here we experience the Father's unconditional love. Lord, have mercy.

Here you enlighten us with your word, and nourish us with the bread of eternal life. Christ, have mercy.

Here we experience the love and support of our fellow Christians. Lord, have mercy.

PRAYER OF THE FAITHFUL

Celebrant: Through Christ we have become heirs to eternal glory. Let us pray with confidence to our heavenly Father for all our needs.

Response: May your love be upon us, O Lord.

Reader(s): For the followers of Christ: that they may listen to him and live by his teachings. [Pause] Let us pray to the Lord.

For our political and civil leaders: that God may sustain them in their efforts to create a just and peaceful society. [Pause] Let us pray to the Lord.

For those who are going through the dark valley of suffering: that they may know that God is with them. [Pause] Let us pray to the Lord.

For all gathered here: that our earthly journey may be illuminated by the light of a steadfast faith. [Pause] Let us pray to the Lord.

For our loved ones who have died: that they may enjoy the vision of God's glory in heaven. [Pause] Let us pray to the Lord.

For our own special needs. [Longer pause] Let us pray to the Lord.

Celebrant: All-powerful God, let your radiant glory free us from the darkness of evil, and bring us safely through the shadows of this world to our homeland of everlasting light. We ask this through Christ our Lord.

OUR FATHER

As God's precious daughters and sons, let us pray to our heavenly Father as Jesus the beloved Son has taught us.

SIGN OF PEACE

Lord Jesus Christ, on the mountain you revealed your glory to the apostles, and they were filled with joy. Reveal yourself to us now in the breaking of bread, so that we may enjoy the peace and unity of your kingdom where you live for ever and ever.

PRAYER/REFLECTION

Jesus was transfigured on the mountain.
We too can have moments of transfiguration.
Sometimes a blessedness comes down around us,
a glory falls upon us from God, and life is sweet.
In his love for us, God allows us to taste on earth
the joys of the world to come.
Lord, give us confidence in your unchanging love for us.
Help us to follow you with courage,
and lead us to the glory that never fades.

FINAL BLESSING

May you never forget that we are but pilgrims on the earth, and that our true home is in heaven.

May you live lives that are worthy of the glory to which you are called.

And may the peace of God, which passes all understanding, guard your hearts and minds in Christ Jesus our Lord.

Sharing the Word of God today

SCRIPTURE NOTE

First Reading (Gen 12:1-4). How does God act in history? God acts by calling key individuals, and it is by their responses that a channel for the execution of God's purpose is carved out in the world. Abraham was one of those key individuals.

The call of Abraham marks the beginning of a special relationship between God and man. In leaving his country, clan and family, and setting out for an unknown destination, Abraham demonstrates extraordinary faith in God's guidance. Through his faith the whole human race would be blessed because from his descendants would come the Saviour of all people. (That Saviour is revealed in the Gospel.)

Second Reading (Tim 1:8-10). This picks up the theme of call, and speaks of the call to be a Christian. This call is based, not on our merits, but on God's grace granted to us in Christ. The power of God and the vision of immortality enable the Christian to face the sufferings which faithfulness to the Gospel inevitably brings (just as the 'Tabor' experience helped Jesus to face his passion).

Gospel (Mt 17:1-9). The story of the transfiguration, like that of the temptations, is a contrived story. It is no longer possible to say what happened on the mountain. But something did happen, because years later Peter still remembered it and wrote: 'We were eye-witnesses of his glory on the mountain' (2 Pet 1:17-18).

The story is concerned with the identity of Jesus. The few details that are given are highly significant. We are told that it happened on a mountain – in the Bible a mountain is a place of divine manifestation. (The name of the mountain is not given, and is not important. There is a tradition that connects it with Mount Tabor in Galilee, and for convenience that is how I refer to it.)

On the mountain Jesus is flanked by two of the most important figures from the Old Testament – Moses and Elijah. Moses represents the law, Elijah the prophets. Thus Jesus is seen as bringing the law and the prophets to fulfilment. In other words, he is the Messiah.

The cloud overshadowing them signifies the presence of God, who cannot be seen by human eyes. From the cloud comes a voice that declares something greater still about Jesus, namely, that he is the God's beloved Son.

As for the event itself, its first and chief significance was for Jesus himself. It was meant to confirm him in the course he had taken and prepare him for the ordeal ahead. (Luke's version brings out more clearly the story's connection with the passion.) But it also benefitted the apostles. In the transfigured Jesus they got a glimpse of the glory that was his as the Son of

God. Coupled with their later experience of his resurrection, it confirmed them in the belief that Jesus was the Messiah and Son of God.

Meaning of the transfiguration

The story of the transfiguration is a beautiful story. But how are we to understand it? Like the story of Jesus' temptations, it is a contrived story. Therefore, we don't have to take it literally.

That's not to say that nothing happened on the mountain. Something did happen, because years later Peter still remembered it and wrote in one of his letter: 'We were eye-witnesses of his glory on the mountain' (2 Pet 1:17-18).

The question to ask is: What is the evangelist telling us in this story? He is telling us about the identity of Jesus. Only a few details are given but they are very important.

We are told that the setting was a mountaintop. In biblical tradition a mountain is a place of encounter with God. The name of the mountain is not given, and it's not important. However, there is a tradition that connects it with Mount Tabor in Galilee.

On the mountain Jesus was flanked by Moses and Elijah. Moses and Elijah are two of the most important figures in the Old Testament. Moses represented the Law; Elijah the prophets. Thus Jesus is seen as bringing the Law and the prophets to fulfilment. In other words, he is the Messiah.

Then a cloud overshadows them. The cloud is a symbol of the presence of God, who cannot be seen by human eyes. And a voice from heaven declares something greater still about Jesus, namely, that he is God's Son. Here we have the full identity of Jesus: he is both Messiah and Son of God. That's what the evangelist is telling us in this story.

The Tabor experience came at a crucial moment in the life of Jesus – at the start of his journey to Jerusalem. He knew the fate that awaited him in Jerusalem – the same fate that had befallen many of the prophets, namely, a violent death. The experience confirmed him in the course he had taken. It was comforting to know that the road he was travelling was marked by the feet of prophets such as Moses and Elijah.

And he was boosted when he heard again the words of affirmation he had heard at his Baptism, assuring him that he enjoyed the Father's favour. And thus he was able to face the ordeal ahead.

What significance has the story for us? We too are journeying towards Jerusalem – the heavenly Jerusalem. And we too can have moments of transfiguration – rare moments of light and joy. In his love for us, God allows us to taste on earth the joys of the world to come.

And at times we too can hear a voice whispering to us in our hearts: 'You are my beloved son', or 'You are my beloved daughter.' And, like Jesus, we are reassured and strengthened. And so we are able face the future with confidence.

It is also comforting to know that the road we are travelling is marked by the feet of countless holy people who have gone before us. Better still, it is marked by the feet of Jesus himself.

Abraham's journey and ours

There are many great journeys in the Bible. One of the most important is that of Abraham (First Reading). At the word of God he left all the usual securities of life – home, family, country – and set out for a foreign country.

Abraham's journey is one that emigrants can identify with in a special way. But all of us can identify with it, because all of us are travellers on this earth. This is true even for the person who has never left home. And while we are on a common journey, each one's journey is unique.

Abraham's journey was fraught with difficulties. It literally was a journey into the unknown. However, he had one marvellous asset, namely, faith in God. That faith provided him with a compass for his journey.

In many respects the journey of life is a journey into the unknown. Blessed are those who possess the compass of faith. To have faith is not to have all the answers. It is to have a set of bearings.

It is very important that a journey should have a destination. Abraham had a clear destination – the land God promised to show him. We also need to know that our earthly journey has a destination.

Here again the value of faith becomes evident. Faith assures us that our journey has a destination – the kingdom of God. It is a goal that defies our imagination, and gives an eternal dimension to our lives.

Truly blessed are those whose earthly journey is lit by the lamp of such a hope. This splendid hope rests not on anything human, but on the word and power of God.

Without that hope, the journey of life, no matter how pleasurable it might be, would be robbed of ultimate meaning. In essence, it would be a journey to nowhere. With that hope, life is a voyage to the promised land of eternal life. The very hardships and difficulties encountered on route will add to the joy of arrival.

Because God had called him, Abraham knew that God would not abandon him. He trusted that God would guide him to his unknown destination. In his love for us, God has sent us a special guide – his Son, Jesus. Jesus guides us on the unfolding road to the eternal joy of God's kingdom. We go forward more confidently and hopefully because he has gone ahead of us.

Often we have our own mini 'Tabors' or transfigurations. We get a taste of the ultimate goal, a hint of the blessed state that lies beyond this life. In his goodness, God allows us to taste on earth the joys of the world to come.

The journey of faith is a mysterious and wonderful one. But we don't have to, and shouldn't, make it alone. We make it with our brothers and sisters in the Christian community.

Glimpses of glory

On Mount Tabor God's light burst forth from the body of Jesus, and he was transfigured. The three apostles were overcome with the beauty and brilliance of it. It was not a surface thing, but something inside shining through. In short: God was in Jesus.

We too have the splendour of divinity in us because we are made in the image of God. Therefore, we too can have moments of transfiguration. Vincent Van Gogh said, 'The poorest woodcutter or miner can have moments of emotion and inspiration which give him a feeling of an eternal home to which he is near.'

A poor man living in a Dublin hostel for the homeless told me the following story. One day he was walking along a street in Dublin. At a certain point he found himself outside a church. Before he realised it, he was inside. He couldn't recall whether or not he said any prayers. But his soul was flooded with light. His depression lifted, and a great peace descended on him. He felt that he belonged on this earth after all. He felt close to God and loved by God.

The experience seemed to last for a long time, yet he had a feeling it may have lasted only a few minutes. But he said he'd gladly give the whole of his life for those few moments. What made the experience so wonderful was the realisation that he had done nothing to deserve it. It was a pure gift from God to him. For one short moment he tasted glory.

However, when it was over he found himself out in the streets once more, going along aimlessly as before. The effects of the experience faded. Though he went back to that church many times afterwards, he was never able to recapture that moment.

That homeless man wanted to hold on to that experience. He wanted to go backwards instead of forwards. He might have used the experience to illuminate the darkness in his life, and to go forward more hopefully and courageously.

Peter made the same mistake. He wanted to stay on the mountaintop. He wanted to hug and hold onto the blessedness of the experience. He did not want to go back down to the everyday and common things again, but to remain for ever in the enchanted land. But Jesus summoned him to go back down the mountain and to face the future. That experience was not meant to provide an escape from the struggle that lay ahead, but to help him face it. The hour of light was meant to help him face the hour of darkness.

And it's clear that something of the wonder of that day remained with Peter and illuminated his life, because many years later he wrote: 'We were eye-witnesses of his glory on the mountain ... A voice came to him saying, "This is my beloved son in whom I am well pleased"' (2 Pet 1:17-18).

We too can experience rare moments of light and joy. We get glimpses of the promised land towards which we are travelling in faith. In his love for us, God allows us to taste on earth the joys of the world to come. But these moments of transfiguration are given to us to strengthen us for our everyday tasks, and to enable us to face the cross that in some shape or form comes to everyone. The moment of glory does not exist for its own sake. It exists to clothe the common things with a radiance they never had before.

Religion is not escapism. It is meant to help us face life with all its difficulties and challenges, to embrace the high and low moments of life, the hilltop and the pit. In between, we travel in the darkness of faith.

THIRD SUNDAY OF LENT
The thirst that only God can quench

Praying with the Word of God today

INTRODUCTION AND CONFITEOR

Today's Gospel tells about the moving encounter between Jesus and a Samaritan woman. Jesus told her about the gift God wanted to give her – the gift of the 'living water' of his grace. Here Jesus offers us the same gift. Let us dispose ourselves to receive the 'gift of God.' [Pause]

Like a deer that yearns for running streams, so our souls are yearning for you, O Lord. Lord, have mercy.

Those who trust in you are like a tree planted beside a flowing stream. Christ, have mercy.

Near restful waters you lead us, to revive our drooping spirits. Lord, have mercy.

PRAYER OF THE FAITHFUL

Celebrant: Let us pray with confidence to God who alone can quench our deepest thirst.

Response: Lord, hear our prayer.

Reader(s): For the followers of Christ: that they may turn away from the murky waters of sin, and seek instead the clear waters of grace. [Pause] Let us pray to the Lord.

For the Pope and the bishops: that God may bless them with the gifts of wisdom and courage. [Pause] Let us pray to the Lord.

For those who are lonely or dejected: that Christians may befriend them. [Pause] Let us pray to the Lord.

For agencies working to bring clean water to people: that God may prosper their work. [Pause] Let us pray to the Lord.

For those who are preparing for Baptism: that they may grow in faith and friendship with Christ. [Pause] Let us pray to the Lord.

For our deceased relatives and friends: that the Lord may lead them to the springs of eternal life. [Pause] Let us pray to the Lord.

For our own special needs. [Longer Pause] Let us pray to the Lord.

Celebrant: Heavenly Father, you sent your Son into the world to quench our thirst with the living water of your grace. May we seek his gift with eager hearts, so that it may sustain us in our journey to the promised land of eternal life. We ask this through the same Christ our Lord.

PRAYER/REFLECTION

There is a thirst in every human heart,
a thirst that only God can quench.
To experience this thirst is not a curse but a blessing.
Lord, in your goodness, give us some of the living water
you offered to the Samaritan woman.
May it become a spring within us welling up to eternal life.

FINAL BLESSING

May you go on growing in the knowledge and love of our Lord and Saviour Jesus Christ.

May God, who has called us to eternal glory in Christ, strengthen and support you with his grace.

May the Lord watch over you, keep you in his care, and bless you with his peace.

Sharing the Word of God today

SCRIPTURE NOTE

First Reading (Ex 17:3-7). In spite of having experienced God's help in various ways, the liberated slaves remain apathetic and sullen towards Yahweh, and complain bitterly against Moses, his spokesman. Here they are complaining about lack of water. Despite their ingratitude, God shows his care for his people by providing water for them in the desert. This prepares us for the Gospel, and the 'living water' God offers us through Jesus.

Second Reading (Rom 5:1-2.5-8). Paul says that we have abundant grounds for hope. Our hope lies in what God has done for us in Christ. God has proved his extraordinary love for us by the fact that Christ died for us while we were still sinners. The Christian life is a response to something that has already been accomplished on our behalf by a loving God.

Gospel (Jn 4:5-42). For this Sunday and the next two, the Gospel readings are taken from John. John doesn't give us parables. He gives us extended discourses built around images. The lectionary presents the stories of the Samaritan woman, the man born blind, and the raising of Lazarus. In the first story Jesus speaks of water; in the second he speaks of sight; and in the third he speaks of life. There is a double level of meaning in all three.

There is a clear baptismal dimension to these stories – the symbols of water, sight and new life are closely associated with Baptism. They are of major importance in regard to Christian initiation, and therefore may also be read in Year B and Year C, especially in places where there are catechumens.

Today's Gospel tells the story of Jesus' encounter with a Samaritan woman. As the Israelites journeyed through the desert, Moses provided them with the life-saving gift of ordinary water (First Reading). Jesus, the new Moses, offers us something infinitely better. He offers us 'living water', that is, a share in the very life of God. It is through the waters of Baptism that we receive a share in the life of God.

Our passage is an invitation to faith. But in it we also see the goodness of God in the compassion Jesus showed to a poor lost woman.

The gift of living water

What is the most precious commodity on earth? Oil? No, even though a lot of wars have been fought over it. Gold? Diamonds? No, even though many people have given their lives trying to acquire them. The most precious commodity with which our earth has been blessed is water. Yes, ordinary water. Why? Because without it there would be no life on earth.

In some countries there is such an abundance of water that it tends to be taken for granted. Moreover, it is readily available – all one has to do is turn on a tap. But in other countries water is extremely scare, and people have to travel long distances to get it. In those countries people have a great appreciation of water.

Water is used for cleaning and cooking. But its chief property is to give life. Nothing can live or grow without water. We water a plant. We take it into ourselves by drinking it. We could live for several weeks without food, but we couldn't survive for more than a few days without water. Water is not so much a necessity of life; it *is* life.

Jesus too needed water. In today's Gospel, St John presents him as completely human. He shows him sitting by a well in the noonday sun, weary and thirsty. We don't often think of Jesus in that way. When a Samaritan woman came to the well to draw water he asked her for a drink, and she gave it to him. The woman was a lost woman, and an outcast from her community. Yet Jesus started up a conversation with her. It is one of the most profound conversations in the Gospel.

Besides being the first necessity of life, water is also a powerful symbol. Jesus used water to talk to the woman about something deeper. He began to talk to her about another kind of thirst and another kind of water.

At first she had had no idea what he was on about. Physical thirst she understood. Yet, when she reflected on her life, she began to understand. Yes, there was another kind of thirst – the thirst for love and happiness and meaning. She had been married not once but five times. Yet she still hadn't found what she was looking for.

She had been searching for love and happiness. Jesus didn't judge her. Ever so gently, he showed her that up to now she had been looking for the right thing (love), but in the wrong places. He explained to her that what she was experiencing was only the deeper thirst that affects everyone – the thirst no earthly water can satisfy. For this deeper thirst we need another kind of 'water'. What is this water? It is the life of God inside us.

To be in touch with God, is to be in touch with a fountain of life. The discovery of God is like a spring within us. Only God can give us what we are looking for.

There is a thirst in the human heart that only God can quench. To experience this thirst is not a curse but a blessing. This thirst disposes us to receive the 'living water' Jesus wishes to give us.

Ordinary water is a very precious commodity. But the 'water' Jesus gives is infinitely more precious. Jesus gives us this 'water' in Baptism. In the waters of Baptism we are given a share in the undying life of God.

Loved in our sins

One theme is common to all three of today's scripture readings. It is a very important and comforting theme. You could say that it is the heart of the Good News. That theme is: God's compassion for sinners.

We see this in the First Reading. In spite of the ingratitude and grumblings of the people, God didn't write his people off, but showed his love for them by providing water for them in the desert. The message is explicitly stated in the Second Reading. There Paul says, 'What proves that God loves us is that Christ died for us while we were still sinners.' And we see this compassion in action in the Gospel.

Jesus' approach to that outcast woman was ever so gentle. He didn't force himself into her life. Had he done so she would have immediately closed up. There is a world of difference between asking people for the key to their house, and battering the door down.

In fact, he began from a position of weakness. He began with a request for a drink of water. In this way he disposed her to receive the gift he wanted to give her. His heart was already open to her. Now she opened her heart to him. A wonderful dialogue ensued, and a marvellous exchange took place.

We marvel at the respect with which Jesus treated her. There wasn't a hint of judgement in his approach. The holier a person is, the less he is inclined to judge others. Right from the start, Jesus was looking into her heart, yet he didn't make her feel bad. She didn't feel judged. Rather, she felt understood.

Before she realised it, she had shared with him the whole story of her sad and confused life. Jesus explained her life to her more sympathetically than she'd been able to explain it to herself.

How could someone as pure as Jesus understand a woman like her? Kahlil Gibran says, 'Only the pure of heart understand the thirst that leads people to drink from muddy waters.'

Jesus was able to see into her secret being, into that part of her that longed for true love, and that was thirsting to be seen as a person and not as an object. She was a deeply wounded woman, wounded by a series of broken relationships, something that is becoming more and more common in our times.

Jesus knew the woman's situation. He might have said to her, 'Come back after you have straightened out your life.' But he didn't. Instead he offered her grace (love). It was that grace that helped her to change her life.

Jesus meets us where we are, and accepts us as we are. It doesn't do us much good to be loved for being perfect. We need to be accepted and loved precisely as sinners. Only the person who has experienced this kind of love can know what it is.

Being loved like that gives one surprising courage and energy. It puts us in touch with our true nature, and to touch our true nature is a kind of homecoming.

Jesus says to us what he said to that lost woman: 'If you only knew the gift God wants to give you.' That gift comes to us through the waters of Baptism – the gift of God's love and the gift of God's life.

The Israelites were finding the going tough in the desert, but God sustained them with water from the rock. When we are finding the going tough, we should turn to God whose love sustains us when things are too much for us.

The giver who began by asking

The greatest good we can do for another person is not to give him of our own wealth, but to show him his own. [*Repeat*] There is a delightful parable by Tagore that illustrates this.

One day a poor man was sitting by the side of the road begging. By his side lay a sack which contained a handful of wheat grains, just enough to make one last cake of bread. But at the end of the morning he had nothing to show for his efforts.

Suddenly he saw the king's carriage approaching. 'The king is a kind man. He will surely give me something,' the beggar-man said to himself. To his delight the royal carriage began to slow down and came to a halt directly opposite the spot where he stood with outstretched hand.

Down came the window, and the king put his head out. The beggar-man bowed low and was about to say, 'Your Majesty, could you spare a little money for me, your most unworthy servant?' But the king got in the first words. Reaching out his hand towards the beggar-man he said, 'Friend, could you spare a little corn for your king?'

Completely taken aback, the beggar-man said, 'Certainly, your Majesty.' With that he opened the sack, picked out the smallest grain of wheat he could find, and gave it to the king. The king thanked him, and the carriage moved off.

The man continued on begging during the afternoon. When evening came on he made his way home, tired and dejected. Once home, he took a pan and emptied the last of the wheat from the sack into it. As he inspected the meagre heap of grains, he made a startling discovery – the smallest grain had turned into a grain of pure gold.

Then he bitterly regretted that he had been so miserly with his king. If only he had known the gift the king wanted to give him, he would have given him all the wheat he had. Then he would never have to beg again.

The story reminds us of the story in today's Gospel. There we read about a poor, outcast woman who came to a well to draw water. At the well she had an unexpected encounter with Jesus, though as yet she knew nothing about him.

Clearly she was the one in greatest need. Yet, like the king in the story, Jesus began by asking something from her – a drink of water. She gave him that drink. In exchange, he offered her a priceless gift – the gift of a 'water' that would quench her thirst for ever. What was this water? It was the life of God inside her.

There is a thirst in every human heart. To experience this thirst is not a curse but a blessing. Only God can quench the thirst of the heart. To be in touch with God, is to be in touch with a fountain of life.

The woman went away greatly enriched as a result of her encounter with Jesus. Yet he didn't give her any *thing*. He did something better. He restored her lost dignity as a human being and a child of God.

The story shows us the astonishing kindness of Jesus. He meets us where we are. He knows our deeper thirst – the thirst of the heart, which ultimately only God can quench. For this deeper thirst we need another kind of 'water', water Jesus said he could give and wanted to give. What is this water? It is the life of God bubbling up inside us, bubbling up into eternal life.

What one would not give for a drop of that 'water' which Jesus offered to the Samaritan woman? The fact is we have already got it through Baptism. In the waters of Baptism we are given a share in the undying life of God.

FOURTH SUNDAY OF LENT
Jesus the Light of the World

Praying with the Word of God today

INTRODUCTION AND CONFITEOR

The Gospel of today's Mass contains these wonderful words of Jesus: 'I am the light of the world.' Let us reflect for a moment on how much we need his light for our own lives and for the world. [Pause]

Lord Jesus, you help us to walk in the light of a steadfast faith. Lord, have mercy.

You help us to walk in the light of a joyful hope. Christ, have mercy.

You help us to walk in the light of an untiring love. Lord, have mercy.

PRAYER OF THE FAITHFUL

Celebrant: Once we were darkness, but now we are light in the Lord. Let us bring our prayers before God in whom there is no trace of darkness.

Response: Lord, hear our prayer.

For all Christians: that they may cause the light of Christ to shine in the world. [Pause] Let us pray to the Lord.

For all those in positions of authority: that they may be able to judge wisely and act justly. [Pause] Let us pray to the Lord.

For those who are in the darkness of unbelief: that the Lord may enlighten them with the gift of faith. [Pause] Let us pray to the Lord.

For medical practitioners who specialise in the diagnosis and treatment of eye diseases. [Pause] Let us pray to the Lord.

For our departed relatives and friends: that they may see the light of God's glory. [Pause] Let us pray to the Lord.

For our own special needs. [Longer Pause] Let us pray to the Lord.

Celebrant: Heavenly Father, in this life we see as in a glass darkly. Strengthen our faith so that we may walk with confidence along the road that leads to your Kingdom, where we shall see as we are seen. We ask this through Christ our Lord.

OUR FATHER

God has called us out of darkness into the wonderful light of his Son. Let us pray to our heavenly Father as children of the light.

SIGN OF PEACE

Lord Jesus Christ, you looked at the blind man, and where others saw a sinner being punished by God, you saw a lonely human being, crying out for healing. Look with compassion on us, and grant us the peace and unity of your kingdom where you live for ever and ever.

PRAYER/REFLECTION

Jesus made a wonderful promise to those who follow him:
'Anyone who follows me will never walk in darkness
but will always have the light of life.'
Lord, you are the light of the world,
a light that no darkness can overpower.
May we follow you faithfully on earth,
and come to the light that shines for ever in heaven.

FINAL BLESSING

May the Lord enable you to shun the works of darkness and to live as children of the light.

May you go on growing in the knowledge and love of our Lord and Saviour Jesus Christ.

And may your earthly journey be illuminated by the light of a steadfast faith.

Sharing the Word of God today

SCRIPTURE NOTE

First Reading (1 Sam 16:1.6-7.10-13). This passage tells the story of how Samuel identified and anointed David as the future king of Israel. The story shows the depth of God's seeing. While people look at appearances, God looks at the heart. This is illustrated in the fact that God chose David, the last and most insignificant of Jesse's sons, to be king of Israel. Seeing is the connection with the Gospel.

Second Reading (Eph 5:8-14). Paul tells the Ephesians that now that Christ has enlightened them, they must adopt a life-style in keeping with their new state. They must shun the works of darkness and live as children of the light.

Gospel (Jn 9:1-41). On the surface this is a story about a blind man receiving sight. But on a deeper level it is a story about a man coming to faith in Jesus. The man's journey from blindness to sight symbolises the journey from unbelief to faith, which is a journey from darkness to light, as St Paul tells his converts at Ephesus: 'Once you were in darkness, but now you are light in the Lord' (Second Reading).

In particular, the story illustrates growth in faith. There is a beautiful progression in the man's understanding of who Jesus is. At a first stage, he calls him 'a man'. Then he calls him 'a prophet'. The climax of the story comes when he calls him 'the Lord.' Notice how his faith grows stronger and deeper the more he is called upon to defend it.

In the story Jesus is proclaimed to be 'the light of the world'. Not only does he give sight to the physically blind, but the light of faith to the spiritually blind. Sadly, while the blind man opens more and more to the light, the Pharisees, who are physically sighted, become more and more spiritually blind.

There is a clear baptismal dimension to the story. As the blind man got sight by washing in the pool of Siloam, so we are enlightened by washing in the waters of Baptism.

The journey from unbelief to belief

The story of the man born blind is essentially a faith story. The climax of the story is the man's profession of faith in Jesus: 'Lord, I believe.'

The man was suffering from physical blindness. At that time a disability like that was seen as a punishment from God for sin. Hence, the apostles' question: 'Who sinned, this man or his parents?'

Jesus didn't go along with the view that suffering was a punishment for sin. He saw suffering as part of the human condition, and used it as an opportunity to show the compassion of God for his wounded children.

But the Gospel story is not really about physical seeing. Jesus did not come on earth to give us physical sight, but the kind of 'sight' that enables us to perceive heavenly realities. The story is about how a man came to believe in Jesus.

His journey from blindness to sight symbolises the journey from unbelief to belief, which is a journey from darkness to light. St Paul tells his converts at Ephesus: 'Once you were in darkness, but now you are light in the Lord' (Second Reading).

Healed quickly of his physical infirmity, the man experiences a gradual spiritual illumination. There is a beautiful progression in his understanding of who Jesus really is. His understanding went through three stages.

At a first stage, Jesus was just a man, though a wonderful man. He referred to him as 'the man called Jesus'. He went on to declare that Jesus was 'a prophet', and clearly a man of God. Finally, he came to understand that human categories were not adequate to describe him. He called him 'the Lord.' In other words, he professed the divinity of Jesus.

It shows that the more we know about Jesus, the greater he becomes. It's also worth noting that the more the man was called upon to defend his faith, the stronger and deeper it became. This is one of the most remarkable aspects of faith – it seems to thrive in adversity.

The story shows that there's a blindness worse than physical blindness – the blindness of unbelief. While the blind man opens more and more to the light of faith, the Pharisees, who are physically sighted, refuse to believe in Jesus and remain in darkness.

Physical sight is a marvellous gift which we should never take for granted. But faith is more precious still. Without faith there is a sense in which we will always be in the dark.

In giving sight to a blind man Jesus shows that he is the 'light of the world'. To believe in him is to have an unfailing lamp for our path. We show that we are following his light by the way we live. St Paul says that the effects of the light are seen in 'goodness, right living, and truth' (Second Reading).

There is a clear baptismal dimension to the story. As the blind man got sight by washing in the pool of Siloam, so we are enlightened by washing in the waters of Baptism.

It's the heart that matters

Israel needed a king. The first king of Israel, Saul, on whom such great hopes and expectations had been placed, had proved a failure and had been rejected by God. The prophet Samuel was commissioned by God to look for a new king.

Samuel's search led him to Bethlehem and the household of Jesse. There, one by one, he was introduced to seven of Jesse's sons. All of them possessed outstanding physical attributes. They were tall, strong, good-looking, etc. They created a very good image. Samuel was impressed. Yet he wasn't quite satisfied. So he continued his search.

He was looking for something else, something not so obvious, but which he felt he would recognise if and when he saw it. Then, almost as an afterthought, David was introduced to him. A mere youth, he was still physically underdeveloped. Judged by appearances, he didn't have a lot going for him. He didn't cut a good image.

Today the image has become more important than the reality, the appearance more important than the substance. Hence, we tend to judge by appearances. And to judge by appearances is to judge superficially. Appearances can be very deceptive. Everything that makes up the kernel of a person's character is hidden from us. In the memorable words of the Little Prince, 'What is essential is invisible.'

Now while David didn't cut a good image, he did have something going for him. Samuel, a wise and perceptive man, noticed it at once. We are told that he had 'fine eyes and a pleasant bearing'. This tells us that there was another side to young David – an inner side. Though this other side was largely invisible, there were some outward manifestations of it. It showed itself in his pleasant personality. But above all it showed itself in his eyes. His clear and bright eyes pointed to a good heart.

As soon as Samuel saw David he knew that his search for a successor to Saul was over. David made a good king and is one of the most important figures in the Old Testament. This doesn't mean that he was perfect. He sinned and sinned grievously. But he always repented. Several times in the Gospel Jesus is called 'Son of David'. It was meant as a compliment.

David's heart was good. When all is said and done it is the heart that matters. Emptiness of heart is the greatest poverty of all. A heavy heart is the most wearisome burden of all. A broken heart is the most painful wound of all. Darkness of heart is the blackest night of all.

In the Gospel story we see that the hearts of the Pharisees were in darkness. And not even Jesus, 'the light of the world', was able to bring light to them. As for the poor blind man, not only did his eyes become bright, but his heart also was filled with light as a result of his encounter with Jesus.

While we tend to look at appearances, God looks at the heart. God sees what is in the heart. That is why only God can truly judge people.

Work while you have the light

The question of human suffering was a big problem in Biblical times. It still is a big problem.

An Old Testament view saw a connection between suffering and sin. Suffering was seen as God's punishment for sin. Suffering served as a stark reminder to people of this side of God. But this left them with a very negative image of God. It made God out to be spiteful and vindictive. And, by and large, this was the view that prevailed.

Hence, when the apostles saw the blind man they immediately concluded that his blindness was the result of sin. But there still remained the problem: for whose sin was he suffering – his own or his parents'? So, hoping that Jesus would solve the problem for them, they asked him, 'Why was this man born blind? Who sinned? Was it the man himself or his parents?'

Jesus said, 'Neither this man nor his parents, but in order that the works of God might be displayed in him.' Thus he rejected the connection between suffering and sin. The man's blindness was not a punishment from God. God does not do evil. God does good.

We are no wiser as to the actual cause of the man's blindness. It might have been the result of a genetic flaw, or the poor health practices in Palestine at that time, or just a random thing. We simply don't know. And it really doesn't matter.

Jesus went on to say, 'This is an opportunity for me to show you what the works of God are really like.' Then he proceeded to heal the man. So the man's blindness did reveal something about what God is like. It showed God's compassion in the face of human suffering. The disciples may not have found Jesus' answer fully satisfying. But it was the perfect answer to the blind man. Talking about a problem will never solve it. Only action will.

Evil is a reality. The best response to it is good. What this man needed was not a lecture on the origins of evil but healing. Thus, what was a problem for the apostles became an opportunity for Jesus – an opportunity to do the work of God, to show what God is really like.

Jesus went on the say that for himself time was running out. The day of his earthly life was drawing to a close; the night of death was fast approaching. The time for works of love and mercy was limited. 'As long as the day lasts I must carry out the work of the one who sent me.'

The suffering of others is an opportunity for us too – an opportunity to show that we care. The night is coming for us too. We do not know how much of life's day remains to us. Hence, we must try to make use of every opportunity that comes our way to do good.

There are things that people could have done, and should have done, but unfortunately they often leave them until they are too sick or too weak.

We shall pass through this world but once. Any good, therefore, that we can do, or any kindness that we can show, to any human being, let us do it now; let us not defer it or neglect it, for we shall not pass this way again.

FIFTH SUNDAY OF LENT
Jesus, the resurrection and the life

Praying with the Word of God today

INTRODUCTION AND CONFITEOR

In today's Gospel we see a scene that, sadly, is very familiar to us, namely, people weeping over the death of a loved one. However, Jesus is at the centre of this scene. Let us turn to him who comforts those who grieve, and gives hope to those who walk in the shadow of death. [Pause]

Lord Jesus, you raise the dead to life in the Spirit. Lord, have mercy.

You bring pardon and peace to the sinner. Christ, have mercy.

You bring light to those who walk in darkness and in the shadow of death. Lord, have mercy.

PRAYER OF THE FAITHFUL

Celebrant: With confidence we raise up our prayers to God with whom is mercy and fullness of redemption.

Response: Lord, let your ears be attentive to the voice of our pleading.

Reader(s): For the Church: that it may proclaim to all the good news of eternal life won for us by the death and resurrection of Jesus. [Pause] Let us pray to the Lord.

For political leaders: that they may facilitate the work of those engaged in caring for and in preserving life. [Pause] Let us pray to the Lord.

For those who care for the sick and the dying: that they may have gentle hands and warm hearts. [Pause] Let us pray to the Lord.

Jesus comforted Martha and Mary: may he comfort all those who are grieving because of the death of a loved one [Pause] Let us pray to the Lord.

For ourselves: that we may treasure the beautiful but fragile gift of life. [Pause] Let us pray to the Lord.

For all those who have gone before us trusting in the words of Jesus: that the Lord may keep them safe in his love. [Pause] Let us pray to the Lord.

For our own special needs. [Longer Pause] Let us pray to the Lord.

Celebrant: God of love and mercy, your promise gives us the hope that one day tears will be wiped from our eyes, and death will be no more. May our faith in you never falter, and our hope in what you promise never grow dim. We ask this through Christ our Lord.

OUR FATHER

St John says, 'God so loved the world that he gave his only Son, so that everyone who believes in him may not perish but may have eternal life.' Let us pray to the God of love as Jesus taught us.

REFLECTION

We are born to die so that we may live more fully.
Every time we pass from one stage of life to another,
something in us dies and something new is born.
We taste death in moments of loneliness,
rejection, sorrow, disappointment, and failure.

We are dying before our time
when we live in bitterness, in hatred, and in isolation.
Each day we are creating our own death by the way we live.
For those with faith, death is not extinguishing the light;
it is putting out the lamp because the dawn has come.

FINAL BLESSING

May you never forget that we are but pilgrims on the earth, and that our true home is in heaven.

May God, who has called us to eternal glory in Christ, strengthen and support you with his grace.

May you walk before the Lord with blameless hearts.

Sharing the Word of God today

SCRIPTURE NOTE

First Reading (Ezek 37:12-14). All three readings are concerned with resurrection to newness of life. In the First Reading Ezekiel describes the Babylonian exile of the Israelites and their promised restoration to their homeland in terms of death and resurrection. They are like a mass of dry bones strewn about a valley; but they will soon be reassembled and re-clothed with flesh and sinews. When the Spirit of Yahweh enters them, they will live again and inhabit their land once more.

Second Reading (Rom 8:8-11). This contains one of the most forceful of Paul's expressions of Christian hope. The God who raised Jesus from the dead will raise us also because the same Spirit dwells in us. The present indwelling of the Spirit is an anticipation of the complete renewal of life that will come at the general resurrection.

Gospel (Jn 11:1-45). John's main aim here is to elicit faith in Jesus. Jesus says, 'Lazarus is dead; and for your sake I am glad I was not there because now you will believe.' And the story ends with the words: 'Many of the Jews ... who had seen what he did, believed in him.' Martha is presented as a model of faith. In defiance of the evidence, she declares, 'I believe that you are the Christ, the Son of God, the one who was to come into the world.'

Lazarus returned to earthly life. There is no suggestion that he was glorified, or that he wouldn't have to die again. He got a few more years added to his earthly life. But this was not Jesus' purpose in coming into the world.

Jesus came to offer us the life that cannot be touched by death, the kind of life that only God possesses, and that Jesus as God's Son makes possible for those who believe in him. The key words in the story are: 'I am the resurrection and the life. Anyone who believes in me will never die [eternally].'

The delay in coming to Martha and Mary, and the fact that Lazarus has been dead for four days, serve to underline the point the evangelist is making, namely, that Jesus is the master of life and death.

There is a clear baptismal dimension to the story. It is through Baptism that we receive a share in the undying life of God.

The life that cannot be destroyed by death

The raising of Lazarus constituted a mighty deed. On witnessing it, many of the Jews believed in Jesus. But what are we to make of it? And how are we to understand it?

We can take it at two levels – a superficial level and a deeper level. If taken on a superficial level what does the miracle amount to? Just a once-off wonder performed for the benefit of one individual, Lazarus. In which case it would have no meaning for us. All it would mean is that Lazarus got a few more years added to his earthly life.

But Jesus didn't come into this world to add a few more years to our earthly existence. Fortunately we can do this for ourselves. In happens regularly in our hospitals. There, people are brought back from the brink of death, and in some cases even resuscitated.

But this is not what the miracle is about. The miracle has a deeper and broader meaning, one valid for all time. The story is about another kind of life, a life no doctor can give, but that Jesus can give, namely, eternal life.

Jesus offers us the life that death cannot destroy. The key to understanding the story is contained in Jesus' declaration: 'I am the resurrection and the life. Anyone who believes in me will never die [eternally].' Just as the miracle of the changing of water into wine at Cana was more than a once-off wonder performed for the benefit of a couple of newly-weds, so the raising of Lazarus is more than a once-off wonder performed for the benefit of one individual, Lazarus.

Jesus came on earth to give the life that cannot be touched by death, the kind of life that only God possesses, and that Jesus as God's Son makes possible for those who believe in him. Those who believe in Jesus and who follow him, enter into a relationship with God that death cannot end. This is what the evangelist is telling us. This is the core message of the story.

Before Jesus could confer eternal life on us, he first had to undergo death himself. By rising from the dead in our humanity, he broke the power of death forever. The Scriptures seldom say, 'Jesus rose from the dead.' What they say is, 'God [the Father] raised Jesus from the dead.'

Now the raising of Lazarus was a wonderful thing, but it doesn't compare with the raising of Jesus. Lazarus returned to natural life or earthly life. There is no suggestion that he was glorified, or that he wouldn't have to die again.

Jesus, on the other hand, having been raised from the dead, will never die again. He is portrayed as conquering death, as returning immortal and glorified. Lazarus came out of the tomb still wearing the wrappings of death (Jn 11:44). Jesus is seen as having left the burial cloths in the tomb (Jn 20:6-7).

Eternal life is not something that begins when we die. It has already begun in Baptism, though in a hidden way. Through Baptism we already share in the risen life of Jesus.

In the story Martha is presented as a model of faith. In defiance of the evidence, she placed her faith in Jesus. Christian faith means trusting that Jesus' promise will be fulfilled: 'Though a man die, yet shall he live.' This kind of faith enables us to live our earthly lives under the brightness of immortality. And it makes it possible for us to enter the dark kingdom of death with hearts buoyed up with hope.

Jesus: the source of eternal life

Everybody needs friends, even Jesus. In the village of Bethany he had three very special friends – Martha and Mary, and their brother, Lazarus. Their house remained open to him when many other houses were being closed against him.

When Lazarus got sick, it was only natural that the sisters should turn to Jesus for help. They sent an urgent message to him: 'Lord, the man you love is ill.' Who could resist a request like that? Surprisingly, Jesus didn't drop everything and rush to the bedside of his dying friend. Instead, he stayed on where he was for two more days. His delay in coming must have been heart-breaking for the sisters. Right in front of their eyes their brother's life was ebbing away. And the one they believed could save him wasn't there.

We can identify with their disappointment. When something bad happens to us or to a loved one, we may feel abandoned by God. We can't help thinking that if God really loved us, he wouldn't have allowed this thing to happen.

Lazarus died. The Gospel shows the desolation his death caused to Martha and Mary. It's a desolation many of us have experienced around the death of a loved one. While they had sympathetic people around them, the one they most wanted to be with them was not there. Jesus, their friend and the friend of Lazarus, was absent.

When he finally came, Martha said to him, 'If you had been here, our brother would not have died,' thereby suggesting that he could have prevented his death. But he challenged her to believe that he could still save Lazarus: 'I am the resurrection and the life. Those who believe in me, even though they die [to this life], will live. Do you believe this?' In defiance of the evidence, she declared, 'I believe that you are the Christ, the Son of God, the one who was to come into the world.'

There was a happy ending for Martha and Mary – Lazarus was restored to them. However, there is no suggestion that he wouldn't have to die again. Clearly he did die again. But that is not the main point of John's story. The point of the story is contained in Jesus' declaration: 'I am the resurrection and the life. Anyone who believes in me will never die [eternally].'

Jesus' purpose in coming into this world was not to add a few years to our earthly existence. He came to give the life that cannot be touched by death, the kind of life that only God possesses. Those who believe in Jesus and who follow him, enter into a relationship with God which death cannot end. That's what the story is about.

In telling us this story St John's aim is to elicit faith in Jesus as the resurrection and the life. Even though there are no happy endings in our stories, we are called to imitate the faith of Martha.

The story shows Jesus as a faithful friend. It shows that even in death we are not beyond the reach of his help. He understands the anguish caused by death. He experienced it himself. He overcame death, not by avoiding it, but by undergoing it and conquering it. He did so, not just for himself, but also for all of us. Thus he has become a pathfinder and a beacon of hope for us.

An invincible spring

The Gospel story presents us with a scene, which is all too familiar to us – people weeping over the death of a loved one. Death is like winter – only worse. In nature's winter, despite appearances to the contrary, life doesn't cease. The outward dies, but not the core. But in the winter of death, life ceases altogether. Death robs us of everything.

When the winter of death came for Lazarus, his sisters, Martha and Mary, were plunged into grief. Jesus didn't leave them alone in their grief. He came to them, and wept with them. In so doing, he has joined himself forever to those who mourn. But he didn't leave it at that. He challenged them to believe that he could still save Lazarus. He said to them, 'I am the resurrection and the life. Those who believe in me, even though they die [to this life], will live. Do you believe this?'

Martha rose to the challenge and declared, 'I believe that you are the Christ, the Son of God, the one who was to come into the world.' It can't have been easy for her to believe as all the evidence was against it.

Faith isn't easy for us either. Death constitutes the severest test for our faith. At the same time faith is our great ally in facing death. It doesn't mean we have all the answers. And it doesn't dispense us from the painful work of grieving. But it does add a vital element to our grieving. That element is hope. We grieve as people who believe that death doesn't have the last word.

There are puzzling elements in the Gospel story. Indeed it stretches our credulity to breaking point – and beyond. However, the main thrust of it is clear. Jesus is the master of death and the source of eternal life for all who believe in him. The key point is Jesus' pronouncement: 'I am the resurrection and the life.' This is one of the greatest statements in the Gospel.

Jesus didn't come into the world to add a few years to our earthly existence. He came to give the life that cannot be touched by death, the kind of life that only God possesses. Those who believe in him and who follow him, enter into a relationship with God which death cannot end. That is what the story is telling us.

Though Jesus himself experienced the winter of death, by rising from the dead in our humanity, he broke the power of death forever. He entered the dark kingdom of death, and emerged victorious. Thus he has caused a new and invincible spring to dawn on all who believe in him.

We feel sad at the onset of winter. And it's hard to believe in spring when we see snow on the hills and feel a bitter wind in our faces. However, we are not too despondent because we know that spring will eventually renew everything again. In the same way, we are sad when the winter of death claims the life of a loved one, and when we think of our own death. Nevertheless, we are not overwhelmed. What sustains us is our faith in Jesus, the resurrection and the life. Just as the expectation of spring takes the sting out of winter, so the resurrection of Jesus takes the sting out of death for us.

Eternal life is not something that begins when we die. It has already started. It started in Baptism when receive a share in the undying life of God. Thus, even in the midst of winter, we know that spring is already quietly at work, though its full blossoming is still in the future.

PALM SUNDAY OF THE LORD'S PASSION

Praying with the Word of God today

INTRODUCTION AND CONFITEOR

The solemn entrance takes the place of the Confiteor. But if the solemn entrance cannot be celebrated, this Introductory Rite could be used.

Holy Week gives us the opportunity to accompany Jesus on his final journey. On that journey, he suffered betrayal, torture, crucifixion, and death. It gives us an insight into the fickleness of the human heart, but also into the immense compassion of God.

As we call to mind our sins, let us also call to mind God's great love for us in Christ. [Pause]

Lord Jesus, you were pierced for our faults. Lord, have mercy.

You bore our sufferings and sorrows. Christ, have mercy.

Through your sufferings you won pardon for all of us. Lord, have mercy.

PRAYER OF THE FAITHFUL

Celebrant: Let us pray that all of God's children may be gathered into the kingdom of salvation.

Response: Lord, hear our prayer.

Reader(s): For the followers of Christ: that they may not be afraid to profess their loyalty to him before an indifferent and sometimes hostile world. [Pause] Let us pray to the Lord.

For all those who administer our justice system: that they may exercise their office in a just and compassionate manner. [Pause] Let us pray to the Lord.

For all those who are suffering: that they may unite their sufferings to those of Jesus, and know his power in their weakness. [Pause] Let us pray to the Lord.

For all gathered here: that we may be sensitive to the sufferings of those around us, and ensure that they do not have to carry their cross alone. [Pause] Let us pray to the Lord.

For all the dead: that the Lord may free them from the shadows of death and gladden them with the light of his face. [Pause] Let us pray to the Lord.

For our own special needs. [Longer pause] Let us pray to the Lord.

Celebrant: Heavenly Father, look with compassion on all who suffer. Make fruitful for good the tribulations of the innocent, the pains of the sick, and the sorrows of the bereaved. We ask this through him who suffered in our flesh and died for our sake, and who now lives and reigns with you and the Holy Spirit, one God, for ever and ever.

OUR FATHER

God did not spare his own Son, but gave him up to death for our sake. Let us pray to the God of love as Jesus taught us.

SIGN OF PEACE

Lord Jesus Christ, you looked on the holy city of Jerusalem, and with tears in your eyes you said, 'If only you understood the message of peace. But, alas, it is hidden from your eyes.'

Look with pity on our world, marred by violence and tragedy, and grant that all of God's children may enjoy the peace and unity of your kingdom where you live for ever and ever.

REFLECTION

The day on which Jesus died
might well have been called '*Bad* Friday'.
But we call it '*Good* Friday'.
We do so because that dark day
was made luminous by the goodness of Jesus,
and because we see it in the light of Easter.
His death may have seemed a defeat,
it was not a defeat; it was a victory;
the victory of love over hate,
of good over evil, and of life over death.

FINAL BLESSING

May the example of Jesus help you to bear your sufferings with patience and fortitude.

May the example of Jesus in forgiving those who put him to death help you to forgive those who have hurt you.

You have professed your faith in Christ here in church; may you have the courage to witness to him in everyday life.

Sharing the Word of God today

SCRIPTURE NOTE

Gospel for procession (Mt 21:1-11). Here Matthew tells us that Jesus, the Messiah, enters Jerusalem, not as an all-conquering warrior on horseback, but as a humble, gentle bearer of Good News riding on a donkey. Thus he fulfils the prophecy of Zechariah (9:9). The garments provide an improvised saddle. The spreading of garments and branches on the road was a form of homage for an important person (somewhat like our red carpet).

First Reading (Is 50:4-7). This contains verses from the third of the Servant Songs of Second Isaiah. The servant must first be a disciple, prayerfully receiving God's word, before presuming to teach others. His message evidently meets with opposition and results in persecution. But he absorbs all the physical and mental abuse directed at him without retaliating. The insults don't really touch him, because he is confident that God will help and vindicate him. (As we read this passage we think of Jesus standing alone and unarmed before Caiphas, Herod, and Pilate.)

Second Reading (Phil 2:6-11). Jesus took on himself our human condition. He went even further: he humbled himself to the point of accepting the most shameful kind of death – death on a cross. God rewarded his obedience and humility by raising him up and making him Lord of heaven and earth. The self-emptying and self-abasement of Christ should serve as a model for every Christian.

Gospel (Mt 26:14-27:66). In his Passion narrative, Matthew follows Mark closely. Like Mark, he presents Jesus as being abandoned by his followers and having to face his hour alone. There is no friend or supporter by the cross; Jesus dies rejected and mocked.

Both have a Jewish trial of Jesus and a Roman trial. The Jewish authorities sought to convict Jesus of planning to destroy the Temple, and of blasphemy. The Roman trial centred on Jesus' claim to be the king of the Jews. Both authorities failed to grant Jesus justice and both maltreated him.

Throughout his narrative, Matthew stresses two factors in particular: the passion fulfils the prophecies of Scripture (in other words, it falls within God's purpose), and because of his foreknowledge and free decision, Jesus was in control of the situation.

Matthew has extraordinary events following the death of Jesus: darkening of the sky, rending of the temple curtain, splitting of the rocks, earthquakes, lightning, the rising of the dead, and the appearance of angels. What are we to make of all these?

These were events that were expected to happen at the end of time when God returned as Lord and Judge. Matthew has them happen at the death and resurrection of Jesus. However, this is not the end of time. But it is 'the turning point of the ages'.

The rending of the curtain of the temple signified that the privilege of Israel has ended; henceforth access to the divine presence is open to all. The earthquake marked the death of Jesus as an epoch-making event and serves as a prelude to the resurrection of the dead. The raising of 'many bodies' is not the general resurrection. It characterises the death of Jesus as the event that makes possible the resurrection of others.

Those who put Christ to death

At the end of World War II the leaders of the Nazi regime were tried before an international tribunal at Nuremberg. For all the horrific things they did, they were not devils incarnate. They were human beings, though bad human beings.

The people who put Jesus to death were not a uniquely evil bunch of people, acting from the vilest possible motives. They belonged to the same human family as we do. In each we glimpse something of ourselves, of our failings, and of our need of grace. This may be a troubling kinship but we cannot reject it. Let us look briefly at the main characters in the Passion Story and the motives out of which they acted.

The Pharisees: These were austere, religious men, who devoted all their energy to doing good and the study of God's Law. But they were convinced of their own rightness, and history shows that such people are capable of appalling evil. Examples: the unconverted Paul; the Crusades; the Inquisition; the torture of suspects by governments, the atrocities of guerrillas, and so on.

Caiphas: He was, perhaps, thinking mainly about religious orthodoxy and how easily people get led astray by false messiahs. The Church condemned heretics to burn at the stake, thinking it was doing a service to God.

Pilate: He was thinking about the preservation of law and order at a time of great unrest. He knew that Jesus was innocent, but he feared that trouble would ensue if he did not give the religious leaders what they wanted. No doubt he was also thinking about his own job. Most people know what is right, but don't always have the courage to do it.

Judas: Most likely he was a disillusioned man. But even he came to recognise and condemn the evil he had done. He could not live with the killing of an innocent man. Plenty of people today seem to have no such problem. Think of executioners, abortionists, terrorists, and death squads. At times we all betray our ideals, if not our friends.

Peter: Here we have a man who was simply weak and cowardly. Any one of us would probably have denied Jesus in the same circumstances. Peter at least shed tears over his denials. How many of us shed tears over our denials?

The soldiers: They were simply carrying out orders. The Nazi leaders made the same excuse at the Nuremberg trials. We too frequently blame others for our sins. We refuse to accept responsibility for our cowardly acts and evasions.

The crowd: It was a highly emotional occasion. They simply got carried away. They didn't really know what was happening. Do we not often take refuge in the crowd? 'Everybody is doing it,' we protest.

But we must not lose sight of the central character in this sordid story, namely, Jesus himself. He shows us that the only way to overcome evil is by good.

Dark evil sleeps in us all. The Passion of Jesus helps us to confront the evil that is within us. It also helps us to deal with pain, rejection, failure, and death. Furthermore, it helps us to find healing for the wounds inflicted on us by the sins of others.

The tracks we leave behind

It's a winter's afternoon and the fields are covered with soft, clean snow. The snow is full of tracks made by birds and animals. On looking closely at those tracks it is possible to identify some of the birds and animals, and even to tell what they are up to.

Most of what you see there is harmless – the tracks of little creatures trying to stay alive in a hostile climate. For instance, you see the scratchings of sparrows in their quest for a worm, and the rootings of rabbits looking for a blade of grass. You see the beaten snow where sheep have passed. But then you see a spatter of blood on the snow where a fox or a bird of prey has made a kill.

On a normal day you could cross these fields, and you would see nothing of the doings of the birds and animals. Everything would be covered up. But today their cover is blown. Everything is written there in the snow – innocence, resourcefulness, pain, cunning, and red murder.

This can happen in the world of humans too. For instance, something happens in the neighbourhood or in the workplace, and people are forced to take a stand. Suddenly, their minds and hearts are revealed. Some come out well, but others are shown up in a poor light.

The trial of Jesus was such an event. He was such a transparently good person that when he was put on trial, the snow of his innocence fell from heaven and covered the earth. All who were abroad on that day left clear tracks behind them.

When we look at those tracks we see some ugly things. We see the hatred and fanaticism of Caiphas and the religious leaders who plotted his death. We see the cold, calculating evil of Judas who betrayed him. We see the weakness of Peter who disowned him. We see the cruelty of Herod who mocked him. We see the cowardice of Pilate, who, though knowing he was innocent, signed his death warrant. We see the unthinking hostility of the mob who shouted, 'Crucify him!' We see the dutiful obedience of the soldiers who carried out the execution.

But we also see some lovely things. We see the compassion of Veronica who wiped his face. The courage of Simon of Cyrene who helped him to carry the cross. The sympathy of the women of Jerusalem who wept for him. And the steadfast loyalty of a little group of friends who stayed with him to the end, among these his mother and the disciple John.

It wasn't Jesus who was judged on that day. It was his disciples, and especially his accusers and executioners. But it wasn't he who judged them. They judged themselves – by the tracks they left behind. And we too will be judged by the tracks we leave behind us.

The long silence

I had a dream that it was the end of time. Billions and billions of people were assembled on a great plain before the throne of God, waiting to be judged. Some were fearful but others were angry.

A woman said, 'How can God judge us? What does *he* know about suffering? We endured terror, torture, and death.' Then she pulled up her sleeve to show a tattooed number from a Nazi concentration camp on her arm.

Then a black man lowered his collar to show an ugly rope burn around his neck. 'What about this?' he asked. 'Lynched for no crime but being black. We have suffocated in slave ships, been wrenched from loved ones, toiled till only death gave us release.'

Next a girl with the word 'illegitimate' stamped on her forehead said, 'To endure my stigma was beyond, beyond ...' and her voice trailed off to be taken up by others.

All had a complaint against God for the evil and suffering he had permitted during their lives on earth. How lucky God was to live in heaven where all was sweetness and light, where there was no weeping, no fear, no hunger, no hatred. What did God know about human suffering?

They decided that God should be sentenced to live on earth – as a man. But because he was God, they would set certain safeguards to be sure he could not use his divine powers to help himself.

Let him be born a Jew. Let the legitimacy of his birth be doubted so that none will know who is really his father. Give him a work so difficult that even his family will think he is out of his mind when he tries to do it.

Let him be betrayed by his dearest friends. Let him be indicted on false charges, tried before a prejudiced jury, convicted by a cowardly judge.

Let him see what it means to be abandoned by everyone. Let him be tortured and mocked. Then let him die. Let him die so that there can be no doubt he died. Let there be a great host of witnesses to verify it.

As each portion of the sentence was announced, loud murmurs of approval went up from the great throng of people assembled. When they had finished pronouncing sentence, a long silence ensued. No one uttered a word. No one moved. For suddenly all knew. God had already served his sentence.

Our God came to live among us. Put God on trial if you will. Shake your fist at him, spit in his face, scourge him and finally crucify him. What does it matter? It's already been done to him. On the cross the innocent and sinless Jesus gathered up all human pain and made it his own.

The road of suffering is narrow and difficult. But it is not the same since Jesus travelled it. A bright light illuminates it. And even though it leads to Calvary, it doesn't end there. It ends at Easter. Those who suffer with him on earth will share his glory in heaven.

Eastertide

EASTER SUNDAY
The Lord is risen

Praying with the Word of God today

INTRODUCTION AND CONFITEOR

For Christians, Easter is the greatest feast of all. This is the day Jesus broke the chains of death and rose in triumph from the grave. This is truly the 'Day of the Lord.'

But it is our day too, because Jesus wants to share with us the fruits of his victory. Let us open our hearts to the joy of this great day. [Pause]

Lord Jesus, through the power of your resurrection you dispel evil and wash guilt away. Lord, have mercy.

You restore lost innocence and bring joy to mourners. Christ, have mercy.

You cast out hatred, humble earthly pride, and bring us peace. Lord, have mercy.

PRAYER OF THE FAITHFUL

Celebrant: Christ, the Morning Star, has come back from the dead, and now sheds his peaceful light on the world. Let us pray to him with confidence for all our needs.

Response: Lord, hear our prayer.

Reader(s): That the Lord's light may shine on his followers, and inflame them with new hope. [Pause] Let us pray to the Lord.

That his light may shine on world leaders, encouraging them in their search for justice and peace. [Pause] Let us pray to the Lord.

That his light may shine on the sad and the lonely, the sick and the troubled. [Pause] Let us pray to the Lord.

That his light may shine on those who are grieving the loss of a loved one, and scatter the shadows of death. [Pause] Let us pray to the Lord.

That his light may shine on all gathered here, confirming our faith and strengthening our hope. [Pause] Let us pray to the Lord.

That the radiance of eternity may shine on our deceased relatives and friends, and on all the faithful departed. [Pause] Let us pray to the Lord.

We pause to pray for our own special needs this Easter night (day). [Longer pause] Let us pray to the Lord.

Celebrant: God of power and love, through the resurrection of your Son you have kindled in our hearts the hope of eternal life. Guard this hope with your grace, and bring it to fulfilment in the kingdom of heaven. We ask this through Christ our Lord.

OUR FATHER

As God's adopted daughters and sons, we are destined to share in the resurrection of Jesus. Let us pray to our heavenly Father as Jesus taught us.

SIGN OF PEACE

Lord Jesus Christ, on Easter Sunday evening, you appeared to your frightened and disheartened disciples and said to them, 'Peace be with you'. And on seeing you they were filled with joy.

Grant that we, who today (tonight) hear anew the message of Easter, may enjoy the peace and unity of your kingdom where you live for ever and ever.

PRAYER/REFLECTION

During the course of our lives
we experience many losses and disappointments.
This brings home to us how fragile are our hopes,
and how brittle our dreams.
Lord, may the splendour of your resurrection
scatter the shadows of death,
and enable us to walk in radiant hope
towards the kingdom where there are
no more shattered hopes or broken dreams.

FINAL BLESSING

May the risen Lord inflame your hearts and raise your spirits, so that we may journey towards his kingdom with undimmed hope.

May you be good witnesses for the resurrection by the joy and hope you radiate.

And may the peace of God, who brought Jesus back from the dead, be with you all.

Sharing the Word of God today

SCRIPTURE NOTE

First Reading (Acts 10:34.37-43). From now until Pentecost inclusive, the First Reading is taken from Acts of the Apostles. In Acts, Luke is concerned with showing the triumphal progress of the Gospel throughout the whole known world. Behind this progress, he sees the power of the Holy Spirit.

Our reading is part of Peter's sermon in the house of the Roman centurion Cornelius. In it he gives a brief sketch of the ministry of Jesus, ending with the narrative of his death and resurrection. He stresses that he and his companions were witnesses to all this. Now they have been sent to proclaim the risen Jesus to be Judge of the living and the dead. He is the one the prophets spoke about. All who believe in him will have their sins forgiven.

Second Reading (Col 3:1-4). This could be seen as a message for the newly baptised. But of course it applies to all the baptised. We Christians died and rose with Christ at the moment of our baptism. Therefore, we must seek the things of heaven (the things of God) rather than the things that belong to the earth (all that is opposed to God). We must live, not by the world's standards, but model ourselves on Christ. The hiddenness of such a life in Christ does not take away one whit from its reality.

Alternative Second Reading (1 Cor 5:6-8). Here Paul is concerned with a case of incest in the Corinthian community. He argues that this 'immoral' person affects the whole community, like yeast within a lump of dough. The passage can also be seen as applying to the baptised. The baptised must rid themselves of the 'yeast' of evil and wickedness, and live in sincerity and truth.

Gospel (Jn 20:1-9). Almost every element in this story is charged with symbolism. The darkness of 'the first day of the week' evokes the darkness of Genesis 1, suggesting that Jesus' death is the prelude to a new creation. The burial clothes, and especially their arrangement, are a sign that Mary Magdalene's interpretation of the empty tomb is not the correct one. Jesus has not been 'taken' anywhere. Rather he has left the things of mortality behind him.

However, only the beloved disciple correctly interprets this sign. He realises what has happened – and he believes. It is not what he has read in scripture that convinces him that Jesus had risen. (Later, of course, the words of scripture would confirm him in his belief).

The hope Easter gives

It would be impossible to exaggerate the value of hope. We can't live without hope. Hope is to the spirit what bread is to the body. It is amazing what the human spirit can endure and overcome provided it is nourished by the bread of hope.

Hope is the daily bread of the spirit. Hope may come only in intermittent flashes, like the beams of a lighthouse, but that is all that is needed. However, human hope is very fragile. And it is constantly under threat because there is so much tragedy in life.

The apostles knew all about this. The crucifixion of Jesus reduced their hope to rubble. Why then wasn't that the end of the story? Because something happened to change it. That something was the resurrection of Jesus. Without the resurrection we probably would never have heard of Jesus.

It has been claimed that it was the faith of the apostles that produced the resurrection. The Gospels show that the opposite was the case. The faith of the apostles was born from the direct experience of the risen Jesus. That experience transformed them from a group of cowardly people into people who were prepared to – and did – die for his message.

The death of Jesus, which had seemed to be a defeat, turned out to be a victory – the victory of love over hate, of good over evil, and of life over death. By rescuing his beloved Son from the power of death, God shows us that he vindicates those who trust in him.

Easter provides us with an enormous injection of hope. It is not a temporary fix, but an intravenous feeding of love and hope from Christ's heart to ours. Even though we still feel the pain of the world, nevertheless, there is a quiet joy among us because we know that good is stronger than evil, and that life is stronger than death. The resurrection assures us that beyond suffering lies glory, beyond defeat is triumph, beyond death is life.

Our disappointments may be many, our joys may be small, but our hope is great. The resurrection of Jesus is the basis of our hope. We must ask God to guard this hope with his grace. Because for those who lose hope, the stones of the road will be rougher under their feet, the brambles more spiky, and the load will weigh heavier on their backs.

But how different things are for those who have hope. In the beautiful words of Isaiah: 'Those who hope in God renew their strength. They put out wings like eagles. They run and do not grow weary, they walk and never tire' (Is 40:31). 'Those who hope in God renew their strength. They put out wings like eagles. They run and do not grow weary, they walk and never tire.'

To profess belief in the resurrection is not to affirm an absurd miracle but to affirm the power of God. The power of God is greater than the power of death.

It was in our fragile, mortal nature that Jesus overcame death. In this way he has become a pathfinder for us. If his humanity can be glorified then so can ours.

His resurrection enables us to live our lives under the brightness of immortality. And it makes it possible for us to enter the dark kingdom of death buoyed up with hope.

O happy fault!

The Easter Vigil is the most important ceremony in the Church's liturgical year. It is also the most moving. We gather in darkness – darkness represents death. But we gather around a flickering fire. The fire represents the undying life of God. From the fire we light the Easter candle, thereby symbolising Jesus rising from the dead. From that candle we light our own candles to symbolise that the resurrection is for us too.

A key moment in the Easter Vigil is when we all stand with lighted candles in our hands as the *Exultet* is sung. The *Exultet* (or Easter Proclamation) is an inspired composition. (It is believed to have been compiled in Gaul in the fifth century.) It is an invitation to rejoice in Christ's victory over death, and spells out the implications of his rising for us and for the entire world.

To quote from it: 'This is the night when Jesus Christ broke the chains of death and rose in triumph from the grave.

'The power of this holy night dispels all evil, washes guilt away, restores lost innocence, and brings joy to mourners.

'Christ, the Morning Star, has come back from the dead, and now sheds his peaceful light on the world.'

These are marvellous words. 'Christ, the Morning Star, has come back from the dead, and now sheds his peaceful light on the world.'

It goes so far as to suggest that the sin of Adam was somehow necessary: 'O happy fault, O necessary sin of Adam, which gained for us so great a Redeemer!'

In other words, a universe with fault and with Christ is preferred to a universe without fault and without Christ. Here is a boldness never before equalled in Christian thought.

But what authority stands behind the *Exultet?* The *Exultet* draws its inspiration from the Scriptures, and especially St Paul. Paul draws a contrast between Christ and Adam. Sin came into the world through Adam; abundant grace came through Jesus Christ (Rom 5:12-15). Paul says that the gift far outweighed the fall: 'where sin increased, grace overflowed all the more' (v. 20).

Paul is not justifying the sin of Adam; he is redeeming it. What he is telling us is that God can bring good out of evil, even a moral evil caused by his creatures. From the greatest moral evil ever committed (the crucifixion of Jesus), God brought the greatest of goods: the glorification of Jesus and our redemption. But for all that, evil never becomes a good.

The death of Jesus is the most powerful example of God's love for us. To quote the *Exultet* again: 'Father, how wonderful your care for us. How boundless your merciful love. To ransom a slave you gave away your Son.'

Here we see the amazing generosity of God and the breadth of his forgiveness. It almost sounds too good to be true. It involves a generosity beyond what our human nature may expect.

Can our God really be that good? The answer is a resounding 'yes'. God's goodness utterly transcends human goodness. The power of God is greater than the power of sin, and the love of God can use even sin for his glory and our good.

The great message of Easter: God in his goodness brings good out of evil, and life out of death. This is not to say that God wills bad things to happen. No. It means that though all that happens is not determined by God's will, all is encompassed by his love.

(This homily is especially suitable for Easter Vigil.)

The triumph of the light

Once a priest installed a stained glass window in the atrium of the parish church. The window depicted the traditional Calvary scene – Jesus hanging on the cross, flanked by the standing figures of Mary his mother, and the apostle John. The sky was dark and threatening; the earth steeped in darkness. Across the middle of the picture there was a faint brightness. And in the distant background there was a hint of dawn coming over the hills.

One day the priest was passing through the atrium when he noticed a man standing in front of the window, deep in thought.

'Well, what do you think of it?' he asked the man.

'It's far too dark for my liking,' came the answer.

'I agree with you,' the priest responded. 'It *is* a very dark painting. But that is what Calvary was like. The evangelists tell us that as Jesus was dying a great darkness descended on Calvary. We don't know if they are talking about an actual darkness, or if they are using darkness in a figurative sense, as a way of saying that Jesus, the Light of the World, was dying. But one thing is certain: Calvary was a dark place. It was made dark by the cruelty inflicted on Jesus, and the mockery and hatred that was directed at him as he died.'

'I never thought of it like that,' the man said.

'But to get back to the window,' the priest resumed. 'Right now we're looking at it at the wrong time of day.'

'What do you mean?' the man asked.

'The window faces the rising sun. As the sun comes up, it shines right through the window. If you see the window when that happens, you'll see it in a completely different light.'

The following morning the man put the priest's words to the test. He arrived in the atrium just before dawn, and headed straight for the window. As the sun rose, the window was transformed. The mostly unclothed body of Jesus began to glow. So did the haloes of Mary and John. Every bit of brightness in the picture was magnified to such an extent that the darkness was completely eclipsed. After that, whenever he looked at the window, he saw it in the light of dawn.

Jesus died in darkness. To his disciples his death, especially the manner of it (crucifixion), seemed to be the defeat of goodness, and the triumph of evil. And that is exactly what it would have been without Easter. Without Easter darkness would have had the last word. But because of the resurrection darkness did not have the last word. God vindicated the faithful love of Jesus by raising him from the dead on the third day.

We have to see Jesus' death in the light of Easter. His death may have seemed a defeat. It was not a defeat; it was a victory – the victory of love over hatred, of good over evil, and of life over death.

In the Gospel (vigil Mass and morning Mass) we read how some women disciples of Jesus came to his tomb towards dawn on the first day of the week. They came in darkness – the pre-dawn darkness and the darkness of grief and despair. At the tomb they were told: 'He is not here; he has risen.' They left the tomb bathed in light – the light of day and the light of hope and joy.

We have heard the same glad tidings: 'He is not here; he has risen.' May we go away from here bathed in light.

Jesus shared the darkness of death with us – the darkness that surrounds all deaths, but violent and tragic deaths in particular. He went into the heart of that darkness, and scattered it by the light of his resurrection. This means that we can walk through the valley of death without fear. This is the hope of Easter. This is the hope that is granted to believers.

Victory already won

We can't appreciate the greatness of Jesus' resurrection unless we acknowledge the full reality of his death. Jesus conquered death, not by avoiding it, but by passing through it. In the Creed we say, 'He descended to the dead' or 'He descended into hell'.

This was not the hell of the damned. This was *Sheol* or the abode of the dead. But he descended there as Saviour, proclaiming the Good News to the spirits of those souls who awaited their Saviour.

The point of this is to make it clear that he truly died. So fully did he join his lot with ours, that he endured not only the act of dying but also the *state* of being dead.

Jesus died in darkness. But he trusted enough in God to face the darkness, and to wait for the resurrection on the third day. He too had to make that leap of faith that we will one day be called upon to make. His leap of faith was not in vain. The Father raised him up.

The Scriptures and the early Church seldom said, 'Jesus *rose* from the dead.' What they said was, 'God *raised* Jesus from the dead.' The Father did not save Jesus *from* death, but *in* death. This action of God set the seal of divine approval on his life and work.

Jesus entered the dark kingdom of death, and emerged victorious. He has won *his* victory. But that victory has to work its way through and become a reality in us. How can this happen? It can happen because Jesus' victory was won in *our* nature. Jesus was raised in our flesh and blood. If the battle had not been fought and won in our nature, we would be incapable of profiting from his victory. We would still be under the power of death.

Now if it happened to the human flesh of Jesus, then it can happen to ours. If his humanity can be glorified, then so can ours. The surprise and gift of Easter is that the resurrection is for us too. It is *our* death that has been defeated.

For Christians, joy is found in the fact that the thing we fear most (death) has been overcome in Christ. Eternal life is not something that is guaranteed to us by nature. There is nothing inherent in human nature that qualifies us for it. Our hope lies in the resurrection of Jesus.

To profess belief in the resurrection is not to affirm an absurd miracle. It is to affirm the power of God, which is greater than the power of death.

Good Friday, day of darkness and death, comes to everyone. So does Holy Saturday, day of emptiness and sorrow. On such days it's hard to believe. But Easter Sunday, day of life and joy, will come as surely as the dawn. Death, the last enemy, has been overcome.

We go forward more confidently and hopefully because Jesus our Brother has gone ahead of us. He has become a pathfinder for us. His Easter victory enables us to live our lives under the brightness of immortality. And it makes it possible for us to enter the dark kingdom of death buoyed up with hope.

SECOND SUNDAY OF EASTER
Blessed are those who have not seen and yet believe

Praying with the Word of God today

INTRODUCTION AND CONFITEOR

On this Sunday each year the Gospel focuses on the apostle who has become known as Doubting Thomas. Thomas is a consolation to us because we too are troubled by doubts.

Let us bring our doubts to the Lord, and ask him to dispel them as he dispelled the doubts of Thomas. [Pause]

Lord Jesus, you help us to believe in God's unconditional love for us. Lord, have mercy.

You help us to believe in God's all-embracing forgiveness. Christ, have mercy.

You help us to believe in God's promise of eternal life. Lord, have mercy.

PRAYER OF THE FAITHFUL

Celebrant: As a people who have not seen and yet believe, we turn in prayer to the God of life with all our needs.

Response: Lord, hear our prayer.

Reader(s): For the disciples of Jesus: that they may be good witnesses to his resurrection by the hope and joy they radiate. [Pause] Let us pray to the Lord.

For the leaders of governments: that they may work together to bring about a just and peaceful world. [Pause] Let us pray to the Lord.

For those whose faith is weak, and those who have no faith. [Pause] Let us pray to the Lord.

For those who are grieving: that the Lord may comfort them, and restore them to full fellowship with the community. [Pause] Let us pray to the Lord.

For the members of this community: that we may be blessed with a strong faith that expresses itself in deeds of love and service. [Pause] Let us pray to the Lord.

For our deceased relatives and friends: that the Lord may receive them into the kingdom of his glory. [Pause] Let us pray to the Lord.

For our own special needs. [Longer pause] Let us pray to the Lord.

Celebrant: Almighty and ever-living God, strengthen our belief that beyond death there is a life, where broken things are mended and lost things are found; where there is rest for the weary and joy for the sad; where all that we have loved and willed of good exists, and where we will meet again our loved ones. We ask this through Christ our Lord.

OUR FATHER

God did not allow his beloved Son to know decay. Let us pray to the God of power and love as Jesus taught us.

SIGN OF PEACE

Lord Jesus Christ, you appeared to the apostle Thomas, and after showing him your wounded hands and side, you said to him, 'Cease doubting and believe.'

Look with compassion on us. Strengthen our faith and deepen our love, so that we may enjoy the peace and unity of your kingdom where you live for ever and ever.

BEFORE COMMUNION

Jesus said to Thomas, 'You believe because you can see me. Blessed are those who have not seen and yet believe.' Happy are we who recognise our risen Lord in this broken bread.

Lord, I am not worthy ....

We are asked to believe without seeing.
Sometimes this can be very difficult.
There can be dark moments in our lives
when God seems far away,
and we seem to be on our own.
Lord Jesus, in those dark moments,
may your gentle words echo in our hearts:
'Blessed are those who have not seen and yet believe.'
And through the power of those words,
we will cease doubting and believe.

FINAL BLESSING

May you never doubt that God will fulfil the promises he has made to us in Christ.

May the Lord keep you steadfast in faith, joyful in hope, and untiring in love.

And by his holy and glorious wounds may Christ our Lord guard you and keep you.

Sharing the Word of God today

SCRIPTURE NOTE

First Reading (Acts 2:42-47). This is the first of three summaries in Acts that describe the life and activities of the earliest Christian community. (The other two are 4:32-35; 5:12-16).

Here Luke describes, in an idealised way, the final result of Peter's preaching at Pentecost. All those who received the word committed themselves to a new way of living centred on the teaching of the apostles, fellowship, the breaking of bread (Eucharist), and prayer. The Church is necessarily a worshipping community. But this worship is related to loving service towards one another.

Second Reading (1 Pet 1:3-9). Until the seventh Sunday of Easter inclusive, the Second Reading is taken from 1 Peter. Peter's aim is to encourage Christians, and help them to hold on to the basic tenets of their faith in times of trial.

In today's text the author thanks God for the new birth of baptism. However, the new life we receive at baptism is never quite perfected in this life. Our full sharing in the glory of Christ lies in the future. This hope not only enables the Christian to cope with trials and difficulties, but also to rejoice in them because he is sure that they will him lead to salvation.

Gospel (Jn 20:19-31). Here we have John's version of Pentecost, birthday of the Church. The risen Jesus appears to his apostles, shows them his wounds (which serve to identify him as the same one who died), and bestows peace on them.

Then he inaugurates the mission of the Church. This mission is the exact same mission he received from the Father (a mission accomplished by his death and resurrection): the reconciliation of people with the Father, through the forgiveness of sins. To carry out their mission he gives them the gift of the Spirit and the power to forgive sin.

All three synoptic Gospels mention doubt when Jesus appears to his followers after the resurrection (Mt 28:17; Lk 24:37-38; Mk 16:14). But John dramatises that doubt in an individual. Paradoxically, however, from the lips of this 'doubting Thomas' comes the highest profession of faith in all of the Gospels: 'My Lord and my God.'

Writing for a generation that has not 'seen' the Lord, the evangelist adds the comment: 'Blessed are those who have not seen and yet believe.' He is telling these later disciples (and us) that they share the same blessedness as those who actually saw the risen Lord. Originally John's Gospel ended where today's passage ends.

Seeing in not necessarily believing

Thomas was not the only apostle to doubt the resurrection. The three synoptic Gospels make it clear that all the apostles initially doubted (Mt 28:17; Mk 16:14; Lk 24:37-39). But John dramatises that doubt in an individual.

John has already told his readers about Thomas. When the other disciples were trying to persuade Jesus not to return to Bethany at the time of Lazarus' fatal illness, Thomas declared, 'Let us also go with him, that we may die with him' (11:16). And at the Last Supper he interrupted the discourse given by Jesus and said, 'Lord, we do not know where you are going; so how can we know the way?' (14:5). It's clear that by nature Thomas was loyal, but also impulsive and questioning.

He was not with the other apostles the first time Jesus appeared to them. When they said to him, 'We have seen the Lord', he said, 'Unless I see the holes that the nails made in his hands and can put my finger into those holes, and unless I can put my hand into his side, I refuse to believe.'

When Jesus appeared to the apostles the second time Thomas was present. Jesus seemed to have come primarily to meet Thomas (as he meets Peter in chapter 21), and to meet him in the full presence of his fellow apostles. Having greeted the others he turned to Thomas and said, 'Put your finger here; look, here are my hands. Give me your hand; put it into my side.' So at last Thomas was offered the proof he desired. Now was his chance to demonstrate that 'seeing was believing'.

Yet it's clear from John's narrative that Thomas did not accept the invitation to touch the Lord's hands and feel his side. Instead he responded: 'My Lord and my God.' This is the highest profession of faith in all of the Gospels.

In the mere seeing of the glorified Lord, Thomas had learnt that touch and sight were not the sufficient things he had supposed. In a strangely paradoxical way he had found through seeing that seeing was not believing. And this makes Thomas the link between the first believers (the apostles) and the believers of every age who make the same confession of faith.

The modern believer, like Thomas, may at times think: 'If only I could touch the wound prints on his hands, or see the spear mark in his side, then I would know for sure.' But were he to be put into a situation where that was possible, he would know at once that he could well be as sceptical about sight and touch as about sheer belief.

Belief is not the inevitable result of sight as such; it is, as the whole NT makes clear, always the work of the Holy Spirit.

Physical sight is of physical objects (and no more). But the eye with which a person 'sees' the One who sent Jesus Christ into the world is not located in any physical body as a sense organ. It is distinct from physical sight.

The story of Thomas makes plain to all believers that there is no advantage to the apostle in 'seeing', because physical seeing can be as seriously questioned as any other experience of sense. The vision of Jesus as the Word of God incarnate is the gift of the Spirit both to those who 'see' certain things, and to those who do not.

The blessedness of belief applies to those who believe, not to those who see. This is the universal beatitude with which John closes his Gospel. It includes Thomas as well as contemporary men and women, and contemporary men and women as well as Thomas.

Blessed are those who believe

Jesus said to Thomas: 'Blessed are those who have not seen and yet believe.' The blessedness of those who believe runs right through the Gospel. You could say that it is the central theme of the Gospel.

It is impossible to exaggerate the value of faith. Faith fills our lives with things without which they would have no ultimate meaning.

Some people are born into a religious faith, and with the passage of the years find this faith increasingly strong and sustaining. To possess a faith like that is a tremendous blessing. But for others faith is a constant struggle. The latter will draw comfort from the story of Doubting Thomas.

Some may be surprised to find a doubter among the apostles. They wonder why the editors didn't remove the story as likely to cause scandal.

Fortunately for us they left it in. We need it.

Incidentally, Thomas was not the only one of the apostles who doubted. The Gospels show that the other apostles also had problems believing. St Mark tells us that when Jesus appeared to them on Easter evening, 'he upbraided them for their unbelief and hardness of heart, because they had not believed those who saw him after he had risen' (Mk 16:14). (See also Mt 28:17; Lk 24:37-39).

This shows that the apostles were not supermen; they were human beings like us. Even though Thomas is not proposed as a model, he is a consolation to us in our doubts. And we can learn from him.

It seems that after Good Friday Thomas cut himself off from the other apostles, and walked alone. It was a mistake. In cutting himself off from the other apostles he made things more difficult for himself. But we must remember that he was in deep grief. People who are grieving have a tendency to isolate themselves.

However, it seems that he hadn't cut himself off completely.

The other apostles claimed that they had seen Jesus. But Thomas refused to take their word for it. He had to be sure.

We can sympathise with him. He was merely echoing the human cry for certainty. However, here on earth there is no such thing as absolute certainty about spiritual things. If there were, faith would not be necessary.

But Tomas was being stubborn too. However, he did one good thing. He rejoined the apostles. It was only when he rejoined the community that he encountered the risen Jesus, and so found faith again.

To be a believer in today's world can be a lonely business. We need support. Here is where the community comes in. We live as members of a community of believers whose common faith strengthens the faith of each individual. The first Christians supported one another by praying and worshipping together, and by a loving service of one another.

Only faith can answer the most important questions of life. But we must not expect that because we believe we know all the answers. But we don't need to know all the answers. Faith is trust, not certainty.

The story of Doubting Thomas brings home to us just how frail is the human container in which the gift of faith is carried. And it also shows us that Christian faith is essentially faith in a person who loves us – and has the wounds to prove it.

Healed by his wounds

On Easter Sunday evening the apostles were gathered in the upper room behind locked doors. They were wounded men. They were wounded, not in body, but in heart and in spirit. They were wounded individually by fear, doubt, guilt, and grief. And they were wounded collectively because one of their number, Judas, had killed himself. Like all people in pain, they had erected a barrier around themselves.

Jesus knew how they were feeling. In one bold move he broke through the barrier, and stood among them. He didn't scold them for failing him. Instead, he greeted them with the lovely words, 'Peace be with you.' He repeated those words to make sure they got the message. In receiving his peace, they received his forgiveness.

Then what did he do? He showed them his wounds. Now we would have expected his risen body to be without spot or blemish. Yet that body still bore the wounds of his crucifixion. Why was this?

Firstly, those wounds helped the apostles to recognise him as the same one who died. Secondly, those wounds were the proof of his love for them. They were the mortal wounds the Good Shepherd suffered when he laid down his life for his sheep.

Jesus didn't just talk about love. He gave an example of it, and had the wounds to prove it. He didn't insulate himself against human pain. On the contrary, he made himself totally vulnerable by taking to himself our fragile, mortal humanity. And he paid the price. He bore the marks of our violent world on his body.

Jesus showed his wounds to Thomas. On seeing those wounds, Thomas' doubts vanished, and his faith was re-born. More marvellous still – through the wounds of Jesus, he and his fellow apostles found healing for their own wounds. (1 Pet 2:24)

In one way or another all of us are wounded. Many people carry wounds in their bodies. But the part of us that is most deeply wounded is the heart. The heart is wounded by such things as disappointment, ingratitude, grief, rejection, and betrayal.

We have a tendency to hide our wounds, because wounds seem to suggest weakness, and displaying weakness does not create respect. Jesus didn't hide his wounds. For him they were not things to be ashamed of. They were more like badges of honour. They were eloquent witnesses to how costly real love can be. Wounds are the greatest form of witness.

The sacred wounds of Jesus are a source of consolation, courage, and hope to us. They help us to believe in Jesus' love for us. And they help us to find healing for our own wounds. By his wounds we are healed of self-pity and the sense of victimhood.

Those who do not disguise their own struggles, and who live through them, give hope to others and become a source of healing for them. What does it matter if our struggles leave us a little fragile. This fragility makes us gentler and more sensitive in dealing with the wounds of others.

Stories

1. Rose is a single, working mother, who lives in New York. In a period of six years she saw her three sons shot dead. The youngest of them was shot dead right in front of her door. It has left a deep wound in her heart. She says she relives her grief every time a child gets killed in the neighbourhood.

Yet she has refused to be trapped by fear and a sense of victimhood. Instead, she has reached out to others. She has become an eloquent advocate for gun control and community responsibility, talking at schools and other places. She started a support group for mothers in a similar position. And when a child dies, she calls on their parents to comfort them.

The frame of her door still bears the marks of the bullets that killed her youngest son. Although she doesn't always notice them, she knows they are there. Why doesn't she have the frame repaired? 'I want those holes to be a constant reminder that a young man lost his life at that spot. When you fix things, people tend to forget.'

Maybe that is why Jesus kept the marks of his wounds on his risen body – lest we forget the price he paid for our redemption.

2. There was a man who was very attached to his father, who had been a labourer all his life. When the father died the son was grief-stricken. As he stood quietly gazing down into the coffin in which his father's body was laid out, he was particularly struck by his father's hands. Even small things can reveal the essence of a person's life.

Later he said: 'I will never forget those magnificently weathered old hands. They told the story of a countryman's life in the eloquent language of wrinkles, veins, old scars and new. My father's hands always bore some fresh scratch or cut as adornment, the result of his latest tangle with a scrap of wire, a rusted pipe, or a stubborn root. In death they did not disappoint even in that small and valuable particular.

'It is not given to sons to know everything about their fathers, but I have those hands in my memory to supply evidence of the obligations he met, the sweat he gave, and the honest deeds he performed. By looking at those hands I was able to read the better part of the old man's heart.'

THIRD SUNDAY OF EASTER
They recognised him in the breaking of bread

Praying with the Word of God today

INTRODUCTION AND CONFITEOR

The story of the two disciples on the road to Emmaus is one of the loveliest stories in the Gospel. The risen Jesus joined them on the road, explained the Scriptures to them, and then revealed himself in the breaking of bread.

The risen Jesus journeys with us too. And we have the same means of recognising him, because the Scriptures and the Eucharist are the essential components of our Sunday service. [Pause]

Lord Jesus, you are with us as we gather to celebrate the Eucharist. Lord, have mercy.

You speak to us when the Scriptures are read. Christ, have mercy.

You nourish us with the bread of eternal life. Lord, have mercy.

PRAYER OF THE FAITHFUL

Celebrant: As we travel in hope towards the kingdom of heaven, let us bring our needs before God, confident that he will listen favourably to them.

Response: Stay with us, Lord.

Reader(s): For the Pope and the bishops: that they may lead the people of God with courage and love. [Pause] Let us pray to the Lord.

For our political and civil leaders: that God may bless them with the gifts of courage and integrity. [Pause] Let us pray to the Lord.

For those who have lost heart: that the risen Lord may strengthen their faith and renew their hope. [Pause] Let us pray to the Lord.

For all gathered here: that we may know God's consolation in times of sorrow, and God's help in times of difficulty. [Pause] Let us pray to the Lord.

For those who have accompanied us on life's journey, and who are no longer with us: that the Lord may give them a place at the banquet of eternal life. [Pause] Let us pray to the Lord.

For our own special needs. [Longer Pause] Let us pray to the Lord.

Celebrant: Lord, grant that through our participation in the Eucharist, we may know that you are with us. May your gentle light guide us on the unfolding road, so that we may walk with confidence towards the light that never fades and the life that never ends. We ask this through you, Christ our Lord.

BEFORE COMMUNION

The disciples recognised Jesus when he broke the bread. Happy are we who recognise our risen Lord in this broken bread.

Lord, I am not worthy ...

PRAYER/REFLECTION

All of us have some experience of the road to Emmaus.
That road represents the road of disappointment,
failure, sorrow, and broken dreams.
But the risen Lord journeys with us.

His resurrection opens all our stories to the prospect,
not just of a good ending, but of a glorious ending.
Stay with us, Lord, and let your presence inflame our hearts
and raise our spirits, so that we may journey towards your kingdom
   with undimmed hope.

FINAL BLESSING

May Christ, who rose from the dead, enflame your hearts with his love.

May the risen Lord fill your hearts with joy and make you courageous heralds of his Gospel.

May you not be afraid of anything the world can throw at you, because Christ has overcome the world.

Sharing the Word of God today

SCRIPTURE NOTE

First Reading (Acts 2:14.22-28). Preaching to the Jews assembled in Jerusalem for the feast of Pentecost, Peter interprets the Jewish scriptures in the light of Jesus' life, death and resurrection.

In our passage we should note two points. Firstly, the crucifixion of Jesus was not a tragic accident of fate. It was foreseen and provided for in the eternal purpose of God. Secondly, the centrality of the resurrection in the early preaching cannot be overstated. The crucifixion and death of Jesus are viewed as only a prelude to the mighty act of God in raising him up.

Second Reading (1 Pet 1:17-21). This reading contains a strong reference to the resurrection. It reminds the Christian what his redemption cost – nothing less than the life and death of Jesus Christ. Since the Christian is destined to share in the glory of Christ, his life must be characterised by holiness.

Gospel (Lk 24:13-35). The Emmaus story is more than a story. It is a sophisticated eucharistic catechesis: a 'liturgy of the Word' followed by a 'liturgy of the Eucharist'. The expression 'breaking of bread' is a technical term for the Eucharist. The gestures and words used are those of the Last Supper and of the Eucharist: 'He *took* the bread ... *blessed* it ... *broke* it ... and *gave* it to them.' No doubt this reflected the Eucharistic practice of the Lukan Church.

By the time Luke wrote his Gospel half a century had gone by since the Lord's death and resurrection. So his readers might look back with envy at the people who were fortunate enough to have seen the risen Lord with their own eyes. But in this story he makes the point that those who were in that enviable position did not truly know Jesus until the Scriptures were expounded and the bread was broken.

The Christians of Luke's time had those same means of recognising him – the Scriptures and the breaking of bread. And so have Christians ever since, for the Scriptures and the Eucharist are the essential components of our Sunday service. In the matter of encountering Jesus with faith, a past generation is no more privileged than the present one.

Luke is faithful to the understanding of the first Christians that Jesus was not the Messiah in spite of his suffering but because of it.

Our story too

The story of the two disciples on the road to Emmaus is one of the loveliest stories in the Gospel. But how does it connect with us?

There is a painting by the Dutch painter, Rembrandt, of Jesus sitting at table between the two disciples. The painting tries to capture the rapture on the faces of the disciples at the moment they recognised Jesus.

There was a guide whose job it was to show Rembrandt's painting to visitors to the museum where it hung. He always began by telling them the story behind the picture, the story we just read in the Gospel. Sadly, for many years he told the story mechanically and without conviction.

Then his wife, whom he loved dearly, got cancer, and died a slow, agonising death. He could see absolutely no meaning in her terrible suffering and untimely death. She was a good person. She didn't deserve to die like that.

He was heart-broken. For him it was as if the world had come to an end. Nevertheless, sometime after the funeral, he was persuaded to go back to work at the museum. So once again he found himself telling the story, only more mechanically than before.

Then one day something clicked inside him, and suddenly he realised that the story was not just about those two disciples. It was about him too.

Like those two disciples, he was going down a sad and lonely road. Even though he was a believer, up to this Jesus had been little more than a figure who lived only in the musty pages of the Gospels. But now Jesus came alive for him. He felt his presence at his side, the presence of a friend who knew all about human suffering.

At that moment his eyes were opened and he saw things differently. It was as if he was hearing the Easter message for the first time. His heart began to burn within him. Jesus was alive! Therefore, his beloved wife, who believed in Jesus, was alive too, because Jesus overcame death not just for himself but for us too.

He went on telling the story at the museum, only now he told it differently. He told it with feeling and conviction. As he did so, a healing process was at work inside him. And he began to hope and live again.

So what's the connection with us? The connection is that all of us have some experience of the road to Emmaus. The road to Emmaus represents the road of disappointment, failure, sorrow, grief, and broken dreams.

The risen Lord is with us on this road, even though we may not recognise him. He shows us that God brings good out of evil, life out of death, and glory out of pain and suffering.

The resurrection of Jesus opens all our stories to the prospect, not just of a good ending, but of a glorious ending. He has made it possible for us to enter the dark kingdom of death with hearts buoyed up with hope.

A story too good to be true?

The story of the two disciples on the road to Emmaus is surely the most wonderful story in the Gospel. But is it too good to be true?

The resurrection is the supreme truth of our Christian faith. Without it there wouldn't have been any Church, and our faith would be in vain. The first Christian community was founded on the resurrection. And that was the main thing they preached (see First Reading).

What grounds have we for believing in the resurrection? In the Gospels we have a number of resurrection stories. These begin with the story of the empty tomb. In itself this is not a proof of the resurrection. The absence of his body from the tomb could be explained otherwise.

The Gospels go on to tell of a number of appearances of Jesus. These appearances were the primary way the disciples came to know that he was risen from the dead.

All these appearance stories stress that Jesus is the same person. This is the reason why he shows his wounds to the apostles. The wound-marks inflicted during the crucifixion serve to identify him as the same one who died.

Yet all the stories make it clear that he is somehow changed, and therefore not immediately recognisable. This is a way of making the point that resurrection is not a return to earthly life as before.

The raising of Jesus was not like the other restorations to life mentioned in the Bible. Take the raising of Lazarus. He returned to ordinary human existence; there is no suggestion that he was glorified, or that he would not have to die again.

Jesus, on the other hand, is portrayed as conquering death, as returning immortal and glorified. He has risen to a new life beyond death, a life with God. Even though he was radically transformed, it was *Jesus* who was seen. He is still *who* he was but not *as* he was.

All the stories also stress the bodily resurrection of Jesus: the tomb is empty; he walks and eats with the apostles. But his risen body possesses new properties: it is no longer subject to the ordinary laws of nature, or to the human boundaries of time and space.

It has been claimed that it was the credulity of the apostles that produced the resurrection. But the Gospels show that the apostles were slow to believe in the resurrection. Even when Jesus showed himself to them, they still doubted (Mk 16:14: Lk 24:37-39). The theory that the resurrection was produced by the faith of the apostles doesn't hold up. On the contrary, the faith of the apostles was born from the direct experience of the risen Jesus.

The most convincing argument for the resurrection is the change that came about in the apostles. The crucifixion dealt them a shattering blow. Why then wasn't Jesus' death the end of the story? Because something happened to them which they could describe only by saying that they had 'seen the Lord'. This transformed them from a cowardly group into people who were prepared to – and did – die for his message.

To profess belief in the resurrection is not to affirm an absurd miracle but to affirm the power of God, which is greater than the power of death.

Jesus has become a pathfinder for us because what happened to him is meant to happen to us. How can this be? Because it was in our humanity that he rose from the dead. If his humanity can be glorified, then so can ours.

The Easter victory of Jesus enables us to live our lives under the brightness of immortality. And it makes it possible for us to enter the dark kingdom of death buoyed up with hope.

Sharing the story

After every death our relationship with the one who has died is changed but goes on. It is even intensified for a time. But it is now one-sided. This is illustrated in the story of the two disciples on the road to Emmaus.

As they made their way homewards, they were talking about Jesus. He had filled their lives with meaning, hope and joy. And now that he was dead they were haunted by his absence. They had believed that he was the long-awaited Messiah. But the crucifixion had reduced that dream to rubble. So now they were going away from Jerusalem.

Peoples' lives are shattered by the death of someone they love, especially if that death was sudden or tragic. Life comes to a standstill on the day the loved one dies. The bereaved stay fixed there, without plans or interests. They may even feel guilty about living, especially about enjoying themselves. After the death of Jesus his disciples experienced all of this – and more.

But help came to them from outside. The risen Jesus joined them, only they didn't recognise him. This is a feature common to all the resurrection stories – Jesus is not immediately recognisable. This is a way of making the point that resurrection is not a return to earthly life as before.

The raising of Jesus was not like the raising of Lazarus. Lazarus returned to ordinary human existence; there is no suggestion that he was glorified, or that he would not have to die again. Jesus, on the other hand, is portrayed as conquering death, as returning immortal and glorified.

With a simple, direct question, asked in a kindly manner, Jesus got the two disciples to open up. And they began to pour out their sad story to him. He listened patiently as all that was dammed up inside them poured out.

Only when they had finished did he begin to talk. He took up the story where they had left off. He opened their minds to a new way of looking at the Scriptures. He showed them how all the prophets had foretold that the Messiah would suffer and die, and *thus* enter into glory.

Later, when they were having supper, he took the cake of bread, blessed it, broke it, and gave each of them a piece – just as Jesus had done at the Last Supper. Suddenly their eyes were opened and they recognised the stranger. He was none other than Jesus! But at that moment he disappeared from their sight.

So their beloved Jesus was alive, and had entered into glory! And what was that glory? It was his triumph over evil and death. So his death, far from being the end of the dream, was precisely the way it was realised.

This encounter with the risen Jesus enabled the disciples to turn their lives around. They returned to Jerusalem, and resumed their discipleship and their ties with the community.

The life of each of us can be looked on as a series of stories that coalesce over time to form one story. However, the sad fact is, all our stories end in death. We do not like stories that end like that. We want our stories to end happily. The resurrection of Christ opens all our stories to the prospect, not just of a good ending, but also of a glorious ending.

Death seems to be the destruction of every relationship. But this is not so. The ties we had with the deceased in life are not ended in death. Our loved ones have gone from us. But they have not disappeared into nothingness. The first and last words in each of our stories belong to God.

Story

There is a story about a dying Buddhist monk who asked a Catholic priest to instruct him in the truths of the faith. The priest did his best to comply with the monk's wishes. Afterwards the monk thanked him, but added, 'You filled my mind with beautiful thoughts, but you left my heart empty.'

Emptiness of heart is a sorry state. Beautiful thoughts can nourish the mind. But they can't nourish the heart. Only an experience of love can nourish the heart.

What did Jesus do for those two forlorn disciples on the road to Emmaus? He certainly illuminated their minds. But he did something better. He set their hearts on fire. 'Were not our hearts burning within us as he explained the scriptures to us?'

Christian faith is concerned with the mind in so far as it has to do with doctrines. But it is even more concerned with the heart. It consists essentially in a relationship of love with the God who first loved us. Without this, faith is like a fireplace without a fire.

Each of us has a unique story to tell – the story of our lives. However, the sad fact is, all our stories end in death. We don't like a story that ends like that. We want our stories to end happily. The resurrection of Jesus opens all our stories to the prospect, not just of a good ending, but also of a glorious ending. Surely that should set our hearts on fire.

FOURTH SUNDAY OF EASTER
I came that you may have life

Praying with the Word of God today

INTRODUCTION AND CONFITEOR

This Sunday is known as Good Shepherd Sunday. The Good Shepherd is, of course, Jesus. Let us pause for a moment to see how we respond to the love and care of the Good Shepherd. [Pause]

Lord Jesus, you came that we may have life and have it to the full. Lord, have mercy.

You seek us out when we stray, and bring us back to the flock you nourish. Christ, have mercy.

You are the shepherd and guardian of our souls. Lord, have mercy.

PRAYER OF THE FAITHFUL

Celebrant: God brought Jesus back from the dead and made him the chief Shepherd of the flock. Let us place our needs before him with great confidence.

Response: Lord, hear our prayer.

Reader(s): For the leaders of the Church: that they may faithfully and lovingly watch over the flock of Christ. [Pause] Let us pray to the Lord.

For doctors, nurses, and all in the caring professions: that they may be blessed with gentle hands and warm hearts. [Pause] Let us pray to the Lord.

For those who have strayed from the Christian community: that they may find their way back to the flock Christ nourishes. [Pause] Let us pray to the Lord.

For vocations to the priesthood and religious life: that more people may hear the call to become ministers to their brothers and sisters in the Christian community. [Pause] Let us pray to the Lord.

For all gathered here: that we may imitate the love of the Good Shepherd by the concern we show for others. [Pause] Let us pray to the Lord.

For our deceased relatives and friends: that they may dwell in the house of the Lord for ever. [Pause] Let us pray to the Lord.

For our own special needs. [Longer pause] Let us pray to the Lord.

Celebrant: God of compassion, you sent your Son into the world that we might have life. Grant that we may follow him faithfully on earth, and come to enjoy eternal life in heaven, where he lives and reigns with you and the Holy Spirit, one God for ever and ever.

OUR FATHER

God wants us to have life here and hereafter. Let us pray to our heavenly Father as Jesus, the Good Shepherd, has taught us.

SIGN OF PEACE

Lord Jesus Christ, you said to your apostles, 'I am the gate of the sheepfold. Anyone who enters through me will be safe and be sure of finding pasture.'

Help us to listen to your voice and to follow you, so that we may enjoy the peace and unity of your kingdom where you live for ever and ever.

PRAYER/REFLECTION

Life is a gift from God, a gift to be lived and enjoyed.
It is possible to enjoy life to the full
while being devout and religious at the same time.
Those who live fully will not feel cheated at death.
Lord, give us the kind of faith
that will enable us to live out joyfully
the mystery of our fragile human condition,
which sees us suspended between earth and heaven,
and between time and eternity.

FINAL BLESSING

May Christ, the Good Shepherd, guide you along the right path.

May he give you a sense of his comforting presence when you walk through the valley of darkness.

And when your earthly journey is over, may he lead you to the green pastures of eternal life.

Sharing the Word of God today

SCRIPTURE NOTE

First Reading (Acts 2:14.36-41). This is the conclusion of Peter's sermon to the Jews assembled in Jerusalem for the feast of Pentecost. The first paragraph gives in a nutshell what the whole sermon is about. Jesus whom they crucified has, by his resurrection, been constituted Lord and Christ. The purpose of the sermon was to make them realise what they had done to Jesus, with a view to getting them to repent and be baptised.

Second Reading (1 Pet 2:20-25). Addressing slaves, Peter urges them to bear their unjust sufferings with patience as Christ, the Good Shepherd, bore his sufferings for love of us.

Slavery was a fact of life in New Testament times. The New Testament writers do not, as might have been expected, lead a campaign against it. Even if they had wanted to do so, they must have been aware that such a stance could only be judged subversive and would jeopardise the tenuous foothold Christianity was gaining in the world of the day.

Peter's words have a wider application. He singled out slaves only because their burden of suffering was heavier than that of others. Suffering is the lot of all Christians. Christ, the shepherd and guardian of our souls, is the one who gets us through it.

Gospel (Jn 10:1-10). Jesus presents himself as the shepherd of God's flock. The sheepfold was a walled enclosure in a field. At night the sheep of various shepherds were gathered there. There was a gate and a guard. In the morning the shepherds came in by the gate and led their own sheep to pasture.

Unlike some other shepherds who come only to steal the sheep, Jesus has come that the sheep may have abundant life. He leads his sheep out and goes before them as their guide. He calls each by name: there is a close, personal relationship between each Christian and Jesus.

Jesus also describes himself as the gate of the sheepfold. Through him Christians have access to God and the life of God. The image of a caring shepherd is a challenge to all who hold pastoral office.

That you may have life

In the Gospel Jesus says, 'I came so that you may have life and have it to the full.' This is wonderful news. It means that God wants us to *live* life, and live it *to the full*. Mere existence is not enough for us. We are summoned to the fullness of life.

Henry David Thoreau was an American writer and philosopher. At one point in his life he decided to take time out. He went to live for two years in a shack in the woods in Maine. In his book, *Walden,* he tells us why. He says: 'I went into the woods to confront the essential facts of life, lest when I come to die I should discover that I had never lived.'

We should live in such a way that we won't look back and regret that we have wasted our life. G. K. Chesterton talks about how sad it is when someone dies 'with all the music inside him.' We could add: how sad it is to die with all the life, all the love, and all the joy inside one.

Life is generous to those who seize it with both hands. Those who live fully and intensely will not feel cheated at death. Thoreau says, 'Fear not that your life will end; fear, rather, that it may never have begun.'

In the past the Christian religion tended to be identified with restrictions and prohibitions. Many of us were brought up on a theology of detachment from the world. This present life was viewed as nothing more than a time of trial. Life was something to be survived rather than lived. That kind of spirituality discouraged enjoyment of life.

But the message of today's Gospel is this: God wants us to have a full and fruitful life here on earth, and eternal life in the hereafter. To live fully is not the same as to live it up, which means to grab all the pleasures for oneself that one can. It is possible to enjoy life to the full while being devout and religious at the same time.

Religion addresses our deepest longings. It fuels the life deep inside us, that fleeting but precarious life that we are called upon to live and live to the full. Religion should enhance our lives in every way. It should enlarge our lives, not shrink them.

It is not possible to have abundant life if one is disconnected from God. God is the source of life. If we remain close to God, we will receive life in abundance.

Life is a gift from God, a gift to be lived and enjoyed. To use a gift well is the best way of saying 'thanks' to the donor. We are called to live deeply, to love the world, but also to look beyond it.

'The days come and go life muffled figures sent from a distant friendly land. If we do not use the gifts they bring, they carry them as silently away' (Ralph Waldo Emerson).

Story

There is a delightful Spanish legend that goes like this. When people arrive at the gate of heaven seeking to enter, St Peter asks them a strange question. He says to each one, 'Tell me this. Have you taken advantage of all the earthly joys which God in his goodness made available to you while you were on earth?'

If a person replies, 'No, I haven't,' Peter shakes his head sadly and says, 'Alas, my friend, I can't let you in – not yet at any rate. How can you expect to be ready for the heavenly joys if you have not prepared yourself for them through the medium of earthly ones? I shall be obliged to send you back down to earth until you learn better.'

Jesus, the image of the invisible God

A psychiatrist who lives in San Francisco says he regrets how little he can do to help his clients. He says, 'The people who come to me for help are in the end all saying to me, "Is there somewhere a friend who will not in the final resort betray one?" I would love to be able to say, "Yes, there is." But I cannot do so because I am an agnostic, and only if you believe in God can you say, "Yes."'

We who believe have such a friend in God. If we want to know what God is like all we have to do is look at Jesus. He is the translation into human reality of what God is. And what is Jesus like? He is the Good Shepherd.

Of all the images we have of Jesus, that of the Good Shepherd is the loveliest. It is an image that is rooted in the Gospels. (See today's Gospel). It was treasured in the early Church, and was one of most common representations of Jesus. The image speaks of love and care – things that are easy to talk about but difficult to live.

In Jesus' time the sheepfold was a walled enclosure in a field. At night the sheep of various shepherds were gathered there. There was a gate and a guard. In the morning the shepherds came in by the gate and led their own sheep to pasture.

That some came to steal obviously was a reality then as it is for us now. The thief was unlikely to come in through the gate. He had to find another way in.

Whereas some shepherds came to steal or to kill the sheep, Jesus, the Good Shepherd, came that his sheep might have life. He leads his sheep out and goes before them as their guide. He calls each by name. This implies that there is a close, personal relationship between each Christian and Jesus. Jesus wants us to have a full and fruitful life here on earth, and eternal life in the hereafter.

Jesus also refers to himself as the gate of the sheepfold. A gate can enable us to gain access or it can bar the way for us. A famous film star once said, 'I've been blessed; almost any door is open to me.' That is generally true for the rich and the famous. But for those who are poor and without influence, there are few doors, few avenues, few opportunities open to them. In our world, admittance depends on *who* you are rather than *what* you are.

Not so with Christ's sheepfold. Through him we have access to God's mercy and forgiveness here on earth, and to eternal life in the hereafter. He scandalised the Pharisees by opening the gate to sinners and outcasts.

In Jesus the compassion of God has come into our world. In one Eucharistic Prayer we proclaim: 'He was moved with compassion for the poor and the powerless, for the sick and the sinner; he made himself neighbour to the oppressed. By his words and actions he proclaimed to the world that

God cares for us as a father cares for his children.'

We, in our turn, can reveal the face of Jesus. The example of Jesus challenges us. If only we could overcome our selfishness we would discover how much we have to give.

'Through his wounds you have been healed'

In the Second Reading St Peter is addressing slaves. He urges them to bear their unjust sufferings with patience as Christ, the Good Shepherd, bore his sufferings for love of us. (This doesn't mean he approved of slavery. Slavery was a fact of life in those times. As yet the infant Church was in no position to fight for its abolition.)

Peter's words have a wider application. He singled out slaves only because their burden of suffering was heavier than that of others. Suffering is the lot of all Christians. Christ, the Good Shepherd, is the one who gets us through it. St Peter says, 'Through his wounds you have been healed.' How can the wounds of another heal our wounds? The following true story shows how it can happen.

Anne's husband died of a heart attack. He was only in his mid-forties. After the funeral, Anne was consumed by grief. Friends advised her to go on a weekend for the bereaved. Somewhat reluctantly she agreed to go.

She was surprised to find that most of the people on the weekend were not widows but separated people. At a certain stage the participants were divided into groups, and it was Anne's bad luck to find herself the only widow in her group.

She felt she didn't belong in the group. The other members *had* their husbands. It was their own fault that they had broken up. They could get back together if they really wanted to. But her husband was dead and gone – a good man who didn't smoke or drink, but lived for his family. She felt she had nothing in common with these people. She refused to share with the group.

Even though she didn't talk she did listen. As she listened, she began to realise that the other people had suffered a great deal. Some of them had put up with a terrible amount of abuse. She had no idea what went on in some homes. She thought that all marriages were like hers. She realised that she had had it very good.

Whereas earlier she had felt no sympathy for the others, now she felt very close to them. Eventually she began to talk about herself. One woman said to her, 'What I wouldn't give for just one of your days.' The weekend proved to be a turning point for Anne. Her wounds began to heal.

Suffering can soften our hardened hearts and enable us to enter a world of suffering where all people live at some time. In reaching out to others, we move out of our isolation into a world of shared suffering. In the simple act of showing sympathy for others there is healing.

Compassion is not learned without suffering. Unless you have suffered you really don't understand what compassion is, nor can you comfort someone who is suffering. But if you have suffered, you can become a pathfinder for others.

The wounds of others can help us to cope with and recover from our own wounds. It is by reaching out to others that we ourselves are healed. Shared pain is a bit like shared bread; it brings its participants closer to each other. Intimacy is the fruit that grows from touching each other's wounds.

If we can draw encouragement from the wounds of others, how much more so from the wounds of Christ, the Good Shepherd. His wounds help us to recognise our own wounds. The sacred, the precious wounds of Jesus are a source of consolation, courage, and hope to us. By his wounds we are healed of self-pity and the sense of victimhood.

Story

Ellen set out to deliver flowers to a friend. Out of the blue, a wasp stung her in the arm. What had been a sweet journey suddenly turned sour. She stopped to inspect the damage. The spot in which she had been stung felt very sore, and was swelling up alarmingly.

As she sat there wincing with pain and feeling very sorry for herself, a kind passer-by stopped and applied some ointment to the wound. The ointment had a soothing effect on the wound, and soon Ellen was on her way again.

She insisted on telling everyone she met along the way about the wasp sting. With every telling, the wasp got more vicious and the wound more serious. Her confidants could see that she was very bitter about it. All of them were sympathetic, and told her to forget the sting.

She tried to forget it. However, no matter how hard she tried, she could not forget it. And every time she remembered it, she felt a stab of pain. Eventually she had the good fortune to meet up with an old friend, Sheila. She told Sheila about the sting and how everyone was telling her she should forget it.

'Why should you forget it?' asked Sheila.

'Because every time I remember it, I feel the pain all over again,' Ellen replied.

'It's *how* you remember it that matters,' said Sheila. 'You're on a mission of love, aren't you?'

'Yes.'

'Well then, don't let the sting distract you from that. Above all, don't let its poison diminish your love. Then when you arrive at your friend's house, your gift will be all the more precious because you suffered a wound in delivering it.'

After they parted, Ellen reflected on what her friend had said. Gradually she came to see the sting in a new light. With that the bitterness left her, and once again she found herself going along with a happy step.

FIFTH SUNDAY OF EASTER
Jesus, the way, the truth and the life

Praying with the Word of God today

INTRODUCTION AND CONFITEOR

During the Last Supper Jesus said to the apostles, 'I am the Way, the truth and the life.' These words, which we hear in today's Gospel, are now addressed to us.

To be a follower of Jesus is to follow his way. We don't always do this. For this we ask pardon and strength. [Pause].

Lord Jesus, you are the way that leads to the Father. Lord, have mercy.

You are the truth that sets us free. Christ, have mercy.

You are the life that makes our joy complete. Lord, have mercy.

PRAYER OF THE FAITHFUL

Celebrant: Jesus is the way, the truth, and the life. Let us pray with confidence to him who shared our earthly exile in order to bring us to our heavenly home.

Response: Lord, hear our prayer.

Reader(s): For the Pope: that God may bless him with wisdom and courage so that he may lead the Church in the footsteps of Christ. [Pause] Let us pray to the Lord.

For political leaders: that they may seek the guidance and help of God in all their deliberations. [Pause] Let us pray to the Lord.

For those who are trouble or fearful: that the risen Lord may inflame their hearts and raise their spirits. [Pause] Let us pray to the Lord.

For ourselves: that our lives may bear witness to the faith we profess with our lips. [Pause] Let us pray to the Lord.

For all the faithful departed, but especially our deceased relatives and friends: that the light of heaven may shine on them. [Pause] Let us pray to the Lord.

For our own special needs. [Longer Pause] Let us pray to the Lord.

Celebrant: Lord, may you support us all day long, till the shadows lengthen, and evening falls, and the busy world is hushed, and the fever of life is over, and our work is done; then, in your mercy, grant us a safe lodging, a holy rest, and peace at last. We ask this through Christ our Lord.

OUR FATHER

God has called us out of darkness into his own wonderful light. Let us pray to our heavenly Father as children of the light.

SIGN OF PEACE

Lord Jesus Christ, at the Last Supper, you said to your sad and frightened apostles, 'Do not let your hearts be troubled. Trust in God still, and trust in me.'

Take pity on our troubled minds and fearful hearts, and grant us the peace and unity of your kingdom where you live for ever and ever.

PRAYER/REFLECTION

For Jesus, to die was to return to the Father
from whom he had come.
In other words, it was to go home.
So it is with us. When we die,
we do not so much go to God as return to him.
Like homesick cranes flying night and day back to their mountain nests,
let all our life take its voyage to you, O Lord,
for you have made us for yourself,
and our hearts will never rest until they rest in you.

FINAL BLESSING

May you keep firm in the hope we profess, because the one who made the promise is faithful.

May you live a life worthy of God, who is calling you to share the glory of his kingdom.

May the peace of God, who brought Jesus back from the dead, be with you all.

Sharing the Word of God today

SCRIPTURE NOTE

First Reading (Acts 6:1-7). The rapid growth of the Christian community created problems. The impoverished widows of the Hellenists (Jews raised in a Greek cultural environment)) were not getting the material help that the native poor of Jerusalem received.

The Twelve wisely chose seven men of good repute from among the Hellenists and commissioned them to supervise the charitable works of the community. This enabled the apostles to devote all their energies to their top priority – the ministry of the word (preaching and teaching). The passage shows how concerned the early Christians were to give practical expression to their Christianity.

Second Reading (1 Pet 2:4-9). This describes the responsibility and special dignity of Christians as members of the community of Christ, the Church. The community is likened to a building. The suffering and risen Lord is the foundation stone of this building. But he is also a stumbling block for those who will not believe. The lives of Christians are an acceptable offering to God, and a source of blessing for others.

In vv. 9-10 Peter switches to the idea of covenant. He transfers titles formerly bestowed on Israel to the new community of Christ. It is a chosen race, a royal house and community of priests, a holy nation God has called out of darkness into his wonderful light.

Gospel (Jn 14:1-12). The Gospel contains a number of related themes. Jesus consoles his disciples who are distressed over his words about his going away. They ought not be troubled; he is not abandoning them; he is going to prepare a home for them in the ample house of the Father.

He himself is the way to the Father. So close is the communion of Father and Son that one who looks on Jesus with the eyes of faith sees the Father, and sees that the 'works' of Jesus are the achievement of the Father. And because Jesus is now the risen Lord present in their lives, they can do 'greater works' than Jesus did in his public ministry.

One theme is common to all three readings: Christ continues his words and works in the world through his disciples.

Jesus, the Way

All of us have had some experience of getting lost and having to ask for directions. We have approached a stranger and asked, 'How do I get to such and such a place?' There are three common responses.

The person says: 'Sorry. I can't help you. I'm a stranger around here.' Needless to say, that's no help to us.

Or the person proceeds to give us a set of complicated directions that leaves us totally confused. That's not much help either.

Or we might be lucky enough to meet a kind person who says, 'I know where it is. But it's a bit complicated. I'll tell you what. Just follow me and I'll take you there.' Here the person is not content just to give us directions and leave us to it. Here is a person who is willing to be our guide. It's a tonic to meet someone like that.

The way to God is the most important way of all. It is a way that has baffled many. At the Last Supper the apostle, Thomas, asked Jesus, 'Show us the

Father.' The most important thing in the life of Jesus was his relationship with the Father. So Jesus knew the way to the Father.

But he might have given Thomas a set of complicated directions. He didn't. He did something better. He said, 'I am the way. No one can come to the Father except through me.' What he was saying in effect was: 'Follow me and I'll take you to the Father.' In other words, he was offering himself as a guide.

Jesus says to us what he said to Thomas, 'I am the way.' And he invites us to follow him. If we follow him we will have a star that will not betray us, and a compass that will not lie to us. He will lead us to the Father's house. The joy of the one who knows he has set the compass of his life on the right path is a recurrent theme in the Bible.

What does following Jesus involve? It involves following his way. In the Bible the word 'way' is often used in a metaphorical sense. Often it designates a way of life and conduct. The early Christians called themselves followers of the Way. By 'way' they meant a Christian way of life.

At the Last Supper Jesus told the apostles that he was 'going away'. They rightly understood 'going away' to mean that he was going to die. On hearing this they we overcome with sadness. But Jesus didn't speak of death as life ending. He spoke of death as going to the Father.

God is the destination of our earthly journey. To die is to go to God. And to go to God is to go home. Meanwhile in the Church we have a spiritual home, built on the foundation stone of Christ (Second Reading). Here we have brothers and sisters who accompany us on our journey to that other home, our heavenly one. Sadly, there are those who have left the Church or the Christian faith, and who have travelled far, searching for what they left behind.

Faith in a time of crisis

There comes a time in the lives of all believers when things get very dark, and they have to believe even though they cannot prove, and to accept even though they cannot understand or make sense of what is happening. It is at such times that we really need a strong faith, but it is precisely at such times that our faith may fail us.

It's easy to convince ourselves that we have a strong faith when things are going well. It's only when a crisis arises that we discover what kind of faith we have, or if we have any faith at all. By faith here I mean trust in God.

There are people who think that if God was with them, and if he really loved them, then no storm would ever hit them. Life would be all plain sailing. So, when a storm hits them, they experience a crisis of faith, thinking that God has abandoned them.

During the Last Supper the apostles were thrown into crisis when Jesus started to talk about his death. Their hearts were troubled and filled with fear – and with good reason. That was a terrible night, not only for Jesus, but also for them. It was a night of upheaval and terror. Seeing their distress, Jesus said to them, 'Do not let your hearts be troubled. Trust in God still, and trust in me.' Since the apostles already believed, in effect what he was saying to them was, 'You must *go on believing* in God and in me.'

Often at a time of crisis people feel that God has abandoned them. But Jesus assured the apostles that, even though he was leaving them, he was not abandoning them. Rather, he was going to prepare a home for them, and would return to take them to that home. Hence, no matter what happened, they must go on believing, go on trusting in him and in the Father.

At a time of crisis that is the only thing we can do – go on stubbornly trusting in God. What faith does is assure us that God is with us *in the midst of the crisis*. It is the conviction that we are not alone, that we are not abandoned, that enables us to get through the crisis.

Those who have faith have a source of comfort and support, especially when trouble strikes. It is not we who keep the faith; it is the faith that keeps us. 'A person with a grain of faith in God never loses hope, because he believes in the ultimate triumph of truth' (Gandhi).

So when things are bad, let us remember the words of Jesus: 'Believe in God, and believe also in me.' The words of Jesus have a power to console and uphold us that no other words have. In times of difficulty one's spirit seems to drink them in, to savour them, and to feel the divine power in them.

The words of Jesus have come down to us across the centuries, bringing light to those in darkness, and hope to those in despair. In him, who conquered death, we have the assurance that ultimately good will triumph over evil, and life will triumph over death.

Not all that happens to us is determined by God's will, but all is encompassed by his love. The fact that life is fragile and fleeting serves to bring home to us just how precious is the treasure we carry in earthen vessels.

An eternal home

It's impossible to exaggerate the importance of home. But we have to go out into the world to know how lovely our own home is. But imagine if we had no home to go to.

Nelson Mandela told of how during the long years of his imprisonment on Robben Island he had a recurring nightmare. He said: 'In the dream, I had just been released from prison – only it was not Robben Island but a jail in Johannesburg. I walked outside the gates into the city and found no one to meet me. In fact there was no one there at all, no people, no cars, no taxis.

'I would then set out on foot towards Soweto. I walked for many hours before arriving in Orlando West, and then turned the corner towards No. 8115. Finally, I would see my home, but it turned out to be empty, a ghost house, with all the doors and windows open but no one there at all.'

Truly it is impossible to exaggerate the importance of home. When things fail, when we feel tired and lonely, there is always home to go to. 'Let's go home.' 'I want to go home.' How many times, and in how many different circumstances, have we heard people say those words, or have said them ourselves. Home is the place where we are safe, where we can relax. If you know you're going home, the trip is never too long or too difficult.

To have a home is not just to have a house. It is to have a set of close ties with people who accept us for what we are, and who give us a feeling of belonging. But in spite of all the buildings we put up and the roots we put down, here on earth we do not have a lasting home. All we have, as Paul says, is a kind of tent. At death the tent is folded up.

Hence, it is not only on earth that we need a home. We also need a home to go to when death brings down the curtain on the day of our life. Without such a home life would be a journey to nowhere.

During the Last Supper Jesus began to talk to the apostles about the fact that he was leaving them. By this they understood that he was going to die. On hearing this, they were plunged into sorrow. But he consoled them with these words, which are among the loveliest in the Gospel: 'There are many rooms in my Father's. I am going to prepare a place for you. I shall return to take you with me; so that where I am you may be too.' This means that we have an eternal home to go to, namely, the Father's house.

For a child home is not so much a place as a relationship of love and trust. A child can move around a lot and not feel homeless, as long as its parents are there. It is the same for those who have a close relationship with God.

We spend our lives searching for God, and groping our way towards God. To die is to go to God, and to go to God is to go home.

There remains the question of how to get there. Jesus says to us what he said to Thomas: 'I am the way.' And he invites us to follow him. Those who follow him will have a star that will not betray them, and a compass that will not lie to them. He will lead us to the Father's house.

Stories

1. Young Martin was so tense that he had to talk to someone. So he told his story to a complete stranger who was sitting next to him on the train. He told him that he had just been released from prison where he had spent three years for robbery. While there he had undergone a change of heart. He felt he had let his family down, and wondered if they wanted him back.

All the time he had been away, they had neither written to him nor come to visit him. But he was hoping against hope that they had forgiven him and wanted him to come home. However, in order to make it easy for them, he had written to them. If they wanted him back into the family, they were to give him a sign.

Their house was close to the railway line. In the back garden grew an old apple tree. If they wanted him back, they should put up a white ribbon on the apple tree. If they didn't, they were to do nothing. In that case he would stay on the train until it reached the first large city, where he would get lost.

As the train neared his house the suspense became so acute that he was unable to look out the window. So he asked the man to keep a lookout for the apple tree. The man agreed to do so. After a while he touched Martin on the shoulder, and said, 'Take a look'.

Martin looked, and there before his eyes stood the old apple tree, covered in ribbons. Tears began to run down his face, and with those tears all the bitterness that had poisoned his young life up to this was washed away. The other man said later, 'I felt I had just witnessed a miracle. I had never realised until that moment what it means for a young lad to have a home to go to.'

Without faith, life is like a journey that leads nowhere. To have faith is to believe that we have a lasting home to go to.

2. John B Keane was an Irish playwright who lived in Listowel, Co Kerry. He wrote some very hard-hitting plays. But he was a man of deep faith. Towards the end of his life he contracted cancer, which proved to be terminal. Around that time he was asked on a TV show if he believed in a life after death. By way of an answer he old the following story.

He had a friend, Jack, who lived in Co Donegal. Trouble was they hadn't seen each other for years. One day John B phoned him. They arranged to meet in Galway at noon on a particular day, Galway being about halfway between Kerry and Donegal.

As John B was about to leave home, his wife said to him, 'But you haven't seen him in years. How can you be sure that he'll show up?'

To which John B responded, 'Jack is a reliable man. If he says he'll be there, he'll be there.'

Then, turning to the interviewer, he said, 'As for your question. I firmly believe that Jesus is a reliable person. He has told us that he has gone to prepare a place for us. He will be there. And so will our loved ones.'

SIXTH SUNDAY OF EASTER
Keeping his commandments

Praying with the Word of God today

INTRODUCTION AND CONFITEOR

We can't truly call ourselves disciples of Jesus unless we listen to his words and make an effort to live by them. We know we fail, and our lives are the poorer for that.

Let us ask the Lord for forgiveness and the help to do better in the future. [Pause]

Lord Jesus, your words are a lamp for our steps and a light for our path. Lord, have mercy.

You call those who belong to you, to listen to your voice and to follow you. Christ, have mercy.

To those who follow you, you give the light of life. Lord, have mercy.

PRAYER OF THE FAITHFUL

Celebrant: God has called us out of darkness into his own wonderful light. Let us pray that we may walk in the light of his truth and love.

Response: Lord, hear our prayer.

Reader(s): For the Pope and the bishops: that they may help God's people to obey Christ's commandments not out of fear, but out of love. [Pause] Let us pray to the Lord.

For government leaders: that they may be guided by the commandments of God. [Pause] Let us pray to the Lord.

For those who are suffering persecution because of their belief in Christ: that they may have the strength to persevere [Pause] Let us pray to the Lord.

For all gathered here: that we may never lose sight of Christ's commandment to love one another. [Pause] Let us pray to the Lord.

For our loved ones who have died: that they may rest in the peace of God. [Pause] Let us pray to the Lord.

For our own special needs. [Longer Pause] Let us pray to the Lord.

Celebrant: Father, your Son, innocent though he was, died for our sins in order to lead us to you. Help us to listen to his words, and to let those words guide our journey to your kingdom. We ask this through the same Christ our Lord.

PRAYER/REFLECTION

A thing you notice about birds
is how they are able to take advantage of the wind.

They go with it, they go against it,
they soar into the sky, they plunge back to earth.
All the time they are availing of the power of the wind.
And I think of how we, the disciples of Jesus,
are so easily blown off course by the winds of adversity.
Lord, through the power of the Holy Spirit,
help us to turn the hard and the easy to our advantage,
so that everything that happens to us
may bear us along the road to your kingdom.

FINAL BLESSING

May the Holy Spirit keep you faithful in times of trial and difficulty.
May you live in such a way that your lives will be an example for others.
May you know the joy of those who live by the Lord's commandments.

Sharing the Word of God today

SCRIPTURE NOTE

Now that we are in the latter part of the Easter season, the attention shifts from the resurrection appearances to the continued presence of the glorified Christ with his Church through the Spirit. This is the connection between the First Reading and the Gospel.

First Reading (Acts 8:5-8.14-17). Luke marks each stage of the spread of the Gospel with a 'Pentecost'. The Gospel was preached in Samaria by Philip, one of the seven deacons, with marked success. Our reading describes a Samaritan Pentecost. It tells of the joy and enthusiasm with which the Samaritans received the Gospel.

The statement that the Samaritan converts, baptised in the name of the Lord Jesus, had not received the Holy Spirit has puzzled many. The explanation lies in the fact that Luke required that each new stage in the growth of the community had to be authenticated by an official representative of the Church. Here Peter and John put their stamp of approval on the work of Philip. It doesn't mean that the Spirit is bestowed only in a 'second baptism'.

Second Reading (1 Pet 3:15-18). Peter encourages Christians to remain steadfast under pressure in their attachment to Christ. The Christian way of life is to be defended but this should be done with courtesy and respect. Their good lives will be the best way to counter false accusations. If they suffer for doing good, they should remember that Jesus, though innocent, suffered and died to lead us to God.

Gospel (Jn 14:15-21). This is part of Jesus' farewell discourse. Loving Jesus means listening to his word and putting it into practice. To those who respond in this way he promises the gift of the Spirit. Jesus will not leave his disciples orphaned. By their faith, they will be able to 'see' him and share in his life and in the life of the Father.

From this we learn that we cannot claim to be one with Jesus, and to be living according to the Spirit, unless we observe his commands in our lives.

Love and obedience

In today's Gospel passage we have part of the farewell discourse of Jesus during the Last Supper. In those last hours with his apostles he spoke about essentials. Many of the things he said were naturally directed towards the future, at how he wanted them to live when he was gone. One of the things he said to them was: 'If you love me, keep my commandments.'

We are not talking about keeping a specific set of commandments but rather about following his way of life. What is involved here is Christian discipleship. We can't truly call ourselves disciples of Jesus if we don't listen to his words and make an effort to live by them. One wouldn't be much of a Christian if one didn't try to live as Jesus taught.

But we must be clear about one thing. We don't keep his commandments so that he will love us; we keep his commandments *because* he loves us. During that same supper Jesus said, 'Love one another *as I have loved you.*' It was he who first loved the apostles, and loved them unconditionally.

The greatest need each one of us has is for real, unconditional love. Yet we find it hard to believe that this is how God loves us. We tend to believe that God will love us only if we are good. God loves us, not because we are good, but because he is good. Our very existence is a sign of God's love. God's unconditional love for us *is* the Good News. Our response is to return that love.

Jesus knew that the Father loved him. He responded by loving the Father. He showed his love for the Father through his obedience, even though that obedience cost him his life. And it is through obedience that we are to show our love for Jesus. What does this mean in practice? It means to listen to his word and to put it into practice. To love is to obey. And to obey is to love.

There are those who proclaim their love for Jesus in words, but who deny him in their deeds. Real love is shown in deeds. People know us by our acts, not by what we say with our lips.

It's not easy to live as a disciple of Jesus in the modern world. It never was an easy thing. But for this reason Jesus has given us the Holy Spirit. When we are weak we must pray to the Spirit. The Spirit comforts us in times of sorrow, enlightens us in times of darkness, and strengthens us in times of weakness.

The word Jesus used for the Spirit was the word *Advocate,* a legal term for one who supports a defendant at a trial. The Spirit will be the great defender of the disciples in time of trial. And the follower of Jesus can expect to suffer. But, as St Peter says (see Second Reading), it is better to suffer for doing the right thing than for doing the wrong thing. Knowing that our cause is right gives us great strength. Besides, we have the example of Jesus, who, though innocent, suffered and died for our sins.

The apostles knew that Jesus loved them. And we know that Jesus loves us too. There is no mistaking love. You feel it in your heart. It is like a flame that warms your soul, energises your spirit and supplies passion to your life. Love is our connection to God and to one another. Love is the climate in which the Christian lives. Jesus commandment, 'Love one another as I have loved you', sums it all up.

The leave-taking

The parting of friends is never easy. But some partings are harder than others. The most painful parting of all happens when someone dies. What makes this parting different from all others is the finality of it.

It was the night before Jesus' death. For some time he had been giving the apostles hints of his death. Now he talked to them openly about it. Except he didn't speak of death in the way we tend to do – in the sense of life ending. He spoke of his death as a going away, 'going to the Father'. But all the apostles heard was the fact that he was leaving them. Yes, he was indeed leaving them. But there are degrees of leaving.

There is a leaving that implies abandonment. Sadly, now and again we read in the newspapers about babies that are abandoned at birth. To be abandoned is the most painful and damaging thing that can happen to anyone, particularly in the case of the young and the elderly. In the Gospel we are not dealing with this. Jesus is not abandoning the apostles.

There is a leaving that implies rejection. For instance, a girl had hopes of marriage but her fiancé suddenly leaves her for someone else. The girl feels rejected. Rejection causes a deep wound. We are not dealing with that here. Jesus is not rejecting the apostles.

There is a leaving that is necessary because it is for the good of the one leaving. For example, a person is leaving to return home, or leaving to take up a better job somewhere else. This is certainly true here. Jesus' leaving is for his own good. He is returning to his Father. To return to the Father is to go home. It is to go to honour and glory.

Finally, there is a leaving that is for the good of the one leaving and of those left behind. This is the full truth of what is happening here. Jesus' leaving is, or will be, good for the apostles because he will send them the Holy Spirit. His departure will not leave them unsupported and unguided as they feared. 'I will not leave you orphans,' he said.

But there was another thing that would have been a great consolation to the apostles at this sad and painful hour. Even as he spoke about leaving them, he spoke about coming back to them. He would come to them through the Spirit, and he would come to them himself. They did encounter him after the resurrection. And even though after the ascension they would see him no more, he assured them that he would still be with them, yes, even to the end of time.

Jesus did not leave his disciples orphaned or desolate. By their faith they were able to 'see' him, and through their obedience to his commandments, they were drawn into a loving communion with him and with the Father.

Nor does Jesus leave us orphaned. We have the same access to his presence, and to the help of the Holy Spirit as the first Christians had. Jesus is not present as a vague memory of a person who lived long ago, but as a real, life-giving presence that transforms us.

Nowhere do we feel so close to him as when we receive him in the Eucharist. When we receive the Eucharist we are not just in communication with him, but also in communion with him – a *holy* communion. Here he nourishes our hearts with his love. The food of the Eucharist gives us the strength to do his word and to live as his disciples.

Keeping his commandments

A number of times during the Last Supper Jesus said these or similar words to his apostles: 'If you love me, keep my commandments.' Clearly he was not talking about the Ten Commandments. He said: '*My* commandments', not '*Moses'* commandments'. What commandments was he talking about?

A look at the Gospels will provide the answer. There we find certain *Dos* and *Don'ts* he talked about. However, we are not talking so much about a set of commandments as about a set of values he wanted his followers to live by. Keeping this in mind, let us consider some of the *Dos* and *Don'ts* he talked about.

DONT'S

Jesus says: 'Do not to return evil for evil.' Nothing is achieved by retaliation, except to pile darkness upon darkness.

Jesus says: 'Do not judge your neighbour, and you yourself will not be judged.' Society needs courts and judges. But here we're talking about our ordinary dealings with one another. In these cases we should leave judgement to God.

Jesus says: 'Do not condemn your neighbour, and you yourself will not be condemned.' This follows from the last. If we are not to pass judgement on our neighbour, neither are we to pass sentence on him.

Jesus says: 'Do not worry about food, and drink, and clothes, like the pagans do.' He is telling us not to make these things the be-all and the end-all of life. Our first concern should be to live a life worthy of our status as God's sons and daughters.

Jesus says: 'Do not store up treasures for yourselves here on earth.' Earthly treasures (such as property and money) are like chaff in the eyes of God, chaff to be blown away in the first winds of judgement.

Jesus says: 'When you put your hand to the plough, do not look back. Anyone who looks back is not worthy of the Kingdom.' He is telling us that once we have decided to follow him, we shouldn't quit.

He says: 'Do not let your hearts be troubled. Trust in God still, and trust in me.' Here he is telling us that we shouldn't give up hope when times are rough. We should remember that we are infinitely precious to God.

DO'S

Jesus says: 'Let your light shine before people.' He is telling us to live in such a way that our lives will become an example for others. In which case we will help others find their way into the Kingdom, and God will be glorified.

Jesus says: 'Love your enemies, and pray for those who persecute you.' This is a huge challenge. Only God's grace can help us to accomplish it.

Jesus says: 'Give generously. The measure you give to others, will be the measure you receive from God.' In other words, if we are generous to others, God will be generous to us.

Jesus says: 'Forgive those who sin against you, and God will forgive you your sins.' That needs no comment.

Jesus says: 'Clean the inside of cup and dish, and the outside will become clean too.' Here he is telling us to see that our minds and hearts are clean. If we do, then all your thoughts, words and deeds will be clean, like water coming from an unpolluted spring.

Jesus says: 'Take this bread and eat it. Take this cup and drink it. Do this in memory of me.' He is telling us that his disciples are to nourish themselves at the banquet of the Eucharist.

And last but not least Jesus says: 'Love one another, the way I have loved you. Then all will know that you are disciples of mine.'

These are some of the values Jesus wants us to live by. One wouldn't be much of a Christian if one didn't try to live as Jesus taught.

In all of these, Jesus in not laying a burden on us. Rather, he is offering us a gift. If we live by his commandments, we will have a deeper, richer, and happier life here on earth, and eternal life in the hereafter.

THE ASCENSION OF THE LORD
Called to share his glory

Praying with the Word of God today

INTRODUCTION AND CONFITEOR

The ascension of Jesus is the climax of his victory over sin and death. What happened to him is meant to happen to us. God wants to bring us to the place where Jesus is, so that we can share his glory.

Let us call to mind the sins that prevent us from walking freely and joyfully towards the glory of God. [Pause]

Lord Jesus, you have gone before us to prepare a place for us. Lord, have mercy.

You plead for us at the right hand of the Father. Christ, have mercy.

You are the Good Shepherd leading us to everlasting life. Lord, have mercy.

PRAYER OF THE FAITHFUL

Celebrant: Christ now sits at God's right hand in glory. Let us bring our needs before God, confident that he is praying with us and for us.

Response: Lord, hear our prayer.

Reader(s): For Christians: that they may realise that Jesus depends on them to ensure that the Gospel is preached and lived. [Pause] Let us pray to the Lord.

For those who govern our country: that God may bless them with the gifts of wisdom and integrity. [Pause] Let us pray to the Lord.

For those who have nothing to hope for beyond this life: that they may be granted the gift of faith. [Pause] Let us pray to the Lord.

For all gathered here: that our lives may bear witness to the hope we carry in our hearts. [Pause] Let us pray to the Lord.

For all the faithful departed: that the Lord may receive them into the kingdom of his glory. [Pause] Let us pray to the Lord.

For our own special needs. [Longer pause] Let us pray to the Lord.

Celebrant: God of love, your Son has passed beyond our sight, not to abandon us, but to be our hope. By your unceasing care, guide our steps towards the life of glory. We ask this through him who lives and reigns with you and the Holy Spirit, one God, for ever and ever

OUR FATHER

God raised Jesus up, and gave him a name which is above all other names. Let us pray to the God of love in the words our Saviour gave us.

This feast shows us the goal of our earthly journey.
It is a goal that defies our imagination,
and that gives an eternal dimension to our lives.
However, we know nothing of the mystery of the beyond.
All we have are the words of Jesus:
'Where I am, you too will be.'
Lord, grant that the glitter of this world
may not dim our hopes of eternal glory.
And by your unceasing care,
guide our steps towards the life of glory.

FINAL BLESSING

May God, who have given us such a sure hope, comfort and strengthen you in everything good that you say or do.

May you live a life worthy of God, who is calling you to share the glory of his kingdom.

May you never be ashamed of witnessing to the Lord.

Sharing the Word of God today

SCRIPTURE NOTE

First Reading (Acts 1:1-11). Luke has the Ascension happening on the Mount of Olives in Jerusalem and coming some forty days after the resurrection, as a solemn finale to his resurrection appearances. (The Ascension marks the termination of his earthly appearances).

At the beginning of his second volume (Acts), he gives a brief recapitulation of the Gospel. Then he passes to a summary of the conversation of Jesus with the apostles after his resurrection.

We then have a final appearance during which he promises to send them the Holy Spirit, a power that will enable them to be his witnesses. Through them the message of Jesus would reach out from Jerusalem in ever-widening circles. The passage concludes with a description of the Ascension.

Second Reading (Eph 1:17-23). Here Paul expresses the theological meaning of the Ascension: God has glorified Jesus, raising him above all earthly powers, and making him head of the Church and Lord of creation.

However, Paul is more interested in the consequences of all this for Christians. He talks about the hope the Ascension holds out for us: we are destined to share in the glory of Jesus.

Gospel (Mt 28:16-20). Matthew has the Ascension happening in a mountain in Galilee. But, as in the First Reading, Jesus gives a mission and a promise to his followers.

Jesus solemnly declares that the Father has given him total power over the universe. He is, therefore, in a position to launch a universal mission. So he commissions his representatives and sends them into the world to make disciples of 'all nations'. His own ministry was confined to Israel; now the good news is for all.

One becomes a disciple through baptism in the name of the Father, Son and Holy Spirit – undoubtedly the formula that was in use in the baptismal liturgy of Matthew's church. The apostles are to teach all the commands they received from the Lord.

Matthew rounds off his Gospel with a word of encouragement for the disciples: the promise of the Lord to be with them always. The ascension does not represent his removal from the earth. It represents his liberation from all restrictions of time and space, so that he can be present everywhere on earth.

The meaning of the Ascension

St Luke gives us what appears to be an eyewitness account of Jesus ascending into heaven. However, we must not take it literally. The Ascension of Jesus is a mystery that is beyond words. Nevertheless, it stands for something real that happened to Jesus.

For Jesus his ascension was not a journey into outer space, but a journey home. He was returning to the Father to be glorified. The ascension means that the humble Jesus who suffered and died now reigns in glory at the right hand of the Father. God has raised him above all earthly powers, and made him head of the Church and Lord of creation (Second Reading). That's what we are celebrating today.

The ascension doesn't mean that Jesus was abandoning his apostles, and that he would no longer be present on earth. The glorified Jesus had no intention of abandoning his apostles. Indeed, he promised to remain with them to the end of time.

But how can this he if he has ascended to heaven? The ascension does not represent his removal from the earth. It is his liberation from all restrictions of time and space. During his earthly ministry he could only be in one place at a time. But now that he is united with God, he is present wherever God is present; and that is everywhere.

The first Christians understood this very well. They knew that Jesus was still with them, even if not in the same way as before. They believed he still shared their lives, and that death would mean being united with him in glory for ever.

In the meantime he had given them a task to perform, namely, to preach the Gospel to the world. He had preached the Gospel only to Israel. But now he commissioned the apostles to preach the Gospel *to all nations*. It was a daunting task. He gave them only one assurance, namely, that he would be with them: 'I will be with you always; yes, to the end of time.'

How do we account for the fact that an institution such as the Church, with all its human faults, has lasted for 2,000 years, while parties and kingdoms have come and gone? The explanation surely lies in the promise of Jesus: 'I will be with you always, to the end of time.'

The baton has now been handed over to us. We are his witnesses before the world. The most effective witness is a Christian life.

This feast is as much about us as about Jesus. His ascension shows us the goal of our earthly journey. It is a goal and a destiny that defies even our imagination. It gives an eternal dimension to our lives.

The path that led Jesus to glory was not an easy one. But if it was easy it would not be of much use to us. Glory can only be attained through struggle and suffering.

Story

Lech Walesa worked for years as an electrician in the Gdansk shipyards in Poland. During those years he and his fellow workers founded the movement that became known as *Solidarity*. Walesa became its leader. This brought them into open conflict with the Communist rulers.

Eventually the Communist regime collapsed and democracy returned to Poland. On Dec 9, 1990, Walesa, the shipyard worker, was elected first president of a free and democratic Poland.

It was a great honour for Walesa. His fellow workers were delighted for him. They also felt honoured because of their association with him. But there was sadness too. They knew that he was leaving them. His elevation to presidency would change for ever the way they related to him.

The day after his election, Walesa went back to the Gdansk shipyard. He emerged from the bulletproof Volvo that was now his official car, and went directly to his former workshop. Workers in overalls congratulated him. They expressed the hope that he would not forget them and that he would help them from his new and more influential position.

This helps us to understand something of the mystery we are celebrating today. Just as after years of humble labour and dangerous struggle, Walesa achieved the great honour of being elected president of his country, so after his years of ministry on earth, a ministry that ended in his crucifixion, Jesus was crowned with glory by his heavenly Father, and became Lord of all creation.

During the years of his public ministry Jesus ate and drank in the company of the apostles. They experienced his love and care every day. In many ways he was just like one of them. Did the ascension mean the end of all this intimacy and familiarity? Yes and no.

He would no longer be physically present to the apostles, but he hadn't left them entirely. He had simply attained to a new and more exalted position. His new and exalted position meant that he was in a better position to help his apostles.

His witnesses

There is a story that says that when Jesus returned to heaven after his death and resurrection, the Archangel Gabriel was surprised to see him back so soon. Thirty-three years is not a long time, especially when you think about the enormity of the task he had been given to do.

'Back so soon?' Gabriel said to Jesus.

'Well, I would have stayed longer but they crucified me,' Jesus replied.

'Oh, so they crucified you,' said Gabriel. 'That means you failed.'

'Not necessarily,' said Jesus. 'You see I called together a little group of disciples. They will carry on my work.'

'And what if they should fail?' asked Gabriel.

'I've no other plans,' Jesus answered.

Jesus had preached the Gospel only to Israel. But now he commissioned the apostles to preach the Gospel to all nations. It was a daunting task. However, he promised that he would send them the Holy Spirit. He also assured them that he himself would always be with them: 'I'll be with you always; yes, to the end of time.'

But how could he always be with them if he was ascending to heaven? The Ascension did not represent Jesus' removal from the earth. The Ascension was his liberation from all restrictions of time and space. During his earthly ministry he could only be in one place at a time. But now that he is united with God, he is present wherever God is present; and that is everywhere.

Other than the promise to be with the apostles, he gave them no assurances. However, that assurance gave them the courage and strength to face whatever difficulties lay ahead.

A sense of the presence of Christ with us doesn't change the world for us, but it can give us the courage to face it. God's closeness shields us against a sense of abandonment and despair.

In spite of the grave failings of his followers, and many terrible persecutions let loose on the Church, the Gospel has come down to us across two thousand years. The explanation for this surely lies in the promise of Jesus: 'I will be with you always, to the very end of time.'

Jesus now depends on us to preach the Gospel. We are his witnesses before the world. It is a daunting task but a great privilege too.

How are we to witness? The great Mahatma Gandhi said, 'My life is my message.' The most effective way to witness to Jesus is to live a Christian life. Those who truly live their faith give a powerful witness.

But we are weak and fail often. However, we must not be discouraged by our weakness or demoralised by our failures. We should draw encouragement from the words of Mother Teresa: 'I don't pray for success; I pray that I may be a faithful witness.'

Presence and absence

St Luke's account of the ascension seems to emphasise the fact that Jesus is *going away*. This means that he will no longer be with the apostles, or with us. However, the story is not so much about Jesus leaving as about Jesus *being glorified*. That's where the emphasis is, and that's what this great feast is about.

It is true that on Ascension Day Jesus withdrew his physical presence from the apostles. The ascension marked the termination of his earthly appearances.

Now physical presence is a great thing but it isn't everything. In fact, it can sometimes actually get in the way of intimate communication. Many of our disappointments in life are caused by the fact that seeing and touching do not always create the closeness we seek.

Two people can be physically close, and yet live separate, lonely lives, because there is no meeting of minds and hearts. They are like shells lying on the same piece of shore.

On the other hand, people can be separated by thousands of miles and yet feel close to one another. When people think of each other with love, a spiritual bond is created between them, and they enter into a new intimacy. For those who love one another there is no such place as 'far away'.

If we are able to be fully present to our friends when we are with them, our absence too will bear fruit. The memory of that presence, the warmth of it, will continue to nourish them. Thus, not only our presence but also our absence becomes a gift.

Jesus' ascension was not a journey into outer space. It was a journey back to the Father to be glorified. We must not think that he has abandoned us, that he once lived on earth but has now gone back to where he really belongs. If this were so then Christianity would be no more than a remembrance religion.

Today's Gospel ends with Jesus' promise to remain with his disciples always, right to the end of time. How can this be if he has ascended to heaven? It can be because the ascension does not represent his removal from the earth. It represents his liberation from all restrictions of time and space. During his earthly ministry he could only be in one place at a time.

But now that he is united with God, he is present wherever God is present; and that is everywhere.

The first Christians understood this very well. They knew that Jesus was still with them, even if not in the same way as before. They believed that they encountered him when the Scriptures were expounded and the bread was broken (in the Eucharist). And they believed that death would mean being united with him in glory for ever.

We Christians of the present day have those same means of encountering Jesus – the Scriptures and the breaking of the bread.

Jesus gave the apostles a great task to perform, namely, to preach the Gospel to the world. That task has been handed on to us. We draw strength from the conviction that the risen and glorified Christ is with us as he was with the apostles.

SEVENTH SUNDAY OF EASTER
Waiting for the Spirit

Praying with the Word of God today

INTRODUCTION AND CONFITEOR

After the ascension of Jesus, the apostles went back to Jerusalem and 'joined in continuous prayer' as they awaited the coming of the Holy Spirit. We are gathered here to wait for the coming of the Spirit. Without the Holy Spirit we cannot live the life of a Christian. [Pause]

Lord Jesus, through the gift of the Holy Spirit you strengthen us in times of trial. Lord, have mercy.

You console us in times of sorrow. Christ, have mercy.

You guide us in times of darkness and doubt. Lord, have mercy.

PRAYER OF THE FAITHFUL

Celebrant: Let us pray for the coming of the Holy Spirit on us, on the Church, and on the world.

Response: Come, Holy Spirit.

Reader(s): For the Church: that the Holy Spirit may renew its members in their commitment to Christ. [Pause] Let us pray to the Lord.

For all those who guide the destiny of nations: that the Holy Spirit may open their ears to the voice of conscience. [Pause] Let us pray to the Lord.

For those whose spirits are crushed by misfortune: that the Holy Spirit may breath new life into them. [Pause] Let us pray to the Lord.

For all gathered here: that the Holy Spirit may warm our hearts with his love, and strengthen our wills with his grace. [Pause] Let us pray to the Lord.

For our deceased relatives and friends: that the Lord may keep them safe in his love. [Pause] Let us pray to the Lord.

For our own special needs. [Longer Pause] Let us pray to the Lord.

Celebrant: God of love, open our hearts to the coming of the Holy Spirit, so that we may follow your Son more faithfully on earth, and come to share his glory in heaven, where he lies and reigns with you and the Holy Spirit, one God, for ever and ever.

REFLECTION

Our spirit is our greatest source of energy.
However, while it can be very strong,
it can also be very brittle.
What is it that enables the spirit to soar,
and what is it that causes it to sink?
Sadness weighs it down; joy lifts it up.
Criticism erodes it; praise builds it up.
Failure shrinks it; success enlarges it.
Despair causes it to wilt; hope breathes new life into it.
Rejection wounds it; acceptance heals it.
Hatred poisons it; love purifies it.
Fear cripples it; solitude calms it; prayer strengths it.

FINAL BLESSING

May you never be ashamed to suffer for being a Christian.

May you not be afraid of anything the world can throw at you, because Christ has overcome the world.

May the Holy Spirit keep you united in prayer and fellowship.

Sharing the Word of God today

SCRIPTURE NOTE

First Reading (Acts 1:12-14). Here Luke sets the stage for the coming of the Holy Spirit that for him marks the dynamic beginnings of the Church.

The disciples are gathered in the upper room, waiting in prayer for the coming of the Holy Spirit. The apostles are mentioned by name (except Judas). So also is Mary the mother of Jesus – a model of faith during the earthly life of Jesus.

Second Reading (1 Pet 4:13-16). Throughout this short letter the author again and again alludes to suffering as part of Christian living. He seeks to encourage those who suffer for their faith in Christ. Joy and glory await the person who remains faithful through thick and thin.

Gospel (Jn 17:1-11). This solemn prayer is part of the farewell discourse of Jesus at the Last Supper. In the first part (vv. 1-5) Jesus talks about the 'hour', that is, the hour of his death and resurrection. During his life on earth Jesus' whole concern had been to make the Father known. Now it is the Father's turn to glorify him.

The second part (vv. 6-19) is the opening part of Jesus' prayer for his disciples. He prays for those whom he leaves behind to carry on his work. He had made the Father known to them. Now he commits them to the Father's care and prays that they may know among themselves the warm communion of Father and Son.

Our need of the Spirit

St Paul tells us that no one can say, 'Jesus is Lord' without the help of the Holy Spirit (1 Cor 12:3). In other words, we can't do anything in the spiritual life without the Holy Spirit. We may be tempted to protest: 'This can't possibly be true. St Paul is exaggerating. We can do lots of things. All we need is some will-power.'

St Paul is not exaggerating. All the great artists were painfully aware of their need of inspiration. Van Gogh put it like this: 'In order to do beautiful things, you need a certain dart of inspiration, a ray from on high, things not in ourselves.'

Anyone who has made serious attempts at living a spiritual life will know that without God's grace we are powerless. We need a strength we ourselves do not possess. In this 'do-it-yourself' age, this truth will come as a blow to our pride. It is especially in times of difficulty and crisis that we come face to face with our limitations.

When Jesus died the apostles were like sheep without a shepherd. Worse, during the passion they learned some uncomfortable things about themselves. Before it they thought they were brave, strong, and generous. During it they discovered they were cowardly, weak, and selfish.

But Jesus had foreseen all this. He knew they needed strengthening. That was why he told them to do nothing until they received 'power from on high', that is, the Holy Spirit. Only with the help of the Spirit would they be able to go out and preach the Gospel. The experience of their own weakness during the passion disposed them to receive the Spirit.

We all have experiences that make us painfully aware of our own weakness. A sudden illness, or perhaps a brush with death, and we are face to face with our powerlessness and mortality. We find that we are not capable of the simplest prayer. All the saints knew such moments. Far from being moments of damnation, these can become moments of enlightenment and salvation. They convince us of our need of the Spirit.

During the nine days between the Ascension and Pentecost the apostles, with Mary in their midst, assembled in the upper room to prepare for the coming of the Holy Spirit. Their preparation consisted in prayer and mutual support. This is the oldest and most important novena in the Church. We must try to make these days, days of prayer. Jesus prayed for those he left behind to carry on his work, as we see from today's Gospel. Each Pentecost renews the gift of the Holy Spirit in the Church as a whole, and in us as individuals.

What the Spirit means to us

As we approach the great feast of Pentecost we naturally think of the Holy Spirit. But we ought also to think of the human spirit.

It would be impossible to exaggerate the importance of the spirit. The human spirit is more powerful than any drug. Our spirit is our most precious possession. It is our greatest source of energy. It is to us what wings are to a bird, or roots are to a tree.

However, while the human spirit can be very strong, it can also be very brittle. It can ascend the heights, or it can plumb the depths. It can be an oak unmoved in a storm, or a frail reed swaying in the wind. It can be as tough as a piece of granite, or as fragile as a piece of china.

The human spirit can be broken. And when the spirit is broken, terrible harm is done to the person. 'Sickness, the spirit of man can endure, but when the spirit is broken, who can bear this?' (Prov 18:14). There is an African story that illustrates this very well.

The story concerns the Bush-people of Africa, or the *Bushmen* as they were called. The Bush-people were the first people of Africa. But down the centuries they suffered persecution at the hands of both white people and black people. Today there is only a remnant of them left in Southern Africa, in and around the Kalahari desert. Most people would find such an environment almost unbearable. Not so the Bush-people. For them it is their natural element.

Once a Bushman was arrested for killing a giant bustard, which was a crime, since the bustard is a protected species. He was locked up in a small cell. For someone used to living in wide-open spaces, this was a crucifixion. He began to waste away like a candle. Even though he was not ill treated, and had sufficient food and drink, he continued to pine away.

Puzzled and alarmed, the authorities called in a doctor to examine him. The doctor gave him a thorough examination, but could find nothing wrong with him physically. Finally, when asked through an interpreter why he was ill, all the man could say was, 'I can't live without being able to see the sun go down over the Kalahari desert.'

I don't know how the story ended, but I hope the authorities had the good sense to release him. His problem was not lack of food for his body, but lack of nourishment for his spirit. It was his spirit, not his body, that was dying.

Because the spirit is easily broken, easily crushed, it needs strengthening and nourishing every bit as much as the body does. If strengthened and nourished the spirit has great powers of recovery.

The death of Jesus left the apostles sad and wounded in spirit. The resurrection of Jesus revived them. But they were not yet courageous and strong enough to face the world. They needed the Holy Spirit to lift their spirits and to breathe new life into them.

The Holy Spirit continually breathes new life into our spirits. So, as we prepare for the feast of Pentecost, we might make our own the prayer: Spirit of the living God, fall afresh on us.

The waiting room

Before leaving his apostles Jesus told them to wait in Jerusalem for the coming of the Holy Spirit. So they returned from the Mount of Olives to the upper room. There they gathered with Mary the mother of Jesus and other disciples, and waited in prayer for the promised Spirit. The upper room became a waiting room.

All of us are familiar with waiting rooms of one kind or another. We have waited for people. We have waited for planes, trains, and buses. We have been in the waiting rooms of doctors and dentists and hospitals. No two waiting rooms are the same. In some you feel close to heaven; in others you feel close to hell.

There is no comparison between waiting in a comfortable airport lounge for a loved one to arrive home, and waiting in a hospital room for news of a loved one who is clinging to life by a slender thread.

We are familiar with the peculiar atmosphere that prevails in waiting rooms. An air of uncertainty prevails which makes us feel nervous and apprehensive. In general, the people we meet in waiting rooms are strangers to us. Still, it's better than being alone. But of course it's so much better if you have a friend or friends by your side.

What makes the experience so difficult is precisely the waiting. Waiting is not easy. It means being idle. Idleness can be unbearable, especially for active people. The poor do more waiting than the rich. The rich are able to skip the queue.

But the hardest thing of all about waiting is the sense of powerlessness that usually accompanies it. Things are out of our control. Our destiny is in the hands of someone else. There is nothing we can do but wait. This can be excruciating for capable people who like to take control of things.

When we are waiting we tend to feel lonely, nervous, anxious, and fearful. We look for some distraction, something to make the time pass more quickly and to keep our minds off the future. In many waiting rooms you will find reading material left there for that purpose. But often you find yourself unable to concentrate on it.

But waiting, though painful, can be a graced thing. The soul is nurtured by want as well as by plenty. Waiting brings home to us how interdependent we are. We need others. Besides, waiting is part of life. The earth has to wait for the rain. The farmer has to wait for the spring. Waiting is necessary for change, growth, and healing to happen.

One psychologist says that people need to be empowered – that is her definition of health. But there are also times when we may need to be weak and powerless, vulnerable and open to experience.

What was it like for the apostles? I'm quite sure that they would have experienced most of our emotions as they waited in that room. They put their trust in the word of Jesus. But that doesn't mean they weren't apprehensive about the future. And as they waited, they became aware of their own powerlessness. But that only served to dispose them to receive the gift of the Holy Spirit. As they waited, they prayed and supported each other.

We must try to make these days, days of prayer. Each Pentecost renews the gift of the Holy Spirit in the Church as a whole, and in us as individuals.

PENTECOST SUNDAY
Power from on high

Praying with the Word of God today

INTRODUCTION AND CONFITEOR

Today we celebrate the coming of the Holy Spirit on the apostles. As a result of his coming, they left the upper room where they had been hiding for fear of the Jews, and set out courageously to preach the Gospel to the world.

The power of the Holy Spirit is available to us too. Let us reflect for a moment on our need of the Spirit. [Pause]

Lord Jesus, through the gift of the Holy Spirit you strengthen us when we are weak, and give us courage when we are afraid. Lord, have mercy.

You guide us in times of doubt, and console us in times of sorrow. Christ, have mercy

You bind us together as a community, dedicated to living and spreading the Gospel. Lord, have mercy.

PRAYER OF THE FAITHFUL

Celebrant: Let us now bring our prayers to the Father, who sends the Holy Spirit to renew the face of the earth.

Response: Spirit of the living God, fall afresh on us.

Reader(s): For the Church: that the Holy Spirit may empower its members to bear witness with their lives to the values of the Gospel. [Pause] Let us pray.

For the human family: that the Holy Spirit may gather people of every race, language, and way of life to share in the one eternal banquet. [Pause] Let us pray.

For those who are imprisoned by doubt, fear, depression, addiction, or habits of sin: that the Holy Spirit may set them free. [Pause] Let us pray.

For those who suffer persecution for the name of Christ: that the Holy Spirit may keep them strong. [Pause] Let us pray.

For all gathered here: that the Holy Spirit may bind us together in a community of faith and love. [Pause] Let us pray.

For our deceased relatives and friends: that the Holy Spirit may cause the light of heaven to shine on them. [Pause] Let us pray.

For our own special needs. [Longer Pause] Let us pray.

Celebrant: God of power and love, may the Holy Spirit enlighten our minds, purify our hearts, and strengthen our wills, so that we may give effective witness to our Christian faith. We ask this through Christ our Lord.

OUR FATHER

Through the gift of the Holy Spirit, people of many languages learned to profess one faith. Let us pray to our Heavenly Father in union with all those who profess the same faith, though in different languages.

SIGN OF PEACE

Lord Jesus Christ, on Pentecost Day, you sent the Holy Spirit on the apostles, and with hearts on fire, they went forth to preach the Gospel to the world.

Send your Spirit into our world to gather people of every race, language, and way of life, into the peace and unity of your kingdom where you live for ever and ever.

REFLECTION

St Paul warns us against self-indulgence.
Self-indulgence leads to fighting, jealousy,
cruelty, meanness, and revenge.
Things such as these make life miserable.
Paul urges us to allow ourselves to be guided by the Holy Spirit.

If we do, then our lives will be characterised by
love, joy, peace, patience, kindness,
goodness, faithfulness, gentleness, and self-control.
These are beautiful things and make life joyful.
Spirit of the living God, fall afresh on us.

FINAL BLESSING

May the Holy Spirit bless you with the gifts of unity and peace.

May the Holy Spirit inflame your hearts and raise your spirits.

May the Holy Spirit kindle in your hearts the fire of his love, and make you courageous followers of Christ.

Sharing the Word of God today

SCRIPTURE NOTE

VIGIL MASS

First Reading (Gen 11:1-9). After the flood, the people were charged by God to spread out and repopulate the earth. But instead of doing this they decided to settle at Shinar where they planned to build a great city and a tower so as to 'make a name' for themselves. Their sin was that they rejected God's will. And (as in the case of Adam and Eve) that sin alienated them from God and from one another.

This reading is chosen for today because Pentecost is seen as reversing the disaster of Babel. Whereas Babel divided and confused the unity of the human family, Pentecost creates from the many languages of people one voice to profess one faith.

Any of the following may be used as alternatives: Exodus 19:3-8.16-20; Ezekiel 37:1-14; Joel 3:1-5.

Second Reading (Rom 8:22-27). This talks about the role of the Holy Spirit in our lives. As we wait (together with the whole of creation) for our salvation to be accomplished, the Spirit comes to our help in our weakness, especially in helping us to pray as we ought.

Gospel (Jn 7:37-39). On the last day of the feast of Tabernacles, there was a ritual pouring of water. This provides the context for the words of Jesus: 'Let anyone who is thirsty come to me ...' John interprets the words as referring to the outpouring of the Holy Spirit that would result from the glorification of Jesus (through his resurrection and ascension).

DAY MASS

First Reading (Acts 2:1-11). Luke has the giving of the Holy Spirit happening on the feast of Pentecost. Jewish tradition saw Pentecost as the feast of the giving of the Law on Mount Sinai. According to a legend a mighty wind turned to fire and a voice proclaimed the Law. In a further refinement, the fire split into 70 tongues corresponding to the 70 nations of the world, to convey that the Law was proclaimed not only to Israel, but also to all nations.

Luke exploits this tradition. He, too, has the mighty wind and tongues of fire coming upon the group of disciples. But for Luke the universal proclamation was not that of the Law, but of the Good News, a proclamation that has undone the sentence of Babel and re-united the scattered nations.

Second Reading (1 Cor 12:3-7.12-13). Here Paul is concerned with charismatic gifts which have become a source of disunity among the Corinthians. He admits that there are many gifts but insists that they all have the same source – the Holy Spirit. These gifts are given by the Spirit for the good of the Church, the Body of Christ. There is no place for divisions within the community of Christ.

Gospel (Jn 20:19-23). John has the giving of the Spirit happening on Easter Day. However, we must avoid any impression of a two-fold initial solemn bestowal of the Spirit. Luke and John are saying the same thing: the risen Lord gives the gift of the Spirit, and inaugurates the mission of the Church. That they differ in their dating is due to theological concerns.

In our passage, the risen Christ appears to his apostles, shows them his wounds (these serve to identify him as the same one who died), and bestows peace on them. Then he entrusts his mission to them. This mission is the exact same mission he received from the Father: the reconciliation of people with the Father (through the forgiveness of sins). To carry out their mission he gives them the gift of the Spirit and the power to forgive sin.

Small beginnings

Today the Catholic Church contains over one billion members. Scattered all over world, they come from every race, tribe, and tongue. Anyone who has been to Lourdes or Rome has got the feeling of being part of something great. This is a wonderful experience. You feel buoyed up, supported, and carried along. It is nice to experience this now and again.

Pentecost is the birthday of the Church. It was the coming of the Holy Spirit that launched the Church. The Holy Spirit came down on the apostles in the form of wind and fire. Wind is a symbol of power – the power of God. Fire is a symbol love – the love of God. These are connected; love is the greatest power of all.

Prior to the coming of the Holy Spirit the apostles were hiding in the upper room. Afterwards, empowered by the Holy Spirit, they left the upper room, and set out courageously to preach the Gospel.

Even though the launch of the Church is described in very dramatic terms, in reality it began very simply. The Church was born in frailty and weakness. It had no property, no buildings, and no money. Its only resource was people, and there weren't many of them. As they waited for the Holy Spirit, they were all able to fit into one room. The Church should never forget its humble origins.

Though small in numbers, thanks to the coming of the Holy Spirit, they were strong in spirit, and united in prayer and charity. The Church is sustained, not by organisational structures and membership statistics, but by the quality of its members.

While it's nice to belong to something big, it can be a drawback. Sometimes the global is just too big. When an organisation becomes big there is a loss of closeness. And the individual tends to get lost.

We need to experience the Church as small. We need to belong to a specific community. We need a sense of closeness and of belonging, a sense of interdependence and of mutual service, such as Paul talks about (see Second Reading). Our faith is nourished at a local level.

In this gathering, we have all we need. Though we have no pomp or grandeur, we have the essentials. Here the Church is stripped down to essentials. Here we have the simplicity of the Gospel – a group of disciples listening to the Word of God, and receiving the broken bread in memory of Jesus.

And, of course, we have the Holy Spirit. The Holy Spirit was not given just for one time and one place. The Holy Spirit abides with us. The Holy Spirit is present in the Church as a whole – guiding it. And the Holy Spirit is present in each member; we are temples of the Holy Spirit (1 Cor 6:19).

It is the Holy Spirit who binds us together in a community of love. And it is the Spirit who gives us the courage to witness to Christ in the world.

Empowerment

Prior to the coming of the Holy Spirit the apostles were living in hiding in the upper room. A great task had been entrusted to them, yet they had neither the strength nor the will to begin it. But after the coming of the Holy Spirit they were changed people. They left their hiding place, and set out courageously to preach the Gospel.

What was it that the Spirit did for them?

In promising the Spirit Jesus said to them, 'You will receive *power* when the Holy Spirit comes on you, and then you will be my witnesses not only in Jerusalem, but also to the ends of the earth' (Acts 1:8).

The key word here is the word *power*. Power was precisely what they needed. At present they felt completely *powerless*. They were crippled with fear and a sense of inadequacy. They needed someone to *empower* them.

Empowerment is one of the 'in' words nowadays. And with good reason. We have seen what individuals or groups of people have been able to do when someone empowered them. We have seen what a good motivator can do for a football team.

What does empowerment mean? In the first place, it means to give or delegate power or authority to someone, to authorise someone. This wouldn't apply to the apostles – they had already been given that by Jesus.

In the second place, it means to *enable* someone to do something. This is the usual sense in which the word empowerment is used, and it certainly applies to the apostles at Pentecost.

When people are empowered, they become able and willing to take charge of their situation. They no longer wait for someone else to do it for you. They accept that they and they alone have to do something about it.

The Holy Spirit *empowered* the apostles. He came down on them in the form of wind and fire. Wind and fire are symbols of power. Wind has the power to move. Fire has the power to refine and transform. The power they symbolise here is the power of God.

The Spirit provided the apostles with the energy, the courage, the love and the passion to get on with the task Christ had given them. Yet, even though the Holy Spirit would help them, he wouldn't do it for them.

After the coming of the Spirit the apostles were changed men. They come out of their shells. This is the real miracle of Pentecost. However, we mustn't think that the change in them came about in an instant. It had to be a gradual thing. It had to be a growth process. And growth can be slow and painful.

We too need someone to empower us so that we are able to take charge of our lives, and live them responsibly. This means being willing to change what needs to be changed. But we especially need empowerment in order to witness to our Christian faith. The power that changed the apostles is available to us too.

The Church is invited to live the mystery of Pentecost as a community in which fatalism is challenged, in which every child of God should be empowered to do more than he/she ever believed possible. St Paul says that the Holy Spirit is 'no cowardly spirit' (2 Tim 1:7). The Holy Spirit can breathe confidence into us all.

The miracle of change

After Pentecost the apostles were changed people. That is the real miracle of Pentecost. However, it is a mistake to think that the change came about in an instant. It had to be a gradual thing, a growth process set in motion by the action of the Holy Spirit. Growth happens gradually.

Though we are dealing with mystery, that doesn't mean we can't understand anything about it. Let us look at how spring goes about its work of change and renewal.

Each year in Ireland towards the middle of March you will see patches of green begin to appear in the fields and on the hillsides, new patches on an old garment. Day by day the patches get bigger. A month or so later spring will have woven a completely new garment.

Yet spring doesn't make anything happen. It is only a facilitator. It merely creates a climate in which things can grow. The new life comes from within. It cannot be imposed. All these brand-new things that we see, come from within. What spring does is provide living things with the opportunity, gives them the impulse to realise what is already inside them in a germinal state.

Spring's task is to awaken and call forth. This calling forth is a gentle process. Force is out of the question. Persuasion is the only effective weapon. For unless there is a response from within, all spring's efforts will be in vain.

If a tree has no life in it, all the sunshine of all springs that have visited this earth will not succeed in producing a single bud in it. One good thing about nature – it is incapable of deception. It does not put on an outward show when there is nothing inside.

People too need to renew themselves. This renewal, however, cannot be imposed. If this is attempted it will merely result in an outward show, a dressing up. It will not enrich the person, and will soon fade and eventually wear out like a garment.

Many people have violence done to them. People try to form them, to press them into shape from the outside, or squeeze them into a mould as if they were lumps of clay. These people betray them.

What we need is someone to awaken us to what is inside us, to bid us live, and help us grow. But growth is slow and painful. We don't let go easily of the old garment, woven out of old attitudes, old ways, and old habits. This probably accounts for the fact that many people are left unawakened, and die without having experienced even one spring.

This gives us some understanding of what happened to the apostles at Pentecost, and what can happen to us too. The power that changed the apostles is available to us too. The Holy Spirit is the most a wonderful facilitator of all. The Spirit awakens us to the mysterious power within us, bids us live, and helps us grow.

St Paul says that the Holy Spirit is 'no timid spirit' (2 Tim 1:7). The Holy Spirit can awaken us and breathe new life into us.

Solemnities of the Lord

TRINITY SUNDAY
A mystery of love

Praying with the Word of God today

INTRODUCTION AND CONFITEOR

Today we are celebrating the great mystery of the Blessed Trinity. The Trinity is not something that is remote from us. Because God's Son, Jesus, befriended us, we are no longer strangers and outsiders. We are part of God's family.

As we call to mind our sins, let us also call to mind our own greatness as God's children. [Pause]

Lord Jesus, you reveal to us the mystery of the Father, and of his unconditional love for us. Lord, have mercy.

You reveal to us the mystery of your own divine sonship, and share your divine inheritance with us. Christ, have mercy.

You reveal to us the mystery of the Holy Spirit, who binds us together in a community of faith and love. Lord, have mercy.

PRAYER OF THE FAITHFUL

Celebrant: As we pray to the Father for our needs, we pray in the name of Jesus, the Son, and the Holy Spirit prays with us.

Response: Lord, to you glory and praise for evermore.

Reader(s): For Christians: that they may be united in praising and honouring the Father, the Son, and the Holy Spirit. [Pause] Let us pray to the Lord.

For the nations and races of the earth: that they may see themselves as members of one family under God. [Pause] Let us pray to the Lord.

For all those who are searching for God: that they may find God by seeking the truth with sincerity. [Pause] Let us pray to the Lord.

For the members of this community: that we may see God as a God of love, who inspires us to love one another. [Pause] Let us pray to the Lord.

For our deceased relatives and friends: that they may enjoy fellowship with the Blessed Trinity in heaven. [Pause] Let us pray to the Lord.

For our own special needs. [Longer pause} Let us pray to the Lord.

Celebrant: Father, source of all life, be our guide when we stray, our strength when we are weak, and our comfort when we downhearted. We ask this through your Son, our Lord Jesus Christ, who lives and reigns with you and the Holy Spirit, one God, for ever and ever.

OUR FATHER

God is love, and anyone who lives in love lives in God. Let us pray to the God of love as Jesus taught us.

REFLECTION

Nowadays, thanks to the security camera,
we are frequently being watched by a cold, dispassionate eye,
intent only on catching us in wrongdoing.
The feeling that someone is *watching* us
is not a pleasant feeling.
But the feeling that someone is *watching over* us
is a lovely feeling.
God is not watching us; God is watching over us.
This conviction gives us strength in times of weakness,
comfort in times of sadness, and hope in times of despair.

FINAL BLESSING

May the Lord surround you with his favour as with a shield.

May the Lord be a refuge for you in times of distress, and a fortress in times of danger.

May you live in such a way that the love and peace of God will reign among you,

Sharing the Word of God today

SCRIPTURE NOTE

First Reading (Ex 34:4-6.8-9). The Old Testament knows nothing of the Trinity. This reading was chosen because it has to do with God's self-revelation. The context is the second giving of the Law to Moses, after he had broken the first set of tablets.

God is the One who is always present to and for his people. This is because he is a God of tenderness and compassion. Moses begs God to forgive the sins of his stubborn people and to stay with them on their journey.

Second Reading (2 Cor 13:11-13). In this, the conclusion to his Second Letter to the Corinthians, Paul encourages them to live in such a way that the love and peace of God will reign among them. The reading ends with a trinitarian blessing that is used as a greeting at the start of Mass.

Gospel (Jn 3:16-18). God (the Father) has shown his love for us by sending his Son to save us; all who believe in him will have eternal life. Those who deliberately reject Jesus condemn themselves; they have rejected the source of life.

Part of the family

The Trinity is a mystery. When we say that something is a mystery, it doesn't mean we can't know *anything* about it. It just means that we can't know *everything* about it. Faith doesn't contradict reason; it transcends it. We should keep this in mind when discussing the mystery of the Trinity.

There is a beautiful Russian icon of the Blessed Trinity painted by a monk by the name of Rublev. (Reproductions of this are widespread nowadays.) The picture must not be seen as a literal representation of what the Trinity is. Nevertheless, it conveys an important truth about the relationship between the Trinity and ourselves.

The picture depicts the three Divine Persons sitting at a table. A dish of food lies on the table. This tells us that we are dealing with a banquet. But the thing that immediately strikes you is the fact that at the front of the table there is a vacant place. The vacant place is meant to convey openness, hospitality, and welcome towards the stranger and the outsider.

That vacant place is meant for each of us, and for all the human family. It signifies God's invitation to us to share in the life of the Trinity. God invites us to come in and sit at his table. He wants to share his life with us.

Because God's Son, Jesus, befriended us, we are no longer strangers and outsiders. We are part of God's family. We are God's children. This is a mystery of love. In the words of today's gospel: 'God loved the world so much that he gave his only Son, so that everyone who believes in him may not be lost but may have eternal life.'

Our response can only be one of trust in God and love towards one another. What St Paul says to the Corinthians (Second Reading) is meant also for us: 'Help one another. Be united; live in peace, and the God of love and peace will be with you.'

Rublev's icon conveys something of the immense hospitality of God. At the same time it challenges us by forcing us to see how hospitable we are towards others. Today there is more need than ever for hospitality and friendliness, because there are many strangers and displaced people in the world.

Hospitality to a friend is no big deal. But hospitality to a stranger is a great thing. Christ calls us to welcome the strangers in our midst. For the followers of Christ, hospitality is not an optional extra. It is at the very heart of the Gospel.

Many are intimidated by the great mystery of the Blessed Trinity. This is a pity. We are people for whom God is a mystery but no stranger. We should see the Father, the Son, and the Holy Spirit as friends to whom we can relate, and to whom we can talk in prayer. God has already given us a place at the banquet of earthly life. But he wants us to have a place at the banquet of eternal life too. Only at God's table can we find the nourishment our hearts are hungering for.

A God of love

It is impossible for us to understand God. God is a mystery. However, to say that something is a mystery doesn't mean we can't know *anything* about it. It just means that we can't know *everything* about it. Faith doesn't contradict reason; it transcends it.

It is possible to know of the existence of God by our own reasoning. At the sight of something or other, a person will know in an instant that things do not exist through themselves, and that God is. As a house implies a builder, a dress a weaver, a door a carpenter, so the world implies a Creator.

But we would know very little about God if God hadn't revealed himself to us. It is especially through the Scriptures that we know God. From the Scriptures we learn that God is Father, Son and Spirit.

And from the Scriptures we learn what God is like. For instance, today's First Reading says that God is 'a God of tenderness and compassion, slow to anger, rich in kindness and faithfulness.' And the gospel says: 'God loved the world so much that he gave his only Son, so that everyone who believes in him may not be lost but may have eternal life.'

Both readings have the same message: God is a God of love. This is something tremendously important to know about God. If we knew nothing else about God, that would be enough.

God loves us, not because we are good, but because he is good. Our very existence is a sign of God's love. God's love for us *is* the Good News. That love has taken flesh in the person of Jesus. And that love has been poured into our hearts by the Holy Spirit.

What should our response be? We must strive to become imitators of God's goodness. This means that we must love one another. What St Paul said to the Corinthians (Second Reading) is meant also for us: 'Help one another. Be united; live in peace, and the God of love and peace will be with you.' Where love is, God is. The Trinity is a great mystery, but it is a mystery of love.

Story

One day two learned men were walking along the seashore, discussing the mystery of God. However, they weren't making much progress. Suddenly they came upon a small boy playing on the beach. He had dug a hole in the sand and kept running down to the sea, dipping his toy bucket in the water, and running back up the beach to empty the water into the hole.

The two men watched him for a while as he ran back and forth, filling and emptying his bucket. They found the scene amusing. They went up to the boy and asked him what he was doing. Very seriously he told them he was emptying the ocean into the hole he had dug in the sand.

The two smiled, and walked on, resuming their discussion about God. After a while, one of them stopped and said to the other, 'You know, we were amused just now when that child told us what he was trying to do. Yet what we have been trying to do in our discussion about God is just the same. It is just as impossible for us to understand the mystery of God as it is for that child to put the water of the ocean into that hole. Our minds are but tiny thimbles, whereas the reality of God is as great as the ocean.'

The story must not be used to justify laziness or superficiality in our efforts to understand something of the mystery of God.

The Trinity is central in our lives

(This homily draws attention to the references to the Trinity in the text of the Mass. Its aim is to show the centrality of the Trinity to our lives as Christians. It could be given as a series of inputs as we celebrate the Mass. If this approach is adopted, it has to be done with a light touch, and with the minimum of words.)

There is a tendency to regard the mystery of the Blessed Trinity as something remote, mysterious, abstract, and largely irrelevant to our lives. Nothing could be further from the truth. Far from being something that is remote form us, the Trinity is central to our lives as Christians.

This will become clear if we pay attention to what we say and hear in the liturgy every time we attend Mass. Thanks to the liturgical reforms of Vatican II, the text of the Mass draws attention to the centrality of the Trinity in our lives.

Anyone who seeks to understand this most central mystery could do no better than pay close attention to what is set before us, spoken and heard, at every Mass. Here are some parts of the text of the Mass we might pay attention to.

We begin the Mass by invoking the names of the Blessed Trinity: 'In the name of the Father, and of the Son, and of the Holy Spirit.'

The *Gloria* is a prayer of praise. It is meant to be *prayed*, not just said. In it we address in turn the Father, the Son, and the Holy Spirit. We acknowledge them as possessing equal glory, of being equally deserving of worship, and working together for our salvation.

The Creed is not a prayer but a profession of faith. It is essentially a summary of what we believe about the Father, the Son and the Holy Spirit, and about their respective roles in our salvation.

The Eucharistic Prayer constitutes the heart of the Mass. This great prayer is addressed to the Father. It begins with the *Preface*. Today's Preface sums up for us what the mystery of the Trinity is about. The rest of the prayer deals with the great things the Father has done for us, and continues to do for us, in and through his Son and the Holy Spirit.

The Mass ends with a solemn blessing that includes the names of the Blessed Trinity: 'May almighty God bless you, the Father, and the Son, and the Holy Spirit.'

These are some of the things we should pay attention to as we celebrate the Mass. If we do pay attention to these things, it will lead us to a better understanding of the Trinity, and of the Mass itself. Each celebration of the Eucharist should deepen our relationship with the persons of the Blessed Trinity.

THE BODY AND BLOOD OF CHRIST
One loaf, one body

Praying with the Word of God today

INTRODUCTION AND CONFITEOR

This is the feast of *Corpus Christi* – the Body of Christ. St Paul says that *we* are the Body of Christ. When we gather to celebrate the Eucharist, the Body of Christ becomes visible.

The Eucharist celebrates and strengthens our unity in Christ. Let us reflect for a moment on how we live out our unity with Christ and one another. [Pause]

Lord Jesus, you are the vine, we are the branches. Lord, have mercy.

Separated from you and from one another our lives become barren. Christ, have mercy.

But united with you and with one another our lives become fruitful. Lord, have mercy.

PRAYER OF THE FAITHFUL

Celebrant: Jesus wanted his followers to be united. Gathered around the table of the Lord on this special feast, let us pray for the gift of unity.

Response: Lord, hear our prayer.

Reader(s): For the Church: that the Eucharist may form its members into a community of love. [Pause] Let us pray to the Lord.

For the world: that all of God's family may be gathered together in unity and peace. [Pause] Let us pray to the Lord.

For those who minister in the Church: that they may be filled with Christ-like love. [Pause] Let us pray to the Lord.

For those who have cut themselves off from the Church: that they may be drawn back into communion with it. [Pause] Let us pray to the Lord.

For the sick, the lonely, and the unloved: that in their pain they may know God's comforting. [Pause] Let us pray to the Lord.

For all gathered here: that as we meet around the Lord's table, he may strengthen our unity and deepen our faith. [Pause] Let us pray to the Lord.

For our departed relatives and friends, who partook of the Eucharist: that they may have a seat at the banquet of eternal life in heaven. [Pause] Let us pray to the Lord.

For our own special needs. [Longer pause] Let us pray to the Lord.

Celebrant: Heavenly Father, may our celebration of Christ's farewell meal keep us strong in faith, and enable us to offer loving service to one another. We ask this through the same Christ our Lord.

SIGN OF PEACE

Lord Jesus Christ, the night before you died you said to your friends, 'Peace I leave with you; my own peace I give you. A peace which the world cannot give, this is my gift to you. So do not let your hearts be troubled or afraid.'

Take pity on our troubled minds and fearful hearts, and grant us the peace and unity of your kingdom where you live for ever and ever.

BEFORE COMMUNION

Jesus says, 'I am the living bread that has come down from heaven. Anyone who eats this bread will live for ever.' Blessed are those who are called to his supper

Lord, I am not worthy ...

PRAYER AFTER COMMUNION

Heavenly Father, the bread we have eaten in the Eucharist was once scattered over the fields in the form of grains of wheat, but then was gathered together and became one loaf. So may your Church be gathered together from the ends of the earth into your kingdom. To you belong glory and power through Jesus Christ, for ever and ever. Amen.

FINAL BLESSING

May you always hunger for the bread that only God can give us.

May the food of the Eucharist sustain you on your journey to the promised land of eternal life.

May the mystery of Christ's love that we have celebrated here, inflame your hearts with love for your brothers and sisters.

Sharing the Word of God today

SCRIPTURE NOTE

First Reading (Deut 8:2-3.14-16). The author exhorts the Israelites to remember their past history and especially the period of wandering in the desert. It was there in particular that God's care for them was made manifest. The manna with which they were nourished was the special sign of God's care.

The desert experience taught the Israelites the importance of bread. But it also taught them that they couldn't live on bread alone. They needed the word of God. They must never forget that they are God's chosen people.

The manna is a type of the Eucharist, the food Jesus provides for the new people of God on their journey to the promised land of eternal life.

Second Reading (1 Cor 10:16-17). Here Paul stresses the role the Eucharist plays in uniting the community. Through their sharing in the body and blood of Christ, believers are united with him and with one another. Sharing the one loaf signifies and strengthens the unity among Christians.

Gospel (Jn 6:51-58). John's account of the multiplication of the loaves (6:1-14) is followed by two discourses on the 'bread of life'. In the first (6:35-50) the 'bread' is the revelation of Jesus. The second discourse (6:51-58) is clearly eucharistic.

In the Hebrew idiom the term 'flesh and blood' stands for the whole person. 'Eating and drinking' implies communion. Eucharistic eating and drinking is a personal encounter with Jesus who shares his life and the life of the Father with us. A source of life here and now, Jesus is the pledge of eternal life beyond death.

The Bread of Life

As human beings we cannot live on bread alone. We suffer from many kinds of hunger. In the Gospels we see the various kinds of 'bread' Jesus offered to people, thus satisfying their many hungers.

To the people who followed him into the desert, and who were starving, he offered ordinary bread, and so satisfied their physical hunger.

To the leper whose body was falling apart, he offered the only bread that mattered to him – the bread of physical healing.

To the lonely woman at Jacob's well, he offered the bread of human kindness, and thus satisfied her hunger for acceptance.

To sinners he offered the bread of forgiveness, and thus satisfied their hunger for salvation.

To the rejects and outcasts, by mixing with them and sharing their bread, he offered the bread of companionship, and so satisfied their hunger for self-worth.

To the widow of Nain who was burying her only son, and to Martha and Mary who had just buried their brother Lazarus, he offered the bread of compassion, and showed them that even in death we are not beyond the reach of God's help.

With Zacchaeus, the rich tax collector who had robbed the bread from the tables of the poor, he began by inviting himself to his table. Then, having awakened within him a hunger for a better life, he got him to share his ill-gotten money with the poor.

To the thief who died at his side, he offered the bread of reconciliation with God, thus bringing peace to his troubled soul.

But, surprisingly, there were some who refused his offer of bread. There was the rich young man to whom he offered the bread of discipleship, but who refused it because he was not willing to part with his riches. There were the scribes and Pharisees to whom he offered not once, but several times, the bread of conversion, but they refused to eat even a crumb of it. There were the people of his beloved city of Jerusalem to whom, with tears in his eyes, he offered the bread of peace, but they refused it with the result that their city was destroyed. There was Pilate to whom he offered the bread of truth, but he had no appetite for it because it meant putting his position at risk.

Jesus shared himself with others in many different ways, and under many different forms, before offering himself to them as food and drink at the last supper.

Jesus nourishes us in all of the above ways, and of course especially in the Eucharist. The real presence of Christ in the Eucharist becomes a problem only for those who have lost their sense of God's presence in creation. Those who have a deep sense of the presence of God in the whole of creation will not have great difficulty in believing that he is present in a very special way in the Eucharist.

God alone can satisfy all the longings and hungers of our hearts, because he alone can give us the bread of eternal life. This is the bread we receive in the Eucharist. St Ignatius of Antioch defined the Eucharistic Bread as 'a medicine of immortality, an antidote to death.'

A human being does not live on bread alone

'Man does not live on bread alone'. We have heard that message a thousand times, but each time we tend to miss the word 'alone'. Our dualistic nature – flesh and spirit – require sustenance from both material and transcendent realities. This suggests that it is as natural for human beings to become attached to earthly realities as to long for something beyond.

Ethiopia suffered a terrible famine during the years 1984-86. The late

Cardinal Basil Hume of Westminster told about an incident that happened when he visited Ethiopia in the middle of the famine. One of the places he visited was a settlement up in the hills where the people were waiting for food that was unlikely to arrive. He was taken there in a helicopter.

As he got out of the helicopter, a small boy, aged about ten, came up to him and took his hand. He was wearing nothing but a loincloth round his waist. The whole time the cardinal was there the little child would not let go of his hand.

As they went around he made two gestures: with one hand he pointed to his mouth, and with the other he took the cardinal's hand and rubbed it on his cheek.

Later the cardinal said, 'Here was an orphan boy who was lost and starving. Yet by two simple gestures he indicated our two fundamental needs or hungers. With one gesture he showed me his hunger for food, and with the other his hunger for love.

'I have never forgotten that incident, and to this day I wonder whether that child is still alive. I remember that as I boarded the helicopter he stood and looked at me reproachfully.'

Today's First Reading says, 'Man [a human being] doesn't live on bread alone but on every word that comes from the mouth of God.' It was with these words that Jesus rebuffed Satan during his temptations in the desert.

We need ordinary bread. That is our first and most basic necessity. However, ordinary bread nourishes only half of us – the physical side. But we also have a spiritual side. It too cries out for nourishment. Even that starving little child realised that.

For this spiritual we need another kind of bead, bread that only God can give us. We get this bread abundantly in the Eucharist. In the Eucharist we receive the bread of God's word in the Scriptures. This nourishes our mind, our heart and our spirit. And in Holy Communion we receive Jesus, the bread of eternal life. Jesus is not present as a vague memory of a person who lived long ago, but as a real, life-giving presence that transforms us.

And the Eucharist also addresses our hunger for love. By inviting us to partake of the sacred food of the Eucharist, Jesus makes us his companions and friends. And in doing so we ought to become companions and friends to one another.

Having been nourished with the food of the Eucharist, we are sent forth to nourish others. When we depart from here we must take out into the world some of the love we have experienced here.

One loaf, one body
St Paul stresses the role the Eucharist plays in uniting the Christian commu-

nity (see Second Reading). Sharing the one loaf signifies and strengthens the unity among Christians. Indeed, a loaf of itself is a splendid illustration of the unity Paul is talking about.

Consider this loaf. (Hold up a loaf for all to see). It is an amazing thing. It is a kind of miracle. It is a gift of God. But like most of God's gifts, it doesn't fall ready-made into our hands.

Many agents contributed to the making of this loaf. First of all, there are the agents of nature – the soil, the sun, and the rain. Then there are the human agents – the farmer, the miller, the baker, and the merchant. This loaf comes to us not from one hand but from many hands. And of course we must not forget God's part in it. Though it is people who bring forth the bread, it is to God that we give thanks. Without God none of this would be possible.

All this is beautifully expressed in the prayer we say over the bread at the Offertory of the Mass: 'Blessed are you, Lord God of all creation, for through your goodness we have received the bread we offer you, fruit of the earth and work of human hands, it will become for us the bread of life.'

Many grains of wheat went into this loaf. Those grains were once scattered over the fields. But at the harvest time they were gathered together and later ground into flour. And from the flour of all those grains this loaf resulted.

This loaf symbolises our unity in Christ. St Paul says that though there are many of us, we form a single body – the Body of Christ, the Church (Second Reading).

During the week we are separated from one another. But here we are gathered together, so that the Body of Christ becomes visible. Here we become living witnesses of God's desire to bring all peoples and nations together into one family. Everyone of us is important. Each individual matters. I may be only a little grain but of such grains is a loaf formed.

Here we lay down our differences and become one family. Here we are in from the cold and experience the warmth of community. Love is the atmosphere we breathe here. We must try to rise above the things that prevent us from experiencing and expressing our unity – shyness, coldness, and indifference.

The Eucharist is the sign and source of our unity. We form a single body because we all share in the one loaf (the Eucharistic bread). We can't truly be in communion with Jesus without being in communion with one another. When we depart from here we must take out into the world some of the warmth we have experienced here.

The celebration of the Eucharist is at the heart of the life of the Church. The Church is where the Eucharist is, and the Eucharist forms the Church.

Sundays of Ordinary Time

SECOND SUNDAY OF THE YEAR
Jesus, the Lamb of God

Praying with the Word of God today

INTRODUCTION AND CONFITEOR

In the words of today's Gospel, Jesus is the Lamb of God who takes away the sins of the world.

Let us begin our celebration by bringing our sins to the Lord and asking for his forgiveness and healing. [Pause].

Lord Jesus, you were pierced for our faults. Lord, have mercy.

You bore our sufferings and sorrows. Christ, have mercy.

Through your wounds we are healed. Lord, have mercy.

PRAYER OF THE FAITHFUL

Celebrant: Let us pray that the light of God's salvation may reach the ends of the earth.

Response: Lord, hear our prayer.

Reader(s): For the Church: that it may be a sign of unity and an instrument of peace in the world. [Pause] Let us pray to the Lord.

For political leaders: that through goodwill and co-operation they may strive to make the world a better and safer place. [Pause] Let us pray to the Lord.

For those who do not know Christ: that they may see him and meet him in Christians. [Pause] Let us pray to the Lord.

For all the innocent victims of war and violence: that they may find fellowship with Jesus, the innocent Lamb of God, in the kingdom of heaven. [Pause] Let us pray to the Lord.

For the members of this community: that we may not be discouraged by our weakness or demoralised by our failures. [Pause] Let us pray to the Lord.

For our own special needs. [Longer Pause] Let us pray to the Lord.

Celebrant: Father, we make all our prayers through Christ, who came on earth to reconcile us to you and to one another, and who now lives and reigns with you and the Holy Spirit, one God, for ever and ever.

BEFORE COMMUNION

Before we receive Jesus we echo the words of John the Baptist: 'Behold the Lamb of God, behold him who takes away the sins of the world.' Blessed are those called to the supper of the Lamb.

Lord, I am not worthy ...

REFLECTION

Jesus, the gentle lamb of God, died for our sins.
Ours were the sufferings that he bore,
ours the sorrows that he carried.
For we had all gone astray like sheep,
and God burdened him with the sins of all of us.
Though harshly treated, he bore it humbly,
never opening his mouth to complain.
Nor was there anyone to plead his cause.
Through his sufferings he has won pardon for all of us,
and through his wounds we are healed.

FINAL BLESSING

May the Lord keep your feet from stumbling and your hearts from straying.

May the Lord deliver you from your sins so that you may walk in the joy and freedom of the children of God.

May the sufferings of Jesus, the innocent Lamb of God, help you to bear your sufferings with patience and fortitude.

Sharing the Word of God today

SCRIPTURE NOTE

First Reading (Is 49:3.5-6). This reading is part of the second Servant Song of Isaiah. It stresses the early call and formation of the servant. God assures him that he will not only lead back Jacob and reassemble and teach Israel, but also be a light for all nations, enabling God's salvation to reach to the ends of the earth. The New Testament writers saw the Servant Songs of Isaiah as being perfectly fulfilled in Jesus.

This is one of the most universalist passages of the Old Testament. The theme of universalism and inclusion is echoed in the other two readings, as is the theme of the divinely appointed servant.

Gospel (Jn 1:29-34). Even though this is the year of Matthew, we begin with a reading from John. The Second Sunday of Ordinary Time respects an old liturgical theme of different epiphanies or manifestations of Jesus.

In the first chapter of his Gospel, John brings forth a number of witnesses to tell the reader who Jesus is. Chief among these is John the Baptist. In our reading the Baptist refers to Jesus as the 'lamb of God' and the 'Chosen One of God', two Messianic titles.

The designation 'lamb of God' suggests the Passover lamb, whose blood delivered the Israelites from the destroying angel. But it also suggests the suffering servant of Isaiah who is likened to a lamb being led to the slaughter (53:7). Jesus is the one who will suffer and die for the sins of the world. He is also God's Chosen Servant, and thus fulfils Isaiah's prophecy (First Reading).

Thus at the beginning of his Gospel, John outlines a whole Christology of Jesus: the eternally existing One (prologue), who is to die as the Paschal Lamb and Suffering Servant for the sins of men and women, and then pour forth the Holy Spirit on a new Israel.

Second Reading (1 Cor 1:1-3). Here we have the opening verses of Paul's letter to the Corinthians. Paul presents himself as divinely appointed 'apostle of Jesus Christ'. He then reminds them of their call to holiness and their membership of the universal church of Christ.

Taking away the sins of the world

When John the Baptist saw Jesus passing by he suddenly declared, 'There is the lamb of God who takes away the sin of the world.' Thus he pinpointed the essence of Jesus' mission. Jesus was that Servant, whose coming was foretold by Isaiah, and whose mission was to bring sinners back to God (First Reading).

Jesus is the one who 'takes away the sin of the world'. How are we to understand this expression? Sin is not *an object* that can be removed from us. Sin is *a condition* in which we live, a condition of brokenness and woundedness, a condition from which we need to be redeemed. Jesus came to redeem us from this condition.

There is no such *thing* out there as sin that can be taken away and disposed of like a piece of garbage. What you have out there are sinners. Jesus' mission was directed at sinners. He came to bring sinners back to God. To sin is to stray from the right path. Jesus brings us back to God by bringing us back to the right path.

How did Jesus get sinners to change their lives? He didn't shun them – you never improve people by shunning them. He befriended them. In his presence sinners felt accepted and loved. It is not surprising that many of them changed their lives. Through his own luminous goodness he evoked goodness in them.

Jesus befriends us also. And he evokes goodness in us too. That is the only way to go if we wish to overcome sin. Evil can be overcome only by goodness.

Through Jesus we have forgiveness for our sins, and so are able to put them behind us. When we are forgiven, a load is lifted from us, and we are able to go forward freely and joyfully.

Here the Sacrament of Reconciliation (Confession) is a great help. It is a place where we can experience the love of Jesus for us in our sins. It is not an impersonal getting rid of sins. Rather, it is a loving encounter with

Jesus our Saviour, who calls us away from sin to goodness of life.

But Jesus does not *bear* our sins. We have to bear the burden of our own sins. We are responsible for them. And even when we are forgiven, everything doesn't magically come right for us. We don't suddenly become new people. Our weaknesses, habits, and compulsions are still with us. This means we still have to struggle.

There is no once-and-for-all victory over sin. It is a life-long struggle. We must not become discouraged when we see ourselves making what seems like very little progress. What is important is the struggle for goodness.

Besides personal sin and personal redemption, there is social sin and social redemption. The whole human family is damaged because of sin. Jesus came to bring us back into relationship with God and with one another. Jesus died suspended between heaven and earth, with arms outstretched, so as to gather together God's flock, dispersed by sin.

Story

Once upon a time there was a beautiful porcelain teapot. One day a careless servant dropped it. The lid and spout got broken. The beautiful teapot was now considered to be useless and was thrown out.

For a long time it lay in a refuse dump. Coats of dirt settled on it, blotting out whatever traces of beauty it still possessed. From time to time people came to the dump, hoping to find something of value. On seeing the teapot they would say, 'What a pity it got broken! It must have been beautiful when it was in one piece.'

Then one day a famous flower grower visited the dump. He found the teapot. The first thing he did was clean it up. In spite of its brokenness, he found it very beautiful, and wondered how anyone could have thrown it away. Then he had an inspiration. He would take it home and use it as a flowerpot.

He filled it with soil, planted a seed in it, and placed it in the front window of his house. Time passed. The seed grew and blossomed into a beautiful flower. Passers-by stopped to admire the flower, and also the handsome pot in which it grew.

Sin is not a physical stain that we can just wash away. Nor can we take it away as if it was a thing. Sin is not a thing. Sin is a *condition* – a condition of brokenness and woundedness. Each of us is damaged and broken.

Jesus came to redeem us. He considered no one as beyond redemption. To be redeemed is to be made whole and well. It is to be restored to our original brightness through the grace of the Holy Spirit. However, this is a lifelong process. We are not things to be repaired. We are people, people to be brought back into relationship with God and with one another.

The Lamb of God

One day John the Baptist was standing on the bank of the river Jordan with some of his disciples when he saw Jesus passing by. Suddenly he declared: 'Look, there is the lamb of God.'

Notice that John referred to Jesus as 'the *lamb* of God'. Now when you consider the mighty task ahead of Jesus (the salvation of the world), you would think John might have said, 'There is the *lion* of God, or 'There is the *tiger* of God.' But he didn't. Instead he said, 'There is the *lamb* of God.'

Of all God's creatures, the lamb is the gentlest, and most lovable. No one could be afraid of a lamb.

John also said he saw the Holy Spirit coming down on Jesus like a *dove.*' Notice again, the Spirit didn't come down on Jesus like a *hawk* or a *vulture*. These are killer birds. The Spirit came down on Jesus like a *dove*. A dove is a gentle bird, a symbol of peace and goodwill.

What do the images of the lamb and the dove tell us about the approach Jesus would adopt? They suggest that his approach would be a gentle one.

Jesus' approach to people was indeed a gentle one. He didn't impose his will on people. He respected their freedom. He invited rather than commanded. He was especially gentle towards the weak and the wounded. He would not break the crushed reed, or extinguish the smouldering wick (Mt 12:20).

He was gentle because he chose the way of love and persuasion over the way of power and compulsion. Power offers an easy substitute for the hard task of love. It is easier to control people than to love people. But Jesus refused the way of power. He had come, not to rule people, but to serve them.

Jesus was gentle, but this doesn't mean that he was weak. When the occasion demanded it he could be very assertive – as when he drove the traders out of the Temple (Jn 2:13-22).

Besides all this, the term 'lamb of God' had rich biblical connotations. It suggested the Passover lamb, whose blood delivered the Israelites from the destroying angel. And it also suggested the suffering servant of Isaiah who is likened to a lamb being led to the slaughter (53:7).

What exactly was Jesus' mission? In the words of the Baptist it was to 'take away the sin of the world.' Jesus is the one who will suffer and die for the sins of the world. His mission was directed at sinners. He didn't come to call the virtuous; he came to call sinners.

Jesus was that faithful servant, whose coming was foretold by Isaiah, and whose mission was to bring sinners back to God. He was also to be a light for the nations, so that God's salvation might each the ends of the earth (First Reading).

Jesus, the gentle Lamb of God, died for our sins, so that we could live in the joy and freedom of the children of God. He was God's gentle servant. He came 'not to be served, but to serve and to give his life as a ransom for many' (Mk 10:45).

A lesson from John the Baptist

The incident described in today's Gospel is found at the start of St John's Gospel. Jesus had only recently arrived from Nazareth. As yet he was completely unknown. This was his first appearance on the public stage. He needed someone to introduce him to the public. He found that person in John the Baptist.

John had already prepared the way for him. Now he had the further task of introducing him to the people. That opportunity came along shortly after he had baptised Jesus. One day he saw Jesus passing by. Turning to his disciples he declared, 'This is the one I spoke of when I said: A man is coming after me who ranks before me.' With these words John introduced Jesus to his own disciples and to the public.

In introducing Jesus, what role did he ascribe to him? He introduced him as 'the lamb of God who takes away the sin of the world.' Through these words John was telling them that Jesus was that Servant, whose coming was foretold by Isaiah, and whose mission was to bring sinners back to God (First Reading).

Though the focus is on Jesus, the incident tells us a lot about John himself. John might have ignored Jesus. Or he might even have seen him as a threat. Nothing of the kind. He regarded Jesus as a friend and ally. He knew what his God-given task was, namely, to prepare the way for Jesus. He did that to the best of his ability. And now that Jesus had appeared on the scene, he pointed him out, and began to direct people to him.

In doing this he knew he was inviting his disciples to leave himself. And that is what happened. From this point on John's disciples began to leave him and follow Jesus. Yet there was no jealousy on John's part. Far from resenting this, he encouraged it. He said, 'He must increase; I must decrease' (Jn 3:30). And so, as the light of Jesus dawned, the light of John waned.

In this we see the greatness of John. In particular we see his humility and generosity of spirit. There is no harder task than to take second place especially when one has enjoyed the first place. It is not easy to make way for another. It is harder still to give up your place to him, and let him take over. But that is exactly what John did.

How desperately hard it is to be a forerunner, to point beyond oneself to another and praise his greatness. To be content to be a supporting actor, not the star. For many powerful people, the 'younger person', full of the energy, is their worst nightmare as it heralds the decline of their own power.

We can learn from John. To know what our task is, and do it to the best of our ability, while being careful not to block the path for others. And we must be conscious of the debt we owe to others who prepared the way for us.

Beyond this it has implications for us as Christians. Through our baptism we have been called to be disciples of Jesus. Our task is to make Jesus known, and to the direct people towards him. Indeed, people should be able to encounter Jesus in us.

THIRD SUNDAY OF THE YEAR
A great light has dawned

Praying with the Word of God today

INTRODUCTION AND CONFITEOR

St Matthew describes the arrival of Jesus on the scene as the coming of a great light into the darkness of the world.

Let us call to mind the darkness that still overshadows our world, and the darkness in which we ourselves sometimes walk. [Pause]

Lord Jesus, you bring pardon and peace to sinners. Lord, have mercy.

You bring light to those who live in darkness and in the shadow of death. Christ, have mercy.

To those who follow you, you give the light of life. Lord, have mercy.

PRAYER OF THE FAITHFUL

Celebrant: The Lord is our light and our help. Let us bring our needs before God with confidence.

Response: Lord, you are our light and our help.

Reader(s): For the Church: that the power of the Holy Spirit may make it one body, healed of all division. [Pause] Let us pray in faith.

For all Christians: that the Lord may make them one in the fullness of faith, and keep them one in the fellowship of love. [Pause] Let us pray in faith.

For all rulers: that Christ, the light of the world, may show them the path to peace. [Pause] Let us pray in faith.

For those experiencing the darkness of grief: that Christ's comforting light may brighten their darkness. [Pause] Let us pray in faith.

For all gathered here: that we may live in such a way as to be good witnesses for the light of Christ. [Pause] Let us pray in faith.

For our departed relatives and friends: that the Lord may bring them into the light no darkness can overpower. [Pause] Let us pray in faith.

For our special needs. [Longer Pause] Let us pray in faith.

Celebrant: Almighty God, may the presence of your Son light up our lives, and bring us safely through the shadows of this world to our homeland of everlasting light. We ask this through Christ our Lord.

OUR FATHER

God has called us out of darkness into the wonderful light of his Son. Let us pray to our heavenly Father as children of the light.

PRAYER/REFLECTION

Christ is the light of the world.
His light was not lit once in Palestine and then extinguished.
It continues to shine for all who believe in him.
It is a persistent and defiant light
that no darkness can overpower.
Lord Jesus, may your gentle and sure light
guide us along the unfolding road,
so that we may walk with confidence
towards the light that never fades
and the life that never ends.

FINAL BLESSING

May the Lord keep you united in the fellowship of love.
May he make your lives radiant with his light.
And may you follow his light faithfully on earth, and come to the light that shines for ever in heaven.

Sharing the Word of God today

SCRIPTURE NOTE

First Reading (Is 8:23-9:3). Here Isaiah is addressing people who had known better times and were now walking in the darkness of servitude to a foreign power. The territory occupied by the tribes of Zebulun and Naphtali (later known as Galilee) was the most northerly part of Israel. It was the first province of Israel to be conquered by Assyria in 732 BC. Isaiah predicts liberation for the oppressed people of that region.

Gospel (Mt 4:12-23). (Shorter form recommended. The call of the four apostles occurs again on the Third Sunday of Ordinary Time, Year B, and is dealt with there).

Jesus' ministry begins under the symbol of light. Matthew sees him as fulfilling Isaiah's wonderful prophecy. He joyfully introduces him as 'the great light that has dawned.' Though Jesus begins his ministry in Galilee, his mission will extend to the whole world.

Jesus takes up the torch from the hand of John the Baptist who has been arrested. 'Repent, for the kingdom of heaven is at hand', continues the Baptist's call to conversion. As the light of John wanes, the light of Jesus dawns.

Second Reading (1 Cor 1:10-13.17). A number of rival factions have sprung up in the community at Corinth. Paul names four, and issues a passionate appeal for unity. He reminds them that all of them were baptised into the same Christ. Therefore, there can only be one loyalty – loyalty to Christ.

The arrival of the light

Some Alpine valleys are so deep that the rays of the sun do not reach them for days or even weeks in the middle of winter. These days can be very depressing ones for the people who live in those valleys. It's almost as if life was one long night. A priest who ministered in one of those valleys tells the following story.

One winter's day he was in the classroom of the local school, chatting with the children, who hadn't seen the sun for several days. Then all of a sudden a ray of sunshine shone into the classroom. On seeing it the children climbed onto their desks and cheered and shouted for joy. It shows that even though the sun may not touch the skin it can still warm the soul.

St Matthew compares the arrival of Jesus on the scene to the coming of a great light to a people who had been living in deep darkness. He saw Jesus as fulfilling the great prophecy of Isaiah: 'The people that lived in darkness have seen a great light; on those who dwell in the land and shadow of death a light has dawned.' Jesus described his mission in similar terms: 'I am the light of the world' (Jn 8:12).

The teaching of Jesus was truly a source of light to all who accepted him. His words have echoed down the centuries, bringing light to those in darkness and hope to those in despair.

But it was above all through his deeds and encounters with people that his luminous goodness manifested itself. Many people came to him in darkness and went away bathed in light. Sinners came to him in the darkness of sin, and went away bathed in the light of God's mercy and love. Outcasts came to him in the darkness of rejection, and went away bathed into the light of acceptance. The sick came to him in the darkness of pain and illness, and went away bathed in the light of well-being.

How dark the world would be if the light of Christ had never shone. The great Russian writer, Dostoevsky, goes so far as to say that but for the precious image of Christ before us, we would lose our way completely and perish. It is to Christianity that we owe the foundational ideals of liberty, justice, charity, compassion and mercy.

And yet, though Jesus brought God's light into the world, not everybody welcomed it. Sadly, some refused his light and opted to remain in darkness. This is why he began his preaching with a call to repentance: 'Repent, for the kingdom of heaven is close at hand.' To repent means to acknowledge our darkness, and to open ourselves to the light.

The light of Jesus was not lit once in Palestine and then extinguished. It continues to shine. Here in church we bask in the light of Christ. But let us not be like the person who stands under a street lamp for a while, and then goes out into a dark world. We must carry a lantern away with us from here.

We must live as children of the light. What does that mean? St Paul tells us. He says that the effects of the light are seen in goodness, right living, and truth (Eph 5:9). By living in the light, we become a source of light to others.

Allowing the light to enter

Jesus began his ministry under the symbol of light. Matthew saw him as fulfilling the great prophecy of Isaiah: 'The people that lived in darkness have seen a great light; on those who dwell in the land and shadow of death a light has dawned.'

And St Luke has similar words. He says that Jesus came 'like the dawn from on high, to give light to those who live in darkness and in the shadow of death' (1:79). These are marvellous words.

Normally light is something we welcome. However, in certain circumstances we might fear it. Why? Because it shows up everything, things we want to see and things we would prefer to keep hidden.

Once in America a woman asked me to bless her house. As I performed the blessing, she escorted me around the house. I noticed that not a thing was out of place. Everything was neat and orderly. Not a cobweb or speck of dust was to be seen.

I sprinkled each room with holy water. I blessed the living room, the 'den', the kitchen, the laundry room, the bathroom, and the bedrooms. We ended up at the top of the stairs that led down into the basement. Seeing me hesitate there, the woman said, 'Oh, you wouldn't want to go down there.' So I left it at that.

Afterwards I wondered why she had refused to take me to the basement, arguably the part of the house that most needed a blessing. Was it that she didn't want to embarrass me? Or was it that she didn't want to embarrass herself by letting me see all the junk that was piled up down there?

How typical this is. The parts of ourselves and of our society that most need to be redeemed are the parts we tend to hide. We don't allow the light to shine into the dark areas of our lives and of our society. Yet the dark areas are the ones that have most need of the light.

Every house, indeed every person, has a 'basement' area. What can we do about these grubbier parts of ourselves? We should open them to the light of Christ. The light of Christ comes as a friend. He did not come to judge us, but to save us, to show us how to live, to show us the way to the Father's kingdom.

Jesus shed light through his teaching, but more especially through the way he treated people. Numerous people came to him in darkness and went away bathed in light.

Still, there were those who refused to acknowledge their need of his light, and so rejected it. We need to acknowledge our darkness and our need of the light. This is why Jesus began his preaching with a call to repentance: 'Repent, for the kingdom of heaven is close at hand.'

To repent is to admit our darkness. There is no need to get depressed about it. It is a grace even to recognise it, because it opens us to the light. To be saved is to have come out of darkness into the light.

Once we have been enlightened by Christ, we in our turn can become a source of light to a darkened world. Indeed each of us is called to that task. But unless our own lamp is lighting, we won't be able to enlighten anyone else.

There is great joy in being in the light. But there is even greater joy in being a source of light to others.

Divisions among Christians

Of all the things that endanger organisations, divisions, factions, and cliques are the worst. The Christian community has not been immune to this threat. Jesus foresaw this. That is why he prayed for unity among his followers during the Last Supper: 'Father, may be one as we are one' (Jn 17:21).

Nothing has so undermined the credibility of Christianity as the divisions among Christians. Indeed, those divisions are a scandal to outsiders. The scandal lies not in the fact that there are differences, but in the competition, rivalry, and enmity these divisions have given rise to.

This is a problem that has plagued the Christian community right from its origin. Already in Paul's lifetime rival factions had sprung up in the community at Corinth, as today's Second Reading shows.

In the case of the Corinthians, there is no indication that the divisions were caused by doctrinal differences. Rather, the Corinthians appear to have split into cliques, each claiming the patronage of one of the great leaders of the Church.

Deeply worried, Paul met these dissensions head-on, and issued a passionate appeal for unity: 'I appeal to you, for the sake of our Lord Jesus Christ, to make up the differences between you, and be united in your belief and practice.'

He reminded the Corinthians that all of them were baptised, not in the name of any human leader, however exalted, but in the name of Christ. Since they have been baptised into the same Christ, there can only be one loyalty – loyalty to Christ.

The problem persisted, indeed could be said to have gotten worse down the centuries. Some of us Catholics can remember how bad our relations were with the other Christian churches before the Second Vatican Council. But then along came a smiling Pope (John XXIII) who urged us to reach out to 'our separated brethren'. We have made a lot of progress since then. But complete unity still eludes us.

However, we must keep in mind that unity is not the same thing as uniformity. Unity doesn't deny difference. Unity means recognising that each member is different and that each has a different gift to contribute, but all are united around the same goal by mutual love.

Each of us must open ourselves to others and welcome their gifts. We are called from many different backgrounds to form one body in Christ. By rising above our many differences, we become witnesses for God who allows his light to shine in a variety of ways.

'What the world needs now is not one religion, but mutual respect and tolerance between the adherents of the various religions' (Gandhi).

FOURTH SUNDAY OF THE YEAR
The beatitudes

Praying with the Word of God today

INTRODUCTION AND CONFITEOR

In the beatitudes we see the values a Christian should live by. While they present a great challenge, they also offer great rewards.

Alas, the values we live by often have little to do with the values of the Gospel. For this we ask the Lord's pardon and help. [Pause]

Lord Jesus, you help us to be gentle and merciful in our dealings with others. Lord, have mercy

You help us to see right living as the most important thing in life. Christ, have mercy.

You help us to be pure of heart and makers of peace. Lord, have mercy.

PRAYER OF THE FAITHFUL

Celebrant: Let us pray to our heavenly Father for those qualities Christ wants to see in his followers.

Response: Lord, hear our prayer.

Reader(s): For all Christians: that they may set their hearts on the kingdom of God and on its justice. [Pause] Let us pray to the Lord.

For all in positions of authority: that they may be gentle and just in their dealings with those they serve. [Pause] Let us pray to the Lord.

For those who mourn: that they may know God's comforting. [Pause] Let us pray to the Lord.

For those who are working for peace: that their efforts may bear fruit. [Pause] Let us pray to the Lord.

For those who suffer for doing what is right: that they may have the strength to persevere. [Pause] Let us pray to the Lord.

For all here present: that we may hunger for a life of goodness. [Pause] Let us pray to the Lord.

For our own special needs. [Longer Pause] Let us pray to the Lord.

Celebrant: Heavenly Father, give us the grace to imitate you Son more closely, and to follow him more faithfully, so that we may know the blessedness of belonging to your kingdom. We ask this through the same Christ our Lord.

REFLECTION

The beatitudes are the badges of a true disciple of Christ.
The things they stand for are very beautiful –
things such as peace, goodness, joy, love,
gentleness, compassion, mercy, and integrity.
A person who lives according to the beatitudes
is already living in the kingdom of heaven.
Eternal life will merely be the full blossoming
of a plant that is green with life.

FINAL BLESSING

May you know the blessedness of those who put their trust in God.

May you know the blessedness of those who hunger and thirst for what is right.

And if you should suffer for the Gospel, know that the wounds you bear will be honourable wounds.

Sharing the Word of God today

SCRIPTURE NOTE

First Reading (Zeph 2:3;3:12-13). The two texts brought together in this reading are the earliest texts that use the term *anawim*. The term referred to the poor and lowly, who put their trust in God and practised integrity and humility. God becomes the champion of this 'faithful remnant'.

The reading gives us one of the most complete pictures of the meaning of poverty to be found in the Old Testament. It is against this background that we must understand the beatitudes, and the first beatitude in particular.

Gospel (Mt 5:1-12). Today we have the first of six extracts from Matthew's Sermon on the Mount (5:1-7:29). There are parallels between Moses and the Matthean Jesus. The old law was given to Moses on a mountain; the new law is given by Jesus also on a mountain.

The sermon begins with the beatitudes. In the beatitudes we see the values Christ preached, and the blessedness promised to those who live by them.

While Matthew has eight beatitudes, Luke has only four, but with four corresponding 'woes' (6:20-26). In Luke the beatitudes are stated more starkly. It seems that Matthew has spiritualised them, because his community includes people who are not physically poor or hungry.

Second Reading (1 Cor 1:26-31). This continues the theme of the blessedness of the poor and the lowly. A cursory glance at the Bible reveals that the poor and the lowly are God's favourites. But it is not for this reason alone that God chooses them. God chooses them because, conscious of their limitations, they rely on God rather than on themselves. Then the success of the work will clearly be seen as God's doing.

The Beatitudes (shorter version)

In the beatitudes Jesus lists the qualities he wishes to see in his followers. Does one need to have all eight of them? No. Any one of them, lived to the full, will suffice. A mere glance will show that they are a complete reversal of conventional standards and values. (Two voices could be used).

The world says: Happy are you who put your trust in money. Be glad and rejoice when it is coming in fast. You'll be the envy of all.

Jesus says: Happy are you who put your trust in God. Remember that it's not the amount of money you possess that makes you rich, but what you are in the sight of God.

The world says: Happy you who are hard and ruthless. People will be afraid of you, and you'll get results.

Jesus says: Happy you who are gentle and kind, and who refuse to get on by trampling on others. Gentleness is a form of strength. There are many vital tasks which only gentleness can accomplish.

The world says: Happy are you who live it up. Remember you only live once. So let your hair down. You'll have great fun.

Jesus says: Happy are you who remember that the most valuable things in life have to be bought with pain and sacrifice. Happy are you who don't confuse real happiness with passing thrills. Even though you may sow in sorrow, you will reap in joy.

The world says: Happy are you who hunger for power, status, and fame. You will always be in the limelight.

Jesus says: Happy are you who have standards and values, and who are prepared to live up to them. Happy are you who realise that to live rightly is the most important thing in life. Those who rate this as important as eating and drinking will taste real happiness even here on earth.

The world says: Happy are you who show no tolerance to those who make mistakes, and no mercy to those who oppose you. You'll be the boss, and everybody will know it.

Jesus says: Happy are you who make allowance for the sins of others, and whose greatness lies in your ability to forgive. The sun of God's mercy will shine warmly on you.

The world says: Happy you whose main concern is to have a clean skin, and who keep up to date with the latest style in clothes. You'll be really with it.

Jesus says: Happy are you whose main concern is to a have clean heart. It is from the heart that all our thoughts, words, and deeds flow. If the heart is clean, all that flows from it will be like water flowing from an unpolluted spring.

The world says: Happy are you troublemakers and warmongers. People will fear you, and you will get sensational headlines.

Jesus says: Happy are you peacemakers. You who spread understanding among people, who welcome the stranger, and who work for a just society. You are true children of God.

The world says: Happy are you who don't hesitate to lie, steal, and cheat, and who manage to get off scot-free. You'll have a great laugh over a pint with your cronies.

Jesus says: Happy are you who make a stand for what is right. If you suffer for your stand, the wounds you bear will be honourable wounds, and will mark you out as a true disciple of mine. You will gain honour on earth and glory in heaven.

The Beatitudes (longer version)

The beatitudes are at the heart of the Gospel. Yet many regard them as impractical and far too demanding for human beings. What follows is an imaginary discussion between a disciple and the Lord. It tries to show that the beatitudes are extremely practical, and are within the reach of human beings – with a little help from above, of course.

(Five or six would be enough to present at one time. The second and the fifth are very similar, as are the fourth and the eight. Two voices should be used).

1. Happy the poor in spirit: theirs is the kingdom of heaven.

Happy the poor! Surely you mean: Happy the rich, because they can have whatever they want?

But rich people are never satisfied, so how can they be happy?

By 'poor' I take it you don't mean living in a hovel.

Of course not. People need a certain amount of material things in order to be able to live with dignity.

What then do you mean by 'poor in spirit'?

I mean those who put their trust in God rather than in money.

Lord, in our world, money is the name of the game. It opens all doors.

All doors but the one that really matters, namely, the door to the kingdom of God.

2. Happy the gentle: they shall inherit the earth.

Happy the gentle! You must be kidding! If you're gentle, people will walk all over you.

You mean if you want to get on, you must be hard.

Exactly. In this world gentle people get left behind. Aggressive people get on.

Yet, is it not true that deep down we all pine for gentleness, and we can't open up and grow without it?

That may be so. But people see gentleness as a form of weakness.

Gentleness is not a form of weakness. It is a form of strength, and is one of the most necessary qualities in life. It takes a strong, self-confident person to be gentle.

3. Happy those who mourn: they will be comforted.

Happy those who mourn! Are you out of your mind, Lord?

Surely everybody is entitled to get some joy out of life?

Indeed. But joy is not the opposite of suffering. It is the opposite of sadness and bitterness. If you love and are loved, you can be joyful even in the midst of suffering. Sorrow is a part of life, and can make life deeper and richer.

But sorrow usually means tears, and some people are ashamed of tears.

Tears are a kind of riches. They show that we have feelings. In short, that we have a heart. Without a heart, a person is no better than a block of marble.

But if you open your heart to others, you're sure to get hurt.

True. But to open your heart is to begin to live. To close it is to begin to die.

4. Happy those who hunger and thirst for what is right: they shall be satisfied.

Lord, the only hunger most people understand is bodily hunger.

I don't agree. People hunger for a lot of things besides food.

For example?

People hunger for something to believe in. People hunger for hope. And, of course, people hunger for love. One cannot live without love.

So then to nourish human beings is not the same as to fatten cattle?

I couldn't have put it better myself. To life rightly is what life is about. Those who rate that as important as eating and drinking will taste real happiness even here on earth.

5. Happy the merciful: they will have mercy shown them.

Mercy! That makes even less sense than gentleness.

Oh, so we're back to hardness and toughness again.

If you're merciful, people will take advantage of you.

Are you saying that the world doesn't need mercy?

I'm not saying that it doesn't need it, but that it's got no room for it.

Well then, it's got to make room for it. How many barriers would fall down, how many broken relationships would be mended, if people were prepared to show mercy and forgiveness to one another. The merciful will receive mercy from God for their own sins.

6. Happy the clean of heart: they shall see God.

People talk about clean teeth, clean skins, and so on. But you never hear anyone talk about a clean heart.

That's because people are more concerned about outer cleanness than inner cleanness.

Inner cleanness? What do you mean?

I mean cleanness of mind and heart, which results in moral living.

Lord, today people are more concerned about hygiene than about morality. See how big an issue pollution is.

People are right in wanting clean water, clean air, and so on. But they should be even more concerned about the most dangerous pollution all, namely, evil.

So what must we do?

We have to purify the source. The heart is the source. It is the wellspring from which all our thoughts, words, and deeds flow. If the heart is clean, then all that flows from it will like water flowing from an unpolluted spring.

What about being able to see God?

Just as you can't see the sun through a murky sky, so you can't see God through a murky heart. But if the heart is clean, we will be able to see God in all that is good and beautiful in the world.

7. Happy the peacemakers: they shall be called the children of God.

It's more like: Happy the troublemakers.

Troublemakers are very unhappy people.

But we have peace. We're not at war with anybody right now.

Peace! People can be almost as cruel to one another in times of peace as in times of war.

How come there's so little peace in the world?

Because there are so few peacemakers. Peace doesn't just happen. It has to be made.

But try reconciling warring factions, and you'll see what a dangerous and thankless business it is.

I couldn't agree more. Peacemaking is a tough business. The peacemaker has to be armed, not with the sword or the gun, but with courage, determination, and patience. Still, everyone could do something.

What in practice can one do?

Forgive those who offend you. Welcome the strange. Do not provoke others to anger. Heal what is wounded. Bind up what is broken. And above all, be just in your dealings. Justice is the foundation of peace.

8. Happy those who are persecuted in the cause of right: theirs is the kingdom of heaven.

Some people would say: Happy those who lie, steal, cheat, and who get off scot-free.

No one can escape the eye of God, or the eye of one's own conscience, for that matter.

Lord, some people have no conscience. Their only commandment is the eleventh commandment – Thou shalt not get caught.

But are they happy?

I don't know, but they seem to prosper.

Perhaps. But how dark the world would be if everyone adopted that attitude. Those who stand up for what is right are the light of the world and the salt of the earth

But it's not easy to stand up for what is right. It won't bring you any honours in this world. It is much more likely to bring you insults and injuries.

If you pick up wounds in taking a stand for what is right, those wounds will be honourable wounds. Besides, it is a wonderful feeling to know that you are living the kind of life God wants you to live. It is a foretaste of heaven.

FIFTH SUNDAY OF THE YEAR
Salt of the earth and light of the world

Praying with the Word of God today

INTRODUCTION AND CONFITEOR

As disciples of Jesus we are called to be the salt of the earth and the light of the world. Unfortunately, we allow the salt to lose its taste and the light to grow dim.

Let us ask the Lord to pardon our failings and help to be better witnesses for him in the future. [Pause]

Lord Jesus, you strengthen us when we are weak. Lord, have mercy.

You forgive us when we fail. Christ, have mercy.

You give us courage when we are afraid. Lord, have mercy.

PRAYER OF THE FAITHFUL

Celebrant: Called by Christ to be the salt of the earth and the light of the world, let us pray to our heavenly Father for all our needs.

Response: Lord, hear our prayer.

Reader(s): For Christians: that the light of their good deeds may be clear for all to see. [Pause] Let us pray to the Lord.

For our political and civil leaders: that we may keep society good and healthy by promoting truth and justice. [Pause] Let us pray to the Lord.

For those Christians whose salt has lost its taste and whose light has gone out. [Pause] Let us pray to the Lord.

For all gathered here: that the world may recognise us as disciples of Christ by the love we have for one another. [Pause] Let us pray to the Lord.

For our deceased relatives and friends: that the Lord may lead them to the fullness of the resurrection and gladden them with the light of his face. [Pause] Let us pray to the Lord.

For our own special needs. [Longer Pause] Let us pray to the Lord.

Celebrant: Lord Jesus, help us to live in such a way that those who do not believe may come to acknowledge you, who live and reign with the Father and the Holy Spirit, one God for ever and ever.

OUR FATHER

God has called us out of darkness into the wonderful light of his Son. Let us pray to our heavenly Father as children of the light.

PRAYER/REFLECTION

Each of us has a capacity for goodness.
We have hands that can care,
eyes that can see,
ears that can hear,
tongues that can speak,
feet that can walk,
and, above all, hearts that can love.
Lord, help us to believe in our own goodness,
and to let the light of that goodness shine.
On seeing this light others find their way,
and you will be glorified.

FINAL BLESSING

May the Lord give you joy in the profession of your faith.

May you live in such a way that your lives will be an example for others.

May you not be discouraged by your weakness or demoralised by your failures.

Sharing the Word of God today

SCRIPTURE NOTE

First Reading (Is 58:7-10). Isaiah has been talking about fasting. He tells the people that true fasting (and therefore true religion) is necessarily linked with the practice of justice and with concern for the poor and the needy. Here he assures them that if they follow this way their lives will become luminous. This is the connection with the Gospel.

Gospel (Mt 5:13-16). Matthew has already introduced Jesus as the light of a darkened world (4:12-16). Now the function of enlightening and guiding a morally confused humanity is shared with his disciples.

Salt and light are powerful images. In the ancient world, salt was one of the most important necessities of life, especially for preserving and seasoning food. So too was light for obvious reasons. Both images are making the same point: Christians are called to bear witness to Christ before unbelievers through their good deeds. When the disciples stop witnessing through their deeds, they become as useless as salt that has lost its taste or a lamp that doesn't give light.

Second Reading (1 Cor 2:1-5). Paul is at pains to convince the Corinthians that their fascination with worldly wisdom and rhetorical skills can only weaken their faith. He points to himself as an example. When he brought the Gospel to them, he didn't rely on human cleverness. He came in weakness, preaching a crucified (and risen) Christ, to show that their faith doesn't depend on human cleverness but on the power of God.

Salt of the earth, light of the world

Jesus said to his disciples, 'You are the salt of the earth; you are the light of the world.' In the ancient world, salt was one of the most important necessities of life, especially for preserving and seasoning food. So too was light for obvious reasons.

Both images are making the same point: Christians are called to bear witness to Christ before unbelievers through their good deeds. When the disciples stop witnessing through their deeds, they become as useless as salt that has lost its taste or a lamp that doesn't give light.

One day a man visited Mother Teresa's home for the poor and the dying in Calcutta. He arrived just as the Sisters were bringing in some of the dying off the streets. They had picked up a man out of the gutter. He was covered with dirt and sores. Without knowing that she was being watched, one of the Sisters began to care for the dying man. The visitor kept watching the Sister as she worked. He saw how tenderly she cared for her patient. He noticed how as she washed the man she smiled at him. She did not miss a detail in her attentive care for that dying man.

After carefully watching the Sister, the visitor turned to Mother Teresa and said, 'When I came here today I didn't believe in God, and my heart was full of hate. But now I am leaving here believing in God. I have seen the love of God in action. Through the hands of that Sister, through her tenderness, through her gestures, which were so full of love for that wretched man, I have seen God's love descend upon him. Now I believe.'

This is surely an example of the kind of thing Jesus had in mind. When he tells us that we must let our light shine, the light he is talking about is the light of our good deeds, especially our deeds of love. People take notice of deeds. Our deeds don't have to be as spectacular as the above example. Generally they will be much more ordinary. But that doesn't mean they can't give effective witness to the light.

When Jesus tells us to let our light shine before people, he doesn't mean that we should advertise our good deeds, much less boast about them. He is asking us to *do* them. If we do them they will speak for themselves. A good life is a strong and effective witness, and in itself is a proclamation of the Gospel.

Salt does not work by remote control. In order to produce its effect, salt has to be mixed in with the food. And a light has to be put in a high place in order to be able to reach people. So Christians have to be in the world. But they must not allow themselves to be absorbed by the world.

Christians have betrayed their vocation if all they do is reflect the values of society. They are like insipid salt. They are incapable of influencing anyone for good. Christians must not just blend in. They must stand out. 'The world today needs Christians who remain Christians' (Albert Camus).

As Christians we have a very positive role to play in the world. We have something to offer, something the world desperately needs, even though it may not always welcome it. We should not be shy or apologetic about our role. 'The lamp of God's love burns in this world only with the oil of our lives.' (Edward Schillebeeckx)

Effective witness calls for conviction, commitment, boldness and courage – things we don't always find in ourselves. We must learn from Paul (Second Reading). He tells us that he doesn't rely on himself but on the power of God.

The task of witnessing is not one for the individual Christian only but for the Christian community as a whole. It is easier to witness to Christ as a member of a supportive community.

Let your light shine

Christ asks us, his disciples, to be the salt of the earth and the light of the world. What does this imply? It doesn't mean that we have to leave our jobs, rush out, and get involved in a whirlwind of good works. It means that we are called to practise our Christianity, not just in church, but out in the world, in whatever situation we happen to find ourselves. All the more so if, by reason of our position, we happen to be situated on some 'hilltop' where all can see us, and where people look to us for light. Here are some examples.

If I'm a teacher, what do people expect from me? That I teach well, and that I refrain from showing favouritism. If I show favouritism then I bring light to some and darkness to others. If a Christian teacher should show any kind of favouritism, it should be towards the children who find learning difficult.

If I'm a judge, what do people expect from me? Justice. Justice is to society what salt is to food. Solzhenitsyn says, 'A corrupt court is worse than highway robbery.' A good judge causes the light of justice to shine.

If I'm a politician, what do people expect from me? That I work for the good of the country and not just for my own good. A corrupt politician has a lot to answer for. But then a good politician can bring light into the lives of many.

If I'm a doctor, what do people expect from me? That I would treat all the sick alike. A good doctor brings the light of healing to many.

If I'm a police officer, what do people expect from me? That I would not try to bend the law or break it, but uphold it and enforce it fairly.

If I'm an employer, what do people expect from me? That I pay a fair wage and create decent working conditions for my employees. People who do this shed a lot of light around them.

If I'm a worker, what do people expect from me? That I know my job and do it to the best of my ability.

If I'm a reporter, what do people expect from me? That I deal in facts, not in half-truths and lies. A good journalist can shine the light of truth into many dark corners.

If I'm a parent, what do my children expect from me? In a nutshell – that I'm there for them.

If I'm a priest, what do people expect of me? That I would try to practise what I preach.

We could multiply the examples and still not cover everything. Each of us must look at our own situation and ask ourselves how we can practise our Christianity there. How we can be 'salt' and 'light' among the people we meet every day, and in the humdrum situations that occur. We may not be able to be a beacon. But we can at least be a humble candle that sheds light in its own immediate vicinity.

There is a tendency to take big matters seriously and neglect small ones.

Here is where the light goes out, and the salt loses its savour. There is only one remedy. To set aside for the time being the big things, and to take seriously the small things.

This Gospel is basically about goodness. But goodness can't be a put-on thing. The good deeds I do must be an expression of the kind of person I am. The authenticity of their lives is the best witness Christians can give.

Stories

Here are two more stories that could be used in much the same way as the Mother Teresa story is used in the first homily. One at a time of course.

1. Often we think we are good simply because we are not conscious of doing any great evil. But what about the good we fail to do?

Alexander Solzhenitsyn recalls, as he says, 'with shame', an incident he witnessed at the front when he was a captain in the Russian army.

'One day I saw a sergeant of the secret police, on horseback, using a whip on a Russian soldier who had been captured serving in a German unit. The man, naked from the waist up, was staggering under the blows, his body covered in blood. Suddenly, he saw me and cried out, "Mister Captain, save me!"

'Any officer in any army in the world should have put a stop to this torture, but I was a coward. I said nothing and I did nothing. This picture has remained in my mind ever since.'

Solzhenitsyn could have brought light into that dark situation but he didn't.

'Be not simply good,' says Thoreau, 'be good for something.'

2. Once there was a great biblical scholar who was also noted for his great piety. He spent hours every day secluded in his room studying the Scriptures, and praying and meditating. One day a holy man visited the town in which the scholar lived. On hearing about it, the scholar set out to look for him.

He looked first in the church, but did not find him there. Then he looked in a local shrine, but he wasn't there either. He looked in other likely places but failed to find him. Eventually he found him in the marketplace.

On meeting him he told him who he was, and how he spent hours every day studying the Scriptures and in prayer and meditation. Then he said, 'I have come to seek your advice on how I might grow in the service of God.'

The advice he got was simple and direct. The holy man said, 'It's easy to be a sage and a saint in your room. You should go out into the marketplace and try to be a saint there.' We are not told whether or not the scholar had the courage to act on that advice.

It is the kind of advice Jesus gives us in today's Gospel when he says, 'You are the light of the world. No one lights a lamp to put it under a tub;

they put it on lamp-stand where it shines for everyone in the house. In the same way your light must shine in the sight of people, so that seeing your good works, they may give praise to your Father in heaven.'

It is easy to let the light shine in the comfort and safety of one's room. But that can be a selfish thing, because it means we are keeping the light to ourselves. It is not so easy to let the light shine in the rough and tumble of the marketplace. But that is where it is most needed.

SIXTH SUNDAY OF THE YEAR
New and higher standards

Praying with the Word of God today

INTRODUCTION AND CONFITEOR

Jesus says, 'If you are going to the altar, and remember that your brother has something against you, leave your offering there before the altar, and go and be reconciled with your brother first.' These words show how important reconciliation is in the eyes of God. Let us reflect on them for a moment. [Pause] It is the Lord himself who helps us to be reconciled.

Lord Jesus, you heal the wounds of sin and division. Lord, have mercy.

You reconcile us to one another and to the Father. Christ, have mercy.

You plead for us at the right hand of the Father. Lord, have mercy.

PRAYER OF THE FAITHFUL

Celebrant: Let us with confidence approach God in our needs because with him is mercy and fullness of redemption.

Response: Lord, hear our prayer.

Reader(s): For the followers of Christ: that their virtue may be deep and genuine. [Pause] Let us pray to the Lord.

For those who make and enforce our laws: that they may seek the wisdom that comes from God. [Pause] Let us pray to the Lord.

For those who are in the grip of an addiction: that they may seek help. [Pause] Let us pray to the Lord.

For all gathered here: that we may not let the sun go down on our anger. [Pause] Let us pray to the Lord.

For our deceased relatives and friends: that they may dwell in the house of the Lord for ever. [Pause] Let us pray to the Lord.

For our own special needs. [Longer pause] Let us pray to the Lord.

Celebrant: All-powerful God, help us to keep our thoughts clean, our desires pure, our words true, and our deeds kind. We ask this through Christ our Lord.

OUR FATHER

No eye has seen, no ear has heard, what God has prepared for those who love him. Let us pray to our heavenly Father as Jesus taught us.

A PRAYER FOR THE END OF THE DAY

Grant, O Lord, that each day
before we enter the little death of sleep,
we may undergo the little judgement of the past day,
so that every wrong deed may be forgiven
and every unholy thought set right.
Let nothing go down into the depths of our being
which has not been forgiven and sanctified.
Then we shall be ready for our final birth into eternity,
and look forward with love and hope to standing before you,
who art both judge and saviour, holy judge and loving saviour.
  Bishop Appleton

FINAL BLESSING

May you know the happiness of those who follow God's law.

May the message of Christ, in all its richness, find a home in you.

May the Lord confirm your hearts in holinesss so that you may be blameless in his sight.

Sharing the Word of God today

SCRIPTURE NOTE

First Reading (Eccles 15:15-20). Sirach presents obedience to God's law as the road that leads to life, and rejection of that law as the path to death. The choice is set before man: he can opt for life or death. The New Testament good news of grace generously poured out in Christ will transform this stark and forbidding morality.

Gospel (Mt 5:17-37). (Shorter form recommended). In this section of the Sermon on the Mount, Matthew illustrates Jesus' attitude to the Law. Jesus does not dispense with the Law but asks for a deeper observance of it. Every small part of it is to remain, but only as radically interpreted by Jesus.

His justice far surpasses the legalistic approach of the scribes and Pharisees. For the Pharisees the letter of the Law was everything. Jesus proposes new standards of goodness for his disciples. It is not enough for them to become better Pharisees.

This justice is made explicit in six concrete examples. These (called 'antitheses') deal with murder, adultery, divorce, oaths and vows, retaliation, and hatred of enemies. The first four are dealt with in today's Gospel, the other two in next Sunday's Gospel.

Murder and adultery are born in the heart. Jesus reinterprets the fifth commandment so that it embraces those angry feelings and emotions that may lead up to murder. And he reinterprets the sixth commandment so that it embraces lustful thoughts and desires that may lead to sexual sin and infidelity. As for oaths: he encourages his disciples to behave in such a way that oaths are superfluous. The disciples are simply to be truthful.

Jesus intention is to bring us beyond legalism and a literal interpretation of the law (the problem with the scribes and Pharisees) and into the spirit of the law.

Second Reading (1 Cor 2:6-10). Christians have a wisdom unknown to others. True wisdom comes from God, and reveals the wonderful things God has prepared for those who love him.

A deeper virtue

Jesus said, 'If your virtue goes no deeper than that of the scribes and Pharisees, you will never get into the kingdom of heaven.' That statement must have surprised his hearers. And it must have angered the scribes and Pharisees, who liked to think of themselves as truly virtuous people.

Jesus shattered their complacent belief in their own goodness and virtue. He declared that their virtue was superficial, and their goodness skin-deep. His disciples would have to do better.

But you might think: virtue is virtue. Not so. There is a shallow virtue. Virtue is shallow when the motive is not pure – an unworthy motive can spoil even the best deed. Virtue is shallow when it lacks personal conviction, and is practised merely out of convention or conformity or routine. Virtue is shallow and inauthentic when the person is not sincere.

But then there is the genuine article. There is deep, true, authentic virtue. It is not a skin-deep thing, but an expression of what one is inside. Above all, it is a revelation of the heart.

Sin and virtue, badness and goodness, are essentially matters of the heart. And it is from the perspective of the heart that a Christian should assess them. Corruption of heart is the worst kind of badness – it is to be bad at the core. Goodness of heart is the best kind of goodness – it is to be good at the core.

Hence, we must not be content merely to look at the surface of our lives – at our words and deeds. We must have the courage to search our hearts. We need to look at what is going on inside us – at our motives, attitudes, and desires.

When considering our sins, we have to consider the sins of the heart – resentments, jealousies, angers, hatreds, and lusts. These might well be our worst sins, and the root cause of our external sins. They are the kind of things, which, if allowed to go unchecked, can lead, as Jesus says, to murder and sexual sin and infidelity.

And when we are considering our virtues, again we must look at the heart. One the best things we can say about anyone is that he/she is warm-hearted or open-hearted. This means he/she is capable of goodness, kindness, tenderness, pity, compassion, mercy ... These are the virtues of the heart.

Without a warm, compassionate heart one cannot call oneself a true human being, never mind a truly religious or virtuous person. Jesus wasn't taken in by the pious exterior of the Pharisees. Piety is no substitute for goodness. For all their piety, many of the Pharisees were both cold-hearted and hard-hearted people. If one's heart is cold and hard, how can one be virtuous?

When all is said and done it is the heart that matters. It is what's in the heart that matters. The heart is what I am deep down. It is the real me. And what is in the heart will out. The state of the heart will deeply affect how I live.

A person is what the heart is. Our chief concern, then, must be to get the heart right. If the heart is right, then our deeds will be true and genuine. They will flow from what we are, as naturally as good fruit from a good tree. You can't go any deeper than that.

Handling anger

It is impossible to live without getting angry at one time or another. Now, we may have been taught that anger is sinful – in fact, one of the seven deadly sins. As a result, we feel guilty about getting angry, and are tempted to deny it or repress it.

The first thing that needs to be said is that anger is normal and even healthy. If we love and value ourselves, we will naturally get angry if we are treated badly. We shouldn't deny our anger. Anger is just a feeling. In itself it is neither good nor bad morally.

And we shouldn't repress our anger. Psychologists tell us that repressed anger is very dangerous, and can result in self-hatred, depression, and even bodily ills such as asthma and ulcers. However, anger is no resting place. Anger can be very damaging if allowed to fester. 'Anger in the heart is like a worm in a plant' (Talmud). Anger needs to be released, but this must be done in a wholesome way. When anger is given a means of expression relief follows.

When Jesus says to us, 'Do not get angry with your brother,' he is not condemning anger in itself. After all, he himself got angry when he drove the traders out of the temple. There are times when we *ought* to be angry.

An unjust situation should make us angry. Anger need not give rise to a lessening of love, much less to hate.

It is when anger turns into *hostility* that it becomes dangerous. Hostility rather than anger is the real deadly sin. It causes us to act out our anger, and leads to deep resentments, negative attitudes, insults, and so on, directed at the object of our anger. We can't avoid getting angry, but we can avoid *acting out* our anger.

If we find ourselves getting angry often, we should look at the cause of our anger. The cause may lie with us. We may be hypersensitive, or over-impatient, or full of hurt that we haven't dealt with. In which case we have to look at ourselves.

But the cause may lie with others. Some people are full of anger, which makes them very difficult to live with. Instead of owning their anger, they direct it onto others. If the cause of our anger lies with another person, we have to look at our relationship with that person.

Finally the cause may lie in some unjust situation. If so, then we should try to put that situation right. Anger can be a good thing – it can spur us to put right something that is wrong. There is an old saying: 'The size of a person's soul can be measured by the size of the things that make him angry.'

Gandhi, said, 'I have learnt through bitter experience the one supreme lesson, namely, to conserve my anger. And, as heat conserved is transformed into energy, anger controlled can be transformed into a power that can move the world.'

Still, when all is said and done, anger is not a good resting place. Anger is a dangerous thing, and can result in a cycle of negativity. If our heart is filled with anger, there is no room in it for love. Therefore, we would do well to heed the advice of St Paul: 'Do not let the sun go down on your anger' (Eph 4:26).

Jesus and the Law

All of us are subject to law. Jesus himself was subject to law, both human and divine. As he grew up he obeyed Joseph and Mary. He obeyed the law of the land. And of course he obeyed the law of God. Here it is Jesus' attitude to the law of God that concerns us.

He found no fault with the law itself. His problem lay with the way it was interpreted and applied by the religious leaders of his day. For them it was the *letter of* the law that mattered. But for Jesus it was the *spirit* of the law that mattered.

The Pharisees looked only at *the outward act.* But God sees the heart. So Jesus said we have to look, not just at our acts, but also at our *thoughts and desires,* even though they may never actually lead to acts. We may never have killed anyone, but we may have entertained hostile thoughts about people and harboured hostile attitudes towards them. We may never have committed adultery, but we may have entertained lustful thoughts and desires.

Again, Jesus saw that the commandments were interpreted in a very negative way which led to *minimalism* – doing the bare minimum. He interpreted them in a *positive* way. For example, the fifth commandment says, 'Thou shalt not kill.' But he said, 'You must love your neighbour.' The seventh commandment says, 'Thou shalt not steal.' But he said, 'You must share your goods with your neighbour when he is in need.'

He also saw that obedience was often *rooted in fear.* He wanted it *rooted in love.* His whole relationship with his heavenly Father was based on love. When you love someone, you avoid doing anything to hurt that person. Where there is love, there is really no need of law.

But the most significant thing of all that Jesus did was this: he brought in a new and more exacting law – *the law of love.* Far from contradicting or abolishing the old law, the new law goes beyond it, and so brings it to perfection.

He said that all of God's laws could be reduced to two: love of God and love of neighbour. These two, properly understood, include all the others. In a sense, then, there is only one law – the law of love. And there is only one sin – not to love.

Story

As the fiftieth anniversary of his parents wedding approached, Thomas wondered what present he should give them. They had been the best of parents. Eventually he decided to pay for a two-week holiday for them in the sun. He was very pleased with himself.

But their response took him by surprise. They said, 'Son, we thank you for your very generous gift. It must have cost you a lot of money. But there is another and better gift you could give us.'

'What is that?' he asked earnestly.

'You wronged your brother Patrick. Go and be reconciled with him. That would meant more to us than any gift.'

Jesus says that if we are on the way to the altar with an offering, and remember that our brother (or sister) has something against us, we should leave our offering there before the altar, go and be reconciled with our brother, and then come back and present our offering.

Reconciliation is not a holier task than offering a gift at God's altar. It's just that lack of reconciliation damages our gift in God's eyes. The thing that God wants above all is to see his children reconciled.

We should take the words of Jesus very seriously. However, it is not necessary to take them literally. If we are on the way to the altar and remember that someone has something against us, we can sincerely make a decision to seek reconciliation later. That, in effect, is the same thing.

SEVENTH SUNDAY OF THE YEAR
Love your enemies

Praying with the Word of God today

INTRODUCTION AND CONFITEOR

Jesus tells us that God loves all of his children, deserving and undeserving. And he urges us to imitate this all-embracing love of God.

Let us reflect on how difficult love can be, especially in relation to people we don't like. [Pause]. Jesus gives us an example of love.

Lord Jesus, you are kind and full of compassion. Lord, have mercy.

You are slow to anger and rich in mercy. Christ, have mercy.

You do not treat us according to our sins nor repay us according to our faults. Lord, have mercy.

PRAYER OF THE FAITHFUL

Celebrant: God loves all of his children, deserving and undeserving. Let us pray that we that we may imitate the all-embracing love of God.

Response: And crown us with love and compassion.

Reader(s): For Christians of different denominations: that they may reach out to one another in love. [Pause] Lord, hear us.

For countries where the population is made up of different religious and ethnic groups: that peace and harmony may prevail there. [Pause] Let us pray to the Lord.

For the healing of relationships that are strained or that have gone sour. [Pause] Let us pray to the Lord.

For those who have hurt us in any way, and whom we find hard to love. [Pause] Let us pray to the Lord.

For our loved ones who have died: that they may rest in the peace of God. [Pause] Let us pray to the Lord.

For our own special needs. [Longer pause] Let us pray to the Lord.

Celebrant: Merciful God, fill our hearts with your love. Give us the grace to rise above our human weakness, and keep us faithful in loving you and one another. We make this prayer through Christ our Lord.

OUR FATHER

God lets the sun shine and the rain fall on all of his children, deserving and undeserving. Let us pray to the God of love as Jesus taught us.

SIGN OF PEACE

Lord Jesus Christ, you said to your disciples, 'Love your enemies; pray for those who persecute you. In this way you will show that you are true children of your Father in heaven'.

Help us to be merciful and forgiving towards those who make life difficult for us, and thus we will enjoy the peace and unity of your kingdom where you live for ever and ever.

REFLECTION

When Abraham Lincoln was running for president of the United States there was a man called Stanton, who never lost an opportunity to vilify him. Yet when Lincoln won the election he surprised everyone by giving Stanton a post in his cabinet. Asked why he didn't destroy his enemy, he replied, 'Do I not destroy my enemy when I make him my friend?'

FINAL BLESSING

May you resist evil and conquer it with good.

May you choose love and forgiveness over hatred and vengeance.

May you be filled with a joyful trust in God, and never tire of doing what is right.

Sharing the Word of God today

SCRIPTURE NOTE

First Reading (Lev 19:1-2.17-18). This reading is made up of two extracts from chapter nineteen of Leviticus. In the first of these, the Israelites are told that the Lord is holy; therefore they, his people, must also be holy.

The second part of the reading forbids the Israelite to nurture hatred of his fellow-Israelite. V. 18 contains the commandment: 'You must love your neighbour as yourself'.

Gospel (Mt 5:38-48). In Levitcus, the commandment 'You must love your neighbour as yourself' is restricted to fellow-Israelites. Here Jesus broadens it to include everyone, Gentiles as well as Jews, enemies as well as friends. His disciples are to love as God loves.

Love within one's group or fellowship is merely a natural and universal human trait. It does not distinguish the Christian from the non-Christian. What makes the disciples of Christ different from other people is their ability to love even their enemies. In this they are imitating the heavenly Father. He shows equal love towards good and bad, not because he is indifferent to morality, but because he loves without limit. Since God is holy, we are to be holy. We are holy when we imitate the generosity of God by not exacting vengeance, or bearing a grudge against another.

As for 'turning the other cheek' – this is not meant to be taken literally. (Jesus didn't turn the other cheek when slapped on the face during his trial before Caiphas. See Jn 18:22-23). Exaggeration is a way of emphasising a truth. The point Jesus is making is that violence breeds violence.

Second Reading (1 Cor 3:16-23). Paul gives us the most profound reason of all why we should respect one another: we are the Temple of God. Individually and collectively the Holy Spirit dwells in us. This is also the basis of our unity.

Choosing love over hate

Nelson Mandela spent 27 years in South African prisons. When he was finally released, he had every reason to feel bitter, and to come out vowing to get revenge on those who unjustly deprived him of his freedom. Instead, he came out smiling, and seeking reconciliation with the leaders of the regime that had put him in prison. He went on to become the cornerstone of a new South Africa. If he had come out vowing revenge, who knows what would have happened?

In his autobiography, *Long Walk to Freedom,* he tells us, 'I knew that people expected me to harbour anger against whites. But I had none. In prison, my anger towards whites decreased, but my hatred for the system grew. I wanted South Africa to see that I loved even my enemies while I hated the system that turned us against one another. I saw my mission as one of preaching reconciliation, of healing the old wounds and building a new South Africa.'

When Jesus says, 'Offer the wicked man no resistance', he is not telling us to be passive in the face of physical danger or abuse. The point he is making is that is that violence breeds violence. We are not allowed to have hatred in our hearts for anyone, even our enemies.

Hatred is a very dangerous thing, and must be handled with great respect. When we hate we expend more energy than in any other emotion. Hate drives out everything else and corrodes and warps the soul. Hatred should be kept for a cause such as intolerance or injustice, not for an individual.

When Jesus talks about 'the enemy' he is not necessarily referring to an enemy in war. He is talking about someone who is close to us, who is making life difficult for us.

The enemy can arouse hatred in us. When we discover our capacity to hate and harm, it is very humbling. We discover perhaps that the enemy is not outside us but inside us. This forces us to recognise the world of shadows and chaos within us. Our enemies are not those who hate us but those whom we hate.

Jesus' command, 'Love your enemy', is a radical rejection of violence.

Returning love for hate is one of the most difficult things in the world. It's a very high ideal, and a very difficult one, but it makes sense.

As Christians, we are on the side of non-violence. However, this is not an option for weakness and passivity. Opting for non-violence means to believe more strongly in the power of truth, justice, and love than in the power of war, weapons and hatred. We must try to respond to the worst with the best. We must try to imitate the generosity of God in our willingness not to exact vengeance.

Mandela suffered much and suffered unfairly. Yet he achieved the only triumph worth achieving – that of not being soured by his suffering or tempted to the ultimate surrender of dignity by seeking revenge.

A better way

One day a native American was talking to his grandson about the atrocity that happened in New York city on September 11, 2001. Suddenly the grandson asked, 'Grandpa, how do you feel about that atrocity?'

'I feel as if there are two wolves fighting in my heart. One wolf is angry, vengeful, and violent. The other is loving, forgiving, and compassionate,' he answered.

'Which wolf will win the fight in your heart?' the grandson asked.

'The one I feed,' he replied.

Jesus says to us, 'Love your enemy and pray for those who persecute you.' He never said that we would have no enemies – there is no lack of realism here. But he offers us a new way of dealing with our enemies. The injunction 'Love your enemy' is a radical rejection of violence.

But how can we be expected to love our enemies? Do we not find it hard enough to love our friends? We are not expected to *feel* love for our enemy. Love is not a feeling; it is an act of the will. We can make a decision to love someone, even though we do not have feelings of love for that person.

Jesus is telling us to love, not to hate. Hatred is a very destructive thing. When we hate we expend more energy than in any other emotion.

This is why Jesus urges us not to have hatred in our hearts for anyone, not even our enemies. It is not only for the sake of the enemy that he says to us, 'Love your enemies', but for our own sake too. Hatred may not destroy its object, but it will surely destroy the one who hates. 'Ten enemies can't hurt a person as much as he hurts himself' (Proverb).

Jesus' way is not an easy way. It is a hard way, but it is a better way. He challenges us to respond to darkness with light. The escalation of evil can be stopped only by one who humbly absorbs it, without passing it on. Revenge and retaliation only add darkness to darkness. Revenge may satisfy a person's rage but it leaves the heart empty.

We mustn't dissipate our strength in hating but save it for better things. Our hearts were made to love, not to hate. Love is more beautiful than hate. Hate poisons the heart, but love purifies it. At all costs, then, we must keep love in our heart. The image of God is at its best and brightest in us when we love.

The power of love is greater than the power of evil. Love releases extraordinary energies in us. And love is never lost. If not reciprocated, it will flow back and soften and purify the heart. If we pray for our enemies, peace will come to us. And when we love our enemies, we can be certain that divine grace dwells in us.

G. K. Chesterton said, 'Christianity has not been tried and found wanting; it has been found hard and left untried'. More than any other, the exhortation to love one's enemies has been left untried.

On not retaliating

Oskar Schindler was a German industrialist. During the Second World War he set up a factory in Poland. The film, *Schinder's List*, tells the story of how he saved over a thousand Jews by giving them work in his factory. When the Germans surrendered at the end of the war, Schindler abandoned the factory and escaped westwards to avoid the Russians who were approaching from the east. Meanwhile, the liberated workers waited in the factory for the arrival of the Russians.

While they waited, they found a German officer by the name of Amon bunkered inside the factory. Amon had been responsible for several brutal killings. A group of men dragged him out and enthusiastically and mercilessly hanged him. Some inmates tried to intervene, but the executioners were in such a rage that they could not be stopped.

This was the first homicide of the peace. It was an event, which would be abhorred forever by those who witnessed it. The hanging of Amon sickened them as profoundly as any of the executions Amon himself had carried out. After all, Amon was a Nazi, and beyond altering. But these hangmen were their own brothers. Instead of reaping satisfaction from it, all it did was sadden and depress them.

Our pain and hurt can so easily turn into rage, with the result that we inflict on others the injuries inflicted to us. Jesus' injunction 'Love your enemy' is a radical rejection of violence. It is one of the most revolutionary things ever said. All the revolutionaries said the enemy must be destroyed.

Love our enemies? Most of us find it hard enough to love our friends. How then can we be expected to love our enemies? All of us have some enemies, or at least some people we positively dislike.

Enemies bring out the worst in us. They expose a side of us which we usually manage to keep hidden from our friends, a dark side of our nature, which we would rather not know about. The enemy stirs up ugly things inside us. This is the real reason why we hate him.

To love one's enemy is not in the first place to do him good. Rather it is to allow him to be different, to be himself, and not try to turn him into a copy of ourselves so that we may be able to love him.

We are not expected to *feel* love for our enemy. Love is not a feeling; it is an act of the will. We can make a decision to love someone even though we do not have feelings of love for that person.

To love an enemy goes clean contrary to human nature. Only God can help us to love in the way Christ asks us to love. When Christ asks us to be perfect as our heavenly Father is perfect, the perfection he is talking about is the perfection of love. God loves his children unconditionally. He loves them not because they are good but because he is good.

Story

Here is another story that could be used in much the same way as the Nelson Mandela story is used in the first homily (p. 203).

Two farmers, John and James, were good friends until a dispute arose between them over a piece of land. Unable to settle the issue among themselves, they went to court over it. The court decided in favour of John. James was bitter, and put poison in John's well, not a fatal dose, but enough to give the water an obnoxious taste.

John was very angry. His neighbours heard about it. Some refused to get involved. But others were supportive and declared that James should be made to pay for what he had done.

John was about to go by night and poison James' well when a stranger arrived at his house. On hearing the story the stranger agreed that it was a pretty nasty situation, but he wouldn't agree with retaliation. 'Poison is not a thing to play around with,' he declared. 'I've a better idea. I'll tell you about it in the morning.'

His idea was to clean out the well. He offered to help. Reluctantly John agreed. It was a messy business and took them a whole day. Then they ran the fresh water through the well several times. Finally, the stranger took a cup of the water, drank it, and declared that it was clean. John also drank from the well, but insisted that he could still taste the poison. To which the stranger replied, 'Take it from me, the water is perfect. But you will continue to taste the poison until you do one more thing.'

'What's that?' asked John earnestly.

'You must forgive your neighbour. You have got rid of the poison from the well, but not the poison that lodges in your mind and heart. Not until you let go of your bitterness, and forgive your brother, will the water taste right.'

That evening John went over to his neighbour and made peace with him. When he came back he tasted the water again. This time it tasted good.

Hatred is a very dangerous thing. It poisons the heart. Love, on the other hand, purifies it. Jesus says to us 'Love your enemies.' It is not only for the sake of the enemy that he says this but for our sake too, and because love is more beautiful than hate. The greatest gift we possess is the gift to love. There is one thing that can utterly destroy this gift, and that is hatred.

'A man who contemplates revenge keeps his own wounds green' (Francis Bacon).

EIGHTH SUNDAY OF THE YEAR
Trusting God

Praying with the Word of God today

INTRODUCTION AND CONFITEOR

We are gathered in the house of God. Here we are conscious of being God's precious daughters and sons. Jesus urges us to let go of worry, and to trust in God's love and care for us. Let us come into God's presence in a spirit of trust. [Pause]

Lord Jesus, you are our strength in times of weakness. Lord, have mercy.
You are our refuge in times of distress. Christ, have mercy.
You are our hope in times of despair. Lord, have mercy.

PRAYER OF THE FAITHFUL

Celebrant: Trusting in God's unfailing love for us, let us bring our needs before him with great confidence.

Response: Lord, our help comes from you.

Reader(s): For the Church: that through its ministry people may experience the tender and steadfast love of God. [Pause] Let us pray to the Lord.

For all parents: that they may love their children in good times and in bad. [Pause] Let us pray to the Lord.

For our own parents: that the love they shared with us may be returned to them many times over. [Pause] Let us pray to the Lord.

For those who are burdened with problems and worries: that they may know the strength that comes from trust in God. [Pause] Let us pray to the Lord.

For our deceased relatives and friends: that they may rest in the peace of God. [Pause] Let us pray to the Lord.

For our own special needs. [Longer Pause] Let us pray to the Lord.

Celebrant: God of love, give us the kind of trust in you that will enable us to live out joyfully the mystery of our fragile human condition, which sees us suspended between earth and heaven, and between time and eternity. We ask this through Christ our Lord.

OUR FATHER

Those who trust in God renew their strength. They run and do not grow weary; they walk and never tire. Let us pray to our heavenly Father in the words our Saviour gave us.

SIGN OF PEACE

Lord Jesus Christ, you said to your disciples, 'Do not worry about food or drink or clothes. Set your hearts on the kingdom of God, and entrust yourselves to the care of your heavenly Father.'

Help us to live by these words, so that we may enjoy the peace and unity of your kingdom where you live and reign for ever and ever.

REFLECTION

The little cares that fretted me
I lost them yesterday
among the fields above the sea,
among the winds at play,
among the lowing of the herds,
the rustling of the trees,
among the singing of the birds,
the humming of the bees.
The foolish fears of what may happen,
I cast them all away,
among the clover-scented grass,
among the new-mown hay;
among the husking of the corn
where drowsy poppies nod,
where ill thoughts die and good are born,
out in the fields with God. (*Anon*).

FINAL BLESSING

May the Lord be your strength in times of weakness and your refuge in times of adversity.

May the Lord bless you with his protection so that whatever happens in your lives will work for your good.

May the Lord help you to walk in uprightness of heart and bring you to the joys of his kingdom.

Sharing the Word of God today

SCRIPTURE NOTE

First Reading (Is 49:14-15). These consoling words were first spoken to the exiles in Babylon. The prophet assures an afflicted people that God has not abandoned them. God's love for his people is like the steadfast love of a mother for her child – only greater. Trust in God's love is the link with the Gospel.

Gospel (Mt 6:24-34). Jesus says, 'Where your treasure is, there will your heart be also' (v.21). Therefore, one must decide to serve (worship) the one true God or the false god of money. One can't serve both.

Jesus goes on to urge his disciples not to allow concern for their material needs to be the dominant thing in their lives. Their main concern must be to seek God and his righteousness.

Jesus is not forbidding all concern about physical needs, but rather that 'anxiety' that expresses itself in total preoccupation with the goods of this world. He reminds his disciples that they are God's precious children. Therefore, they must put their future in the hands of God and pray only for the modest needs of today.

Worry is essentially distrust in God. Such distrust may be understandable in a heathen who believes in a jealous, capricious, unpredictable god; but not in one who has learned to call God by the name of Father.

Second Reading (1 Cor 4:1-5). Paul sees himself first and foremost as a servant of Christ, a steward who has been entrusted with God's revelation and charged with its propagation. He is willing to leave God the judge of how well he has carried out this charge. God is the only one who can judge rightly, because God alone knows the secrets of the heart.

Can a mother forget her child?

A poor woman in a Dublin parish had a son who was ruining her life. He wouldn't work. He spent his time drinking and hanging around with troublemakers. He robbed everything of value she had in the house. Again and again she pleaded with him to change his life, but he refused to do so. He broke her heart and made her life a misery.

Eventually he ended up in prison. Surely now she would leave him to his fate? Not at all. She visited him without fail every week, carrying cigarettes and other things to him in a little carrier bag. One day one of the priests from the parish met her as she was on her way to the prison.

'This son has ruined your life,' the priest said. 'He'll never change. Why don't you just forget about him?'

'How can I?' she replied. 'I don't like what he's done, but he's still my son.'

You could say that that mother was foolish. Yet she was only doing what any mother worthy of the name can't help doing, that is, loving her child through thick and thin.

Can a mother forget her child? Occasionally it can happen. But thankfully it is something so rare that when it does happen, it shocks us. For most of us, the love of a mother is the most reliable kind of human love we will experience. It's no wonder that the Bible uses a mother's love as an image of God's love for us.

'Does a woman forget her baby at the breast, or fail to cherish the son of her womb? Yet even if these forget, I will never forget you' (First Reading).

These lovely words were spoken (by the prophet) to God's people during a very low ebb in their history. The Temple had been destroyed, Jerusalem sacked, and many taken into exile in Babylon. The people felt that God had abandoned them. But the prophet assured them that God had not abandoned them, no more than a mother could abandon her child.

If a mother, who after all is a mere human being, is capable of such steadfast love, then how much greater is God's love for us who are his children. Even when we are in sin, God doesn't cease loving us.

We all pine for security. People accumulate money and possessions, because they give the illusion of security. People of faith do not rely on those things but on God, who is everlasting love. God is their security, and their chief concern is to do his will. This gives them a deep trust in life, and enables them to live the present moment free from attachments and worries.

When Jesus says, 'Do not worry about tomorrow', he is not condemning human resourcefulness. We have to plan for tomorrow. What he is condemning is the fretting and worrying that keeps us from lifting up our gaze beyond material values and the cares of this world.

We are in constant danger of becoming immersed in the affairs of the world and of becoming enslaved to material things. Jesus reminds us that we are God's precious children, and that only in God can we find security. We must put our future in the hands of God and pray only for the modest needs of today.

Story

(This story could be used in much the same way as the above story.)

A missionary Sister working in Africa tells of a woman who scarcely had any feet at all due to the ravages of leprosy. One day she noticed a spot on her young child. Taking the child in her arms, she somehow managed to walk six miles to the mission health clinic.

'Sister, my child has got leprosy,' she said.

The Sister examined the child. It turned out that the spot was not leprosy after all. The woman took back the child, and walked all the way back home. She didn't even stop to rest, so happy was she on hearing that her child did not have leprosy.

Dealing with worry

Jesus said to his disciples, 'Do not worry about life and what you are to eat, nor about your body and what you are to wear ... Set your hearts on the kingdom of God first, and on his righteousness, and all these other things will be given you as well.'

Jesus' prime concern is the call to decide between the fragile security of earthly things and the true riches of possessing God. He does not forbid all concern about physical needs, but rather that 'anxiety' that expresses itself in total absorption in the goods of this world.

In the time of Jesus people had a lot more reason to be worried than we have today. In those days most ordinary people lived from day to day regarding food. They were happy if they had enough food for the day.

Things are very different for us. Our fridges and freezers are seldom empty. Even if that should happen, a supermarket is not far away. So we should find it easier 'not to worry' about food, and be able to concentrate on essentials – what life is about, and how to live well.

But worry is still something that affects us all. It is part of our daily lives. It results from the duties and frustrations we carry around with us like a camel's tail.

But worry is not caused by external circumstances only, but also by internal disposition. Some people are natural worriers and are perpetually anxious. Anxious people are not thankful enough for the good things that have happened to them, and instead are over-anxious about what might happen to them.

Worry is not only useless, but is positively injurious to one's health. Worry puts a stoop on the shoulders. Even though it is probably impossible to live a life free from all worry, it is possible to reduce its power over us. It is not work that kills people – work is healthy. What kills people is worry.

A famous rabbi said that there are two things we should never worry about – what can be corrected and what cannot be corrected. What can be corrected should be corrected at once, without any worry. As for what cannot be corrected, worrying will not help.

Worry is essentially distrust in God. Such distrust may be understandable in a heathen who believes in a jealous, capricious, unpredictable god; but not in one who has learned to call God by the name of Father.

Worry is banished when trust in God and the desire to please him is the dominant thing in one's life. When we put ourselves in God's hands, we open ourselves to enjoy the full grace of God's protection.

The other way to defeat worry is to live a day at a time. We should strive to handle the demands of each day as it comes, without worrying about the unknown future and things that may never happen. St Augustine says that we should entrust the past to God's mercy, the present to his love, and the future to his providence. (Repeat).

Story

There was a town in which the people were terrible worriers. They called a meeting to see what they could do about the problem of worry. One person suggested that the town should have a park where people could relax. A second suggested that it should have a golf course. A third suggested that it should have a cinema. And so it went on. Finally a man got up and said, 'I've just thought of a much simpler solution. Why don't we ask David, the town cobbler, to do our worrying for us.'

'Wait a minute,' said David. 'Why pick on me?'

'Because if you agree, we'll make it worth your while. We'll pay you €500 a week.'

'Well in that case, why not me?' David exclaimed.

Everybody agreed that the idea was a good one. However, just as the motion was about to be put to a vote, this fellow got up and said, 'Wait a minute! If David earned €500 a week, what would he have to worry about?'

A good question. But since he was a worrier just like the rest of them, I'm sure he would have found something. Worriers always do.

According to a survey, the most common worries people have are: money (45%), other people (39%), personal health (32%), exams (20%), job security (15%).

Our relationship with God

There is an abyss between knowledge about things and immediate perception of things. A child knows practically nothing about its teddy bear, yet it knows it in a way that most grown-ups can never do.

The same holds true with regard to people. We could know a lot of facts about a person, and still not know the person. There is a big difference between the two. Take the example of Mary and Katie, both aged ten.

If you ask Mary to describe her father she says: 'He works in an office. He gets up very early. He comes home very late. He drives a car. He's very tall. He's got black hair ...'

If you ask her does she love her father, she replies, 'I don't see very much of him. He's away a lot'. And if you ask her does she trust him she replies, 'It depends on the mood he's in. If he's in a good mood, yes. But if he is in a bad mood, no.'

Sadly, for Mary her father is little better than an acquaintance. She knows certain facts about him, but doesn't enjoy a close relationship with him. And this colours her whole attitude to him. She does what is right, but only to please him. She avoids what is wrong, only because she is afraid of punishment. Her life is a kind of bargaining – something given for something received. Her moral growth will be stunted like that of a shrub planted in a cold climate.

If you ask Katie to describe her father she says something like this: 'My dad is very funny. He buys me presents, and I buy him presents. He doesn't like it when I misbehave. He takes me for walks in the woods. Once he saved me from running in front of a car. I'm getting a card for him for father's day, but I'm keeping it a surprise …'

Katie is talking about a warm relationship that exists between her and her dad. In a climate like this, Katie will grow like a flower in the sun.

So it is with God. We might know facts about God (learned from our religion books), and still not know God. There is a vast difference between knowing about God and knowing God. Even the devils believe in God's existence and know certain facts about him. But they do not love him.

We might be able to recite the Creed perfectly, but not have the kind of trust in God that Jesus speaks about in the Gospel. Jesus tells us that the heavenly Father loves us. That we are precious in his eyes. God is not an impersonal God, remote from us and from our world. God is near us, and loves us unconditionally.

We are not grains of sand or specks of dust. We are God's precious children. We have a splendid destiny. Sure of God's unconditional love for us, of our own immense dignity as God's children, and of the splendour of our destiny, why worry? The whole of Christianity can be summed up in the concept of God as our Father, a Father who rejoices in his children.

NINTH SUNDAY OF THE YEAR
Building on rock

Praying with the Word of God today

INTRODUCTION AND CONFITEOR

When we think of something solid and reliable, a rock is probably the first thing that comes into our minds. God's word provides a rocklike foundation for our lives. But it is not enough to listen to it; we have to do it.

Let us call to mind our failures to live by God's word. [Pause] Many times in the Bible God is compared to a rock.

Lord Jesus, you are the strength of the weak. Lord, have mercy.

You are the hope of the poor. Christ, have mercy.

You are the joy of the humble. Lord, have mercy.

PRAYER OF THE FAITHFUL

Celebrant: The Lord is the one in whom our hope rests. Let us now bring our needs before him with confidence.

Response: Lord, hear us and speedily rescue us.

Reader(s): For all Christians: that they may strive to live by the values of the Gospel. [Pause] Let us pray to the Lord.

For world leaders: that God may bless and unite them in their efforts to build a just and peaceful world. [Pause] Let us pray to the Lord.

For those who are finding life difficult: that their trust in God may sustain them. [Pause] Let us pray to the Lord.

For all gathered here: that we may listen to the words of Christ, and put them into practice in our lives. [Pause] Let us pray to the Lord.

For all the dead: that the Lord may free them from the shadows of death and gladden them with the light of his face. [Pause] Let us pray to the Lord.

For our own special needs. [Longer Pause] Let us pray to the Lord.

Celebrant: Lord, grant that what we have said with our lips, we may believe with our hearts, and practise with our lives. We ask this through Christ our Lord.

OUR FATHER

God is our rock and our refuge. Those who trust in him will never be put to shame. Let us pray to our heavenly Father as Jesus taught us.

PRAYER/REFLECTION

Human opinions change from day to day,
but the words of Christ do no change or pass away.
Those who listen to his words and act on them,
are building the house of their lives on rock.
Lord, soften our hearts with the rain of your grace,
and warm them with the sun of your love,
so that your word may take root in our hearts,
and bear fruit in our lives.

FINAL BLESSING

May the Lord keep your feet from stumbling and your heart from straying.

May you know the happiness of those who do God's will and seek him with all their hearts.

May you rejoice in God's saving help in time of trial.

Sharing the Word of God today

SCRIPTURE NOTE

First Reading (Deut 11:18.26-28). 'These words of mine' refer to the statutes, ordinances and commandments of the Lord so regularly mentioned in Deuteronomy. Here Moses presents the people with a choice: to accept or refuse the commandments of the Lord. If they accept them they will be blessed. If they reject them they will be cursed.

Gospel (Mt 7:21-27). Here the teaching of Jesus (the new Moses) is presented as the 'rock' on which his followers should build their lives.

Our reading contrasts the fate of those who listen to his words and act on them with that of those who listen to his words but do not act on them. The former are compared to a wise man who builds his house on rock – even the most violent storm will not prevail against it. The latter are compared to a foolish man who builds his house on sand – it is doomed to collapse when the storm hits it.

Second Reading (Rom 3:21-25.28). Since all people have sinned, they are all, both Jews and Gentile, sinners and therefore God's debtors. Nothing they can do is able to put them in right relationship with God. If, therefore, they are to be righteous, this can only happen by the pure gift of God, a gift that is made in Christ.

The good news of grace generously poured out in Christ transforms the stark and forbidding morality of Deuteronomy (First Reading).

Building on rock

Tobias Wolff is an American writer. He had a difficult childhood. After his father and mother divorced, he accompanied his mother as she travelled across America in search of work. He had an anguished adolescence, and was frequently on the verge of delinquency.

During that time he got a rudimentary education in the faith – his mother was a Catholic but didn't go to church. When she married again, the stepfather was very cruel to him. Somewhere along the line he made up his mind that he would be a writer, though it seemed an impossible dream at the time. After high school, he joined the US army and spent a year in Vietnam, an experience he found 'extremely corrupt and corrupting.' He lost good friends there. After leaving the army he managed to get accepted into Oxford University.

At Oxford he had a strange experience. One night he was doing a translation from old English into modern English. The passage assigned to him was from the West Saxon Gospels. The passage began to sound vaguely familiar to him. It told the story of a wise man who built his house on rock, and a foolish man who build his house on sand.

This caused him to reflect on his life. He realised that up to now he had known very little security. There had been nothing solid or reliable in his life. Yet now this amazing thing had happened to him: he was a student in a famous university. And indeed it was truly amazing that a boy from his background should end up in a College such as Oxford. The winds that had blown him here could have blown him anywhere, even off the face of the earth.

But he was here. All the other moments of his life had somehow conspired to bring him here. And with this moment came these words of Jesus. And as he copied out his translation in plain English, he thought that, 'yes, I would do well to build my house upon rock, whatever that meant.'

Gradually he found out what it meant to build one's life on the words of Jesus. How? By observing the lives of some fellow students who were active Catholics. He noticed that while many other students had no solid values, and were blown all over the place, these possessed something. They seemed to know where they were going, and what life was truly about. He wanted what they had. And so it was that he became an active Catholic himself. Notice, he wasn't won over by their arguments (words), but by their lives (deeds).

In comparison with faith, there is nothing sure or lasting in the world. Human opinions are rooted in appearances, and change from day to day, but the words of Christ do no change or pass away. We would do well to build the house of our lives on his precious words.

The people who heard the Sermon on the Mount were enormously impressed. But Jesus told them that it was not enough to listen to his words. They would have to act on them, if they wished to benefit from them.

Jesus said his disciples would be judged, not by their words, but by their deeds. There is only one way in which a person can prove his sincerity, that is, by his practice. Fine words can never take the place of deeds. Sadly, some who confess God with their lips deny him with their lives.

Jesus said that those who listened to his words, but who did not act on them, were building on sand. On the other hand, those who listened to his words and who did act on them, were building on rock. It's never too late to begin to act on the words of Jesus.

Building on his words

Some years ago, while Russia was still under Communist rule, a number of dissidents were arrested. They were subjected to a thorough body search. One man was found to have a small ball of paper in his mouth. It contained a few pages from a book.

The man knew that long years in some remote prison camp lay ahead of him, and that it was quite possible he would never return home. What pages was he taking with him to give him the necessary courage and strength to face such a bleak future? The pages contained the Sermon on the Mount, the conclusion of which we have just read.

It is reasonable to assume that this man was not turning to the words of Christ merely as a last resort. Rather, he was turning to something that had already filled his life with meaning and hope. Which suggests that he was not only a *listener* but also a *doer* of the word.

So it was to these marvellous words of Christ that he now fled. He wanted to take with him a lamp that would illuminate the dark path that stretched out unendingly before him. On these words he would build whatever hopes he still had for himself and for his life on earth.

What were some of those words on which he was pinning his hopes? No doubt it was words such as the following:

Blessed are those who are persecuted in the cause of right; theirs is the kingdom of heaven.

Where your treasure is, there will your heart be also.

No one can serve two masters ... You cannot be the slave both of God and of money.

Look at the birds of the air ... If God looks after them, how much more will he look after you, you of little faith.

Set your hearts on his kingdom first, and on his righteousness, and all these others things will be given to you as well.

Enter by the narrow gate, since the road that leads to perdition is wide and spacious; but it is a narrow gate and a hard road that leads to life.

Only a house built on a sound foundation can withstand the storm. Only a life build on the words of Jesus will be able to withstand the inevitable assaults, temptations and crises of life. However, it is not enough to listen to the words of Christ. We have to *do* them.

The more we listen to the words of Christ, the clearer the path will become for us. And the more we do his word, the happier we will become. It is never too late to begin to act on the words of Christ.

What to build on

If we want a building to last we must build it on something solid. You can plan and construct the most sophisticated building, but if it is not built on something solid, one day the winds will come and blow it down.

Alternatively, you can make an improvised shelter, which looks frail and probably is. But if it is attached to something solid, it has a good chance of withstanding the worst storm.

We also need something solid and reliable on which to build our lives. We need values that will not betray us. Jesus says, 'Everyone who hears these words of mine and acts of them will be like a sensible man who built his house on rock.'

What a wonderful promise. If we build our lives on his words, then we are building them on solid rock. There is no surer source of hope than the words of Jesus. Human opinions are rooted in appearances, and change from day to day, but the words of Jesus do no change or pass away. We would do well to build the house of our lives on his precious words.

However, there are a lot of other voices that, directly or indirectly, tell us to build our lives on very different values. These say something like this:

'If you want to get on in life, if you want to succeed, here are some of the pillars on which you must build.

Look after yourself. If you don't, nobody else will. Follow every path that advances your own interests. Never ask whether something is right, only if it benefits you.

Be ambitious. This means that on occasions you will have to throw your weight around, which means people may get hurt. But don't let that rob you of any sleep. It's all a rat race anyway.

Get to know the people who matter. You may have to grease a few palms along the way, but it will be worth it. But don't neglect your cronies either. Hopefully they will return the compliment. But do not concede as much as an inch to your opponents.

Try to project the image of a successful person. Even when things are far from well, don't let on.

Do not hesitate to raise your hat to religion and to God if you have to. Keep up the facade of outer observance if it enhances your respectability. But do not let religion rob you of a single one of your comforts or pleasures, or interfere in the slightest way with your standard of living.

These are some of the pillars you should build on. These should suffice to see your fortunes soar, and your house to rise steadily.'

What Jesus says is very different. He says, 'You are not a rat, so you don't have to behave like a rat. You are a human being and a child of God. The most important thing about you is your capacity for goodness.

The most important thing in life is to be a person of integrity, and to live rightly.

If you raise your status, make sure to raise yourself too. What sense does it make if you work hard at advancing your career, if you don't work at your character? What does it matter if you are always in the limelight if your soul is in darkness? What does it matter if your bank account is bulging if your heart is empty?

Take care of your conscience, and listen to it. If you live without a conscience, can you still call yourself a human being?

Do not be afraid of sacrifice. If your sole aim is to grab as many pleasures as possible out of life, you are doing a terrible injustice to yourself. Without sacrifice and struggle you can never grow up and discover who you are.

Be faithful to your promises. To live loosely is to discover one day, sooner or later, that you haven't anchored your boat to anything solid. When the storm strikes, you will find that you are alone and adrift. Fidelity is a beautiful thing. It is a precious stone, a true gem.

Do not be ashamed of your beliefs and values. Without beliefs and convictions, you are no better than a ship without rudder or port of destination.'

These are some of the pillars on which the Christian ought to build the house of his/her life. It is not enough merely to listen to the words of Christ. People may think they are religious and pious while failing hopelessly to live by the teachings of Christ.

We have to act on the words of Christ. We have to live them. Otherwise we are building on sand. Those who base their lives on the teachings of Christ are able to withstand all assaults, temptations and crises.

TENTH SUNDAY OF THE YEAR
Jesus. the friend of sinners

Praying with the Word of God today

INTRODUCTION AND CONFITEOR

In today's Gospel we see Jesus eating and drinking with sinners. We are gathered around the Lord's table, not because we think we are saints, but because we know we are sinners.

Let us turn to the Lord for forgiveness and healing. [Pause]

Lord Jesus, you came to heal the broken-hearted. Lord, have mercy.

You came to call sinners to repentance. Christ, have mercy.

You came to seek out and to save the lost. Lord, have mercy.

PRAYER OF THE FAITHFUL

Celebrant: Let us now bring our needs before God, remembering that what he wants from us is love, not sacrifice.

Response: Lord, hear our prayer.

Reader(s): For the Church: that through its ministry sinners may experience the compassion of Christ. [Pause] Let us pray to the Lord.

For those who make and enforce our laws: that they may know how to temper justice with mercy. [Pause] Let us pray to the Lord.

For the rejects and outcasts of our society: that the followers of Christ may show special care for them. [Pause] Let us pray to the Lord.

For all gathered here: that we may grow in closeness to Christ, the friend of sinners. [Pause] Let us pray to the Lord.

For those who have died in sad situations: that the Lord may welcome them into his kingdom as he welcomed the repentant thief. [Pause] Let us pray to the Lord.

For our own special needs. [Longer pause] Let us pray to the Lord.

Celebrant: Heavenly Father, source of life and holiness, you know our weakness. May we reach out with joy to grasp the hand you reach out to us in Christ, so that we may walk more readily in your ways. We ask this through Christ our Lord.

SIGN OF PEACE

Lord Jesus Christ, you did not shun sinners, but befriended them. Look not on our sins, but on the faith of your Church, and grant us the peace and unity of your kingdom where you live and reign for ever and ever.

BEFORE COMMUNION

Jesus dined with sinners. At the banquet of the Eucharist, Jesus is the host, we sinners are the guests. Happy are we who are called to his supper.

Lord, I am not worthy ...

PRAYER/REFLECTION

In hot countries a cloud may appear in the early morning,
only to quickly disappear under the heat of the sun.
'Your love is like a morning cloud'.
Thus God described the fickleness of his people.
Lord, your love is everlasting.
Look with compassion on us in our weakness,
and keep us faithful to you and to one another.

FINAL BLESSING

May you blessed with a steadfast love for God and for one another.

May you never doubt but that God will fulfill the promises he had made to us in Christ.

May you who have experienced Christ's compassion, become ministers of that compassion to others.

Sharing the Word of God today

SCRIPTURE NOTE

First Reading (Hos 6:3-6). The comparison of Israel to an unfaithful wife and Yahweh to a faithful husband is a dominant motif in Hosea. Yahweh was a God of faithfulness to his word. This too was asked of his people. But sadly their love was as fickle as a morning cloud. That is why God unleashed the prophets on them. What God wants from his people is not sacrifices and holocausts but love – a theme repeated in the Gospel.

Gospel (Mt 9:9-13). Jesus scandalised the Pharisees by eating and drinking with people who did not observe the dietary laws or the laws concerning ritual cleanness that were regarded as equally binding as the Law itself. The Pharisees regarded such people as sinners, and avoided social contact with them. Chief among these were tax collectors. Tax collectors were banned from the synagogue and treated as the dregs of society.

Jesus didn't deny that they were sinners. But he said that it was precisely to call sinners that he had come. Just as a doctor devotes his time not to the healthy but to the sick, so he had come to call not virtuous people but sinners to repentance.

In Jesus' eyes, the Pharisees are the descendants of the hypocrites of Hosea's day, who were assiduous at attending the liturgy of the sanctuary while they exploited the poor.

Second Reading (Rom 4:18-25). Abraham's faith in God should serve as a model for our faith in Christ. Abraham believed that God was able to bring life out of death (the 'death' of his old age and his wife's barren womb). We are justified through believing in God's action in the resurrection of Jesus. He was put to death for our sins and raised to life to justify us.

Jesus, the friend of sinners

One of the big temptations of religious people is to be judgemental, and to look down on those who appear not to be living by the same high standards as themselves.

The Pharisees shunned sinners. According to them, sinners were cursed by God, and therefore beyond redemption. Jesus, on the other hand, mixed with sinners. It was not a question of a few kind words, or a gesture or two, on his part. He associated with sinners. He shared their food and drink. He didn't just tolerate them. He *welcomed* them. He didn't wait for sinners to come to him. He went looking for them.

The religious leaders were scandalised. What scandalised them most was the fact that Jesus associated with sinners *while they were still sinners*. Just as today some people see compassion for the criminal as a betrayal of the victim, so the Pharisees saw Jesus' compassion for sinners as a betrayal of the virtuous.

Jesus' defence was straightforward. He went where the need was greatest. Who needed him the most: the virtuous or sinners? Sinners of course. Sinners would be healed, not by shunning them, but by caring for them.

In associating with sinners he wasn't condoning their situation. Rather, he was trying to show them a new way of life. He could not do this without associating with them and being sympathetic towards them. You never improve people by shunning them.

His attitude to sinners was not one of condemnation and denunciation. It was one of kindness and persuasion. He distinguished between the sin and the sinner. In his presence sinners felt accepted and loved just as they were. It's not surprising then that many of them heeded his message and changed their lives. (Matthew is an example of this). His goodness evoked goodness in them.

It would have been easier and more popular for him to go among the good. But he wasn't thinking of himself. He was thinking of others, and of the mission given him by his Father. That mission was to seek out and save the lost. He had been sent not to call the virtuous but sinners to repentance.

If we are sinners – and which of us is not a sinner? – then Christ loves us more, not less. It doesn't do us much good to be loved for being perfect. We need to be accepted and loved precisely as sinners. Jesus who sat down at Levi's table, now (in the Eucharist) invites us to sit at his table.

As sinners who have experienced the love of Christ, we must strive to become ministers of his mercy and compassion to others. We must be careful not to take our standards from the Tabloids, with their phoney righteousness and indignation: 'Lock them up and throw the key away!' 'Let him rot in hell!' Next week they are just as likely to destroy a good person by printing a story that is untrue.

We take our standards from Jesus. As a result, we envisage God less as a stern judge shaking his fist at our waywardness, than as a doctor who tends our wounds.

The call of Matthew

Jesus' choice of Matthew was a surprising one. Matthew was a tax collector. At that time tax collectors were hated by the people – they were seen as collaborators with their foreigner occupiers, the Romans. Besides, those who were in the tax-collecting business were in it for themselves.

But even more surprising was Matthew's immediate and whole-hearted response to the call of Jesus. How do we account for this? It may be that he was finding the job of tax collecting soul destroying. But there must have been positive reasons for his decision to leave everything and follow Jesus.

That decision can't have been an easy one for him. In meant turning his back on a secure and lucrative job. It meant sacrificing his own plans and ambitions. But he knew that he was being called to a new and more abundant life. The call of Jesus was like a warm, fructifying sun which shone especially for him, and which in due time would bring all his gifts to blossom and ripeness.

The great thing about Matthew was that he was open to change. He had the courage to answer a call, even though that call subverted all his values. Thus he challenges us. We can become so focused on our own goals and schedules that we refuse to be involved in anything that threatens those goals and schedules. Without realising it, we can create a world in which the ego is king. The ego is never happier than when controlling the agenda.

Besides, for all our industry, we may be stagnating. Each of us has a greater possibility. In the words of Emerson, 'There is in each of us a chamber, or a closet, that has never been opened.' If we are to realise this greater possibility, we need to be challenged to go beyond what we think we are capable of or have settled for.

All people are capable of bursts of greatness, such as in times of emergency. But when things return to normal they go back to sleep. However, now and again something happens that causes the soul of a particular person to burst into flame, so much so that afterwards he or she is never the same again.

The quality of people's lives is affected, not so much by what is given to them, as by what is asked of them.

Jesus' invitation to Matthew, 'Follow me', is directed at us also. We must try to respond as whole-heartedly as Matthew did. By so doing we will become more committed disciples of the Lord.

What I want is mercy, not sacrifice

It's tragic to find religious people devoid of the attribute that best defines us as human beings, namely, compassion for others. This was the chief fault of the Pharisees. Grim, earnest men, they practised severe virtues while condemning others who did not measure up to their standards.

Once there was an abbot called Anastasius. Anastasius was considered a saint by his fellow desert monks. One day when a monk by the name of Simon sinned and was told to leave the community, Anastasius got up and walked out with him, saying, 'I too am a sinner.' Simon left the monastery and fell very low. Years later he came to visit Anastasius as he was saying his evening prayers.

'Forgive me for interrupting your prayers and making you break your Rule,' Simon said.

'Don't worry,' Anastasius replied. 'My Rule is to receive you with hospitality.' And he gave him food and lodgings for the night.

Now Anastasius had an old copy of the Bible that was worth quite a bit of money. Seeing the book, Simon took it with him when he was leaving next morning. When Anastasius realised that he had stolen the book, he didn't follow him, fearing that he might only make him add the sin of perjury to that of theft. Simon went to a nearby merchant to sell the book, asking a high price.

'Give me the book for a little while so that I can find out whether it's worth that much,' the merchant said.

He took it to Anastasius. Anastasius took one look at it and said, 'Yes, this is a splendid book. In fact, it's worth much more.' The buyer came back and told the thief what Anastasius had said.

'Was that all he said?' Simon asked,

'That's all he said,' the merchant answered.

On hearing this, Simon was deeply moved, and said, 'I've changed my mind. I don't want to sell the book after all.'

He hastened back to Anastasius, and with tears in his eyes, gave him back the book, and begged his forgiveness. Anastasius received him with the same kindness as before. He simply said, 'I forgive you. Keep the book. Read a little from it each day, and pray to Christ who received sinners like us, and brought them back to God's love and friendship. Now go in peace.'

His fellow monks were surprised to see him wasting his time on someone like Simon, but Anastasias said, 'Tell me, if your robe is torn, will you throw it away?' And they replied, 'No, we will mend it and put it back on.' Then he said, 'If you take such care of your robe, will not God be merciful to one who bears his image?'

And the kindness of Anastasius paid off. Simon changed his life. He returned to the life of a monk and became known for his goodness and holiness.

Anastasius placed kindness, hospitality and mercy towards fellow human beings above the practice of penance and the observance of the Rule. He modelled himself on Jesus. Jesus sat down and ate with sinners, which means he became their friend.

To offer sacrifice to God is a great thing. But to show mercy to a fellow human being is an even greater thing, and is harder. After offering a sacrifice we feel good; we have done something, chalked up some merit. To show mercy is not easy, especially when the person involved deserves to be punished, and when it is in our power to punish him.

One thing helps: the conviction that we ourselves stand in daily need of God's mercy. Blessed are the merciful; they shall have mercy shown them.

Stories

(Here are two more stories that could be used in much the same way as the story about Anastasius.)

1. In India the untouchables did not belong to any caste. They were

barred from the temples. In the cities they lived in the slums, and did only the most menial jobs. In the country they were forbidden to use the wells.

Yet it was precisely the untouchables whom the great Mahatma Gandhi befriended. He ate and drank with them, and played with their children.

He once said: 'I do not want to be reborn. But if that should happen, I would like to find myself among the untouchables in order to share the suffering they are subjected to. In this way, I would have the chance to liberate them and myself from their miserable condition.'

2. Andrew had a doctor living on the same street. Since he enjoyed good health, he had no reason to visit the doctor, and so had only a nodding acquaintance with him. But he had heard from others that he was a kind and compassionate man.

Then Andrew got sick and went to see the doctor. The doctor welcomed him, and examined him with patience and thoroughness. He diagnosed what his trouble was and prescribed appropriate medication. Within a week Andrew was well again.

Prior to this Andrew had *heard* that the doctor was a kind man. Now he *knew it* at first hand. But this happened only because he got sick. Later he said to a neighbour, 'No one wants to get sick. But if one should get sick, it's nice to know that there is a doctor like him around.'

It is in and through our sins that we experience the goodness and mercy of Christ. This is not an excuse for sinning. But it's nice to know that this is how Christ receives sinners.

Saints bear witness to God. But so too do repentant sinners. Saints bear witness to God's grace and fidelity. Sinners bear witness to God's love and mercy.

ELEVENTH SUNDAY OF THE YEAR
He had compassion on them

Praying with the Word of God today

INTRODUCTION AND CONFITEOR

Jesus had compassion on the ordinary people of his day because he saw that they were like sheep without a shepherd. Jesus, the Good Shepherd, has compassion on us too.

To prepare ourselves to celebrate the sacred mysteries, let us call to mind our sins. [Pause]

Lord Jesus, you show the path to those who stray. Lord, have mercy.

You bind up hearts that are broken. Christ, have mercy.

You lead us to the green pastures of eternal life. Lord, have mercy.

PRAYER OF THE FAITHFUL

Celebrant: Jesus had compassion for the poor and the powerless, the sick and the sinner. Therefore, let us turn to him with confidence, laying our needs before him.

Response: Lord, hear us in your love.

Reader(s): For Christians: that they may not be content merely to pray for the relief of suffering in the world, but do something about it. [Pause] We pray in faith.

For our political and civil leaders: that they may show special concern for those suffering hardship and deprivation. [Pause] We pray in faith.

For the sick and all those undergoing serious operations: that they may experience God's healing power in their weakness. [Pause] We pray in faith.

For those who are feeling lonely and unloved: that they may know the compassion of Christ in their pain. [Pause] We pray in faith.

For all gathered here: that we who have experienced Christ's compassion, may be willing to show compassion to others. [Pause] We pray in faith.

For our own special needs. [Longer Pause] We pray in faith.

Celebrant: God of compassion, grant that we may never doubt the love of Christ, the Good Shepherd, and help us to love others as he has loved us. We ask this through the same Christ our Lord.

OUR FATHER

We see God's great love for us in the fact that Jesus died for us while we were still sinners. Let us pray to the God of love in the words Jesus gave us.

PRAYER/REFLECTION

The person in misery does not need
a look that judges and criticises,
but a comforting presence.
Jesus looked at the ordinary people,
and seeing how needy they were,
he had compassion on them,
and began to minister to them.
Lord, give us warm and generous hearts,
so that we who have experienced your compassion
may become agents of your compassion to others.

DISMISSAL

At the end of Mass we are not simply dismissed. We are sent out in the Lord's name and with the Lord's power, to help build up his kingdom in the world.

FINAL BLESSING

May you live a life worthy of God, who is calling you to share the glory of his kingdom.

May you treat each other in the same friendly way Christ has treated you.

May the Lord watch over you, keep you in his care, and bless you with his peace.

Sharing the Word of God today

SCRIPTURE NOTE

First Reading (Ex 19:2-6). This passage contains the promise of a covenant that Yahweh would make with the Israelites. Yahweh takes the initiative in choosing the Israelites. But they will be his chosen people only in so far as they keep their side of the pact. They are given a mission – to show forth in their lives the universal saving plan of God. In regarding Israel, all the other nations should be able to see the destiny to which Yahweh is calling them.

Gospel (Mt 9:36-10:8). Matthew 10:1-42 contains the Mission Sermon given by Jesus to the apostles before he sent them out. Today we have the first of three portions of it that are read in the Sunday Lectionary.

Into it Matthew inserts the names of the twelve apostles. Why twelve? Just as the old Israel was founded on twelve tribes, so the new Israel (the Church) will be founded on the twelve apostles.

Matthew stresses the compassion Jesus felt for the ordinary people, dejected because they lacked true leaders. The sight moves Jesus to think of the need for a mission by his disciples. The mission of the disciples mirrors that of Jesus in word and work.

The first task of the apostles was preaching – they were to alert people to the advent of the kingdom and the availability of salvation. Their second task was healing. He gave them the power to heal, and authority over unclean spirits. The birth of Christianity saw a liberation from the fear of demons, something that was all pervasive at the time.

For the moment, they are given a limited mission; they are to go only to 'the lost sheep of the house of Israel'. After his resurrection, they will be formally commissioned to undertake a universal mission (Mt 28:19).

Second Reading (Rom 5:6-11). Here Paul talks about God's amazing love for us. Proof of that love lies in the fact that Christ died for us while we were still sinners.

The Chosen Twelve

Jesus had many disciples. From the ranks of these he picked out twelve leaders. He called them *apostles*. The names of the twelve are given in today's Gospel. Who were these men and what qualifications did they have?

Today companies screen people for management positions. Let us imagine that the twelve apostles were sent by Jesus to a firm of consultants for screening. The following report, marked *private and confidential*, was sent back to him.

Dear Sir,

Thank you for submitting the resumes of the twelve men you have picked for management positions in your new organisation. All of them have now taken our battery of tests. We have run the results through our computer, and also arranged personal interviews for each of them. The results of all the tests are included, and we advise that you study each of them carefully.

Simon Peter: Without doubt he has some admirable qualities, but he has one fatal flaw – he is unreliable. Besides, he is emotionally unstable. Definitely not the man you would want to head your organisation.

Andrew has absolutely no qualities of leadership. He is just a follower.

James and John: are far too hotheaded. Besides, they are two very ambitious characters. They are completely lacking in the team concept. They will cause dissension among the others.

Philip and Bartholomew: These seem willing and sincere but we found it hard to get to know them. We are not convinced they have what it takes.

Thomas demonstrates a questioning attitude. People like him would undermine morale within the group.

Matthew, the tax collector, is undoubtedly a man of ability. But given the contempt in which tax collectors are held, he would project the wrong image for an organisation such as yours.

James (son of Alphaeus) *and Thaddaeus:* These two have no special qualities that we could see. Once again, we doubt if they have what it takes.

Simon has terrorist leanings. Are you aware that he belongs to a band of people called the Zealots. Their aim is to get the Romans out of Palestine by force. Definitely not suitable.

In our opinion all of the above eleven are lacking in background, education, and vocational aptitude for the type of enterprise you are contemplating. Therefore, we would recommend that you continue your search for persons of experience and proven ability.

That brings us to the last of your nominees – *Judas Iscariot.* This is one man who possesses real potential. He is a man of ability and resourcefulness, and has a keen business mind. We recommend him as your controller and right-hand man.

We wish you every success in your new venture.

Sincerely yours, Jordan Management Consultants.

Those assessors had a point. The apostles were just ordinary people. They came from ordinary walks of life – a number of them were fishermen. They had no special qualifications. They were far from perfect. They possessed the same human faults and failings we find in ourselves.

But Jesus saw good in each one of them, even in Judas. It shows that one doesn't have to be perfect or possess all the talents in order to be called by Jesus. Jesus didn't work with perfect material; he worked with ordinary material.

Yet these are the men Jesus chose. Jesus welded them together in friendship. He saw not only what they were, but also what they could be.

In the midst of them was Judas Iscariot, who turned out to be a traitor. God did not predestine Judas to play the role of traitor. Judas became a traitor through the choices he made. But he wasn't a demon. He was made from human material that might have become something very different.

We should learn from Judas never to be surprised or shocked by any sort of betrayal or apostasy in the Church. Judas was personally picked by Jesus. If Judas could go wrong, any of us can go wrong.

Choice is a privilege and an honour. But it is also a responsibility. The Israelites were chosen to be a light to the nations. The apostles were chosen to help Jesus with the harvest.

And through baptism we too are chosen. Though the harvest is immense, there is no need to be discouraged. We can't do everything, but we can do something.

Christ of the Gospels

As Christians we need to keep before us like a beacon the Christ of the Gospels. In his famous novel, *The Brothers Karamazov*, Fyodor Dostoevsky gives a moving portrayal of Christ. The action takes place in Seville during the Inquisition. Christ came to visit his people in their sufferings. Only the day before, a hundred heretics had been burned at the stake by order of the cardinal, the Grand Inquisitor.

Though Christ came without fanfare, the people recognised him at once. They crowded around him. He walked among them with an expression of gentleness on his face. He reached out his hands and blessed them. Many were healed of their diseases just by touching his robe.

He stopped at the steps of the cathedral as an open coffin with the body of a little girl in it was being carried out. A hush fell over the crowd. Then a whisper arose: 'He will raise the child'. And he did. However, no sooner had he done so than the Grand Inquisitor arrived in the square. When he saw what had happened, he had the stranger arrested and thrown into jail.

That night the Grand Inquisitor visited the prisoner in his cell. 'Is it really you?' he asked him. Receiving no reply he said, 'You have no need to say anything. You have said it all before. I don't know if you really are he. All I know is that tomorrow you will burn at the stake as the worst of all heretics, and the people who today kissed your feet, tomorrow will be throwing sticks on your fire. Do you realise that?'

He waited for some reply but none came. Then the stranger approached him, and with great gentleness, embraced him. That was his answer. For a moment the old man was confused. But he soon recovered. He went to the cell door, opened it, and said to him, 'Go, and come back no more – never, never!' And he let him out, and he disappeared into the dark streets and lanes of the sleeping city.

The Gospel of today's Mass gives us a beautiful picture of the compassionate Christ in action.

The religious leaders had nothing to offer the ordinary people in their sufferings – neither guidance, nor comfort, nor support. In fact, the opposite was the case. With their emphasis on the exact observance of the Law, they made life more burdensome for the people.

But Jesus was different. When he looked at the ordinary people, he didn't see a crowd but a collection of individuals, each with problems and worries, joys and sorrows. And far from despising them, he had compassion on them, and gave himself unsparingly to them.

We can forget what Christ was like. The Church can forget. It can put its doctrines and dogmas, its rules and regulations, before people. Individuals can put their private devotions before Christian living. Today there is an increasing preoccupation with revelations and apparitions. If we forget what Christ was like, we will get blown way off course. Today there is a hunger for the Christ of the Gospels.

Knowing how great the harvest was, Jesus decided to summon helpers. From his many followers he chose twelve to be his friends and companions in a special way. He named them *apostles* – people who are sent.

He knew it would be good for them. It would give them a stake in his work and an opportunity to use their gifts and talents.

But first he trained them. Not in a formal way, but by being a model for them. They learned to do things as he did them. Then he sent them out to others.

Today Jesus depends on us. To become an apostle one doesn't need to be an exceptional person or a specialist. First, one must become a disciple. Then all one needs is willingness and a warm heart. Is it not a great privilege to be an instrument of the compassion of Christ?

From disciples to apostles

Parish councils are now part and parcel of most parishes. Once I attended a study day organised for members of a parish council. The facilitator began by asking the members why they had joined the council. Almost all answered, 'because the parish priest asked me to join.'

At first I was disappointed. I had presumed they were all volunteers. And now I was discovering that they were more like conscripts. But then I thought: Was this not the way Jesus did it – as today's Gospel shows.

Jesus saw that the ordinary people were 'like sheep without a shepherd'. The sight moved him to think of the need for a mission by his disciples. Hence, out of the many disciples he had, he chose twelve to be *apostles*, and sent them out. The apostles were not volunteers. But neither were they conscripts. They were *recruits*. Jesus *called* them, and they agreed to join him. Remember the words Jesus said to the apostles at the Last Supper: 'You did not choose me, no, I chose you' (John 15:16).

Becoming an apostle involved a further step. It involved a progression from disciple to apostle. Not that one ever ceases to be a disciple, for we will be learners all our lives

Next the facilitator asked them why they had agreed to join the council. Two main answers were forthcoming: 1) they wanted to be more involved in their parish; 2) they wanted to give something back.

Becoming a member of the parish council involved the transition from passive to active Christians. Instead of being just takers they now become people who were willing to give. Faith is always demanding because it leads us beyond ourselves.

Why did Jesus involved the apostles in his work? He did this first of all for the sake of the people: he couldn't attend to them all himself. And secondly, he did it for the sake of the apostles. It gave them a stake in his work and an opportunity to use their gifts and talents.

Jesus himself is the true shepherd, but he desires his disciples to act as shepherds of the people in his place and after his manner. He makes them his co-workers.

God made human beings partners in the work of creation. And Christ made his disciples partners in the work of salvation. Through our baptism we are called to share in the ministry of Christ. We are co-workers with Christ. At the end of every Mass we are not simply dismissed. We are *sent out* to share with others what we have received from the Lord.

Many lay people are willing to get involved if given a chance. Here it is not academic qualifications that are required but a willingness to serve – to visit sick people, to spend time with the elderly, to comfort the bereaved, and so on.

To be involved benefits the lay people themselves; it does wonders for their faith. And it benefits the Church. It means that the Body of Christ has a lot of arms and legs. And a lot of work gets done that otherwise would not get done. The words of Jesus still ring true: 'The harvest is great, the labourers are few.'

TWELFTH SUNDAY OF THE YEAR
Do not be afraid

Praying with the Word of God today

INTRODUCTION AND CONFITEOR

Jesus asks us to be his witnesses in the world. And he says to us what he said to his first disciples, 'Do not be afraid.' Let us bring our fears to the Lord, and ask his help in overcoming them. [Pause]

Lord Jesus, you give us strength when we are weak. Lord, have mercy.

You give us courage when we are afraid. Christ, have mercy.

You give us new heart when we fail. Lord, have mercy.

PRAYER OF THE FAITHFUL

Celebrant: Just as Jeremiah committed his cause to the Lord, let us commit our needs and concerns to the Father, who knows every detail of our lives.

Response: Lord, in your great love, answer us.

Reader(s): For Church leaders: that they may proclaim the Gospel with courage and conviction. [Pause] Let us pray to the Lord.

For the leaders of governments: that God may guide their minds and hearts so that people everywhere may enjoy religious freedom, security, and peace. [Pause] Let us pray to the Lord.

For all those who are suffering because of their faith in Christ: that they may commit their cause to him, and know his strength in their weakness. [Pause] Let us pray to the Lord.

For the members of this community: that our lives may bear witness to the faith we profess with their lips. [Pause] Let us pray to the Lord.

For our own special needs. [Longer Pause] Let us pray to the Lord.

Celebrant: God of power and love, grant us in all our tasks your help, in all our doubts your guidance, in all our weaknesses your strength, in all our sorrows your consolation, and in all our dangers your protection. We ask this through Christ our Lord.

OUR FATHER

We are more precious to God than all the sparrows in the world. Let us pray to our heavenly Father in the words our Saviour gave us.

A CELTIC PRAYER

I rise today
with God's strength to direct me,
God's wisdom to guide me,
God's eyes to look before me,
God's ear to hear me,
God's word to speak for me,
God's hand to uphold me,
God's pathway before me,
God's shield to protect me,
God's host to save me –
from temptations,
from one man or many
that seek to destroy me. Amen.

FINAL BLESSING

May the Lord be within you to strengthen you, and outside you to protect you.

May the Lord be above you to watch over you, and beneath you to uphold you.

May the Lord be before you to guide you, and behind you to keep you from straying.

Sharing the Word of God today

SCRIPTURE NOTE

First Reading (Jer 20:10-13). Jeremiah's outcry 'terror from every side' (20:3) is now turned against him in derision and mockery. People who once were his friends have now turned against him, hoping to see his downfall so that they can take their revenge on him. Jeremiah, however, keeps faith in God, confident that God will vindicate him. However, he sees his vindication as involving the downfall of his enemies and prays for vengeance.

In this respect Jeremiah was a man of his time and must be judged accordingly. Nevertheless, Christians have always seen him as a figure of Christ. And Christians who suffer in bringing Christ's message to the world are meant to draw inspiration from him. The close relationship between witness and suffering is the connection with the Gospel.

Gospel (Mt 10:26-33). This is the second extract from the Mission Sermon (10:1-42) given by Jesus to the apostles before he sent them out.

Here he exhorts his disciples to open and fearless proclamation of the

Gospel. What he tells them during periods of private instruction must be given the greatest publicity by the disciples on mission.

Anticipating the kind of persecution and possible martyrdom that will greet the apostles in the future, Jesus urges them to have complete trust in the Father, who knows every detail of their lives. The exposure to death must not frighten them. If the Father watches over the life and death of even his smallest and least valuable creatures (sparrows were the cheapest edible birds), how much more will he watch over his children in all their trials.

As long as the apostles are faithful to their mission, they have nothing to fear, not even death itself. Faithful disciples will be vindicated by the Father in heaven.

Second Reading (Rom 5:12-15). St Paul draws a contrast between Christ and Adam: sin came into the world through Adam; abundant grace came through Jesus Christ. Paul says that 'the gift far outweighed the fall'. This thought is echoed in the Exultet of the Easter vigil: 'O happy fault, which gained for us so great a Redeemer!'

Do not be afraid

Fear is something we all have to cope with. All those who have accomplished great things have known fear at one time or another. Little wonder that the phrase 'Do not be afraid' occurs 366 times in the Bible.

Fear is not necessarily a bad thing. Fear sometimes has a protective function – it warns us of the presence of danger. In this case, fear is a grace. But fear can be a handicap. It can make cowards of us. Fear is the enemy of faith. Fear is the measure of our lack of faith.

All those who have accomplished great things have had to overcome fear. Take the example of the prophet Jeremiah (First Reading). He lived out his vocation during a time of great turmoil, which saw the defeat of Israel and the destruction of Jerusalem and the Temple. He lived with constant threats to his life. Fear followed him around like a shadow.

Yet, in spite of everything, he remained faithful to his calling. What was it that enabled him to overcome his fears and remain faithful to his mission? It was the conviction that God was on his side: 'The Lord is at my side, a might hero.' Therefore, he committed his cause to God.

When Jesus sent the apostles out to proclaim his teaching openly, they knew they would have to face persecution and possible martyrdom. Naturally they were afraid. Jesus understood their fears. So, not once but three times, he said to them, 'Do not be afraid.'

In saying this he was addressing their fears and trying to allay them. He was trying to move them beyond fear, knowing that fear could make them so timid as to be unable to fulfil their mission.

How did he suggest they might overcome their fears? He urged them to have complete trust in God. He assured them that God knew every detail of their lives, and would support them in every crisis. The exposure to death must not frighten them. If the Father watches over the life and death of the smallest and least valuable creatures (sparrows), how much more will he watch over his children in all their trials.

The Lord is at our side too. We mustn't allow our fears to cripple us. To live a Christian life requires courage. But then any meaningful living requires courage. What is needed in life is not so much heroism as ordinary courage.

Courage is the most important of all the virtues, because without it we can't practise any other virtue with constancy. Faith is a great source of courage. To be a disciple one needs a brave heart. As people of faith, we believe that God will give us the strength to cope with whatever comes.

Fear and courage are not mutually exclusive. They can and do coexist. Courage is not never being afraid. It is being afraid, and carrying on in spite of it.

Only God can allay our deepest fears. If we keep our eyes directed at God we will be able to move beyond fear to trust. The fact that our cause is right gives us great strength.

Someone to watch over us

When Jesus sent the apostles out to be his witnesses in the world, he knew that they would be putting their lives in danger. He knew that as a consequence they were afraid. He understood their fears, and tried to allay them. He told them not to be afraid of human beings who can kill the body but can do no more. They should fear God who can condemn a person to an even worse fate – eternal damnation.

There is such a thing as a holy fear of God. The Bible says, 'Fear of God is the beginning of wisdom.' It consists of the fear of displeasing God, the fear of losing God, the fear of eternal damnation. These can be powerful motivating forces. Fear sometimes has a protective function, warning us of the presence of danger. In this case, fear is a grace.

But Jesus is not telling us that we should base our relationship with God on fear. Rather, he is urging us to base it on trust. He says, 'Can you not buy two sparrows for a penny? And yet not one sparrow falls to the ground without your Father knowing ... So do not be afraid; you are worth more than many sparrows.'

What Jesus is doing is trying to move us from fear to trust. Fear creates suspicion, distance, defensiveness, and insecurity. Trust leads to closeness, intimacy, and a sense of safety. Good religion makes a person fearless. Bad religion increases a person's fears.

When Jesus says, 'Not one sparrow falls to the ground without you Father knowing,' he wants us to know how far-reaching and all embracing is the knowledge and care of God. Everything that happens to any of his creatures, even the most insignificant of them, is seen by God and is important to him – yes, even the fall of a single sparrow. The fact that God doesn't prevent this fall doesn't mean that God is indifferent to it. God is never indifferent about the fate of any of his creatures.

If then God is concerned about the sparrows, we can be sure that he is concerned about us who are his children. Still, we have no guarantee that nothing bad will happen to us. However, we believe that even should death come, God will take care of us.

Faith is not a comforting illusion that all is well. Rather, it means to know that life is full of risk and insecurity, and yet to rejoice in it – that is the essence of faith.

Nowadays, thanks to the security camera, we are often being watched, watched by a cold, dispassionate eye intent only on catching us in wrongdoing. The feeling that someone is *watching* you is not a pleasant feeling. But the feeling that someone is *watching over* you is a lovely feeling.

God is not watching us. God is watching over us. The conviction that God is watching over us, gives us comfort, strength and hope, especially in times of difficulty and danger. In the end only God can allay our deepest fears.

Witnessing in spite of fear

In the Gospel Jesus exhorts his disciples to open and fearless proclamation of the Gospel. What he tells them during periods of private instruction must be given the greatest publicity by the disciples on mission.

The Gospel must not be kept hidden because of indifference or fear. It has to be put on a stand so that people may see its light and give praise to the heavenly Father. If this is to happen, witnesses are needed, that is, people who are not afraid to be seen to be followers of Christ out there in the midst of a sceptical and sometimes hostile world.

Fear is one of the things that keeps Christians from a bold and generous witnessing to the Gospel. Fortunately, there are always those in the Church who, by the grace of God, are able to overcome fear and witness to the Gospel in the most difficult and dangerous circumstances. Oscar Romero is an outstanding example.

When Romero was made Archbishop of San Salvador in 1977 he was a conservative. But he soon changed when he saw what was happening in the country. Every Sunday he preached at the cathedral. His homilies so electrified the country that national affairs halted when he spoke from the altar. He made public the unspeakable crimes being committed, many by agents of the government.

He was under constant threat of death. Some of his best friends were murdered. And still he would not be silenced. Nor would he go into hiding or exile. 'At the first sight of danger the shepherd cannot run and leave the sheep to fend for themselves. I will stay with my people,' he said. He was shot dead in March 1980 while saying Mass.

Romero's life was a coherent expression of how faith and justice are meant to go hand in hand. According to him it didn't take courage. All it took was the understanding that his enemies dealt in fear, and that if he was not afraid of them, they would have no power over him. They might be able to kill his body, but they could not and would not kill his soul.

To live any kind of meaningful life requires courage. But to live a Christian life in today's world calls for a special kind of courage. People like Romaro are an inspiration to us. The words of Christ surely apply to them: 'If anyone declares himself for me before men, I will declare myself for him before my Father in heaven'.

Every place needs Christian witnesses. Christ says, 'Witness to me *before men*'. It is in the world we have to stand up and be counted. It's not good enough to be secret disciples of Christ. We have to give public witness to our Christian faith.

In some countries to witness to Christ is to place one's life in danger. But in most countries this is not the case. But the latter countries too need witnesses, because faith and Christian values are being eroded. It may be even harder to witness in the latter countries. What we are likely to face is not so much hostility or opposition, but something, which is even harder – a deadly indifference.

When Jesus said to his apostles, 'Do not be afraid,' he wasn't saying that they should never feel afraid. He knew that at times they would be afraid. The issue was what fear might do to them. It might paralyse them, or make them so timid as to be unable to fulfil their mission. What Jesus was doing was encouraging them so that they might be able to move beyond fear.

How were they to overcome their fear? He urged them to have complete trust in God, who lovingly watches over the life and death of even the smallest and least valuable of his creatures – the sparrows.

THIRTEENTH SUNDAY OF THE YEAR
Hospitality

Praying with the Word of God today

INTRODUCTION AND CONFITEOR

We are gathered in God's house. God is the host, we are the guests. We should feel at home here.

Since God accepts us, we should accept one another. Let us reflect on the fact that we are not always as open and welcoming towards other people as we should be. [Pause] The Lord himself sets us the example.

Lord Jesus, you are close to the broken-hearted. Lord, have mercy.

You bring pardon and peace to sinners. Christ, have mercy.

You bring hope to those who walk in the shadow of death. Lord, have mercy.

PRAYER OF THE FAITHFUL

Celebrant: God's love lasts forever. Therefore, let us bring our needs before him with confidence.

Response: Lord, hear our prayer.

Reader(s): For Christians: that they may be known for their generosity to the poor and their hospitality to the stranger. [Pause] Let us pray to the Lord.

For government leaders: that they may be generous towards refugees and displaced people. [Pause] Let us pray to the Lord.

For those who have come among us from other countries: that they may experience true Christian kindness. [Pause] Let us pray to the Lord.

For all gathered here: that we may be sensitive to the sufferings of those around us, and ensure that they do not have to carry their cross alone. [Pause] Let us pray to the Lord.

For our deceased relatives and all the faithful departed: that they may share Christ's victory over death and enjoy the vision of his glory in heaven. [Pause] Let us pray to the Lord.

For our own special needs. [Longer pause] Let us pray to the Lord.

Celebrant: God of love, look with compassion on us as we journey along the paths of time, and when our earthly pilgrimage is over, welcome us into your heavenly home, where we shall dwell with you for ever. We ask this through Christ our Lord.

OUR FATHER

Whatever the world may think of us, in God's house we know what we are

– we are God's precious daughters and sons. Let us pray to our heavenly Father as Jesus our Saviour and our Brother has taught us.

REFLECTION

Our size as human beings can be measured
by the circles we draw to take other people in.
The bigger the circle, the bigger the person.
A strong person isn't afraid of people who are different.
A wise person welcomes them.
By shutting other people out we deny ourselves
the riches of other people's experience.
In the beginning God gave the earth its shape.
He made it round. He included everybody.
So should we.

FINAL BLESSING

May you never be ashamed to suffer for being a Christian.

May you not be afraid of anything the world can throw at you, because Christ has overcome the world.

May the Lord bless you with a noble and generous heart.

Sharing the Word of God today

SCRIPTURE NOTE

First Reading (2 Kgs 4:8-11.14-16). This tells about a beautiful act of hospitality, and how God rewarded it. The episode is designed to enhance the reputation of Elijah, and to encourage the virtue of hospitality, especially towards a 'man of God'. A 'man of God' in this context means a bearer of God's word. This prepares us for what the Gospel says about the importance of showing hospitality to the envoys of Christ.

Gospel (Mt 10:37-42). This is the conclusion of the Mission Sermon (10:1-42) given by Jesus to the apostles before he sent them out.

Here he instructs the apostles on the sacrifices involved, and the priorities they must embrace, in being his envoys to the world. Following him will require difficult choices in relation both to family ties and life.

They must be ready if needs be to sacrifice the dearest things in life. In certain (rare) circumstances they might have to choose between him and their own relatives. But generosity will bring generous rewards.

Jesus also issues a challenge to those who hear the message of the envoys to receive them properly. The smallest act of hospitality to his envoys will not go unrewarded.

To receive a person's envoy is to receive the person himself. Welcome given to an envoy is a sign of openness to his mission and word. Receiving the missionaries is receiving Jesus, and receiving him is receiving the God who sent him.

Second Reading (Rom 6:3-4.8-11). Baptism is a communion with the passion, death and resurrection of Christ. To be baptised means to die to what is sinful in order to live the Christian life that comes to us from the risen Saviour. Just as Jesus emerged from the tomb a totally new being, so we are totally changed by baptism. The challenge then is to live up to what we are.

The cost of discipleship

Jesus says, 'Anyone who does not take up his cross and follow me is not worthy of me' (Gospel). The 'cross' is a metaphor for sacrifice. Jesus is saying that discipleship will involve sacrifice.

Many are put off by the idea of sacrifice. Sacrifice has a harsh ring to it. It suggests hardship, discipline, renunciation, and pain. Yet there is no achievement without sacrifice. It's true that sacrifice can crush people. The poet, W. B. Yeats says, 'Too long a sacrifice can make a stone of the heart.' But sacrifice can also bring out the very best in people.

And experience shows that people are capable of great sacrifice.

Take the example of marathon running. Here we have to consider not only the actual running of the marathon, but also the months of training that precede it. Yet today it is common to see twenty thousand people taking part in city marathons around the world.

There are two things that ease the burden of a sacrifice.

The first is when it is freely chosen. You won't find any conscripts among marathon runners. Those who run marathons do so because they choose to do so. This makes a huge difference. It enables them to bring all their energies to it.

The second is when the participants are highly motivated. People are capable of great sacrifices, provided they are motivated. For marathon runners motivation is everything. It is the fuel in their tank. It is the wind beneath their wings.

Where does the motivation come from? The vast majority do it because of the sense of achievement they derive from completing it. But many are running for charity. Hundreds of charities benefit from the fundraising.

All this shows that people are not afraid of sacrifice. It's amazing what people will endure when they want to do it and when they are highly motivated.

Besides, people respond to a challenge. The quality of people's lives is affected, not so much by what is given to them, as by what is asked of them.

Sacrifice is not the enemy of enjoyment. There are more happy people to be found in conditions of hardship and self-sacrifice than in conditions of ease and luxury. On observing the eagerness of young women to join Mother Teresa's Order, Malcolm Muggeridge said, 'Their obvious delight at being accepted to share a life of sacrifice, contrasts so sharply with the self-indulgence considered today to be synomymous with happiness and "quality of life".'

The greatest happiness of all is that which comes after the achievement of a difficult task that demanded the best of us.

Now to apply this to our following of Christ. The decision to follow Christ has to be a free one. It has to result from personal conviction. And we have to be motivated. We have to see it as something that is worthwhile. And anything worthwhile is rarely easy.

Jesus himself has given us the example. He chose the way of self-sacrifice and suffering. It wasn't that he was in love with suffering. No. It was because he chose the way of love. And love inevitably results in suffering. But it was through his suffering that he attained to glory. If we suffer with him on earth we will be glorified with him in heaven.

We have to follow Christ freely.

And we have to follow Christ out of love. Love is the greatest motivating power of all. Love can make even the hardest sacrifice sweet. And love enables one to give absolutely everything, so that one has nothing left.

Hospitality

Both the First Reading and the Gospel stress the greatness of hospitality shown to the envoys of God, that is, those who are bearers of God's word. But there is another kind of hospitality that is stressed again and again in the Bible, namely, hospitality to the stranger. Hospitality is the hallmark of a Christian.

At long last winter ended and spring came. All along the street the people rejoiced. They drew back their curtains and opened up their windows. Fresh air, sunlight, and warmth poured into their homes. 'Thank God for spring! Thank God for the sunshine!' they exclaimed.

Just then a beggar man appeared at the end of the street. He was quickly spotted through the open windows. One by one, down the length of the street, the windows were quickly closed, the curtains silently drawn, and the locks put back on the doors. The beggar man knocked on every door on the street, but not one door opened to him.

Forlornly he left the street and headed for somewhere else. No sooner had he disappeared than the curtains were pulled back again, and the windows and doors opened up once more. And again the sunshine and fresh air poured in, and all the people rejoiced.

Strange how our homes are always open to receive God's sunshine and fresh air, but not always open to receive a child of God, especially when he comes in poverty.

Hospitality is a beautiful thing. But nowadays hospitality is a very different matter from what it was in the old days when nobody locked their doors. Sadly, those days are gone. Today is the day of locks, bolts, chains, peep holes, alarm systems, dogs ... Yet today there is more need than ever for hospitality and friendliness. In the world today there is a lot of loneliness, and there are lots of strangers and displaced people.

Hospitality to a friend is no big deal. There is no risk involved, and there is every likelihood that the favour will be returned. But hospitality to a stranger is a great thing. However, there is a risk involved.

But Christ calls us to welcome the strangers in our midst. To be hospitable does not mean making them like us. It means accepting them as they are. This enables them to shed their strangeness, and become members of the community.

If Christians retreat into ghettos where they secure themselves and their property against those they consider as socially inferior to them, what hope is there for the world? Christ calls us to reach out. And the rewards are great. He said that even a trivial act of kindness, like giving a cup of cold water, would not go unrewarded in heaven. But there are earthly rewards too, and very great ones – the growth of understanding, friendliness, and co-operation, things our neighbourhoods are crying out for.

This is the kind of spring we ourselves can cause to visit our homes and streets, a spring that will banish from our midst the winter of mistrust, fear, and hostility. For the followers of Christ, hospitality is not an optional extra. It is at the very heart of the Gospel. And the ultimate motivation is clear: to welcome the stranger is to welcome Christ himself.

Hospitality is not so much about open doors as about open hearts. There is a risk in having an open heart. One can get hurt. But to open one's heart is to begin to live. To close it is to begin to die.

A cup of cold water

In Ireland when we want to welcome a person we say, 'Will you have a cup of tea?' How often we have said that to others, and how often others have said it to us. In itself, a cup of tea is a small thing. Yet it can make a person feel welcome.

This shows the importance of small deeds. Small deeds may not look much, but they create a friendly atmosphere. Small flowers give off little scent on their own. But put a bunch of them together, and they can fill a room with fragrance. The dawn chorus results from the singing of many little birds.

Jesus says that anyone who gives one of his disciples even a cup of cold water will be rewarded. Again, a cup of cold water isn't much. It is the biblical equivalent of our cup of tea. To give a cup of cold water is about the smallest thing we could do for another person. Yet in the desert it could be the difference between life and death. Which shows that a deed doesn't have to be big in order to mean a lot. Small deeds and small gifts are very important. Circumstances can magnify the effect of a small deed.

It's not how much we do that matters, but how much love we put into what we do. The spirit in which a deed is done, the person to whom it is done, and the circumstances, can magnify a small deed.

A small deed can bring great comfort to a person provided it has a certain quality. That quality is warmth. All deeds that come from the heart have that quality.

Few of us are given the chance to perform great deeds. But the chance to give 'a cup of water' can come our way several times in the course of a day. The 'cup of cold water' is a symbol of the small kind deed. Little deeds may not look much, but they can bring peace.

Small gestures can tell us more about a person's character than big gestures. Big gestures show us a person's power. Small gestures show us a person's humanity.

Giving is at the heart of the Gospel. It is of the very essence of Christianity. It is through giving that the heart remains open and one becomes a loving person.

Story

The following story shows how important a small deed can be. The Irish writer, Oscar Wilde, made a reputation for himself as a fine writer, and was regarded as a celebrity as well. But then he was sent to prison (for having a sexual relationship with a young man). It was a terrible humiliation for him.

As he was being brought by two policemen from prison to court, a noisy, hostile crowd had gathered. But then a friend of his appeared, who made a simple gesture of friendship and respect that silenced the crowd. As Wilde passed by, handcuffed and with bowed head, this man raised his hat to him. It was a very small thing, yet it meant a great deal to Wilde at the time.

Reflecting on that simple gesture Wilde later wrote: 'Men have gone to heaven for smaller things than that. I do not know to the present moment whether my friend is aware that I was even conscious of his action. It is not a thing for which one can render formal thanks in formal words. I store it in the treasure house of my heart. I keep it there as a secret debt that I can never possibly repay.

'It is embalmed and kept sweet by the myrrh of many tears. When wisdom has been profitless to me, and philosophy barren, and the proverbs and phrases of those who sought to give me consolation as dust and ashes in my mouth, the memory of that lowly silent act of love has unsealed for me all the wells of pity, made the desert blossom like a rose, and brought me out of the bitterness of lonely exile into harmony with the wounded, broken and great heart of the world' (*De Profundis*).

The readings underline the greatness of kindness shown to those who are bearers of God's word. But it is an even greater challenge to show kindness to one who is in disrepute.

FOURTEENTH SUNDAY OF THE YEAR
Come to me, all you who labour and are over-burdened

Praying with the Word of God today

INTRODUCTION AND CONFITEOR

At times life can become very burdensome. But Jesus invites us to come to him with our burdens and promises to give us rest.

Let us come to him now in a spirit of love and trust. [Pause]

Lord Jesus, you are close to the broken-hearted. Lord, have mercy.

You renew the strength of those who trust in you. Christ, have mercy.

You give peace of soul to the humble and the gentle. Lord, have mercy.

PRAYER OF THE FAITHFUL

Celebrant: Let us bring our burdens to the Lord, who supports all who fall and raises all who are bowed down.

Response: Lord, you are kind and full of compassion.

Reader(s): For the disciples of Jesus: that they may have compassion for those who are burdened. [Pause] Let us pray to the Lord.

For those who are burdened with the responsibility of office: that the Lord may bless them with the gifts of courage, wisdom and integrity. [Pause] Let us pray to the Lord.

For those who are burdened with a disability, or illness, or old age: that they may know the Lord's strength in their weakness. [Pause] Let us pray to the Lord.

For the members of this community: that the Lord may give us the strength to carry our own burdens, and the love that makes all burdens light. [Pause] Let us pray to the Lord.

For our loved ones who have died: that they may rest in the peace of God. [Pause] Let us pray to the Lord.

For our own special needs. [Longer pause] Let us pray to the Lord.

Celebrant: God of power and love, you give strength to the weary, and new courage to those who have lost heart. Hear the prayers of all who call on you in any trouble that they may have the joy of receiving your help in their need. We ask this through Christ our Lord.

OUR FATHER

No one knows the Father except the Son and those to whom the Son chooses to reveal him. Let us pray to our heavenly Father as Jesus the beloved Son has taught us.

REFLECTION

The Lord says to us, 'Come to me, all you who are weary
and carrying heavy burdens, and I will give you rest.'
Let us not be afraid then to come to the Lord.
Let us sit in his presence as in the shade of a tree.
Let us refresh ourselves here as at a running stream.
Here we will find rest. Here we will find peace.
And our yoke will become easy, and our burden light.

PRAYER

Lord, we have come to you with our many burdens.
As we go away from here, give us
the wisdom to let go of the burdens we should no longer carry,
the strength to carry the ones we should,
the humility to ask for help when we need it,
and the generosity to help another when we can.

FINAL BLESSING

May the Lord surround you with his favour as with a shield.

May the Lord be a refuge for you in times of distress, and a fortress in times of danger.

May the Lord turn the darkness before you into light, and rough places into level ground.

Sharing the Word of God today

SCRIPTURE NOTE

First Reading (Zech 9:9-10). The prophet announces the joyful news that the messianic king is coming. He portrays him, not as a proud warrior, but as a humble and gentle leader, who will put an end to war and establish peace – the messianic peace of Isaiah 11:1-9.

It was as such a Messiah that Jesus entered Jerusalem before his passion (Mt 21:5). His action was not a sudden inspiration but something wholly in character with his previous ministry. The humble and gentle Jesus (Gospel) came to usher in a peace the world cannot give (Jn 14:27).

Gospel (Mt 11:25-30). The first section contains part of a prayer of Jesus in which he praises God for hiding the mysteries of the kingdom from the learned and the clever (that is, proud religious experts such as the scribes and the Pharisees) and revealing them to the childlike (that is, his disciples).

The prayer reminds us of the discourses and prayers of John's Gospel. It's a celebration of the unique relationship of Jesus with the Father, a relationship that he (the Son) makes possible for those who believe in him.

The second section consists of a two-fold invitation that is matched by a two-fold promise. The Jewish rabbis spoke of the 'yoke of the Law', a yoke that had become an intolerable burden because of the traditions added to it. The yoke of Jesus is easy: it is the demand for love of God and neighbour. The humble and gentle Jesus (echo of First Reading) lightens the burdens of the poor, and brings peace to the humble.

Second Reading (Rom 8:9.11-13). Here St Paul contrasts life 'in the spirit' with life 'in the flesh'. 'Flesh' means human beings in their frailty and transience. 'Spirit' means the power that comes from God though Jesus Christ. If we choose to obey the Spirit rather than the flesh, we are choosing life over death.

Jesus reveals the Father

It gives us joy to know an important person. However, to know often simply means to know facts about the person. This is a very superficial way of knowing a person.

To really know a person we need to have a relationship with the person. Better again if it is a relationship based on trust and love. And also to know that we too are known and loved by the person.

In his biography of George Washington, Richard Brookhiser says, 'George Washington is with us every day, on our dollar bills and quarters. He looks down on us from Mount Rushmore. In the national capital that bears his name he has the most prominent memorial. More schools, streets and cities bear his name than that of any other American, and historians rank him among the greatest Presidents America has had.

'However, the omnipresence of Washington does not translate into familiarity. He is in our textbooks and our wallets, but not in our hearts. The fault is partly Washington's, since he tended to distance himself from the people.'

Some see God as distant and remote, not really concerned about us and our sufferings. Worse still, others see God as a judge, or a spy ready to pounce and punish.

Jesus knows the Father in a way no one else knows him. Because he knows the Father he is able to reveal him to us. You could say that was the reason he came on earth. Jesus revealed God as a loving and compassionate Father. A God who is passionately interested in us. A God whose concern is not to judge and condemn, but to heal and to save.

Simple people are often nearer to God than clever people. Many of the so-called wise people rejected Jesus, whereas the simple people accepted him. This caused Jesus to say, 'I bless you, Father, for hiding these things from the learned and the clever and revealing them to mere children.'

Jesus is not condemning intellectual power, but intellectual pride. It is not cleverness that shuts God out; it is pride. Intellectual pride is a dangerous thing. And it is not stupidity that enables God to come in; it is humility.

Rational argument is not a sufficient condition for acquiring faith, or – more accurately – receiving it. Experience constantly shows us how the mere force of argument is never enough by itself to convert someone to Christian faith. Faith depends on things that go beyond reason. There is need of an interior divine illumination.

Some great thinkers have managed to reason their way towards faith in God. But, just as often, the sharpness of a good brain led many others away.

Because of the coming of Jesus we no longer see God as someone remote. We are people for whom God is a mystery but no stranger. We see God as someone who is very close to us, who knows each of us and is concerned about each of us, because we are his children.

To know God in this way, and to have a close and loving relationship with him, should be a cause of great joy to us. God is like a spring within us from which we can drink and refresh ourselves.

Story

Evelyn Waugh wrote a play about Helena, mother of the Emperor Constantine. In it Helena is meditating on the coming of the Wise Men to the crib. They arrive late, missing the angels. Unlike the simple, barefoot shepherds who just ran over the grass to adore without a second thought, the Wise Men had travelled laboriously with their cumbersome and preposterous gifts. In Jerusalem they made a diplomatic call on Herod – because one does, after all, present one's credentials to the local authorities.

Helena understands and pities them. For her they represent those who are confused by knowledge and speculation, and who stand in danger by reason of their talents. She urges us to pray for them. She says, 'Pray for the great. Pray for the learned. Let them not be quite forgotten at the throne of God when the simple come into their kingdom.'

Waugh is right. Talent can be a barrier to faith. Simple, honest faith is a shining and beautiful thing – the faith of simple poor people, for whom God is all, without any doubt or any intellectual speculation.

But, as Helena says, there has to be a space too for those whose faith is threatened by their very cleverness: for the philosophers, the scientists, the writers and the artists. A few great thinkers have managed to reason their way towards faith in God. But, just as often, the sharpness of a good brain led them away.

Gentleness and humility

The prophet Zecchariah (First Reading) announces the joyful news that the messianic king is coming. He portrays him, not as a proud warrior, but as a humble and gentle leader, riding on a donkey. Jesus fulfilled this prophecy when he rode into Jerusalem on a donkey on Palm Sunday.

Jesus said to his disciples, 'Learn of me for I am gentle and humble of heart, and you will find rest for your souls'. Humility and gentleness are two beautiful virtues, but they don't seem to make much sense in today's competitive world.

Take *gentleness*. There is a belief that if you want to get on in life you have to be hard, because if you're gentle, people will walk all over you. Gentleness tends to be equated with timidity, passivity, and weakness.

Gentleness is not a form of weakness. It is a form of strength. Jesus was gentle. He was especially gentle towards the weak and the wounded (Mt 12:20). But this doesn't mean that he was weak. He was strong. And when the occasion demanded it he could be very assertive – as when he drove the traders out of the Temple.

Nothing is so strong as gentleness, and noting so gentle as real strength. It takes a strong, self-confident person to be gentle. A gentle person knows that growth results, not from forcing, but from nurturing. If you love, you are gentle. And there are certain tasks that only gentleness can accomplish. 'A gentle person treads lightly, listens carefully, looks tenderly, and touches with reverence' (Henri Nouwen).

And take *humility*. Unfortunately, like gentleness, humility is a misunderstood virtue. It is seen as weakness. Humility is not a form of weakness. It is a form of strength. It doesn't mean we have to demean ourselves. It means that we recognise our true greatness, while acknowledging from Whom it comes. Humility is the soil in which all other virtues flourish.

To the gentle and humble Jesus promises peace of soul. If we were gentler in our dealings with one another, we would have more peace in our homes and in the world. And if we were more humble, we would have more peace within ourselves and with others.

Those who are proud and insensitive make life burdensome for themselves and for others. Those who are gentle and humble make life less burdensome for themselves and others. St Seraphim says, 'Acquire inner peace, and a multitude of people will find salvation near you.'

Lightening burdens

'Come to me all you who labour and are overburdened, and I will give you rest.' These are some of the loveliest words in the Gospel. And they have great relevance for us. Nowadays many people live very pressurised lives. Stress has become a big factor in modern life.

During the 30 years he spent at Nazareth, Jesus lived among the ordinary people. He knew at firsthand how burdensome life was for them. Consequently, he had sympathy for the ordinary people and wanted to lighten their burdens. Hence his invitation: 'Come to me, all you who labour ...'

Many people accepted that invitation, and came to him with their burdens of sickness and misery. All had their burdens lightened as a result of meeting him. His mere presence could bring peace to an anguished soul.

What a contrast there was between his attitude towards the ordinary people and that of the scribes and Pharisees. The latter, with their emphasis on the exact observance of the Law, and their multiplication of rules and regulations, placed an impossible burden on the people. And they had little sympathy for those who found this burden too much for them. They wouldn't lift a finger to help them.

We too should accept his invitation and come to him with our burdens. Some of our burdens may be baggage, which we could and should let go of. There is a Zen story about an old man going on a spiritual journey with a heavy bag on his back. On his deathbed he passes on the bag to his disciple. When the disciple opens the bag he finds that it is empty. Yet he wonders why it weighed so much. And the old man says, 'It is the weight of everything in my life that I did not need to carry.'

Jesus doesn't promise that we will have no burdens. Some burdens we just have to bear. But the Lord does give us the strength to carry them. When we trust in God, another power becomes available to us, namely, the power of God. In the lovely words of Isaiah: 'Those who hope in the Lord renew their strength, they put out wings like eagles. They run and do not grow weary, walk and never tire.' (40:31) 'Those who hope in the Lord renew their strength, they put out wings like eagles. They run and do not grow weary, walk and never tire.'

Religion should not make life more burdensome for us. Quite the opposite. If Jesus placed any burden on us at all, it was that of loving one another. But in exhorting us to love one another, he is not laying a burden on us. He is inviting us to open our hearts, and to open our hearts is to begin to live.

Love can make a burden light and a sacrifice sweet. A woman who is deprived of food for a day can barely last out till the end of it. But a mother, who gives up food for a day so that her children may have something to eat, hardly notices it.

Stories

1. It is said that old people are not lonely because they have no one to share their burden. They are lonely because they have only their own burden to bear. Perhaps the same is true of others.

An 85-year old woman was being interviewed on her birthday. 'What advice would you have for people your age?' the reporter asked.

'Well,' said the old woman, 'at our age it is very important to keep using all our potential, otherwise it dries up. It is important to be with people, and, if it is at all possible, to earn one's living through service. That's what keeps us alive and well.'

'May I ask what exactly you do for a living at your age?'

'I look after an old lady in my neighbourhood,' she replied.

The strong should share the burdens of the weak. However, we shouldn't burden ourselves beyond the limit of grace, humanity and survival. Anyone of us can bear the burdens of only a few.

2. Today those who do menial jobs are poorly paid and generally taken for granted. They are valued, not for themselves, but only for the service they provide.

The Irish writer, John McGahern, told of an incident that happened when he was writer in residence at Trinity College, Dublin. A woman came in one day a week to clean his room. In less than an hour she'd have everything shining and in its proper place. She was a charming woman and often they talked as she cleaned. She told him how she waited each morning for the private bus at six o'clock that took the cleaners to Trinity, and that she was able to be home in time to cook the family dinner.

Of the professor who occupied the room before McGahern she said, 'I cleaned his room for fourteen years, and he never once spoke to me. I used to say "Good morning" at first, but after a while I didn't say anything. They say he's one of the cleverest men in the university, but I say he has the manners of a bowsie.'

How a little sensitivity, or a word of appreciation, would help to make a heavy burden light. It makes the world of difference when people are recognised and treated with respect.

3. A rabbi said to his disciples, 'Suppose I asked you to carry a bag for me and leave it in a house down the road, and suppose you generously did that, that would be good. If you thought there was just rubbish in the bag but you carried it because I asked you, that would be good. But if you knew there was gold in the bag, it would make a difference.'

To know the worth of what we are carrying changes everything.

FIFTEENTH SUNDAY OF THE YEAR
The Sower

Praying with the Word of God today

INTRODUCTION AND CONFITEOR

Jesus compared the word of God to a seed. If a seed is to bear fruit it has to be sown in favourable ground. The ground in which the seed of God's word is sown is the human heart.

Unfortunately our hearts are not always receptive. We need the Lord to touch our hearts so that they can receive his word. [Pause]

Lord Jesus, you soften our hearts when they are hard. Lord, have mercy.

You warm our hearts when they are cold. Christ, have mercy.

You open our hearts when they are closed. Lord, have mercy.

PRAYER OF THE FAITHFUL

Celebrant: Let us pray that the word of God may take root in our hearts and bear fruit in our lives.

Response: Lord, hear our prayer.

Reader(s): For the Church: that it may continue to proclaim the word of God to the world. [Pause] Let us pray to the Lord.

For world leaders: that they may seek the help and guidance of God in all their deliberations. [Pause] Let us pray to the Lord.

For parents, teachers, and preachers: that they may go on sowing the word, even when results are not forthcoming. [Pause] Let us pray to the Lord.

For the members of this community: that we may receive the word of God with noble and generous hearts. [Pause] Let us pray to the Lord.

For our loved ones who have died: that the Lord may keep them safe in his love. [Pause] Let us pray to the Lord.

For our own needs. [Longer pause] Let us pray to the Lord.

Celebrant: Lord, grant that what we have said with our lips, we may believe with our hearts, and practise with our lives. We ask this through Christ our Lord.

OUR FATHER

God cares for the earth by sending rain to make it fruitful. God cares for us by sending us his word. Let us pray to our heavenly Father in the words our Saviour gave us.

PRAYER/REFLECTION

The word of God is to the human heart
what a seed is to the earth.
And just as a seed needs favourable soil,
so the word of God needs a receptive heart.
Lord, soften our hearts with the rain of your grace,
and warm them with the sun of your love,
so that the precious seed of your word
may take root in our hearts, and bear fruit in our lives.

FINAL BLESSING

May the word of God be a lamp for you steps and a light for your path.
May the message of Christ, in all its richness, find a home in you.

And may you remember that what we suffer in this life can never be compared to the glory that awaits us in the next.

Sharing the Word of God today

SCRIPTURE NOTE

First Reading (Is 55:10-11). God cares for the earth by sending rain to make it fruitful. God cares for us by sending us his word. Our reading emphasis the effectiveness of God's word. The rain always produces positive results; eventually somewhere the earth responds and becomes fruitful. So God persists with his word until he gets a response.

Gospel (Mt 13:1-23). (Shorter form recommended). In the third great discourse – The Sermon in Parables 13:1-52 – Matthew brings together eight parables which illustrate various aspects of the kingdom. The Lectionary deals with all eight of these during this and the following two Sundays.

The chapter opens with the parable of the sower and its interpretation. Between the parable and its explanation Matthew inserts a piece as to why Jesus speaks in parables.

The shorter form is most likely the original form of the parable. The meaning of the original parable: despite all obstacles the word of God *will* bear fruit. It echoes the idea of the First Reading: the word of God achieves the end for which it was sent.

The early Church adapted the parable to the new situation in which they found themselves. The explanation reflects the missionary experience of the early Church. It accounts for the relative failure of the message of Jesus. Four obstacles have frustrated the growth of the kingdom: the shallow mind, the hard heart, worldly preoccupations, and persecution.

As to why Jesus speaks in parables: on the face of it, it might seem that he did so in order to prevent his hearers from understanding. But such a purpose is completely alien to the character of Jesus. Jesus used parables as an effective way of teaching. Those who were open to him received more. Those who had closed their minds against him received less. The fault lay not with Jesus but with the receivers.

Second Reading (Rom 8:18-23). St Paul says that the glory that awaits us in the next life far outweighs anything we could suffer in this life. Our redemption will be complete only at the resurrection, which includes the redemption of the whole physical universe.

A receptive heart

In the course of our lives we hear an enormous number of words. Most of these go in one ear and out the other, and so have no effect on our lives. But some have a profound effect on our lives. Why? Because they go straight to our hearts.

Jesus compared the word to a seed. It's a beautiful image. A seed has the potential to enrich. But for that to happen it needs to fall into favourable ground. So God's word has the power to enrich our lives, provided we receive it favourably.

Clearly the parable applies to all words. But Jesus was talking specifically about the word of God. The ground in which the precious seed of God's word is sown is the human heart. Just as there are some kinds of ground that are conducive to growth and others that militate against it, so it is with the human heart. There are states of heart that favour growth and states that hinder it.

The seed that fell on the beaten path represents those whose hearts are hard. Sadly, God's call makes no impression on them. A hard heart is a closed heart, so it can't receive. A hard heart inevitably becomes a barren heart.

The seed that fell on stony ground represents those whose hearts are resistant. God's call is heard alright but doesn't make a deep impression. When difficulties occur, it fades away.

The seed that fell among thorns represents those whose hearts are so full of worldly concerns that the call of God gets drowned out. It is not that God is deliberately excluded, but that there is no room for God.

And the seed that fell on good ground represents those who receive God's call with open and generous hearts, and in responding to it, produce a harvest of goodness.

God doesn't speak to us like a dictator speaks to his subjects. God's voice is a very gentle one. This is because it is the voice of love. Yet God's gentle voice has the power to turn our hearts from a desert into a garden.

God's word is essentially an appeal to our hearts. God longs for our hearts, and is continually calling us into communion with himself and with one another. Unfortunately, the heart is not always receptive.

In a *cri de coeur* the psalmist says to God's people: 'O that today you would listen to his voice! Harden not your hearts' (Ps 95:8). We would do well to heed that cry. To harden our hearts against anyone is bad. But to harden them against God would be a calamity.

St Teresa said: 'If God has not got your heart, he has nothing'. The question to ask then is: What place has God got in my heart? If God has no place in my heart, God will have no place in my life. If God has a central place in my heart, God will have a central place in my life. And my life will be more fruitful and joyful as a result.

We are not just hearers but also sowers of the word. Parents, teachers, and preachers sow a lot of words. Jesus' parable is a very encouraging one for sowers. It tells them not to be discouraged if no 'product' is apparent. Their job is to go on sowing and not to get disheartened. We must leave the harvest to God.

The prodigal sower

The prophet Isaiah (First Reading) tells us that God cares for the earth by sending rain to make it fruitful. And God cares for us by sending us his word. Our reading emphasis the effectiveness of God's word. The rain always produces positive results; eventually somewhere the earth responds and becomes fruitful. So God persists with his word until he gets a response.

The parable of the sower echoes that same idea: the word of God achieves the end for which it was sent. Despite the hard ground, predatory birds, stones, thorns, and weeds, the seed finally finds some good soil and produces a harvest, in some cases even a hundred per cent. The parable is telling us that despite all obstacles the word of God *will* bear fruit.

The parable was meant to encourage Jesus' disciples. It assured them that in spite of frustrations and apparent failures, the kingdom of God would grow.

But you might wonder at the carelessness of the sower. The sower sowed the seed haphazardly. Yes, some seed did fall on good ground. But some fell on the hard path, some on ground littered with stones, and some among thorns and briars. You might say that the sower was wasteful and foolish. One couldn't imagine any farmer scattering seed in such a fashion.

But there is another way of looking at this. You could say that the sower was extremely generous, even prodigal, with the seed. He was determined to give every part of the field a chance to produce something. Of course, the poorer parts would not be expected to produce as much as the more fertile parts.

The sower in the parable is an image of God. And God in his extravagance is unlike any farmer that ever lived. God scatters the seed around in a display of reckless generosity. Our God is like that – he sows the precious seed of his word in the most unlikely places.

And God keeps on sowing his word in human hearts even though he knows that much of what he sows will be eaten by the birds, or fall on rocks or among thorns. There is no sinner beyond the reach of God's mercy. God never gives up on anyone.

In his love, God is continually calling us to a better and more fruitful life. God doesn't speak to us like a dictator to his subjects. He speaks to us as a Father speaks to his children. His word is gentle because it is the voice of love. Yet that word is more effective than the word of the most powerful dictator – it can change our hearts.

God speaks to us in the Sacred Scriptures. But he also speaks to us through the events of our lives. But it the words of Scripture that help us to interpret what God is saying to us in those events. We will not be judged by results but only by the efforts we have made.

We are not just hearers of the word, we are also sowers of the word. This is particularly true in the case of parents, teachers, and preachers. But to some extent it is true of us all. Jesus' parable is a very encouraging one for sowers. It tells them not to be discouraged if no 'product' is apparent. Their job is to go on sowing the good seed and not to get discouraged. We must leave the harvest to God.

Importance of the word

How many words were spoken to us when we were young. How many seeds were dropped into the soil of our minds and hearts during the springtime of our lives. Those words came from our parents and from many others. We heard words of greeting and welcome, words of encouragement and affirmation, words of advice and guidance, words of correction and chastisement, words of warning and caution, words of comfort and consolation.

At the time we may not have appreciated those words, but we needed to hear them. Only God knows how many of those words took root in our lives. But one thing is clear: our lives would be immeasurably poorer without the sowing of those words.

As adults we still need the sowing of the word. Pity those people who hear nothing but words of criticism and blame. But happy those who hear words of encouragement, love and peace.

But human words, no matter how necessary, will never fully nourish us. We need God's word because we are God's children. Through his word, God guides and corrects us as a parent does a child. God's word is never a negative word. It is a word spoken in love. Just as food nourishes the body, so the word of God nourishes the spirit. 'Man doesn't live on bread alone but on every word that comes from the mouth of God' (Dt 8:3).

The word of God gives us guidance in times of doubt, reassurance in times of difficulty, comfort in times of sorrow, correction in times of foolishness, challenge in times of laziness, warning in times of danger, and hope in times of despair.

But there are many other voices vying for our attention. In fact, every day we are subjected to a veritable blizzard of words. There has never been so much talk on radio and television. How then can we hear or even recognise God's quiet word in the midst of this din? We can do so only by creating a little bit of stillness and quietness within us.

It is not enough merely to hear God's word; we have to do it. One of the ways of telling a false diamond from a true one is by means of the light. In the case of a false diamond, the light goes straight through the stone. In the case of a true diamond, the light remains inside it, bringing it to life and setting it on fire.

With some people, the word of God goes in and comes straight back out. They are mere hearers of the word. But those who 'keep the word', that is, who act on it, are transformed by it. God's word has the power to turn the human heart from a desert into a garden.

Stories

1. Some grains of wheat were found in the tomb of one of the kings of ancient Egypt. Someone took some of them and planted and watered them. To the amazement of everyone, the grains came to life and began to grow, yes, after five thousand years lying in a tomb.

The seed of God's word, once dropped into the human heart, never dies. It's never too late to act on the word of God. 'A word is dead when it is said, some say. I say it just begins to live that day' (Emily Dickinson).

2. There was a famous violin teacher by the name of Amadeus. Once four pupils were sent to him.

The first was Mary. She had only just started her music lessons when her friends began to pester her. They would come knocking at her door, begging her to come out to play. After a while she gave in, and that was the end of her music lessons.

The second was John. The idea to take music lessons hadn't come from him but from his parents. His heart wasn't in it. Still, for a while, it was exciting to hear the sound of the violin. But soon the novelty wore off. It was just too much hard work. He gave it up.

The third was James. He was multi-talented. He tried to cultivate all his interests. For a while he succeeded. But eventually something had to suffer. It was the music lessons. First he began to fall behind, then to neglect them, and finally he dropped them altogether. Amadeus was sad to see another of his pupils drop out.

The fourth was Anne. She was by no means the most talented of the four, but she really wanted to succeed. Right from the start, she put her heart and soul into it. Even so, there were times when practising got boring, and she would have preferred to be out playing with her friends. But she stuck to her lessons, and in the end graduated with first class honours.

The idea here is to show that the word of God comes to us as a friend. It is a sign of God's love for us. Through his word, God calls us to a fuller and more fruitful life. Its purpose is to enrich us, and a great enrichment does result when a person hears the word and acts on it. If we refuse to receive the word, or if we receive it but don't act on it, we are the losers.

SIXTEENTH SUNDAY OF THE YEAR
Weeds among the wheat

Praying with the Word of God today

INTRODUCTION AND CONFITEOR

We go to church, not because we think we are saints, but because we know we are sinners. Fortunately the Lord is very patient with us.

Let us call to mind our sins and ask for the Lord's forgiveness. [Pause]

Lord Jesus, you are good and forgiving to all who call on you. Lord, have mercy.

You are slow to anger and abounding in love. Christ, have mercy.

You do not abandon us when we stray, but call us back to the right path. Lord, have mercy.

PRAYER OF THE FAITHFUL

Celebrant: Let us now bring our needs before God, who is good and forgiving towards all who call on him with humility and trust.

Response: Give heed, O Lord, to our prayer.

Reader(s): For Christians: that they may strive to imitate the patience and compassion of Christ. [Pause] We pray in faith.

For all those in positions of authority: that they may show wisdom and understanding in the exercise of their authority. [Pause] We pray in faith.

For all those who have been uprooted as a result of bigotry or intolerance: that they may not allow themselves to be poisoned by bitterness. [Pause] We pray in faith.

For prisoners: that they may not allow the light of hope to be extinguished. [Pause] We pray in faith.

For the members of this community: that we may not be discouraged by our weakness or demoralised by our failures.[Pause] We pray in faith.

For our deceased relatives and friends, and all the faith departed: that the light of heaven may shine on them. [Pause] We pray in faith.

For our own special needs. [Longer pause] We pray in faith.

Celebrant: Heavenly Father, on the day of death, the harvest of our life will be poured out before you, wheat and weeds together. Let your wise hand sift through it; then keep what is worth keeping, and with the breath of your kindness blow the rest away. We ask this through Christ our Lord.

OUR FATHER

God governs with great lenience, and never gives up on anyone. Let us pray to our heavenly Father in the words our Saviour gave us.

REFLECTION

In general, we reap what we sow.
We can't expect to reap good if we sow evil.
Even though we have no absolute guarantee
that what we sow will always fall on good ground,
nevertheless, if we are careful to sow good seeds,
we can, within reason, trust our expectations,
because nature has shown,
that if what is planted bears fruit at all,
it will yield more of itself.

FINAL BLESSING

May you go on growing in the knowledge and love of our Lord and Saviour Jesus Christ.

May the Lord help you to resist evil and conquer it with good.

May you be filled with a joyful trust in God, and never tire of doing what is right.

Sharing the Word of God today

SCRIPTURE NOTE

First Reading (Wis 12:13.16-19). God's attitude towards his creatures is fundamentally one of care. Though God has both the knowledge and the power to root out evil people if he so desired, he is patient in the face of human wickedness and gives people the chance to repent. This should be a blueprint for our dealings with one another. Mercy and leniency towards our fellows is an expression not of weakness but of strength.

Gospel (Mt 13:24-43). (Short form recommended). Jesus' parable of the wheat and the weeds originally addressed the problem of sinners in the kingdom. The Pharisees believed that the kingdom was for saints only; sinners should be ruthlessly weeded out. But Jesus didn't agree, as this parable shows. The main point of the parable is clear: up to the last judgement, the kingdom will be a mixed bag, consisting of saints and sinners.

Later the parable was applied to the problem of sinners in the Church. Like the kingdom, the Church is also a mixed bag. It must not play God by trying to purify itself completely through purges and inquisitions. The definitive separation must be left to a future judgement by the Son of Man. Meanwhile, the erring are given time to mend their ways. The Church's part is to preach repentance and practice leniency.

The parables of the mustard seed and of the yeast are two very positive parables: they express the inexorable growth of the kingdom of God on earth. (The parable of the mustard seed reoccurs in Year B, Eleventh Sunday, and is dealt with there.)

Second Reading (Rom 8:26-27). Here Paul is talking of prayer – a profound form of prayer at that. The Holy Spirit helps us to pray when we can't find the words to express what is on our minds. (Paul has already assured us that the Holy Spirit has been given to us: Rom 5:5.) Those who find prayer difficult will take courage from Paul's words.

An inclusive Church

There have always been two views of the Church – one exclusive, the other inclusive. The exclusive view holds that the Church is for good people. The inclusive view holds that the Church must be open to all, to saints and sinners.

For some, the presence of sinners in the Church is a cause of scandal. If they had their way, only saints would be admitted. The issue of sinners in the Church was a big one for the early Christians. How did they resolve it? They turned for guidance to the teaching and practice of Jesus.

As regards his teaching, they had the parable of the wheat and the weeds to guide them. This parable was a response to this very question. The key sentence is: 'Let them *both* grow until the harvest.' This implies an inclusive view.

But it was especially Jesus' practice that guided them. Not only did he not exclude sinners, he directed his mission at them. He sought them out. He befriended them. He called them to a new way of life. And many responded by changing their lives. When self-righteous people (like the Pharisees) criticised him, he responded, 'I did not come to call the virtuous, but sinners' (Mt 9:13).

Jesus knew that human beings are complex. If only there were evil people, and it were necessary only to separate them from the rest of us and destroy them. But the line dividing good and evil cuts through the heart of every human being. To some extent each of us is like that field in the parable: wheat and weeds grow side by side in us. In other words, there is good and evil in each of us.

Jesus also knew that people could change. A weed will always be a weed. Not so people. A person may commit a grave sin, but, by the grace of God, can redeem himself/herself. St Paul is a good example. At one stage he was a leader in the persecution of the early Christians. Yet he was converted, and went on to become one of the greatest champions of the Christian faith.

So what should we do? As far as ourselves are concerned, the best thing we can do is take a good look into our own field. If we find some weeds there, as no doubt we will, there is no law against trying to rid ourselves of them. If we try to do so, we will discover what a painful process this is.

As far as others are concerned, we should try to act towards them as Jesus acted. Isn't it strange that he who had no trace of weed in him could be so understanding towards those who failed to measure up? He refused to weed out Judas. Rather, he loved him to the end. And he refused to weed out Peter. He saw the weeds in Peter's life, but he saw the wheat too. He knew that with encouragement the wheat would prevail. And it did. We too must believe that people can change. Just because someone has a past, doesn't mean he/she can't have a future.

Evil has to be resisted and, if possible, eradicated. But this can't be done by doing more evil. Evil can be overcome only by good.

God is a lot more tolerant than we are. God is lenient to all .. mild in his judgement .. He governs with great lenience (First Reading). God never gives up on anyone.

We must try to be as understanding and tolerant as God is. We must be patient – with ourselves and with others. We won't be judged on one act or on one period in our lives, but on our lives as a whole. The kingdom of God is still at the growing stage. Now is the time for conversion. This is why the sorting out can't come until the end. And the sorting out is God's business, not ours.

To sum up: The Church can do no better than imitate its Founder. It has to be big enough and loving enough to hold sinners in the fold. It if did not do so, it would not be the Church founded by Christ. Besides, a Church that admitted only saints would make as little sense as a hospital that admitted only healthy people.

Story

Reflecting on the years he spent in Stalin's labour camps, Alexander Solzhenitsyn has this to say: 'I learnt one great lesson from my years in prison camps. I learnt how a person becomes evil and how he becomes good. Gradually I came to realise that the line that separates good from evil passes not between states, or between classes, or between political parties, but right through every human heart. Even in hearts that are overwhelmed by evil, one small bridgehead of good is retained. And in the best of all hearts, there remains an unuprooted small corner of evil' (*The Gulag Archipelago*).

Weeds among the wheat

The farmer in Jesus' story planted good seed in his field and expected a bumper harvest. Soon a host of sturdy green shoots sprang up, covering the field from end to end. It looked as if his expectations would be fulfilled.

The farmer was going through a honeymoon period. Everybody goes through a honeymoon period, whether in marriage, or in a vocation, or in an undertaking ...

But then one morning the farmer discovered weeds growing among the shoots of wheat. Not just an odd weed here and there, but weeds everywhere. The honeymoon was over.

He got a terrible shock. He was bitterly disappointed. When he looked at the field now, all he could see were the weeds. The wheat seemed to have disappeared.

Sooner or later the weeds appear in our field too – a friend betrays us, a partner disappoints us or proves unfaithful ... We are shocked and hurt at the appearance of evil. The badness of bad people we expect, and can forearm ourselves against. But the badness of good people takes us by surprise, and hurts all the more. For a while at least, we tend to see everything as bad. We become very negative.

The farmer had done everything right, yet the weeds appeared. What could he do? The simple answer was to pull the weeds up. However, this proved impossible. They were growing so close to the stalks of wheat that he could not uproot them without uprooting the wheat as well.

So what did he do? Well, for one thing he calmed down. This enabled him to see things in better perspective. True, there were weeds in his precious field. But there was wheat there too, wheat that was just as green and vibrant as ever. He would have to work hard on the wheat, coaxing and encouraging it in the hope that it would outgrow the weeds.

We can do our best, yet things go wrong. We mustn't despair. The world is a mixture of light and darkness, good and evil. Wheat and weeds grow side by side in the same person, indeed, in ourselves. But all is not lost – there is good there too. No one understood this better than Jesus. Even in the small garden (the community of the apostles) which he tended carefully for three years, the weeds persisted, yet he didn't write it off.

We have to work on the good. But what about the evil? Evil has to be resisted. But we have to do so in such a way that we not do further evil in the process. Evil can be overcome only by good.

So the farmer set to work. It wasn't easy. But he tried to concentrate on the wheat. This proved a great help. When he looked closely at it he noticed that it was by reaching and straining upwards that it grew. He took heart from this because it meant that by making the wheat struggle harder, the weeds were actually having a beneficial effect on the crop.

Because of the presence of evil we have to struggle. But it is through struggle that we grow. Struggle awakens all that is good and precious within us. Indeed, the presence of evil could even be said to be necessary. Unless we had to make a choice between good and evil no virtue would be possible.

On the day of the harvest the farmer separated the weeds from the wheat. He reaped a fine harvest. Even though it fell short of the hundred per cent he had hoped for, the quality was excellent. And for some strange reason, he got more satisfaction from reaping that harvest than from any other. There is more joy when the victory is hard-won.

The parable is optimistic – in the end good triumphs. Truth and goodness are invincible. We live in a world where Christian values are not adhered to, or are despised. We must hold firm, and not grow discouraged.

Flawed goodness

We have a tendency to divide people into two categories: saints and sinners. However, this division is quite unreal. People are not so easily categorised. Human beings are complex, and we find things that are at odds with one another coexisting in the same human being.

Many people were inspired by the story of Oskar Schindler, who was the subject of the film, *Schindler's List*. Schindler was a German industrialist, who saved over a thousand Polish Jews from the concentration camps. Yet many who saw the film were surprised to discover that Schindler was a man endowed with all the human vices. Hence, he constitutes something of a moral puzzle.

Schindler certainly was no saint. In fact, he was riddled with contradictions. Unfaithful to his wife, he certainly knew how to enjoy the so-called good life – cigars, drink, women ... He was a Catholic, but in name only.

He was also a member of the Nazi party, and his avowed aim was to end the war with 'two trunks full of money'. He exploited the Jews as a source of cheap labour.

Yet there was a basic goodness about him. There was another and better side to him, and in spite of his lapses, he always returned to that better side. As the war went on he became appalled at the horrors of 'the final solution'. At considerable personal risk (he was twice arrested by the Nazis), he protected his workers from the death camps.

But Schindler was no angel. He was a mere human being, an essentially good human being, even though his goodness was seriously flawed. We wonder what he might have achieved had he not been so divided.

Some people don't seem to have any understanding of the divided nature of each human being. Their hero must be perfect. As soon as they discover a weakness in someone, they write the person off. But things are not that simple. Human beings are complex. They are an extraordinary mixture of good and evil. And the roots of good are so entwined with the roots of evil that one can't be pulled up without pulling up the other.

No one understood this better than Jesus. Even in the small garden (the apostolic group) which he tended lovingly for three years, the weeds persisted. Yet he didn't write it off. He refused to weed out Judas. He never rejected him, but loved him to the end. And he refused to weed out Peter. He saw the weeds in Peter's life – contradictions, flaws, and imperfections. But he saw the wheat too – generosity and capacity for leadership. He knew that in time the wheat would prevail. And it did.

It takes wisdom to recognise the frailty of the human character, the occasional unreliability of even the best of people, and the sometimes unexpected goodness of even the worst.

We must learn to be patient and lenient – towards ourselves in the first place. We must acknowledge the dark side of ourselves, without conceding victory to it. We must struggle on, confident that with God's help, the good will finally triumph.

And we must then be lenient towards others. We are too quick to classify people, and once we have classified them as evil, for them there is no redemption. God is the only who has a right and the knowledge to judge, yet God is patient and tolerant. Just because a man has a past, doesn't mean he can't have a future.

A person will be judged, not by a single act or stage in his life, but by his whole life. That is why judgement can't come until the end. And that judgement is for God, not for us. A man may make a great mistake, but by the grace of God redeem himself. Of what else but flawed creatures does God make saints?

SEVENTEENTH SUNDAY OF THE YEAR
The pearl of great price

Praying with the Word of God today

INTRODUCTION AND CONFITEOR

The theme of wisdom dominates today's liturgy. However, the wisdom in question is not worldly wisdom. It is divine wisdom. Through the gift of wisdom God communicates to us the meaning of our life, and the grandeur of our destiny.

Let us now call to mind our need of God's wisdom, and open ourselves to receive that wisdom. [Pause]

Lord Jesus, you guide the humble in the right path. Lord, have mercy.

You seek out and save the lost. Christ, have mercy.

You are close to the broken-hearted. Lord, have mercy.

PRAYER OF THE FAITHFUL

Celebrant: Divine wisdom is more precious that silver or gold. Let us pray to God for the gift of wisdom.

Response: Lord, hear our prayer.

Reader(s): For the followers of Christ: that they may never exchange what is lasting and priceless for what is passing and cheap. [Pause] Let us pray to the Lord.

For government leaders: that God may bless them with the gifts of wisdom and integrity. [Pause] Let us pray to the Lord.

For all those who live only for material things: that they may see the importance of the things of the spirit. [Pause] Let us pray to the Lord.

For all gathered here: that we may know the will of God, and have the strength to do it. [Pause] Let us pray to the Lord.

For our loved ones who have died: that they may rest in the peace of God. [Pause] Let us pray to the Lord.

For our own special needs. [Longer pause] Let us pray to the Lord.

Celebrant: God of love, help us to seek your kingdom as fervently as a merchant seeks a rare pearl, because only you can satisfy the longings of our hearts. We ask this through Christ our Lord.

OUR FATHER

A close relationship with God is a real treasure. Let us pray to our heavenly Father in the words our Saviour gave us.

PRAYER/REFLECTION

Jesus compared the kingdom of Heaven
to a net cast into the sea which catches all kinds of fish.
When it is full, the fisherman hauls it ashore,
and sorts out the good fish from the worthless fish.
The good he keeps, the worthless he throws away.
In a sense, all of us are fishers.
Each day we cast our net into the sea of life.
And at the end of the day we have a catch,
sometimes small, sometimes large.
May we take time to sift through that catch.
And may you, Lord, give us the wisdom to know
what to keep and what to throw away.

FINAL BLESSING

May you know the shortness of life that you may gain wisdom of heart.

May you never forget that we are but pilgrims on the earth, and that our true home is in heaven.

And may the Lord bless you with his protection so that whatever happens to you will work for your good.

Sharing the Word of God today

SCRIPTURE NOTE

First Reading (1 Kgs 3:5.7-12). The youthful Solomon had only just been chosen to succeed David as king, and felt inadequate to the task. Then God appeared to him in a dream and told him that he could have any gift he wanted. Solomon didn't ask for anything for himself. Instead he asked for the gift of wisdom, so that he might make a wise and discerning ruler of God's people. God was pleased with his choice and promised to give him wisdom in abundance. Sadly, the graced Solomon was unable to live up to his promise and his endowment.

This story is telling us that wisdom is the most precious gift anyone can have, that it belongs to God alone, and that it includes everything else that is worth having. Wisdom is the connection with the Gospel.

Gospel (Mt 13:44-52). The parables of the hidden treasure and the pearl of great price have the same message: the inestimable value of the kingdom. The kingdom of heaven is worth investing everything we have to acquire it. But we need the wisdom that comes from God to see this.

Notice that there is no stress here on sacrifice. Both men gladly give their all because they know that they have found so much more. They have discovered the treasure of the kingdom, and realise that it is worth any price.

The parable of the net has the same message as that of the wheat and the weeds (see last Sunday). In its present stage the kingdom contains both good and bad things. Only at the final judgement will they be separated.

The Sermon in Parables (13:1-52) ends with a summary parable of the householder and the new and old treasure. Those who have understood the parables are like a wise scribe who appreciates the new revelation in Jesus and the old revelation in Moses. Both shed light on each other, but the new is the definitive; it is the fulfilment of the old.

Second Reading (Rom 8:28-30). God turns everything to the spiritual advantage of those who love him. Those who base theories of predestination on this text are wide of the mark. God's plan for people is that they should be 'conformed to the image of his Son', and share in his glory. But this can't happen without human cooperation.

The pearl of great price

John Steinbeck has a story about a poor Mexican fisherman who made a meagre living diving for pearls. He dreamed that one day he would find a pearl of great value. One day he dived into the sea and came up with an oyster. He opened it, and there it was – the pearl of great price.

He was overjoyed, and started to make plans for his future. He was not greedy or over-ambitious. His aims were modest. He would sell the pearl. With the money, he would get an education for his son, some new clothes for his wife, and a hunting rifle for himself. It seemed that all his troubles were over. Alas, they were only beginning.

The pearl brought him nothing but trouble. Whereas prior to this he enjoyed good relations with his neighbours, now he didn't know whom to trust. Thieves broke into his hut at night. Having failed to get their hands on the pearl, they burned down the hut. The merchants told him the pearl was worthless. When he tried to sell it in another town, he was pursued by killer-thieves. He had to option but to kill all three of them, not however before one of them discharged a shot that killed his son.

At that point he lost the will to fight on. His house had been burned down, his son shot dead, and he himself had turned into a killer. Completely defeated, he returned to his village and threw the pearl back into the sea. Steinbeck's story is a pessimistic one. But sadly, that's how it often is with the treasures of this world.

Jesus also told a story about a man who found a pearl. But this pearl is guaranteed to bring its finder joy, not misery. It enables him to be at peace with others, not at enmity with them. It brings out the best in him, not the worst. And it is not just for a lucky or privileged few. God wants us all to possess it. And we can. It is closer and more accessible to us than we imagine.

What does this pearl consist in? The pearl is the kingdom of God.

The kingdom of God is really a very simple concept. It consists in being in a deep, loving relationship with God. Those who find this pearl are truly blessed. And even if in the eyes of the world they are poor, in the eyes of God they are rich, and in their heart of hearts they know it.

To taste the joy of the kingdom involves a letting go of all other things. Not in the sense that we have to give them up entirely – we still need a certain amount of them to live. But in the sense that they are no longer the be-all and the end-all of our lives.

The pearl is not an illusion. This sense of God, and of his love for us, is something truly wonderful. It brings peace to he soul, joy to the heart, and beauty to life. A simple but deeply religious woman said to me: 'I'm alone but I don't feel lonely because I have God to talk to.'

Only God can give us what we are looking for. Only God can satisfy the longings of our heart. That God, who St Paul tells us, can make all things work for our good. Not just the good things, but even the bad, the sad, and the painful things too.

The pearl of wisdom

Wisdom is the most precious gift a person can have. Without it all other things are useless because we won't know how to use them. On being told that he could have anything he wanted from God, Solomon asked for the gift of wisdom. God was pleased with his request and granted it to him.

However, this doesn't mean that wisdom was handed to him on a plate, so to speak. If acquired at all, wisdom is acquired gradually and often painfully. However, some experiences enable us to take a giant step forward.

Once there was an architect who desired to make progress in his career and to climb the social ladder. He worked very hard. In fact, his work was his life. He had little time for his family, and even less for the enjoyment of life. It was clear to everyone where his treasure was.

But then he had a heart attack. He was taken to hospital where he lay for days, drifting in an out of consciousness, and not knowing whether he would live or die. During moments of lucidity he saw some shadowy figures by his bedside. One day those figures came into focus and he recognised them. They were his wife and children who had been visiting him faithfully every day, spending hours at his bedside.

In that moment he saw where his true treasure lay – it lay in his family, in his home, in the gift of life, and of course in God. He saw how foolish he had been up to now. And he prayed with all his heart: 'Lord, give me back my life, and I'll be happy.' And he resolved that if he got well, he would turn his priorities upside down.

He made a full recovery. The day he walked out of hospital he was deliriously happy. Yet he didn't have anything that he hadn't before.

Through that painful experience the architect acquired much wisdom. He realised that the happiness he was looking for couldn't be found in material things. Riches bring anxiety; wisdom brings peace of mind.

Prior to this, he was completely focused on himself and his career. Now he decided to open himself to others and to life. Sometimes wisdom consists in appreciating and enjoying what we already have.

Wisdom is not the same thing as knowledge. Knowledge is acquired through hard work; wisdom is a gift of God. Through the gift of wisdom God communicates to us the meaning of life, and the grandeur of our destiny, which is to be with God.

Wisdom *is* the pearl of great price. It means knowing what is truly important in life. It means to be able to see life from God's point of view, and being able to live the way God wants us to live. If we don't have that, then no matter how many possessions we have, or how successful we are, we will not be happy.

Stories

1. There was this poor tailor who lived in Krakow. One night he had a dream in which a voice said to him, 'If you go to Prague and dig beneath a certain tree behind the emperor's castle, you will find a great treasure.'

Since the poor man placed great trust in dreams, he set out the very next day for Prague. However, when he got there he found that the castle was guarded. Unable to get across the bridge, he lived under it for a while. While there he became friends with the captain of the guard.

One day he shared his story with him. He said, 'I had a dream that if I got into the castle grounds, and went to a certain tree and dug there, I would find a treasure.'

'You're a very foolish man,' said the captain. 'You shouldn't believe that sort of thing. I have dreams myself. Once I had a dream that over in Krakow there lived a poor tailor, not unlike you. I dreamt that if I went to his house, and dug behind his stove, I would find a treasure that somebody had buried there a long time ago. Of course, I dismissed it as foolishness.'

The tailor thanked him, went back home, dug behind his own hearth, and found the treasure.

We will never be happy unless we find the treasure that God has hidden in our own field. If we do not find happiness within ourselves, we won't find it elsewhere.

2. Once there was a famer who owned a small farm of land. The land was stony but he worked hard, and for a while was blessed with happiness and contentment. But then he began to feel that something was missing

in his life. There must be more to life, he thought.

One evening a stranger arrived and asked for a night's lodgings. The farmer was only too glad to take him because he was pining for company and excitement.

Around the fire that night the stranger talked about diamonds. He told the farmer that if he could find a diamond the size of the nail of his little finger, he would never have to work again.

Next day the stranger departed leaving the farmer unhappy and restless. As the days went by he got more and more restless. He began to neglect his farm. Finally, he sold it cheaply, and went off roaming the country in search of diamonds. He travelled far but found none.

Meanwhile, the man who bought his farm was working hard. One day, while out ploughing, the plough turned up a stone that shone in the sunlight. It turned out to be a diamond. When he went back to the spot he found lots more. It turned out to be one of the richest diamond mines ever found in South Africa.

While we cannot but feel sorry for the farmer, we have to say that he was a very foolish man. Had he persevered with what he had, he would undoubtedly have found the mine himelf.

There are many people like that. It's not that they are afraid of hard work and sacrifice. It's that they don't know what is important. They pursue wrong goals. They look in the wrong places, and end up selling their birthright.

God turns everything to our good

It's not possible to go through life without some painful things happening to us. Some of these things we bring on ourselves (e.g. an addiction). Others are things we suffer at the hands of others (e.g. a betrayal). And others are things that happen through nobody's fault (e.g. an accident).

We tend to write off these experiences as being worse than useless. That nothing can be salvaged from them. That everything has gone down the river and is irretrievably lost.

This is where St Paul comes to our rescue. In today's Second Reading he says a wonderfully consoling thing. He says that God can turn everything to the benefit of those who love him. This is not to say that God wills bad things to happen to us. No. But when bad things do happen to us, God helps us, not only to pick up the pieces, but also to reap a harvest from the wreckage.

There was a king who owned a very valuable diamond. One day an accident happened and the diamond got deeply scratched. The king consulted experts to see if anything could be done to save the diamond. But they told him that even if they were to polish it, they would never be able to repair the wound it had suffered.

So the king locked the diamond in his vault where it lay hidden and use-less for years. Then one day a very famous diamond cutter arrived in the capital. At the king's invitation he undertook to examine the diamond to see if anything could be done with it. After examining it carefully he said, 'Your Majesty, I will make the diamond look even more beautiful than it was before the accident.'

On hearing this the other diamond cutters laughed. But the king was delighted, and gave him permission to work on the diamond. Bringing all his artistry to bear on it, he proceeded to engrave a beautiful rose on the diamond, using the deep scratch as the stem of the rose. When the king and the diamond cutters saw what he had done they were filled with admiration. It wasn't just a clever cover-up. He had taken the diamond's fault and transformed it into something beautiful.

In the same way, God can help us to transform our worst misfortune into a blessing. God can bring good out of anything – even out of our mistakes, failures, sorrows, wounds, and tragedies. Even our sins can be part of our fumbling attempts to love. Our mistakes belong to our journey to the truth.

The story of redemption is a great symphony that embraces all our er-rors and false notes, and in which beauty finally triumphs. It is not that God wipes out our wrong notes, or pretends that they never happened, but that he finds a place for them in the musical score that redeems them.

When we look back over our lives, we see that the things that hurt us and the things that helped us cannot be separated from each other. We must try to see the guiding hand of a loving God in all that has brought us to where we are now.

Not all that happens to us is determined by God's will, but all is en-compassed by his love. Through God's goodness and mercy, our mistakes, our fumblings, yes, even our sins, become part the process that leads to fruitfulness.

Thus our troubles can bring us closer to God. From painful experiences and difficult times we learn that God is faithful to us. And if the difficult times should return, we will remember what God has already done for us, and we will not lose heart.

EIGHTEENTH SUNDAY OF THE YEAR
Food for the hungry

Praying with the Word of God today

INTRODUCTION AND CONFITEOR

We read in today's Gospel how on one occasion the people forgot everything, including food, and followed Jesus to a lonely place. Taking pity on them, Jesus first taught them and then fed them.

We too have left everything, if only for a while, and have come here to listen to the Lord's words and to be fed with the food of the Eucharist. [Pause]

Lord Jesus, you are kind and full of compassion, slow to anger, abounding in love. Lord, have mercy.

You are just in all your ways, and loving in all your deeds. Christ, have mercy.

Lord, you are close to all who call on you, who call on you from their hearts. Lord, have mercy.

PRAYER OF THE FAITHFUL

Celebrant: The Lord is close to all who call on him from their hearts. Let us bring our needs before him with confidence.

Response: Lord, grant the desires of all who live.

Reader(s): For Christians: that they may be known for their compassion for the suffering, and their generosity to the needy. [Pause] We pray to the Lord.

For government leaders: that they may strive to ensure that people everywhere have food to eat. [Pause] We pray to the Lord.

For the sick, the lonely, and the unloved: that in their pain they may know God's comforting. [Pause] We pray to the Lord.

For all gathered here: that we may hunger for the food that only God can give us. [Pause] We pray to the Lord.

For our departed relatives and friends, who partook of the Eucharist: that they may have a seat at the banquet of eternal life in heaven. [Pause] We pray to the Lord.

For our own special needs. [Longer Pause] We pray to the Lord.

Celebrant: God of love and mercy, grant your children food for soul and body, so that we may walk steadfastly towards the promised land of eternal life, where all our hungers will be satisfied. We make this prayer through Christ our Lord.

OUR FATHER

St Paul says that nothing can separate us from the love of God. Let us pray to the God of love in the words our Saviour gave us.

REFLECTION

I may be poor but no millionaire can be so happy as me,
if they haven't got the love of God in their souls.
Think what it is – not to hate anything but evil;
to be full of love for every creature;
to be frightened of nothing;
to be sure that all things will turn to good;
to know that nothing can separate us from God who loves us,
and who fills our souls with peace and joy.
This blessedness is offered to everyone;
it is the good news that Jesus came to preach to the poor.
   George Elliot

FINAL BLESSING

May you have an unshakeable confidence in God's love for you.

May you be convinced that nothing can separate you from that love.

And may you be good witnesses for the Gospel by the love and joy you radiate.

Sharing the Word of God today

SCRIPTURE NOTE

First Reading (Is 55:1-3). This contains an invitation, addressed to the exiles in Babylon, to come to a banquet at which the food and drink are both free and fully satisfying. The banquet is a metaphor for the new covenant Yahweh wants to make with his people (in place of the old one that had been broken by the people's infidelities). The banquet image is the connection with the Gospel.

Gospel (Mt 14:13-21). After receiving the news of the death of John the Baptist, Jesus withdrew to a lonely place where he and the apostles could be by themselves. This is the context for the miracle of the loaves and fishes.

We cannot get back to what actually happened. But we can see what it meant to Matthew and his readers. For them the miracle recalled the Old Testament story of how, at the intercession of Moses, God provided manna for his people in the desert. Jesus is the new Moses who feeds his people in the desert.

In this feeding they saw an anticipation of the Eucharist. The gestures and words used are the exact same ones that are used in describing the institution of the Eucharist at the last supper: 'He *took* the bread ... *blessed* it ... *broke* it ... and *gave* it to them.' The Eucharist in turn anticipates the final banquet of the kingdom.

Some have attempted to explain the miracle in terms of Jesus touching the hearts of those present so that they opened their knapsacks and brought out hidden food. To go down this road may be tempting, but it is to risk missing the meaning of the miracle.

Second Reading (Rom 8:35.37-39). This is a wonderful reading. No matter what bad times we may have to go through, we remain undaunted, because we are certain that Christ loves us. Nothing in all of creation can separate us from the love of God that we have experienced in Christ Jesus.

Miracle of generosity

Giving is at the heart of the Gospel. Basically, there are two kinds of giving. One is when the giver gives what he/she can live without. This kind of giving doesn't really hurt. But there is another kind of giving that does hurt, namely, when the gift is as desperately needed by the giver as by the receiver. Here a real sacrifice is involved.

Mother Teresa gives an example of the second kind of giving. Once she came across a Hindu family that hadn't eaten for days. She took a small quantity of rice and gave it to the family. What happened next surprised her.

Without a moment's hesitation, the mother of the family divided the rice into two halves. Then she took one half of it to the family next-door, which happened to be a Moslem family.

Seeing this, Mother Teresa said to her, 'How much will you have left over? Aren't there enough of yourselves?'

'But they haven't eaten for days either,' the woman replied.

Generosity such as that humbles us.

There are a number of examples of this kind of generosity in today's Gospel. The miracle of the feeding of the 5,000 was made possible by the gift of five loaves and two fish. Acording to St John it was a small boy who made that gift (6:9). It was a small thing in itself, but for the little boy it was a big thing because it was all he had.

Then there is the marvellous generosity of Jesus. To appreciate this we need to consider the circumstances of the miracle. He had just learned that his cousin, John, had been murdered. He needed peace and quiet. That is why he and the apostles crossed to the far side of the lake. But when he stepped out of the boat he found a throng of people waiting for him. He might have got angry and sent them away. Instead, he had compassion on them and gave himself completely to them.

Finally there is the marvellous generosity with which he fed them. Each got as much as he wanted, and even so there were twelve baskets of leftovers.

The story of the feeding of the multitude was treasured by the early Christians. It is the only miracle that is contained in all four Gospels. Why was it so treasured? Because it recalled the Old Testament story of God's people being fed by manna in the desert. The early Christians came to regard Jesus as the new Moses who feeds his people in the desert.

They also saw in this feeding a foreshadowing of the Eucharist. At the table of the Eucharist Jesus nourished them with something greater than the manna. The manna sustained life temporarily. The food of the Eucharist sustains life eternally.

And it is at the table of the Eucharist that Jesus nourishes us now. Only at God's table can we get the nourishment our hearts are longing for. In the Eucharist we are nourished with the Word of God and the bread of eternal life.

As the people went back to their homes at the end of that day they knew they had experienced the goodness and love of God – that love Paul talks about, a love from which nothing can separate us.

In the Eucharist we taste the love of God. The proof that we have experienced that love will be our willingness to share it with others. It is not so much about giving *things*. It is more about giving of *ourselves*, of our time, and our gifts. We may be able to give only in small ways and in small amounts. However, from the little boy in the Gospel, we see that a small amount can become a big amount when placed in the hands of the Lord.

A modern version of the miracle

Christ fed 5,000 people in the desert. Everyone got as much as they wanted, and still there were twelve baskets of food left over. It was an astonishing display of compassion and generosity on his part. But he couldn't have done it without the five loaves and two fish given him by a young boy (see Jn 6:9), and without the help of the apostles.

Mother Teresa fed 9,000 people every day in Calcutta. But she couldn't have done so without the generosity of many people around the world, and the assistance of her nuns and lay helpers. Here is an example of the kind of generosity that made this daily miracle possible.

One day a young couple came into their house and gave them a large sum of money.

'Where did you get so much money?' Mother Teresa asked.

'We were married two days ago,' they replied. 'We decided not to have a wedding feast, but to give the money to feed the poor instead.'

'Why would you do this?' she asked.

'Because we love each other and wanted to begin our married life with an act of sacrifice,' they relied.

What made their act of generosity all the more amazing was the fact that both of them were high-caste Hindus, who normally will have nothing to do with the poor.

Sometimes a small deed takes on an importance far beyond its actual value. When Jesus told the apostles to give food to the people, they said, 'All we have with us is five loaves and two fish.' On hearing this Jesus might have said, 'That's no good. Forget the whole thing. Send the people home.' But he said no such thing. Instead, he took the five loaves and two fish, and with them fed the people.

There is a tendency today to go in for the big gesture, and to neglect the small gesture. Hence, we may be tempted to think that because our contribution is small, it will make no difference. So we excuse ourselves from doing anything. But everything helps. Enough crumbs make a loaf. Besides, our example may trigger a response in others.

Feeding hungry bodies is one of the corporal works of mercy. It is some-thing we could and should be able to do for ourselves. But there is a food that only God can give.

Jesus was concerned about those who were hungry. However, he didn't just feed people's bodies; he nourished their minds, their hearts, and their spirits. The people Jesus fed in that lonely place that day went home fully nourished, in body and in spirit.

The miracle involved a lot more than giving food to people. It was an expression of the care and love of God for his people. The food is a symbol of the life God wants us to have – life here on earth, and eternal life in the hereafter.

The story of the feeding of the multitude was treasured by the early Christians. The miracle recalled the Old Testament story of manna in the desert. For them Jesus was the new Moses who feeds his people in the desert. Then they saw in this feeding an anticipation of the Eucharist. It was at the table of the Eucharist that Jesus nourished them.

In the Eucharist Jesus nourishes us now. Only at God's table can we get the nourishment our hearts are longing for. In the Eucharist we are nourished with the Word of God and the Bread of Life. In the Eucharist we taste the love of God. The proof that we have experienced that love will be our willingness to share it with others.

Nothing can separate us from the love of God

In July 2002, nine coal miners in Pennsylvania got trapped in a shaft 240 ft below the ground when it was flooded with water. They sought refuge in the one area that remained free of water. From the start they decided that they would live or die as a group. So they bound themselves together so they wouldn't float away from one another in the dark. It was an amazing display of solidarity. Without doubt that bond was a major factor in their survival. Their ordeal lasted three days, after which all were successfully rescued.

It reminds us of what Paul says about God's solidarity with us in Christ. In one of the most memorable passages in the Bible, he assures us that nothing in the whole of creation can separate us from the love of God:

'What will separate us from the love of Christ? Will anguish, or persecution, or hunger, or nakedness, or danger? No. All of these things we can conquer through him who loved us. Neither death nor life, nor angels, nor present things, nor future things, nor height nor depth, nor any creature will be able to separate us from the love of God in Christ Jesus our Lord.'

Paul was talking from experience. He had known lots of troubles, as he tells us in another of his letters (2 Cor 11: 23-29). We are talking about major stuff. He was imprisoned. He was whipped to the point of death. Five times he received 39 lashes from the Jews. Three times he was beaten with sticks. Once he was stoned and left for dead. Three times he was shipwrecked, spending a day and a night adrift in the sea. He travelled thousands of miles, often narrowly escaping death from robbers and enemies. He knew hunger and thirst, cold and nakedness. Yet he overcame all of these through the power of God who loved him in Christ. His strength came from the conviction of God's love for him.

Each of us could draw up a list of troubles we have experienced. The list would be different for everyone. However, as soon as trouble hits us, we begin to think negatively. We feel that God no longer loves us, or has even abandoned us.

We must try to imitate Paul. The more his troubles abounded, the more he clung to God. Only God can provide us with a love that is trustworthy, a love that never changes.

If we do as Paul did, then our trials, far from separating us from God, will actually bring us closer to God, because in them we experience his power and his love.

The love we are talking about here is not our love for God, but God's love for us in Christ. We see a marvellous example of this love in today's Gospel. In spite of his own troubles (he had just received the news of the death of his cousin, John the Baptist), when Jesus saw the people, he had pity on them and gave himself to them – teaching them, healing their sick, and feeding them.

As they returned home at the end of that day those people knew that God loved them and cared about them. This is the love Paul is talking about.

Nowhere do we experience God's love more than in the Eucharist. In the Eucharist we are nourished with the Word of God and the Bread of Life. In the Eucharist we taste the love of God.

But we might think that we don't deserve this love. It has nothing to do with deserving it. God loves us, not because we are good, but because he is good. We are his children. That is reason enough for God to love us.

NINETEENTH SUNDAY OF THE YEAR
Calming the storm and walking on water

Praying with the Word of God today

INTRODUCTION AND CONFITEOR

In times of difficulty we find it natural to turn to God. But in good times we tend to forget God. We must learn to turn to God at all times.

Let us turn to God now, and ask pardon for our sins and strength in our weakness. [Pause]

Lord Jesus, you are our strength in times of weakness. Lord, have mercy.

You are our refuge in times of distress. Christ, have mercy.

You are our hope in times of despair. Lord, have mercy.

PRAYER OF THE FAITHFUL

Celebrant: Let us bring our needs before the Lord, and ask him to give us his saving help.

Response: Lord, grant us your salvation.

Reader(s): For the Pope and the bishops: that they may lead the Church with courage and wisdom. [Pause] Let us pray to the Lord.

For our political and civil leaders: that they may seek God's guidance in times of doubt and difficulty. [Pause] Let us pray to the Lord.

For the Jewish people, the first to hear the word of God: that they may grow in love of his name and in faithfulness to his covenant. [Pause] Let us pray to the Lord.

For those who are finding life difficult: that they may know God's help in their trials. [Pause] Let us pray to the Lord.

For all gathered here: that when in times of difficulty our faith begins to falter, the Lord may uphold us with his divine power. [Pause] Let us pray to the Lord.

For all the dead: that the Lord may free them from the shadows of death and gladden them with the light of his face. [Pause] Let us pray to the Lord.

For our own special needs. [Longer pause] Let us pray to the Lord.

Celebrant: Heavenly Father, strengthen our faith, so that we may walk with confidence over the waves of danger, and steer our little boat to a place

of safety and peace, beyond the wind and the waves. We ask this through
Christ our Lord.

REFLECTION

All day from that deep well of life within
Himself has He drawn healing for the press
of folk, restoring strength, forgiving sin,
quieting frenzy, comforting distress.
Shadows of evening fall, yet wildly still
they throng Him, touch Him, clutch His garment's hem,
fall down and clasp His feet, cry on Him, till
the Master, spent, slips from the midst of them
and climbs the mountain for a cup of peace,
taking a sheer and rugged track untrod
save by a poor lost sheep with thorn-torn fleece
that follows on and hears Him talk with God.

Katherine Lee Bates

FINAL BLESSING

May God be within you to strengthen you, and outside you to protect you.
May God be above you to watch over you, and beneath you to uphold you.
May God be before you to guide you, and behind you to keep you from
straying.

Sharing the Word of God today

SCRIPTURE NOTEE

First Reading (1 Kgs 19:9.11-13). During the reign of Ahab in Israel, Elijah
took on himself the task of combating the Baal-worship fostered by queen
Jezebel. However, he adopted a very militant, even bloodthirsty, approach.
Now on the run for his life, he is directed to Mount Horeb where he takes
refuge in a cave.

There he is taught that the tactics he had been adopting are not God's
tactics. God's ways are not man's ways – even Elijah had to learn this. God's
approach is not a violent one (symbolised by the mighty wind and the
earthquake). Rather, it is a gentle one (symbolised by the breeze).

This passage matches the Gospel story. In each story an encounter with
God or with Christ takes place after the stilling of the storm.

Gospel (Mt 14:22-33). We have no way of knowing what actually happened.
However, the lesson of this passage is abundantly clear. As Matthew relates
it, the story is clearly symbolic. The disciples in the boat represent the
infant Church; the wind and the waves represent the persecution let loose

on the Church. Jesus is not with them physically; he is in heaven, praying to the Father. However, in the Church's direst need, when all seems lost, her Lord comes to save her.

The incident of Peter sinking and being saved by Jesus is probably a reference to Peter's failure during the Passion, and his restoration after the resurrection. The writer would have known this, and almost certainly had it in mind when telling this story.

In any case, Peter represents the typical disciple, caught between faith and doubt. Jesus' rebuke, 'Man of little faith! Why did you doubt?' is directed at us also, who often start out courageously only to lose heart when faced with a crisis.

Second Reading (Rom 9:1-5). St Paul tells of the sorrow and anguish he suffers because his fellow Jews refused to accept Christ as the Messiah. His pain is not unlike what is experienced by those who become separated from family and friends over issues of faith and religion.

The power of faith

If taken literally, the Gospel story has little or no relevance for us. Taken symbolically, however, it has great relevance for us. And that seems to be how Matthew meant it to be taken.

Even though it is meant to be taken symbolically, it does represent something that really did happen to the apostles. The small boat represents the infant Church. The wind and the waves represent the persecutions let loose on it.

And it represents something that really did happen to Peter. It is a reference to his failure during the Passion, and his restoration after the resurrection.

Matthew tells this story to demonstrate the kind of faith that followers of Jesus must develop if they are to weather the storms that are an inevitable part of Christian life.

Some people think that if we have sufficient faith, life will be all plain sailing for us. It doesn't happen like that. Faith doesn't shield us from the hard knocks of life and death. We see this even in the case of the great prophet, Elijah (First Reading).

Elijah was a man of great faith. But because of his opposition to idolatry, queen Jezebel wanted to kill him. So he fled to the desert and took refuge in a cave. A beaten and broken man, he just wanted to die. However, in the cave he experienced the presence of God. And reassured by that experience, he was able to go on.

We see the same thing in the lives of the early Christians. They too were people of faith. Nevertheless, they encountered persecution. Thinking that the Lord had abandoned them, their faith began to wilt. However, they discovered that even though the Lord was not with them physically, he was with them, and could still help them. Hence, their faith revived, and they were able to face their trials and dangers.

It is comforting for us to see that the apostles and early Christians were weak and fearful – just like us. We may think that we have great faith. But when difficulties arise, we may discover that we have very little faith.

The example of Peter is especially enlightening. He represents the typical disciple, caught between faith and doubt. He set out to obey Jesus, but 'as soon as he felt the force of the wind', that is, persecution, his courage failed him. But Jesus upheld him with his power.

So it is with us. Like Peter, we often start out courageously only to lose heart when the going gets tough. Jesus' rebuke, 'Man of little faith! Why did you doubt?' is directed at us too.

There can be many situations in which we feel weak and powerless. At such times we have to cry out to the Lord for help, like the apostles and Peter did. If we do, the Lord will uphold us.

Faith doesn't save us from trials and tribulations. What it does is give us the strength to cope with them. Faith assures us that we are not alone in our trials. God is with us, and his power is available to us.

I believe that most of us, on looking back over our lives, can say that there was some situation we would never have been able to cope with were it not for our faith. This means that we have experienced what Elijah experienced, and what Peter and the apostles experienced – we have been upheld by the power of God.

The Gospel story shows us the power of faith. To those with faith, Jesus is not a ghost from the past. He is the Son of God, who is present with us, and whose grace upholds us when things are too much for us.

Upheld by his power

The story of Peter walking on water, sinking, and then being rescued by Jesus is a strange one. Even a nonsensical one, some might say. What are we to make of it? Taken in a literal sense, the story has no relevance for us. But taken symbolically (which seems to be how Matthew intends it to be taken), it has great relevance for us.

Even though it is meant to be taken symbolically, it represents something that really did happen to Peter. Most likely it is a reference to his failure during the Passion, and his restoration after the resurrection. The writer would have known this, and almost certainly had it in mind when telling this story.

We notice that initially Peter is full of confidence as he sets out across the water. It reminds us of his brave words at the Last Supper: 'Even if all the others should lose faith in you, I will never lose faith in you (Mt 26:33).' He really meant those words. He thought he was brave and strong. Yet a short while later, when Jesus asked him to watch with him in the garden, he fell asleep, and left Jesus to drink the cup of sorrow alone. Peter was already beginning to sink. But worse was to come.

Later that same night, in the courtyard of the high priest's house, some-one turned to him and said, 'Aren't you one of his?' And what happened? Not once but three times he denied Jesus, denied ever having known him. Then the cook crew. At that moment Jesus looked at Peter, and Peter immediately realised what he had done – he had denied his friend. And he went outside and wept bitterly.

It was the lowest moment in his life. He found out a very painful truth about himself. He found out that he wasn't as strong, or as brave, as he thought he was. But Jesus didn't write him off. He continued to believe in him. He knew that there was another and better side to him. After the resurrection he restored a wiser and humbler Peter to where he was before, and made him the chief shepherd of his flock.

And Peter came good. He recovered. It was he who led the apostles in witnessing to the resurrection.

Peter represents the typical disciple of the present time, caught between faith and doubt. Jesus' rebuke, 'Man of little faith! Why did you doubt?' is directed at us too. Like Peter, we often start out courageously only to lose heart when the going gets tough.

Peter has been called a stumbling saint. He is a favourite with many, probably because the weakness we see in him we see in ourselves. Courage fails us all. In the end, all of us are mere mortals who are inconstant in our beliefs. But we must not judge ourselves or others by momentary lapses, but by commitment over a long time to our beliefs.

At some time or other, every disciple of Jesus is faced with very trying circumstances, very difficult decisions, very great sorrows, and very powerful temptations. At those times it is as if we are being asked to 'walk on water'. At such times we need the Lord to uphold us.

To some extent, the whole life of a Christian is a kind of 'walking on water', in the sense that it implies walking in faith, which means relying only on the word of Christ. Many times we are asked to step out on his word. But Christ is not a ghostlike figure from the past. He is the Son of God who lives among us.

God's ways are not man's ways

Ahab was king of Israel from 874 to 853 BC. Under his reign, Baal worship became the official cult in Israel. The Baal-worship was fostered by Ahab's queen, Jezebel (a Phoenician princess). God's prophets were being killed. Those who survived were in hiding. None the less, Elijah took on himself the fearsome task of combating this false worship.

However, he adopted a very militant, even bloodthirsty, approach. For instance, after the defeat of the prophets of Baal at Mount Carmel, he had all of them (400 plus) slaughtered. When Jezebel heard what he had done, she wanted him killed, so he fled into the desert in fear for his life. From there he was directed to Mount Horeb, the mountain sanctified by the theophanies of the Exodus and the giving of the Law.

At Horeb he took refuge in a cave, where he received a strange vision. He witnessed a whirlwind that shattered rocks, then an earthquake, and then a fire. But the vision led him to understand that God was not in any of these things. Then he heard the sound of a gentle breeze. And he realised at once that he was in the presence of God.

And a voice said to him. 'What are you doing here, Elijah?'

And he said, 'I'm here because of my zeal for Yahweh. The Israelites have abandoned your covenant. Your prophets have been killed. I am the only one left, and now they want to kill me.'

Then the voice said, 'You must go and anoint Elisha as your successor.'

Thus Elijah was shown another aspect of his God. He was taught that God's ways are not man's ways – even Elijah had to learn this. The tactics he had adopted were not God's tactics. Violence is evil. Violence committed in the name of God is doubly evil.

God's approach is not a violent one (symbolised by the mighty wind and the earthquake). Rather, it is a gentle one (symbolised by the breeze). God's approach is as gentle as a breeze. God's presence in the world achieves what he wills as gently and relentlessly as a breeze.

And God's voice is the gentlest voice of all. God did not make himself heard to Elijah in the sound of the mighty wind or the earthquake, but in the whisper of a gentle breeze.

Since we live in a very noisy world, if we want to hear the voice of God, we need to create some stillness and quietness in our soul. (Elijah had to go to a cave to hear it). Many other voices clamour for our attention, voices that are loud, strident, and seductive.

Yet, for those who know how to listen, God's gentle voice can make itself heard even in the midst of a storm. Over the roar of wind and the waves, the apostles heard the gentle voice of Jesus saying to them, 'Courage! It is I! Do not be afraid.'

To live by faith means to trust in God and to rely on his power. God won't carry us, but he will uphold us if we let go. We are God's children.

There is an unbreakable bond between God and us. With this conviction our prayer should produce a kind of lightness in us that makes it possible for us to walk over the waves of danger.

TWENTIETH SUNDAY OF THE YEAR
Tough faith

Praying with the Word of God today

INTRODUCTION AND CONFITEOR

We are gathered in the house of God. God wants his house to be a house of prayer. We must ask God to make us one in mind and heart, so that our prayers may ascend to him like fragrant incense. [Pause]

Lord Jesus, you heal the wounds of sin and division. Lord, have mercy.

You reconcile us to one another and to the Father. Christ, have mercy.

You gather the nations into the peace of God's kingdom. Lord, have mercy.

PRAYER OF THE FAITHFUL

Celebrant: Let us turn to God in faith, trusting, that like the Canaanite woman, we will know his saving help in our need.

Response: Lord, be gracious and bless us.

Reader(s): For Christians: that they may draw inspiration from the faith and courage of the Canaanite woman. [Pause] Let us pray to the Lord.

For those who do not belong to our Church but who share our faith in Jesus Christ: that we may be united in the fellowship of love. [Pause] Let us pray to the Lord.

For government leaders: that they may show special concern for the poor and disadvantaged members of society. [Pause] Let us pray to the Lord.

For parents who have a sick or problem child: that they may know God's help in their need. [Pause] Let us pray to the Lord.

For the members of this community: that we may be grateful for the good things we enjoy, and be generous in sharing them with others. [Pause] Let us pray to the Lord.

For our deceased relatives and friends: that they may dwell in the house of the Lord for ever. [Pause] Let us pray to the Lord.

For our own special needs. [Longer pause] Let us pray to the Lord.

Celebrant: God of power and love, grant us in all our tasks your help, in all our doubts your guidance, in all our weaknesses your strength, in all our sorrows your consolation, and in all our dangers your protection. We ask this through Christ our Lord.

OUR FATHER

Let us pray to our heavenly Father as Jesus taught us, and as Christians all over the world pray.

PRAYER

Lord, grant us a strong and courageous faith,
a faith that burns brightly even in times of darkness,
a faith that doesn't falter even when there are no miracles
or happy endings,
a Good Friday faith that trusts in the dawn of Easter,
a faith that is rooted in your love for us
and that expresses itself in love for others.

FINAL BLESSING

May you keep firm in the faith we profess, because the one who made the promises is faithful.

May the God, who has called us to eternal glory in Christ, strengthen and support you with his grace.

May the peace of God, which is beyond all understanding, guard your hearts and minds in Christ Jesus our Lord.

Sharing the Word of God today

SCRIPTURE NOTE

First Reading (Is 56:1.6-7). This reading reflects a time during the period of restoration after the return from Babylon (538 BC onwards). Since the returned exiles constituted a small group, they tended to be inward looking. The prophet encourages them to embrace foreigners because God intends his house to be 'a house of prayer for *all* the peoples'. The theme of inclusiveness forms the link with the Gospel.

Gospel (Mt 15:21-28). The early Church faced a similar problem with regard to the Gentiles. Matthew sees Jesus as having broken down the barrier between Jew and Gentile. Even though his own mission was restricted to Israel, Jesus did reach out to individual Gentiles such as the centurion (8:5-13) and the Canaanite woman. Hence, after the resurrection of Jesus, the early Church extended its mission to the Gentiles.

This story resembles that of the healing of centurion's servant in showing us the great faith of a Gentile. Though a member of a tribe that had been ancestral enemies of the Jews, she had more faith in Jesus than his own people. They wouldn't believe in him unless they saw signs and wonders. Indeed, they saw signs and wonders, and still refused to believe. This nameless pagan woman has remained an exemplar of faith for 2,000 years.

Second Reading (Rom 11:13-15.29-32). Paul declares that he has been sent as apostle of the pagans. The pagans have benefitted from the Jews' refusal of faith because it was their refusal that caused Paul to turn to the Gentiles. The witness of the pagan converts will be a testimony to the Jews of the power of God. Paul hopes that the Jews will see the light through a salutary 'jealousy' of the Gentile Christians.

A tough faith

The Canaanite woman is a great example of faith. We have this on the authority of Jesus himself: 'Woman, you have great faith.' We are familiar with the expression 'tough love.' Well, that woman possessed what we might call 'tough faith'.

First of all she humbled herself to ask a favour from a Jew. Then she refused to give up when her request wasn't granted at once. At first Jesus refused to answer her. Then he announced that he was sent only to the lost sheep of Israel. (She was a Gentile.) Even when the apostles tried to get rid of her, she persisted. So great was her faith in Jesus that she went on pleading. Finally Jesus granted her request.

Sometimes you hear people say: 'Ah, it's easy for you; you have great faith.' Faith doesn't always make things easier. The opposite is sometimes the case. Faith impels us to persevere, to struggle on, with no guarantee of a happy ending. Faith is not a magic wand. It calls for humility, courage, perseverance, and above all love.

Sometimes it would be easier to give up, and to throw towel in. But because we have faith, we refuse to give up. We don't give up on the elderly or the terminally ill. We don't give up on the severely handicapped. We refuse to consider the unborn child as disposable. Because we have faith we refuse to give in to despair in face of the awful things that happen – things such as random acts of violence, horrific accidents, and illnesses that claim the lives of children or young parents. We refuse to give up even before death itself. A person with even a grain of real faith never gives up.

This nameless Gentile woman is an example of that tough faith we all need at times. But she is also a great example of love. Jesus could just as well have said to her: 'Woman, you have great love.' We see the depth of her love in the trouble she went to on behalf of her daughter. She had no thought of the cost to herself.

Hers was not only a tough faith, but also a faith that expressed itself in love. There is an essential link between faith and love. St Paul says that we could have faith strong enough to move mountains, but if we are without love, it will be of no benefit to us (1 Cor 13:2).

Love is the greatest power in the world. It's amazing what people can do and will do when motivated by love. This is especially true of a mother. A mother will do anything, and endure anything, for sake of her child. A mother never gives up.

A mother's love is probably the most reliable human love most of us will ever know. No wonder the Bible uses a mother's love as an image of God's love for us. 'Can a mother forget the child at her breast, or fail to cherish the child of her womb? Yet even if a mother should forget, I will never forget you,' says the Lord (Is 49:15).

Isaiah is telling us that God's love for us is even more reliable than a mother's love for her child. It is on this love – God's love for us – that our faith is based.

Story

Once, during a particularly severe winter in the Arctic, all but two people in a certain camp died of starvation. The two survivors were an Eskimo woman and her baby.

The woman began a desperate search for some means of obtaining food. Eventually she found a small fishhook. It was a simple matter to rig a line, but she had no bait, and no hope of getting bait. Without a moment's hesitation she took a knife and cut a piece of flesh from her thigh. Using this as bait she caught a fish. She fed her child and herself, saving the fish gut for bait. She lived on fish until spring when she walked out of the camp and found some other people.

It was no coincidence that the only adult to survive in that camp was a mother. What kept that mother alive was her concern for her child. There seems to be no limit to what a mother will go through for the sake of her child. A mother doesn't give up easily.

The cry of the poor

At one time or another all of us have been approached by a street beggar. I think it would be fair to say that few of us come out of such an encounter with credit. Often we refuse to help the person. We justify our refusal to help by telling ourselves that it is better not to give money to beggars because it only serves to keep them trapped in a way of life that is degrading.

We might sometimes wonder how Jesus would deal with this kind of situation. Well, today's Gospel tells the story of an encounter Jesus had with a beggar. True, the Canaanite woman was not begging for money. But she was begging, begging for a favour.

Jesus had withdrawn with his apostles to the region of Tyre and Sidon, which was Gentile country. It seems that he had gone there for a break. However, no sooner had he arrived there, than he was approached by a pagan woman who pestered him to cure her sick daughter.

The reaction of the apostles was not unlike our own. For them the Canaanite woman was a nuisance and an embarrassment. They just wanted to get rid of her, and as quickly as possible.

Indeed, Jesus' own initial reaction surprises us. At first he ignored her. Then he refused her with what appears to be a very uncharitable remark. However, the remark didn't produce the desired effect. The woman was a very determined person – most beggars are. She refused to take no for an answer. Finally, Jesus granted her request.

We don't know why he made it so hard for her. Remember she was a Gentile. So there may be a clue in his remark: 'I was sent only to the lost sheep of the house of Israel.' The important thing is that he finally did grant the woman her request.

To come back to ourselves. An encounter with a beggar can be a disturbing experience. Why can't we at least bid this poor person, this fellow human being, the time of day? Why can't we look at him? Why do we try to avoid him? And if we do decide to give him something, why does it always have to be the smallest coin in our pocket?

Such an encounter can stir up unpleasant things inside us. It arouses within us conflicting feelings of pity, discomfort, anger, and guilt. We hate what we discover about ourselves. And unless we are careful we may direct that hate at the poor unfortunate person who has dared to approach us.

An encounter with a poor person can also be a humbling experience. Why? Because it makes us aware of our own poverty. We realise that while the beggar is materially poor, we are poor in a different sense. We are poor in compassion, poor in our willingness to help another person, and poor in our capacity to love.

But an encounter with a poor person can be a blessing. It can awaken within us feelings of tenderness and compassion, kindness and communion. It shows us that it is possible to love more, and to give more of ourselves. It can even change us.

And it reminds us that before God all of us are poor. The priest says the prayers of the Mass with outstretched hands. To pray like this is to acknowledge that before God we are poor, and stand in daily need of his mercy and love. Therefore, we hold up our empty hands to God as a beggar holds out an empty bowl to passersby. We are saying in effect, 'Lord, before you I am as poor as a beggar.'

How can we make a prayer like that in church, and then close our eyes to a beggar out in the street?

Story

When I see a beggar in the street or in the Metro, I tend to put my hand into my pocket and give him the first coin – big or small – that I find there.

As I give it to him, I look into his eyes and say a few words to him. As our eyes meet, there seems to be a moment of communion and of mutual understanding between us that brings me peace. This simple look can give him back a little confidence in himself. Maybe it can give me confidence in myself too.

'Every man who loses confidence in himself, who has fallen into the world of alcohol or drugs, or who has failed in family life or relationships or work, needs someone who looks at him as a human being with tenderness and trust. And it is this moment of communion that enables him, little by little, to rebuild his confidence.' (Jean Vanier, founder of l'Arche)

The house of God

At the time the prophet Isaiah was writing (First Reading) there were a lot of foreigners living in Israel. The question arose as to whether or not the benefits of salvation should be extended to them. Isaiah gave a clear and positive answer: God's house is to be a house of prayer for *all* the peoples.

'My house shall be a house of prayer for *all* the peoples.' This is a tremendous statement. There are so many closed shops, so many exclusive clubs in the world. But God's house is meant to be different. God's house is meant to be open to all his children.

Sadly, instead of being a force for unity, religion has often been the cause of conflict and division. Nevertheless, it has a great capacity to break down barriers. Of all the things that draw people together, worship alone has the power to turn them into a loving family.

In the house of God there are no first and lasts. This is because before God all of us are equal. A great levelling occurs. For one small hour the high and mighty descend and the lowly rise. And in the house of God there are no special seats. This is because in the house of God every place is a place of honour.

The Church is a temple with a hundred gates, and pilgrims enter from every angle. Through every door, and from all kinds of paths, we enter the house of God on a Sunday morning.

For the most part, a church is associated with Sunday worship. But it remains open all week long. Anyone can come here at any hour of the day to talk to God – to seek his help in times of trouble, his guidance in times of doubt, or just to be near the Lord in the hope of tasting the peace this world cannot give.

Many lost, lonely, homeless souls have come to the house of God, or have wandered into it almost by accident, and felt at home there. In God's house we discover who we are. Whatever the world may think of us, in God's house we know we are. We are God's precious daughters and sons.

The house of God is a place beyond earning, deserving, and rewarding. It's a place of surrender and complete trust. It's a place of prayer that through the presence of God becomes a place of blessing. Someone said: 'I like to go into churches to sense the undefinable perfume of transcendence raising mediocre man about his petty destiny.'

We must strive to make this house of worship a house of prayer, joy, and unity. And we must try to take a spirit of joy and welcome towards others with us when we leave it.

Even though we don't have to be saints to enter this house, we know that inside God's house we are called to conversion. We should heed the words of the prophet: 'Have a care for justice, act with integrity' (First Reading). That is a sharp, well-focused message that challenges us to live out what we experience here.

TWENTY-FIRST SUNDAY OF THE YEAR
The call of Peter

Praying with the Word of God today

INTRODUCTION AND CONFITEOR

Jesus chose Peter to be the chief shepherd of his flock. Though Peter had strengths, he also had weaknesses.

We too have strengths and weaknesses. Let us turn to the Lord, confident that he understands our weaknesses and forgives us when we fall. [Pause]

Lord Jesus, you are our strength in times of weakness. Lord, have mercy.
You are our light in times of darkness. Christ, have mercy.
You are our refuge in times of despair. Lord, have mercy.

PRAYER OF THE FAITHFUL

Celebrant: The Lord's love is eternal. Therefore, let us bring our needs before him with confidence.

Response: Lord, hear our prayer.

Reader(s): For the Pope, the successor of Peter: that he may be a worthy representative of Christ on earth. [Pause] Let us pray to the Lord.

For temporal rulers: that God may guide their mind and hearts so that people everywhere may enjoy religious freedom, security and peace. [Pause] Let us pray to the Lord.

For those who have left the Church: that they may return to the flock Christ nourishes. [Pause] Let us pray to the Lord.

For all gathered here: that we may not be discouraged by our weakness or demoralised by our failures. [Pause] Let us pray to the Lord.

For on our deceased relatives and friends: that the light of heaven may shine on them. [Pause] Let us pray to the Lord.

For our own special needs. [Longer pause] Let us pray to the Lord.

Celebrant: Merciful God, fill our hearts with your love. Give us the grace to rise above our human weakness, and keep us faithful to you and to one another. We ask this through Christ our Lord.

OUR FATHER

With our limited minds we can't possibly understand the mind of God. Yet we pray to him with confidence in the words our Saviour gave us.

REFLECTION

Peter has been called a stumbling saint.
He is a great consolation to us
because all of us are inconstant in our beliefs.
But we must not judge ourselves or others
by momentary inconsistencies,
but by commitment given over a long time.
Jesus was well aware of Peter's faults,
but he saw that, in spite of everything, his heart was sound.
Which meant he had the ability to love.
And in the long run love is what counts.

FINAL BLESSING

May you live a life worthy of God, who is calling you to share the glory of his kingdom.

May the God, who has called us to eternal glory in Christ, strengthen and support you with his grace.

May you be good witnesses for the Gospel by the love and joy you radiate.

Sharing the Word of God today

SCRIPTURE NOTE

First Reading (Is 22:19-23). Eliakim was among the leaders in Jerusalem during the critical Assyrian siege (2 Kgs 18:26). Apart from that, little is known about him. Here he succeeds Shebnah to the office of chief steward. He will hold 'the key of the house of David' and will be a firm support to his descendants.

In the New Testament the text is applied to Jesus (Rev 3:7). In the Gospel we will read of the true Son of David bestowing 'keys' on Peter.

Gospel (Mt 16:13-20). Jesus asked his disciples, 'Who do people say that I am?' The various answers show that Jesus was seen as a prophetic figure,

Still, those answers are only approximations to the mystery of Jesus. Jesus rejected these inadequate views of others and demanded that his disciples speak for themselves.

Peter replied, 'You are the Christ, the Son of the living God.' In all probability what we have here is a solemn confessional formula of Matthew's church.

Then Jesus reciprocated. While Peter was simply acknowledging what Jesus always was, Jesus confers a new title on Peter. Peter will be the foundation stone of the new people of God (the Church).

The story shows that the primacy of Peter was not something that was invented by the Church later on. It went right back to the beginning, yes, to the mind and will of Jesus himself. The failures of Popes throughout history do not contradict Jesus' promise that the gates of hell would not prevail against the Church. The Church's true foundation is Christ himself. The Pope is his servant, not his substitute.

Jesus forbade the disciples to speak openly of this confession, given that it would undoubtedly have been misinterpreted, and would have led to false hopes.

Second Reading (Rom 11:33-36). This is a hymn of praise to the wisdom of God, a wisdom that is far too deep for us to fathom. God is the Creator and Sustainer of all.

Making the faith our own

Today we have a glut of opinion polls especially around election times. One thing opinion polls show is the variety and often contradictory views people can have about a particular issue or personality.

In the Gospel we have an example of an early opinion poll. Surprisingly it was Jesus himself who conducted it. Though it was a very limited one, it concerned a vital question, namely, the identity of Jesus.

'Who do people say the Son of Man is?' This is the central question in the Gospel. Everything hinges on this. Get this wrong, and we get everything wrong. Today it is fashionable to regard Jesus as just one of the great religious founders. Get this right, and there's a good chance we'll get everything right.

Jesus knew who he was. The question was for the benefit of the disciples. Questions help people to clarify their thinking. Jesus didn't pluck the question out of the air. Large crowds were coming to hear him. He was doing great deeds – such as healing. The question on everybody's lips was: Who is this man Jesus? The question echoes through the entire Gospel. After he calmed the storm, the apostles asked, 'Who is this that the wind and the sea obey him?'

Jesus' little poll confirms what I said earlier about polls: it shows the different opinions regarding Jesus. Some said he was John Baptist. Others said he was Elijah. Still others said he was Jeremiah or one of the prophets. The various answers show that Jesus was seen as a prophetic figure. Though flattering, the answers were only approximations to the mystery of Jesus.

Jesus rejected these inadequate views of others and demanded that his disciples speak for themselves. So he said to them, 'And you, who do *you* say that I am?' 'You are the Christ (the Messiah), the Son of the living God,' Peter answered.

We mustn't think that it happened just like that. It wasn't that easy or that simple, even for Peter. The mystery of who Jesus was, was only gradually revealed to the apostles. In fact, they didn't fully grasp it until after the resurrection. (See Acts 2:36.)

What we have here, in the mouth of Peter, is the supreme confessional formula of Matthew's Church. This didn't end the question for all time. Various controversies arose. And various heresies denied either the humanity or divinity of Jesus. It had to be settled by the Church in a Council.

Take the Creed that we recite here every Sunday. Two thirds of it relate to what we believe about Jesus. The Creed is a development of that kernel proclaimed by Peter.

It is easier for us today to profess the faith. We have 2000 years of tradition and the teaching of various councils to guide us. But it is important to make the answer our own. To believe, not simply because the Church says so, but out of personal conviction. Each of us must face the perennial question posed by Jesus: Who do you say that I am?

A person can't be baptised without a profession of faith. At baptism we are asked: 'Do you believe in Jesus Christ, his only Son our Lord, who was born of the Virgin Mary, was crucified, died, and was buried, rose from the dead, and is now seated at the right hand of the Father?'

The more people we have in the Church who believe out of personal conviction, the more the Church will be founded on rock. But even though it is important to be able to profess the true faith, that is only the beginning. We must live out the faith. Whether we are conscious of it or not, all of us are shaped by our convictions. So we must allow our lives to be shaped by the faith.

There is a little prayer that sums it all up: Lord, grant that the faith we have professed with our lips, we may believe with our hearts, and practise with our lives.

The highs and lows of Peter

Peter is at the centre of today's Gospel. There he makes a marvellous profession of faith in Jesus. Jesus reacts by conferring the primacy on him. (This shows that the primacy was not something that was invented by the Church later on. It went right back to the beginning, to the mind and will of Christ himself.) But why did Jesus confer the primacy on Peter and not on any of the others?

It's clear that Peter had leadership qualities. In all four Gospels he is the one who is mentioned most frequently, and who speaks most frequently. Indeed, very often, he acts as spokesman for the Twelve. And whenever the twelve apostles are listed, his name is always first. His great profession of faith in Jesus was one of his finest moments.

Yet the Gospels do not spare Peter. True, they show that there was a solid side to his character. But they also show there was an opposite side to his character. On the night Jesus was on trial for his life, instead of standing by him, Peter denied him not once but three times. That was his lowest moment.

The Peter who said, 'You are the Christ, the Son of the living God,' was the same Peter who said, 'I do not know this man' (Mt 26:74). If it was a different Peter, that would explain everything. But it was the same Peter. Still, we might be inclined to say, 'Ah, but the first Peter, was the real Peter.' This would be a mistake. There was only one Peter.

No one would have been surprised had Jesus written Peter off at this point, as being weak, cowardly, and unreliable. But he didn't. Instead, he restored him to where he was before, and made him the chief shepherd of his flock. Why? Because he knew that there was another and better side to Peter. Generosity and selfishness, courage and cowardice, can co-exist in the same person.

Judas' betrayal was a planned thing, and was carried out in a cold, calculating manner. Peter's denial was not a planned thing, and was the result of weakness rather than malice. But he didn't fall simply because he is weak. He fell because he thought he was strong.

In giving authority to the man who denied him, Jesus showed that he was establishing his Church not on human strength, but on his own love and faithfulness.

The denial was a very humbling and chastening experience for Peter. But he learned two great lessons from that it.

Firstly, he learned a painful truth about himself. He learned that he wasn't as strong or as brave as he thought he was. It is important that those in positions of leadership be aware of their weaknesses and limitations.

And secondly, he learned a wonderful truth about Jesus. He learned that in spite of his denials, Jesus still loved him. It was love that enabled him to turn an hour of pain and shame into an hour of grace and salvation.

And this time Peter did not fail Jesus. He led the early Church and, like his Master, gave his life for his sheep.

God doesn't choose perfect people to do his work – there are no such people. God chooses human beings who are flawed, but nevertheless have a capacity for greatness and holiness. In them we see the power of grace working through human weakness and sinfulness.

Peter is a great consolation to us. The frailties we see in him we recognise in ourselves. Courage fails us all. In the end, all of us are mere mortals who are inconstant in our beliefs. But we must not judge ourselves or others by momentary lapses, but by commitment over a long time to our beliefs.

But Peter is also a great challenge to us. He didn't belong to some superior race or species. He was made of the same human material as ourselves. We too can become better than we are.

The formation of a leader

The Gospel story shows Jesus conferring the primacy on Peter. Peter is one of the most interesting characters in the Gospel. It's clear that he had leadership qualities. But it's also clear that he had glaring weaknesses.

It is very interesting to see how Jesus dealt with him, and how he helped him to grow into the man who was ready to lay down his life for him, and eventually did. This will help us as we struggle to grow as human beings and as disciples of Jesus. And it will show us how best to help those we love to grow.

It all began when Jesus *called* him. Obviously Jesus saw potential in him. We all need someone to believe in us.

Peter didn't think he deserved that call. He said, 'Lord, depart from me, for I am a sinful man' (Lk 5:8). Jesus did not deny that Peter was a sinner, but he *challenged* him to grow. We too need to be challenged. The quality of people's lives is affected, not so much by what is given to them, as by what is asked of them.

Jesus *involved him* in his work. Responsibility helps people to grow.

Jesus asked him to *declare his loyalty*. Once when large numbers of people were leaving him, Jesus turned to Peter and said, 'Will you also leave me?' (Jn 6:67). This forced Peter to look into his own heart, and to stand on his own two feet. That helps growth.

When Peter made his great declaration of faith: 'You are the Christ, the Son of the living God', Jesus *praised* him. We all need recognition for work well done. This encourages further generosity.

Jesus *corrected* him. When Peter drew his sword in the garden of Gethsemane, Jesus said to him, 'Put away your sword' (Mt 26:52). It takes courage on the part of the tutor to point out mistakes. And to learn from one's mistakes is an essential part of growth.

Jesus once *told him off*. When Peter wanted to prevent him from going to Jerusalem, Jesus said, 'Get behind me, Satan, you are more of a hindrance to me than a help' (Mt 16:23). At times the tutor may have to reprove. But there is an art in doing it.

Jesus *confronted* him with his failure to stay awake in the garden: 'Can you not watch even one hour with me?' (Mt 26:40). It doesn't help to let someone away with sloppiness and shoddiness.

Jesus even *threatened* to cut him off over the feet-washing incident. One has to be stern at times and refuse to compromise on matters of principle.

Jesus *understood* that when Peter denied him, he did so out of weakness rather than malice. He forgave him and gave him the chance to begin again. We all need someone who can understand our weakness, and who doesn't write us off when we don't produce the goods right away.

But Jesus *never spoilt* Peter. That would be to ruin his chance of growing.

The thread which runs through their relationship is love. Peter knew that Jesus loved him. Love provides the climate in which people can grow.

We can imagine that Peter made a very good leader. A leader has to be aware of his own weakness. The experience of denying Jesus rid him of pride and blind reliance on his own resources. At the same time it enabled him to understand the weakness of others.

Peter's story helps us to understand ourselves. The frailties we see in him we see in ourselves. However, we must not be allow ourselves to be discouraged by our weakness or demoralised by our failures. Peter's story also shows us how to develop a close relationship with Jesus. Without a warm relationship with Christ, we are only on the fringes of Christianity. We are like someone talking about love compared with someone who is in love.

TWENTY-SECOND SUNDAY OF THE YEAR
The cost of discipleship

Praying with the Word of God today

INTRODUCTION AND CONFITEOR

For a Christian suffering is not a likelihood; it is a certainty. But we have the example of Jesus to inspire us. The fact that Jesus suffered gives hope and courage to us in our sufferings.

Let us turn to God now, asking pardon for our failures, and strength in our weakness. [Pause]

Lord Jesus, you give courage to those who are afraid. Lord, have mercy.

You uphold those who suffer in the cause of right. Christ, have mercy.

You renew the strength of those who hope in you. Lord, have mercy.

PRAYER OF THE FAITHFUL

Celebrant: God is the strength of those who trust in him. Let our prayers today be an expression of our trust in God and of our concern for others.

Response: Lord, hear our prayer.

Reader(s): For the Pope: that he may be blessed with wisdom so that he may guide the Church with courage and vision. [Pause] Let us pray to the Lord.

For Christians: that they may not conform themselves to the ways of the world but proclaim the faith by the witness of their lives. [Pause] Let us pray to the Lord.

For temporal rulers: that they may carry out their responsibilities worthily and well. [Pause] Let us pray to the Lord.

For those who are suffering because of their faith in Christ: that they may have the strength to persevere. [Pause] Let us pray to the Lord.

For all gathered here: that we may experience joy in the profession of our faith, and that the depth of our faith may be evident in the way we live. [Pause] Let us pray to the Lord.

For our deceased relatives and friends, who were marked with the sign of Christ's cross in baptism: may they now share his glory in heaven. [Pause] Let us pray to the Lord.

For our own special needs. [Longer pause] Lord, hear us.

Celebrant: Lord, teach us to serve you as you deserve: to give and not to count the cost, to fight and not to heed the wounds, to toil and not to seek for rest, to labour and not to ask for any reward except that of knowing that we do your will. We ask this through you, Christ our Lord.

PRAYER/REFLECTION

Jeremiah had a difficult life as God's prophet.
There were times when he felt like packing it in.
But he kept going because there was a fire burning in his heart,
and imprisoned in his bones.
It was this 'inner fire' that enabled him to remain faithful
to the task God had given him.
Lord, kindle in our hearts the fire of your love,
so that we may follow you faithfully on earth
and come to share your glory in heaven.

FINAL BLESSING

May you live in such a way that the world will recognise you as disciples of Christ.

May God, who has called us to eternal glory in Christ, strengthen and support you with his grace.

May the fire that burned in the heart of Jeremiah inflame your hearts with love for Christ and for the Gospel.

Sharing the Word of God today

SCRIPTURE NOTE

First Reading (Jer 20:7-9). Jeremiah feels overwhelmed by the demands of a task that has brought him nothing but insult and derision. He has come to his wits end. He wants to pack it all in. He feels that God has tricked him into accepting it. Yet, for all that, he cannot quit because he feels a fire burning inside him. Faithfulness in spite of the cross is the link with the Gospel.

Gospel (Mt 16:21-27). This contains the first of three predictions of the Passion that we find in Matthew's Gospel. Peter gladly received the revelation of Jesus as Messiah and Son of God. But he rejected out of hand the apparently contradictory revelation of a suffering Messiah. He obviously had bought into the idea of a political Messiah.

Here Matthew is concerned with discipleship. The 'cross' symbolises the sufferings, persecutions and struggles that every follower of Christ is bound to encounter. Peter represents the typical Christian, for whom the cross is a stumbling block.

In the passage we see the faithfulness of Jesus, and the kind of faithfulness that is demanded of those who would follow him. From this point on, Jesus' disciples must decide if they can follow a Messiah who calls them to suffering and even death. Nevertheless, the disciples do not abandon him.

Second Reading (Rom 12:1-2). St Paul urges the Romans not to model themselves on the people around them, but to live a life in keeping with their redeemed status. If they do this then their whole lives will become a living sacrifice pleasing to God.

The cost of discipleship

Jesus said to his disciples, 'Unless you take up your cross and follow me you cannot be my disciple.' The cross doesn't mean our arthritis, or our indigestion, or a difficult relationship, at least not in the first place. These are things that come to us in spite of ourselves. The 'cross' in the New Testament means that suffering which comes into our lives because of the choices we have made for the Gospel. In that sense it is always something we choose. An illustration.

Nelson Mandela spent 27 years in prison, or 10,000 days (approx.). Before that he was on the run for a number of years. Of the time he was on the run he wrote later, 'I had to separate myself from my wife and children. I had to say goodbye to the good old days when, at the end of a strenuous day at the office, I could look forward to joining my family at the dinner table. Instead, I had to take up the life of a man hunted continuously by the police, living separated from those who are closest to me, facing continually the hazards of detection and of arrest. This was a life infinitely more difficult than serving a prison sentence.'

What was it that drove him to make such great sacrifices? It was his love for his country. This was the 'cross' he carried because of his love for his people.

In the Gospel Jesus asks for commitment from his followers: 'If anyone wants to be a follower of mine, he must renounce himself and take up his cross and follow me. ... anyone who loses his life for my sake will find it.' For the committed Christian, suffering is not likelihood; it is a certainty.

It has been claimed that religion asks too little of people. It is too ready to offer comfort and to console, but has lost the courage to challenge. The result is that for many religion is just a crutch – something to lean on in times of weakness and infirmity, but something to forget in times of well-being.

It's true that religion is the best support we can have in times of weakness. But it is a lot more. It should be a positive force in our lives. It should not be just a crutch. It should be a pair of wings. It should increase our joys. It should give us energy and vitality. It should make us into loving people.

There is a religion of *devotion*, and a religion of *commitment*. A religion of devotion is a religion of comfort, and is often centred on self rather than on others. A religion of commitment is a religion of challenge, of risk, and of unselfishness.

Being a disciple is a serious business. Yet this doesn't mean that suffering is something a Christian should seek. Jesus did not seek suffering; Gethsemane makes that clear. But suffering will inevitably be part of Christian life as it was part of Jesus' life.

There are two extremes that a Christian must avoid. One extreme speaks only of personal self-fulfillment, and denies the demand of Jesus about taking up the cross. The other extreme speaks only the negative language of denial and renunciation, and does not allow for the proper self-love without which true growth is not possible.

The 'cross' is a metaphor for sacrifice. Sacrifice has a harsh ring to it. It suggests hardship, discipline, renunciation, and pain. Yet there is no achievement without sacrifice. Besides, sacrifice can bring out the best in people. The person who selfishly grasps at personal fulfilment will only see it slip through his fingers, while the one who sacrifices himself for Jesus (and others) will find true fulfilment.

Jesus himself has given us the example. He chose the way of self-sacrifice and suffering. It wasn't that he was in love with suffering. No. It was because he chose the way of love. And love inevitably results in suffering. But it was through his suffering that he attained to glory. He promises that those who follow him faithfully here will share his glory in the hereafter.

Refusing to be deflected from his destiny

Nelson Mandela tells us that when he was struggling to establish himself as a young lawyer in Johannesburg, he became friendly with a businessman by the name of Hans Muller. One day Muller pointed out the window, and said:

'Look out there, Nelson. Do you see those men and women scurrying up and down the street? What is it that they are pursuing so feverishly? I'll tell you: all of them, without exception, are after wealth and money. Because wealth and money equal happiness. That is what you must struggle for: money, and nothing but money. Once you have money, you will want for nothing.'

The advice was well meant. But that made it all the more dangerous. Mandela was an intelligent man. If he had taken Muller's advice he could have done very well for himself. Luckily for South Africa, he didn't. Instead of looking after Number One, Mandela decided to dedicate himself to serving his country.

This incident helps us to understand the incident related in today's Gospel. A short time prior to this Peter had recognised Jesus as the Messiah. According to popular expectation, the Messiah would be a great military leader – another King David who would restore Israel to its former military greatness. It seems that Peter had bought into the idea of a political Messiah.

But this wasn't Jesus' idea of the Messiah. He told the apostles that the Messiah would suffer and be put to death. That was what God wanted. Not that God wanted the suffering of his Son, but that he wanted to show us the depth of his love for us in and through the faithfulness and love of his Son, a faithfulness and love that cost him his life.

The notion of a suffering Messiah was completely unacceptable to Peter. So, out of concern for Jesus, he tried to stop him. But no doubt he was thinking of himself too. Being a disciple of a suffering Messiah was not a role to be relished.

But Jesus said to him, 'Get behind me, Satan!' These are strong words. Peter had become a stumbling block to Jesus. And even though Peter had a very important role to play in his plans, Jesus was prepared to lose his friendship rather than allow him to deflect him from his destiny.

When Mandela decided to dedicate his life to his country, he didn't know that it would mean spending twenty-seven years of his life in prison.

But when Jesus set out on the road to Jerusalem he did know the full consequences of that decision. This makes his sacrifice all the greater.

However, when the hour came for him to drink the cup of suffering and death, he didn't find it easy. On the contrary, he underwent a terrible agony, and asked the Father to remove the cup from him. Nevertheless, he remained faithful.

St Paul urged his Roman converts not to model their behaviour on the pagans around them (Second Reading). As Christians we have to be in the world while not allowing ourselves to be absorbed by the world. 'The world today needs Christians who remain Christians' (Albert Camus).

Fidelity to Christ will involve sacrifice. Sacrifice is not an easy road. But it is in this way that our best self takes shape. This is how one becomes a person of character and integrity. And paradoxically this is also the road to happiness.

The only thing that makes sacrifice easy is love. Love enables us to turn the cross from a stumbling block into a stepping-stone. What Jesus did was an expression of his love for us and for his heavenly Father. Jesus supports all those who follow him down the narrow road of sacrifice, and shares his Easter victory with them.

Story

'What will it benefit a man if he gained the whole world but lost his soul?' These are words we ought never to forget. There's nothing like an example to inspire us.

Alexander Solzhenitsyn tells the story of a political prisoner by the name of Ivan. The scene is a prison near Moscow (during the era of Stalin). Ivan was an expert in physics and optics. One day he was summoned by the prison governor. He knew at once that he wanted something from him.

'Would you like a remission?' the governor asked him.

'What do I have to do?' Ivan asked.

'We'd like to transfer you to another prison to take charge of an important project. If you agree, you will be free in six months'.

'What is the project?'

'We want you to perfect a miniature camera that can be fitted to the jamb of a door, and that works when the door is opened. We know you can do this.'

Ivan was perhaps the only person in the whole of Russia who could produce a blueprint for this device. After seventeen years in prison the idea of going home appealed to him. Here surely was the answer to his wife Natasha's prayer. All he had to do was invent a device that would put a few unsuspecting fools behind bars in his place, and he would be free.

'Could I not go on working on television sets as I am at present?' he asked.

'You mean you refuse?' said the governor.

Ivan thought: Who would ever thank him? Were those people out there worth saving? Natasha was his life-long companion. She had waited for him for seventeen years.

'I couldn't do it,' he said at last.

'But you're just the man for the job,' said the governor. 'We'll give you time to make up your mind.'

'I won't do it. Putting people in prison because of the way they think is not my line. That's my final answer.'

A few days later Ivan was on a train to Siberia to work in a copper mine where starvation rations, and probable death awaited him. No fate on earth could be worse. Yet he was at peace with himself.

A fire burning inside

Jeremiah is at the centre of the First Reading. He was called to be a prophet from an early age. He sacrificed everything, including marriage, for his vocation. He lived out that vocation during a time of great turmoil which saw the defeat of Israel and the destruction of Jerusalem and the Temple.

He indicted the official leaders for neglecting their duties towards the people, blaming them for the misfortune that had befallen the people. As a result of his preaching, he lived with constant threats to his life.

There were times when he felt overwhelmed by the demands of his task, and wanted to pack it all in. He felt that God had tricked him into accepting it. He said, 'For me, Yahweh's word has been the cause of insult and derision all day long. I would say to myself, "I will not think about him, I will not speak in his name any more."'

It is comforting to know that even someone as great as Jeremiah could contemplate 'changing his option.' But he didn't pack it in. He tells us why he went on: 'There seemed to be a fire burning in my heart, imprisoned in my bones. The effort to restrain it wearied me, I could not do it.'

It was this 'inner fire' that drove him on. It was this that enabled him to persevere and to triumph over all his external difficulties. It didn't make things easier for him, but it gave him the drive to keep going. So, no matter how hard things got, he remained unflinchingly faithful to the task God had given him.

There is a song which talks about 'something inside so strong'. The greatest motivation of all is that which comes from inside a person. No outward compulsion can compare with it. Jeremiah is a marvellous example of this, and perhaps no one articulated it as powerfully as he.

Jeremiah's life of struggle and fidelity is a source of courage and inspiration to us. Indeed, his faithfulness prefigures the faithfulness of Jesus.

With his example to inspire us, and God's grace to strengthen us, we too can be faithful to our vocation as Jesus' disciples.

Jesus says that anyone who wishes to be his disciple must take up his cross and follow him. It is not the cross for the sake of the cross. It is the cross because of fidelity, because of service, and because of love.

TWENTY-THIRD SUNDAY OF THE YEAR
Fraternal correction

Praying with the Word of God today

INTRODUCTION AND CONFITEOR

Jesus says, 'Where two or three are gathered in my name, I am there among them.' We are meeting in the Lord's name, and at his command. Hence, we are confident that he is with us.

The Lord wants us to be a community reconciled in love. Let us call to mind the sins that damage our unity. [Pause]

Lord Jesus, you heal the wounds of sin and division. Lord, have mercy.

You reconcile us to one another and to the Father. Christ, have mercy.

You gather the nations into the peace of God's kingdom. Lord, have mercy.

PRAYER OF THE FAITHFUL

Celebrant: We are God's people, the flock that is led by his hand. Let us bring our needs before him with confidence.

Response: Lord, hear our prayer.

Reader(s): For the Pope and the bishops: that they may watch over the flock of Christ wisely and lovingly. [Pause] Let us pray to the Lord.

For our political and civil leaders: that they may fulfil their responsibilities faithfully and well. [Pause] Let us pray to the Lord.

For those who are blind to the hurt they cause to others: that they may see the light and repent. [Pause] Let us pray to the Lord.

For the members of this community: that we may remember that when we love one another we fulfil all the commandments. [Pause] Let us pray to the Lord.

For all the dead: that the Lord may free them from the shadows of death and gladden them with the light of his face. [Pause] Let us pray to the Lord.

For our own special needs. [Longer pause] Let us pray to the Lord.

Celebrant: Almighty and eternal God, look kindly on all who follow Jesus your Son. We are all consecrated to you by our common baptism. Make us one in the fullness of faith and in the fellowship of love. We ask this through Christ our Lord.

REFLECTION

'O that today you would listen to his voice.
Harden not your hearts.'
To adopt a hard-hearted attitude is to maim oneself.
A hard heart is a closed heart, so it can't receive.
A hard heart inevitably becomes a barren heart.
A soft heart, on the other hand, is a blessing.
A soft heart can receive and can respond.
Lord, grant that softened by the rain of your grace,
and warmed by the sun of your love,
our hearts may be turned from a desert into a garden.

FINAL BLESSING

May you walk without fault and act with justice.
May the words of your mouth, and the thoughts of your heart, win favour in the sight of God.
May the Lord keep you safe in his tent in the day of evil.

Sharing the Word of God today

SCRIPTURE NOTE

First Reading (Ezek 33:7-9). This contains a message for the prophet himself, reminding him of his pastoral responsibilities. God has posted him as a sentinel on the city wall. It is his duty to bring back others from infidelity and iniquity. It is presumed that he speaks to those under his care with genuine humility and love for them.

The responsibility to point out to a wrongdoer the error of his ways and to try to get him to reform is the link with the Gospel.

Gospel (Mt 18:15-20). This talks about the duty a Christian has to correct an erring brother or sister. It is presumed that the fault in question is serious, but has not necessarily been committed against oneself.

Every effort must be made to bring the erring person to repentance: first in private, then before a few, finally before the whole community. If he is still unrepentant, he must be excommunicated. The decision of the Church will be honoured by God, since God inspired them in making that decision.

This passage presents difficulties. The procedure Matthew outlines here implies a fully developed and organised Church with a system of ecclesiastical discipline. What is more, it speaks of tax collectors and Gentiles as irredeemable outsiders. The harsh epithets reflect a tradition cultivated by the stringent Jewish Christianity out of which Matthew's Church grew.

The biggest problem, however, is that it doesn't sound like Jesus. No doubt it went back to something Jesus did say. At its widest what Jesus was saying was: if someone sins, no effort must be spared to get him to acknowledge his fault and reform.

While each member of the community has the responsibility to correct an erring brother or sister, special responsibility falls on the leaders. They are the 'sentries' posted by God to watch over the community.

Second Reading (Rom 13:8-10). Seven of the Ten Commandments refer to relations with our neighbour. All seven are summed up in the one command: 'Love your neighbour as yourself', because if we really loved our neighbour, we would not harm him in any way.

How to correct a person

The Gospel talks about the duty to correct an erring brother or sister. Jesus says, 'If your brother does something wrong, go and have it out with him.' It is presumed that the fault in question is serious, but has not necessarily been committed against oneself.

If someone is doing serious wrong, we have a duty to point it out to him or her. This duty falls most heavily on the leaders in the community (see First Reading). But it is the duty of every Christian. However, it's something that calls for courage, sensitivity, and above all love.

A famous rabbi said. 'I wonder if there is anyone in this generation capable of accepting reproof.' Another rabbi said, 'I wonder if there is anyone in this generation who knows how to reprove.' One man who seems to have mastered the art of reproving is Nelson Mandela.

In his autobiography, *Long Walk to Freedom,* he talks about his long years of imprisonment on Robben Island. He tells how one day he was called to the main office. General Steyn was visiting the island and wanted to know from Mandela if the prisoners had any complaints. (Mandela had been chosen by his fellow prisoners as their spokesman). Badenhorst, the officer in command on the prison, was also present. Badenhorst was feared and hated by the prisoners.

In a calm, but forceful and truthful manner, Mandela informed the visitor about the chief complaints of the prisoners. But he did so without bitterness or recriminations. The general duly took note of what he had to say, which amounted to a damning indictment of Badenhorst's regime.

The following day Badenhorst went to Mandela and said, 'I'm leaving the island. I just want to wish you people good luck.' The remark left Mandela dumbfounded. He thought about this incident for a long time afterwards. Badenhorst had perhaps been the most callous and barbaric commanding officer they had had on the island. But that incident showed that there was another side to his nature. And Mandela concludes: 'It goes to show that even the most seemingly cold-blooded have a core of decency, and that if their hearts are touched, they are capable of changing.'

We have a duty to correct another. But we must not commit a sin while doing so. We must not humiliate the person we are reproving. And we must not do it in anger, because in that case all we do is cause the person to harden his heart. We must do it out of concern for the other person. It is a way of showing love for him. We don't show love for someone if we allow him to go on doing wrong.

We are responsible for one another. We should not remain silent when silence can be taken to mean that we approve of what is happening. In that case we bear part of the responsibility for the evil.

When God asked Cain where his brother Abel was, he replied, 'Am I my brothers keeper?' It's an excuse that has been widely used to this day. People turn a blind eye, refuse to get involved, declaring that it is none of their business. But we are responsible for one another.

If we confront the offender in the right spirit, and he is genuine, he will want to put it right. If not, he won't be able to plead ignorance, saying, 'Why didn't you tell me?' But the object is not to score a victory over our brother, but to win him over.

God is continually calling us from the error of our ways into a closer relationship with him and with one another. It is usually through human intermediaries that God's call comes.

Seeking to be reconciled

The Gospel talks about the duty to correct an erring brother or sister. Jesus says, 'If your brother does something wrong, go and have it out with him.' Obviously these kind of problems occurred even in the first Christian community.

It is presumed that the fault in question is serious, but has not necessarily been committed against oneself. But let us suppose that it has been committed against oneself. Today's Gospel gives us a way of tackling a problem like this.

First of all, however, let us look at the way we normally tackle the problem. We begin by keeping it to ourselves. It may be that we are ashamed or simply unable to talk about it to anyone. So we pretend that everything is normal. Meanwhile we brood over the injury. This tends to magnify it. We become sullen and sour and depressed, and may cut the offender off as a kind of revenge.

Eventually, unable to keep it to ourselves, we begin to tell others about it – friends, neighbours, and relatives. Sometimes total strangers are brought into it. We bring them in, not as advisers, but as people who will corroborate our reading of the situation and who will sympathise with us. The last person to hear about the hurt is often the person who is causing it.

Today's Gospel shows that there is another approach. We should confront the person who is causing the hurt. Indeed, we have a duty to do so. Failure to do so shows a lack of love for the person. Confrontation takes courage and involves risk. But sometimes a little honest talking can clear the air. The person may not be aware of the extent of the hurt he is causing. He may see the light at once, which means you have won him over.

The confrontation should not be done in anger. Nor should it be done out of a desire to get even. It must be done out of concern for him, not just out of a desire to appease one's own wounded pride. Also, before we do it, we should examine our own conscience to see if maybe we are not partly to blame. We recoil from the self-righteous person who behaves as a self-appointed moral officer.

The highest point we can attain in a confrontation is when we get the other person to see the wrong he has done and to condemn it himself. If he repents, forgiveness must be warm and without limits or conditions.

If he refuses to see the light, what then? We should seek advice. We should get one or two wise people and enlist their help to face him. The rabbis had a very wise saying: 'Judge not alone, for none may judge alone but God'.

If even then we fail, we should go to the community. Community need not necessarily mean the Church. It could mean family, or some other group of concerned and responsible people. But it cannot be repeated too often, that the whole aim of the exercise is not to score points against one's brother, but to help him to amend his ways, and to be reconciled with him. To seek reconciliation is, according to Jesus, more important than offering sacrifice to God (Mt 5:23-24).

If at the end of the day, reconciliation proves to be impossible, then the verdict you (and the community) come to will be ratified by God.

But reconciliation can happen and it leads to great growth for both parties. Reconciliation is hard, but for that reason it should not be left untried. Needless to say, the Christian will pray about it. Prayer disposes one to follow the Christian approach.

Harden not your hearts

Today's readings stress the responsibility to correct an erring brother or sister. This duty falls most heavily on the leaders in the community (see First Reading). But it is the duty of every Christian.

But the readings also stress the onus on the one corrected to repent. The consequences of not doing so are also stressed. 'If the wicked man does not repent, he will die in his sin' (First Reading). And the Gospel says, 'If he refuses to listen … treat him as a pagan or a tax collector.' In other words, excommunicate him.

'O that today you would listen to his voice! Harden not your hearts.' This is a very serious warning, which is contained in today's responsorial psalm. To harden one's heart means to refuse to repent. Then one is faced with the terrifying prospect of dying in one's sins.

The warning is addressed to serious evildoers. But it has relevance for us all. To a greater or lesser extent all of us are drawn towards evil. And once we succumb, it is hard to break free. Each time we repeat an evil choice it becomes more of a habit, to the point where it eventually becomes part of our character.

Every evil act tends to harden a person's heart. The more a person's heart hardens, the less freedom there is to change. But the opposite is also true. Every good deed tends to soften a person's heart. Every time we do something good, we make it easier to do good again.

From a spiritual point of view, hardness of heart is one of the worst things that can happen to anyone. A hard heart is a closed heart, so it can't receive. A hard heart inevitably becomes a barren heart. To adopt a hard-hearted attitude is to maim oneself. 'Fear not that your heart might be broken; fear, rather, that it might turn into a stone' (Oscar Wilde).

God is calling us from the error of our ways into a closer relationship with him and with one another. And it is to the heart that the call of God comes. Unfortunately, the heart is not always receptive.

To harden our hearts against one another is bad enough. But to harden our hearts against God would be the ultimate calamity. It would mean that God himself could not get through to us.

God longs for our hearts, and is continually calling us into communion with him and with one another. When we heed the voice of God everything changes. Softened by the rain of God's grace, and warmed by the sun of his love, the human heart can be turned from a wasteland into fertile ground.

Jesus came not to condemn us but to save us. In order to be saved, we have to confess our sins. But this is seldom easy. Pride makes it difficult for us to confess. However, if we do confess our sins, we have nothing to fear but the mercy of God.

TWENTY-FOURTH SUNDAY OF THE YEAR
Forgiveness

Praying with the Word of God today

INTRODUCTION AND CONFITEOR

In the Gospel Jesus makes it clear that if we want God to forgive us, we must be willing to forgive others. We always begin Mass by asking forgiveness for our sins. As we do so, we should also ask for the grace to forgive those who have sinned against us. [Pause]

God is generous with his forgiveness. Let us open ourselves to God's forgiveness now.

Lord Jesus, you are slow to anger and rich in mercy. Lord, have mercy.

You do not treat us according to our sins nor repay us according to our faults. Christ, have mercy.

As far as the east is from the west, so far do you remove our sins. Lord, have mercy.

PRAYER OF THE FAITHFUL

Celebrant: God forgives all our guilt and crowns us with love and compassion. Let us pray that we may be equally generous in our dealings with others.

Response: Lord, hear our prayer.

Reader(s): For Christians: that they may give an example to the world of the art of forgiveness. [Pause] Let us pray to the Lord.

For all who exercise authority: that they may be kind and forgiving towards those who fail them. [Pause] Let us pray to the Lord.

For those who have been badly sinned against: that they may find healing and peace. [Pause] Let us pray to the Lord.

For all gathered here: that we may have the humility and courage to seek forgiveness of those we have offended. Pause] Let us pray to the Lord.

For our loved ones who have died: that they may rest in the peace of God. [Pause] Let us pray to the Lord.

For our own special needs. [Longer pause] Let us pray to the Lord.

Celebrant: God of love and mercy, may our sharing in this holy mystery bring us your forgiveness, and help us to forgive from the heart those who have sinned against us. We ask this through Christ our Lord.

OUR FATHER

Let us ask our heavenly Father to forgive our sins and to bring us to forgive those who have sinned against us.

PRAYER

Lord, remember not only people of good will
but also people of ill will.
Do not remember only the sufferings
that have been inflicted on us,
but remember too the fruit we have bought
as a result of this suffering:
the comradeship and loyalty,
the humility and courage,
the generosity and greatness of heart
that has grown out of it.
And when they come to judgement,
let all the fruits that we have borne be their forgiveness.
Prayer found in Auschwitz.

FINAL BLESSING

May you bear with one another in complete selflessness, gentleness and patience.

May you do all you can to preserve unity by the peace that binds you together.

May you forgive each other as the Lord has forgiven you.

Sharing the Word of God today

SCRIPTURE NOTE

First Reading (Sir 27:30-28:7). It is a human reaction to hold grudges against those who have hurt us. But Sirach insists that wrath and anger are hateful things. He also admonishes us to show mercy to others, since we look to God for mercy for ourselves.

If we harbour resentment and anger against those who have hurt us, how can we demand compassion from God? And if we show no pity for a fellow human being, how can we plead for pity for ourselves?

All of this ties in closely with the theme of the Gospel, where Jesus warns that an unforgiving spirit will come between us and the God we worship.

Gospel (Mt 18:21-35). Last Sunday's Gospel talked about the duty a Christian has to correct an erring brother or sister. The focus now shifts to the brother who is not recalcitrant, but who sins often, and therefore needs forgiveness often.

The position of the servant in Jesus' story is absolutely hopeless. He owes the king so much money that even if he worked forever, he would not be able to repay him. This is the strong point of the story. All he can do is plead for his mercy.

Our situation before God is similar to that of the servant. We can't win God's forgiveness. All we can do is plead for it. But God is generous with his forgiveness. We then must be willing to extend to others the forgiveness God has extended to us.

To refuse to forgive those who have sinned against us would be to exclude ourselves from receiving God's forgiveness for our own sins. We must forgive, not seven times, but seventy times seven times. This means that forgiveness must be unlimited.

All this has a very real application in church life. The thing that is most likely to turn people away from the Church is when they don't find forgiveness there.

Second Reading (Rom 14:7-9). As Christians, our living and dying, that is, our whole entire existence, must be for Christ and for one another.

Importance of forgiveness

Today's Gospel deals with a subject that touches us all – forgiveness. None of us can go through life without getting hurt. The memory of wrongs done to us seeps into our heart, producing a legacy of bitterness and resentment. Some people have years of stored hurts inside them.

Bitterness and resentment are self-destructive. Bitterness is internal decay. It can poison our spirit, and destroy our capacity to love.

A study done among divorced women has shown that more hurt is caused by the resentment they harbour than by the divorce itself. There is a Yiddish saying that goes like this: 'Ten enemies cannot hurt a person as much as he hurts himself.'

Those who adopt negative attitudes like these will live their lives as severely handicapped as if they had lost a leg or been born deaf. At all costs we must keep the heart free of bitterness. Resentment and bitterness are very dangerous things, and we cannot be healed of them unless we forgive.

However, there is no point in being glib about forgiveness. Forgiveness is never easy. To forgive is, first and foremost, a duty we owe ourselves. We forgive for the sake of our own well-being. We forgive because we don't want to live with feelings of resentment and desire for revenge. We forgive in order to cleanse ourselves of these poisonous attitudes and states of mind, so that we may be able to devote all our energies to loving, which is the only activity that befits a Christian.

One of the things that can motivate us to forgive is an appreciation of our own need of forgiveness. Jesus says that unless we forgive others God won't forgive us. The fault is not with God but with us. When we refuse to forgive we break down the bridge over which we ourselves must pass.

Forgiveness, on the other hand, clears a path for God to forgive us.

'Forgive your neighbour the hurt he does you, and when you pray your sins will be forgiven' (First Reading).

Jesus says, 'You must forgive your brother *from your heart.*' It is only with the heart that we can forgive rightly. If forgiveness is to be effective it must be sincere and warm. A cold forgiveness is not much use.

When we forgive, we ourselves are the main beneficiaries. But forgiveness also benefits the person who is forgiven. It sets the person free to walk in friendship with God and with the person he has offended.

We constantly fall short of complete forgiveness. Perhaps this is why Jesus tells us that we have to forgive seventy times seven. There is no moment when we are not in need of forgiveness nor any moment when we do not need to be forgiving.

Forgiveness doesn't mean forgetting the wrong done to us. It means remembering and letting go. There is a saying: The stupid neither forgive not forget; the naive forgive and forget; the wise forgive but do not forget.

Forgiveness is one of the highest and most beautiful forms of love. It is a holy task. Only God can help us to accomplish it fully.

Stories

1. A former inmate of a Nazi concentration camp was visiting a friend who had shared the ordeal with him. 'Have your forgiven the Nazis?' he asked his friend.

'Yes,' came the reply.

'Well, I haven't. I'm still consumed with hatred for them.'

'In that case,' said his friend gently, 'they still have you in prison.'

2. Too many people take too much unfinished relational business to their graves. A man on his deathbed told the following story.

'I had a very good friend called Bob. But he and his wife moved away to another county. A little while later, my wife, Charlotte, had to have a serious operation. Bob and his wife never got in touch with us. I know they knew about it. I was very hurt because they never called to see her or even to enquire how she was. So I dropped the relationship.

'Over the years I met Bob a few times and he always tried to reconcile, but I didn't accept it. I wasn't satisfied with his explanation. I was prideful. I shrugged him off. A few years ago he died of cancer. I feel so sad. I never got to see him. I never got to forgive him. It pains me so much. My advice is: don't wait.'

The process of forgiveness

Jesus asks us to forgive *'seventy times seven'*. This means forgiveness must be unlimited. There is no point in pretending that forgiveness is easy. It is never easy. Without the grace of God it is sometimes impossible.

When we get hurt, we naturally grow resentful and bitter. Resentment and bitterness are very dangerous things, and we cannot be healed of them unless we forgive.

We all need to forgive because at one time or another we all have been hurt. What can we do? We have to remember that forgiveness cannot be achieved overnight. Forgiveness is *a process,* and like all processes it takes time. There are steps we can take, which, with the grace of God, will lead to forgiveness and healing of the hurt.

1. We must recognise that a wrong has been done to us. There is no point in pretending it didn't happen.

2. We must recognise that we have feelings about this. We feel angry and hurt. These feelings are not sins. In fact, they are natural and healthy.

3. We should talk about these feelings. If we can't do this with the person who has hurt us, we should do it with someone we trust.

4. We should make a decision to forgive. Forgiveness is an act of the will, not of the feelings. But this doesn't mean that feelings of hurt and bitterness will suddenly disappear. The healing of these will take time.

5. Finally, we have to make a decision about our relationship with the person who has hurt us – whether to continue it or discontinue it. Reconciliation is not always possible. It takes two to be reconciled.

It's not a question of forgiving if and when the offender repents. We are expected to forgive even if the offender doesn't repent – that is what makes it so difficult, and why we need God's grace.

We need to pray for the gift of forgiveness. Unless we forgive, we will not be able to let go of bitterness and resentment, and so will not know peace or healing. And unless we forgive others God won't forgive us. The fault is not with God but with us. When we refuse to forgive we break down the bridge over which we ourselves must pass.

Forgiveness doesn't mean forgetting the wrong done to us. It means remembering and letting go. Forgiveness is one of the highest and most beautiful forms of love. It is a holy task. Only God can help us to accomplish it fully.

Story
Even before the six-day war, Israel and Jordan had been mutual enemies. But in the summer of 1994 King Hussein of Jordan and the late President Rabin of Israel signed a peace accord. They said they did so in order that their children would not need to fight anymore.

To prepare the way for the signing of the peace treaty, Israeli foreign minister, Simon Peres, crossed the Dead Sea by helicopter to end nearly half a century of enmity. He was the first high-ranking official from Israel to openly visit Jordan.

He said, 'It took us a mere 15 minutes to ride over. But it took us 46 years to arrive at this time and this place of peace and promise.'

On signing the treaty King Hussein said, 'Out of all the days of my life, I don't believe there is one such as this.'

Peace is a process. So too is reconciliation. They both take time.

Asking for forgiveness

We have an obligation to forgive those who have offended us. But we also have an obligation to ask forgiveness of those we have offended. The former can be very hard. But the latter can be even harder. It can take great courage to ask for forgiveness.

According to Jewish law, sins committed against God can be absolved by sincere repentance. But for sins committed against fellow human beings we must first seek the forgiveness of those whom we have wronged in order to be in a position to invoke divine mercy. (I don't think the Christian position is much different. See Mt 5:23.)

Once in Poland an elderly rabbi boarded a train to travel home to Warsaw. He entered a compartment in which three salesmen were playing cards. In need of a foursome, the salesmen asked the rabbi to join in, but he politely refused, saying he had been busy all day and needed to catch up on his prayers, and that in any case he didn't play cards. They tried to persuade him, but he still refused. At this they got very hostile and started to abuse him. When he still refused, they threw him out of the compartment, so that he had to stand in the corridor for the rest of the journey.

On arriving at Warsaw the rabbi got off the train. So too did the salesmen. The rabbi was met by a large crowd of his followers. On seeing this one of the salesmen asked, 'Who is that man?'

'That's rabbi Solomon, the most revered rabbi in the whole of Poland,' came the answer.

On hearing this the man regretted what he had done. He had no idea who he had offended. So he quickly went up to the rabbi and asked for forgiveness. However, the rabbi refused to forgive him.

The rabbi's followers were taken aback at this. They couldn't figure out how their rabbi, a man renowned for his gentleness and holiness, could refuse to forgive someone. So they asked him, 'When someone who has offended us asks for forgiveness, should we not forgive him?'

'Yes,' the rabbi replied.

'Well then, why didn't you forgive that man?'

'I can't forgive him. The salesman didn't offend me, the chief rabbi of Warsaw. He offended a common man. Let him go to him and ask for forgiveness.'

In other words, he was asking for forgiveness only because he had offended a famous person. But had it been just an ordinary person that he had offended, it would never have occurred to him to ask for forgiveness.

I wonder if God doesn't sometimes feel like saying something similar to us: 'Why do you tell me that you are sorry for offending your neighbour? Why don't you go to your neighbour, tell him you're sorry, and ask his forgiveness? By that very act you would clear a path for me to forgive you.'

Fortunately, in our communities there are many who are willing to forgive others. But, alas, there are very few who are willing to seek forgiveness from others.

Illustrations

It is in forgiving that we ourselves are forgiven. Two illustrations.

1. Once two prisoners shared the same cell. A dank, dark cell it was. One of them was a strong, crude individual. The other was gentle and timid. The prisoners were handcuffed to one another. The strong man was mean and cruel to the timid man.

One day, while his companion was asleep, the timid man found the key to the cell. He desperately wanted to get away from this horrible cell. But at the same time he had no wish to do any favours to his obnoxious companion. However, he soon realised he could not set himself free unless he also set his companion free.

2. It is like two people living in the same room, one of whom closes the blind because he doesn't want the other to enjoy the sunlight. But in so doing he also deprives himself of the sunlight.

TWENTY-FIFTH SUNDAY OF THE YEAR
The workers in the vineyard

Praying with the Word of God today

INTRODUCTION AND CONFITEOR

Often we are small and petty in the way we think and act. Fortunately for us there is nothing small or petty about God. God's ways are as high above our ways as the heavens are above the earth.

Let us ask God for forgiveness for our smallness of heart, while at the same time opening ourselves to God's goodness. [Pause]

Lord Jesus, you are kind and full of compassion. Lord, have mercy.

You are slow to anger, abounding in love. Christ, have mercy.

You are just in all your ways, and loving in all your deeds. Lord, have mercy.

PRAYER OF THE FAITHFUL

Celebrant: Let us now bring our prayers to the God who takes pity on us, and whose greatness cannot be measured.

Response: Lord, hear our prayer.

Reader(s): For Christians: that they may prove themselves faithful workers in the Lord's vineyard. [Pause] Let us pray to the Lord.

For those entrusted with public office: that they may prove themselves worthy of their stewardship. [Pause] Let us pray to the Lord.

For those who are unemployed: that they may not lose heart. [Pause] Let us pray to the Lord.

For all gathered here: that we may serve God out of love, and that our love may be reflected in our dealings with others. [Pause] Let us pray to the Lord.

For our deceased relatives and friends: that they may share Christ's victory over death and enjoy the vision of his glory in heaven. [Pause] Let us pray to the Lord.

For our own special needs. [Longer pause] Let us pray to the Lord.

Celebrant: Lord, give us work till our lives are ended, and give us life till our work is done. We ask this through Christ our Lord.

OUR FATHER

God is just in all your ways and loving in all his deeds. Let us pray to our heavenly Father in the words our Saviour gave us.

PRAYER/REFLECTION

'As high as the heavens are above the earth,
so high are my ways above your ways,
my thoughts above your thoughts,' says the Lord.
Lord, open our minds and enlarge our hearts,
so that we think more like you,
and act more like you.
Let us not to begrudge your goodness to others,
knowing that we too are undeserving of your favours,
and stand more in need of your mercy than of your justice.

FINAL BLESSING

May you treat each other in the same friendly way Christ has treated you.
May you clothe yourselves in sincere compassion, kindness and patience.
May your love not be mere words but something real and active.

Sharing the Word of God today

SCRIPTURE NOTE

First Reading (Is 55:6-9). Here the prophet insists that evildoers must abandon their evil ways, and seek the Lord with humility. If they do, then God, who is rich in forgiveness, will take pity on them. God's ways are as high above our ways as the heavens are above the earth. Just how vast is the difference between God's ways and our ways is illustrated in the parable of the labourers in the vineyard.

Gospel (Mt 20:1-16). The Pharisees were very critical of Jesus because of the way he befriended sinners and outcasts. By means of this parable Jesus tells them that he is only imitating God, who is generous to, and full of compassion for, the poor and the outcast.

The owner of the vineyard is God. The Pharisees were meant to see themselves in the workers who came in early. The latecomers were sinners and outcasts. Just as the owner of the vineyard was generous towards the latecomers, so God is generous towards sinners with his forgiveness and mercy.

In this respect the parable is similar to that of the Prodigal Son. It illustrates that God's gracious giving is not determined by what is earned – a Matthean example of a major Pauline emphasis.

Second Reading (Phil 1:20-24.27). For this and the next three Sundays the Second Reading is taken from Paul's letter to the Philippians. The present lines were written from prison where Paul faced an uncertain future.

Here he speaks of death. However, he doesn't regard death in a morbid way. Rather, he sees it as a way of achieving complete union with Christ, something he longs for. Still, he would be more than happy to continue living, as it would mean carrying on his work on behalf of the Philippians.

Paul exhibits precisely the kind of attitude envisaged in Jesus' parable. Rewards are not denied, but they are not the reason why we work in the Lord's vineyard.

An unfair story?

Some consider the story of the workers in the vineyard an unfair story. What happens seems patently unjust. It seems to favour the idler at the expense of the hard worker. Not so. The story goes out of its way to stress that no injustice has been done. To understand it we need to keep the following in mind.

The eleventh-hour people were not idlers. They wanted to work. It was just that nobody had hired them. In effect, they were rejects. The idea that any employer would take such people on at the eleventh hour, and pay them a full day's wage, was unthinkable. Yet that is exactly what the owner of the vineyard did. This is the strong point of the parable.

Justice is very important. To realise how important it is, all we have to do is think of its opposite. Anyone who has had the experience of being treated unjustly will know what a deep hurt it can cause. Justice is to society what leaven is to bread.

However, the story is not about justice. It is about generosity. Justice is a great thing, but it hasn't the sweetness of generosity. Generosity touches the heart in a way justice never does. Though the story is about generosity, it is not about human generosity. It is about the generosity of God.

God's generosity utterly transcends human generosity. 'My thoughts are not your thoughts, nor are my ways your ways. As high as the heavens are above the earth, so high are my ways above your ways, my thoughts above your thoughts' (First Reading).

To be more specific, the story is about God's generosity to sinners. There were some who criticised Jesus because of his kindness to sinners. In their eyes he was betraying the virtuous. They assumed that God works on the merit system. According to this system, you must earn your graces by hard work. Jesus didn't agree with them. He told them so in this story.

His audience knew exactly what he was getting at. The vineyard was the kingdom of God. Those who had been working all day long were the Pharisees and the Jews in general. The eleventh-hour people were sinners and the Gentiles.

Which of us would like to be treated by God according to strict justice? Do we not all stand more in need of God's mercy than of God's justice. Where God is concerned we should never expect anything as a right.

Therefore, when we come before God, let us not parade our rights and entitlements. We can't put God in our debt. But we don't have to. God is generous beyond our imagining.

God's generosity is a great comfort to us, but it is also a great challenge. If we have experienced that generosity in our own lives, far from begrudging it to others, we will try to imitate it in our dealings with others.

A conversion is required before we can begin to think and act like God. The conversion that is required is not an intellectual conversion, but a conversion of the heart.

Story

The setting is a crossroads on the edge of a shantytown near Cape Town, South Africa. It's mid-morning. A number of men are gathered at the side of the road. Some are lying down under the trees to escape the blazing sun. But most are standing in the open.

What are they doing there? They are waiting – waiting for some farmer or builder to come along and hire them for the day. Some have been there since sunrise. Some have even been there overnight. And still you will find people who say that these kind of people don't want to work.

They are totally exposed. They are on display. Many eyes scan them – indifferent eyes, curious eyes, and hostile eyes. Their value depends on what people want from them. They have no value in themselves. They will settle for the minimum wage. It is already eleven o'clock in the morning. A look of dejection is beginning to settle on their furrowed faces. The day is wearing on. Hope is fading.

For most of these men there will be no eleventh-hour reprieve. They will go home to their shacks and their families empty-handed. In this world the first shall be first, and the last shall be last.

Rejoice in the Lord's goodness

Some people can't bear to see others get things easier than themselves. According to this mentality you get what you earn. If you haven't earned anything, then you don't deserve to get anything. In this kind of world there is no room for grace. Grace is favour extended to undeserving people as a gift.

I encountered an example of this as I was travelling in a hearse to officiate at a burial service. On the way I got chatting with the driver. He told me with pride how he had risen from poverty to relative wealth. But he had his troubles along the way. He had fallen victim to alcoholism but was now in recovery. He had buried a twelve year-old daughter. Even so, he was able to say that God had been good to him.

I warmed to him. It was clear to me that he was a good man, and a spiritual one too. Yet there was something about him that saddened me, namely, his attitude to the poor. As one who had once shared their lot, I would have expected him to be understanding and compassionate towards them. Instead, he was harsh and judgmental. He resented any help given to them, seeing it as a betrayal of people like himself who had worked their way up without receiving help from anyone.

Sadly, such an attitude is not uncommon. Jesus encountered a similar mentality. He met religious people who begrudged his kindness to sinners. In their eyes he was betraying the virtuous. They assumed that God works on the merit system. According to this system, you must earn your graces by hard work. Jesus didn't agree with them. And told them so in the parable of the labourers in the vineyard.

His audience knew exactly what he was getting at. The vineyard was the kingdom of God. Those who had been working all day long were the Pharisees and the Jews in general. The eleventh-hour people were sinners and the Gentiles.

The people taken on at 6 am were happy to get work, satisfied with the wage, and thankful to the boss. But when they saw others being taken on later, and being promised the same wage, they began to grow resentful. The result was that what had been a sweet service turned sour, what had been a labour of love turn into one of resentment.

If one is into worthiness and rewards, Jesus' parable is likely to make one angry and resentful. And from the point of view of strict justice it makes no sense. But the story is not about justice. Thank heavens for that. Which of us would like to be treated by God according to strict justice? Do we not all stand more in need of God's mercy than of God's justice?

Jesus' story is about generosity. However, it is not about human generosity, but the generosity of God. God's generosity utterly transcends human generosity. 'My thoughts are not your thoughts, nor are my ways your ways. As high as the heavens are above the earth, so high are my ways above your ways, my thoughts above your thoughts,' says the Lord (First Reading).

God's generosity is a great comfort to us, but it is also a great challenge. If we have experienced that generosity in our own lives, far from begrudging it to others, we will try to imitate it in our dealings with others.

We must be thankful to be given the opportunity to work in the Lord's vineyard, and not think that we are better and more deserving than others. We ought to look on it as a privilege and a joy, just as it was for Paul (see Second Reading). Though he longs for the reward of complete union with Christ, he is more than happy to carry on doing Christ's work among the Philippians.

The last shall be first

Some people consider the story of the workers in the vineyard an unfair story, because it seems to favour the idler over the hard worker. Here is another story that may help us to understand the point Jesus was making.

The final of the 3000 metres was in progress. The runners stayed bunched together until the last lap. Then the eventual winner eased himself into the lead. As he did so another man fell back into last place, after a desperate effort to keep up. The other runners were strung out in between.

As the leader (a local man) came into the home straight, the spectators rose to him. When the news was flashed up that he had set a new world record, thunderous applause echoed around the stadium. The cameras followed him as he did a lap of honour. He got a standing ovation as he went around. Bouquets of flowers were thrown in his direction.

Afterwards everybody wanted to clap him on the back and shake his hand. Microphones were thrust in front of him. 'How does it feel like to be a world champion?' he was asked. Beaming all over he replied, 'Absolutely wonderful!' Already newspapers were queuing up for the exclusive rights to his story, and company executives, cheque books in hand, were doing likewise for the right to use his name to endorse their products.

While all this was going on, the other runners had finished the race. The last man had to really struggle to finish. Then, with head bowed, he departed for the dressing rooms.

A VIP had been invited to perform the prize-giving ceremony. The first three runners home were waiting, all smiles, to take their places on the victory podium. The first sign that something unusual was about to happen was when the VIP said he wanted all the runners present at the ceremony. The runners were duly called, and all was now set.

Then what did he do? He called the man who came in last and gave the gold medal to him. He gave the silver medal to the man who came second last, and the bronze medal to the man who came third last. There were gasps of astonishment from the crowd, and sighs of embarrassment from the organisers. The mistake was pointed out to him. But he said, 'There is no mistake. This is the way I want it.' Then he proceeded to give a warm handshake to each of the other runners right down to the man who came first.

When the latter came forward he was very angry. 'This is not fair!' he exclaimed.

'So you think it's not fair?' the VIP replied calmly.

'I do,' said the man. 'I won the race. I deserve to get the gold medal.'

'Friend,' said the VIP, 'haven't you got enough already?'

'What do you mean?' the man asked.

'You've had the satisfaction of winning the race. You've had the applause of the crowd and the attention of the media. You've had lucrative contracts offered to you. Now consider the man who came last. He finished the race too. And what did he get for his efforts? Nothing. Would it be fairer if you got everything while he got nothing?' With that the victor was reduced to silence. Still fuming, he turned and went away.

The aim of this story is not to downplay the achievement of the winner but to make a point. It seems wrong that one person should get everything, while another gets nothing. I know this is exactly what happens in our world – the winner takes all.

Some might still say that the story is an outrageous one. But is it any more outrageous than Jesus' story about the workers in the vineyard? What point was Jesus making?

The key to understanding the story in in the phrase, 'Are you envious because I am generous?' The story is not about justice. It is about generosity, a generosity unlike anything we've ever known – the generosity of God.

Which of us would like to be treated by God according to strict justice? Do we not all long for mercy rather than justice? We can't put God in our debt. But we don't need to. God is generous to a degree that far outstrips human generosity. All we have to do is open our hearts to God's generosity. And having experienced it, let it serve as a model for our dealings with others.

TWENTY-SIXTH SUNDAY OF THE YEAR
The two sons

Praying with the Word of God today

INTRODUCTION AND CONFITEOR

We have the freedom to say 'yes' or 'no' to God. Sometimes we abuse our freedom, but God in his goodness calls us to repentance. Let us call to mind our sins, and ask God to give us the grace of true repentance. [Pause]

Lord Jesus, you guide the humble in the right path. Lord, have mercy.

You show the path to those who stray. Christ, have mercy.

You seek out and save the lost. Lord, have mercy.

PRAYER OF THE FAITHFUL

Celebrant: Let us bring our needs before the Lord, who is close to the broken-hearted and hears the cries of the poor.

Response: Remember your mercies, O Lord.

Reader(s): For Christians: that their lives may bear witness to the faith they profess with their lips. [Pause] Let us pray to the Lord.

For all who hold public office: that they may be faithful in carrying out their duties and responsibilities. [Pause] Let us pray to the Lord.

For those who have been the victims of broken promises: that they may find healing and peace. [Pause] Let us pray to the Lord.

For all gathered here: that we may never allow words to take the place of deeds. [Pause] Let us pray to the Lord.

For our deceased relatives and friends: that God may fulfil for them his promise of eternal life. [Pause] Let us pray to the Lord.

For our own special needs. [Longer pause] Let us pray to the Lord.

Celebrant: God of love, save us from the darkness of broken promises, fill our hearts with your love, and keep us faithful to you and to one another. We ask this through Christ our Lord.

PRAYER/REFLECTION

Two words that we use very frequently
are the words 'yes' and 'no'.

In general 'yes' and 'no' are morning words.
However, as the day passes, we can be moved
to turn a morning 'no' into an evening 'yes'.
But the earlier we do this, the better,
because the night is coming when no one can work.
Lord, grant that the night may not come upon us
with our work undone and our promises unkept.

FINAL BLESSING

May you never allow words to take the place of deeds.

May the God, who has called us to eternal glory in Christ, strengthen and support you with his grace.

And may the peace of Christ reign in your minds and in your hearts.

Sharing the Word of God today

SCRIPTURE NOTE

First Reading (Ezek 18:25-28). Here the prophet is responding to an objection that God is unjust because he punishes or rewards the individual for his own actions instead of allowing him to rely on the institution of Israel and the promises made to the nation.

The prophet declares that each individual is responsible for his/her own actions, and will be judged accordingly. But he goes on to state that repentance will win the individual pardon and life. The theme of repentance is the connection with the Gospel.

Gospel (Mt 21:28-32). Matthew now has three parables that are concerned with the judgement of Israel: the two sons, the vinedressers, and the wedding feast. We have the first of these today.

In today's Gospel the focus is on the refusal of the religious leaders to repent and believe in Jesus. Their unbelief is contrasted with the belief of tax collectors and prostitutes. This is pressed home in the parable of the two sons.

The religious leaders were meant to see themselves in the second son. They promised to work for God but failed to do so, and so have excluded themselves from the kingdom.

The first son represents sinners. They originally chose to go their own way but then repented and took God's way, and so gained entry into the kingdom. Repentance is a necessary disposition for entry into the kingdom.

The parable was meant to defend Jesus' invitation of sinners and outcasts to the kingdom, in the face of the sneers of the religious establishment. But it also illustrates the difference between saying and doing – a favourite theme of Matthew.

Second Reading (Phil 2:1-5). Here Paul says that self-seeking and rivalry have no place in the Christian community. We must imitate Christ who humbled himself to the point of accepting death, the most shameful kind of death – death on a cross (Deut. 21:23). God rewarded his obedience and humility by 'raising him on high and giving him a name which is above all other names.' The self-emptying and self-abasement of Christ should serve as a model for every Christian.

Giving one's word

One of the greatest things we can give another person is our word. A person's word is a great test of a person's character. But it's easy to give our word. It doesn't cost anything there and then. The cost comes later, if and when we honour our word.

Some people are very generous with their word. They will promise the sun, moon and stars. But they can't be relied on. Their promises dissolve like salt in water. There is not one of us who has not experienced the pain of being let down by someone who failed to keep his/her word.

There are other people who are slow to give their word. They don't make promises easily. But when they do make a promise, they can be relied on to honour it. How lovely it is to deal with people like that.

When the father in Jesus' story asked his two sons to go and work in the vineyard, one of them said an immediate and definite yes – 'Certainly, sir'. But he didn't go. Nothing is as dangerous as a glib, unthinking 'yes'. It betrays a lack of self-knowledge (we presume we are up to it), and shows no appreciation of what the task involves.

The other son said an immediate and definite no – 'I will not go.' However, he later changed his mind and went.

There is part of both of those sons in each of us. This means we can learn from both.

We can learn from the first son – the one who said he wouldn't go but later changed his mind and went. To change one's mind is sometimes regarded as a weakness. But this is not always the case. To change one's mind can mean to repent, that is, to think again. It takes humility to admit one's mistake, and courage to put it right.

Many of the greatest saints in the history of the Church were sinners who initially said 'no' to God, but later changed their minds (that is, repented), and said 'yes'. St Augustine is perhaps the best-known example, but there are many, many others.

We can also learn from the second son – the one who said he would go but didn't. He is meant as a warning to us. We must not allow words to take the place of deeds. Promises can never take the place of performance. Fine words can never be a substitute for fine deeds.

However, Jesus is not holding up either son as a model. The ideal son would be the son who immediately and willingly carried out his father's wishes. Jesus is the ideal Son.

St Paul says that with him it was always 'yes' (2 Cor 1:20). And in today's Second Reaidng he says, 'Jesus emptied himself and became obedient to the point of death, death on a cross. Therefore, God exalted him, giving him a name that is above all other names.' Jesus is the model for us.

Two important words

There are two words that we use very frequently. Though they are very small words they are very important ones. It is no exaggeration to say that our lives could be summed up in terms of these two words. What are these two words? They are the words 'yes' and 'no'.

Of course, it's not the words in themselves but the spirit in which they are said that makes the difference. They can be said glibly and without sincerity, or they can be said thoughtfully and with sincerity. But that's only the beginning. At the end of the day what matters is whether or not they are acted on.

In Jesus story, when the father asked his sons to go and work in his vineyard, the first son said an immediate and definite no – 'I will not go.' We don't know why he refused to go. Maybe he thought, 'Why does it always have to be me? Let someone else go for a change.' Maybe he had other plans for that day. Maybe he was being rebellious. Or maybe he was just plain lazy.

However, it was early morning when he said that 'no'. A lot can happen between morning and evening. At some point during the course of the day, the word 'yes' began to sound inside him – at first faintly, then loudly. A struggle ensued between it and the initial 'no'. Eventually the 'yes' won the struggle, and he went to work in the vineyard. Of course by that time some of the day was lost. Even so, the father would have been happy to see that he changed his mind. To change one's mind here means to repent (to think again).

Now let us consider the second son. He said an immediate and definite yes to his father – 'Certainly, sir'. But in fact he didn't go. We wonder why not. Maybe he genuinely intended to go but forgot. Maybe he postponed it, and then found it wasn't worth his while. Or maybe he said, 'They'll manage without me.'

At any rate, the day wore on, and the 'yes' he had said so loudly and clearly in the morning grew fainter and fainter. By evening it had turned into a 'no'. His case is worse than that of the first son. He had given his word. His father would have been counting on him, and would feel let down when he discovered that he didn't go.

Jesus' audience knew what he was getting at. The vineyard was the kingdom of God. The son who promised to work but didn't, represented the religious leaders. They promised to work for God but failed to do so, and so excluded themselves from the kingdom. The other son represents sinners. They originally chose to go their own way, but then repented and took God's way, and so gained entry into the kingdom.

Many of the greatest saints in the history of the Church were sinners who initially said 'no' to God, but later changed their minds and said 'yes'? St Augustine is perhaps the most obvious example, but there are many others.

God has given us the freedom to say 'yes' or 'no' – our 'yes' would have no value unless we were free to say 'no'. However, we may say 'yes' to God with our words, and 'no' to God with our deeds. We profess to believe, but fail to translate our belief into active obedience. Words are no substitute for deeds.

We must, therefore, constantly examine ourselves. We must try to turn our promises into fulfilment, and our words into deeds. Every day we can turn one of yesterday's 'nos' into one of today's 'yeses'.

Personal responsibility

Nowadays personal responsibility is being eroded. When something goes wrong, no one takes responsibility. It is put down to 'a systems failure'.

And the whole thrust of modern psychoanalysis seems to be directed at removing responsibility from the individual. Someone else is to blame – one's companions, one's parents, one's environment, and so on.

At the time of the prophet Ezekiel (First Reading), there was a belief that the child was punished for the sins of the parent. There was a popular saying, 'Parents eat sour grapes, and their children's teeth are set on edge.' But the prophet didn't agree with this. He stated clearly and unequivocally that each individual is responsible for his or her actions, and he or she alone will have to answer for them.

He pointed out that we cannot hide behind the goodness or evil of others; each of us stands before God in his own goodness or in his own badness, and is judged accordingly. All of us must, therefore, look into our own hearts. If we do, we will see plenty to blame. But repentance will win us pardon and life. Ezekiel says, 'God does not desire the death of the sinner but that he be converted and live.'

We are, of course, influenced by our upbringing and environment. Still, there must come a time when we stop blaming others, and accept responsibility for our actions. We have to say, 'The buck stops with me.' My own sins are my own, and I and no one else will have to answer before

God for them. It is refreshing to hear someone say, 'I am to blame. I am responsible.' But how seldom that happens.

Unless we accept responsibility for our sins, we will see no need to repent of them. If we do accept responsibility for them, we will want to do something about them, and God will help us. If we confess our sins, we have nothing to fear but the mercy of God.

Jesus' story of the two sons is very relevant here. One son gave his word that he would go and work in his father's vineyard, but in actual fact he didn't go. He probably said to himself: 'They'll get on without me'. Here we have a total abdication of personal responsibility.

The other son at first refused to go. However, later in the day he reflected on his decision, saw that it was wrong, and decided to put it right. In other words, he repented. Here you have an example of someone who took responsibility for his life.

All us are called to conversion, because conversion is a necessary disposition for entry into the kingdom of God. But the conversion that above all Jesus sought to bring about in people was a change of heart. And he succeeded in bringing it about in the most unlikely of people.

Many sinners heeded his call to conversion of heart, changed their lives, and made their way into the kingdom. But many religious people stubbornly resisted his call to conversion of heart, refused to change their lives, and so excluded themselves from the kingdom.

We need the Lord to touch our hearts with his love and compassion. People are essentially good. But this goodness has to be awakened and called forth if we are to enter the Lord's kingdom, which is a kingdom of love.

TWENTY-SEVENTH SUNDAY OF THE YEAR
The fruitless vineyard

Praying with the Word of God today

INTRODUCTION AND CONFITEOR

God bestowed on his people the sort of care that a dedicated vinedresser bestows on a vineyard. But his people failed to produce the fruits of right living. We are the new people of God. God looks to us to produce the fruits of justice, love and peace. Sadly, we often fail God. [Pause] Let us confess our sins, especially those of omission.

I confess to almighty God ...

PRAYER OF THE FAITHFUL

Celebrant: Let us pray that we may respond to God's goodness and produce the fruits of right living.

Response: Lord, hear our prayer.

Reader(s): For the Christian community, the vineyard of Christ: that it may produce the fruits of justice, love and peace. [Pause] Let us pray to the Lord.

For all those in positions of authority: that they may fulfil their duties faithfully and well. [Pause] Let us pray to the Lord.

For those who have been the victims of ingratitude and unjust treatment: that they may find healing and peace. [Pause] Let us pray to the Lord.

For all gathered here: that the fruits of Christian living may be evident in our lives. [Pause] Let us pray to the Lord.

For our deceased relatives and friends: that the Lord may bring them into the light no darkness can overpower. [Pause] Let us pray to the Lord.

For our own special needs. [Longer Pause] Let us pray to the Lord.

Celebrant: God of love, in your unfailing compassion, watch over your Church, and since left to ourselves we are prone to evil, by your grace turn us away for all that is wrong, and direct us into the way of what is right. We make this prayer through Christ our Lord.

PRAYER/REFLECTION

Jesus says to us what he said to his apostles:
'I am the vine, you are the branches.
United with me, you will bear much fruit.
Separated from me, you can do nothing.'
The fruit that Jesus desires from us
is primarily the fruit of love.
Lord, with your patient urging,
help us to produce the fruit of love,
and thus the world know
that we are living branches of you, the True Vine.

FINAL BLESSING

May the Lord bless you with a strong faith, a joyful spirit, and a loving heart.

May you act rightly, love sincerely, and walk humbly with your God.

May the Lord watch over you, keep you in his care, and bless you his peace.

Sharing the Word of God today

SCRIPTURE NOTE

First Reading (Is 5:1-7). This talks about the owner of a vineyard who did everything he possibly could for his vineyard, yet all it produced was

- 327 -

sour grapes. The owner of the vineyard is God. The vineyard stands for the people of Israel. The care lavished on the vineyard by its owner represents God's care for his people. God expected justice from his people, but all he got was bloodshed.

Because the vineyard failed to respond to God's gracious care, it will become what it had been without his favour, namely, a wilderness. The Gospel echoes the theme of the First Reading.

Gospel (Mt 21:33-43). Here we have the second of Matthew's three parables concerned with the judgement of Israel – the evil vinedressers.

The parable is an allegory of God's dealings with his people. The landowner is God. The vineyard is Israel. The wicked tenants are the people of Israel, but more especially the religious leaders who had been given charge of the vineyard by God. The servants are the prophets sent by God and so often rejected and killed. The son and heir is Jesus himself whom they killed. Jesus tells them that the vineyard will be taken from the original tenants (the Jews), and let out to other tenants (the Gentiles).

The original parable was probably a much simpler and more straightforward one, along the lines of Isaiah's parable. By the time Matthew was writing his Gospel, Jesus had been crucified, Jerusalem destroyed, and the Gentiles had replaced the Jews as God's people. So Matthew interprets the parable in the light of these events.

He is making clear that Jesus is the stone rejected by the builders (the Jewish leaders), who, through the power of God (manifested in the resurrection), has become the cornerstone of a new building (the new people of God that includes the Gentiles).

Second Reading (Phil 4:6-9). In this beautiful reading Paul warns the converts at Philippi against anxiety, and advises them as to how they should live in order to enjoy the peace of God.

The stone rejected by the builders

Today's Gospel contains these words from Psalm 118:(22-23): 'The stone which the builders rejected has become the cornerstone; this was the Lord's doing, and it is a marvel in our eyes.'

South Africa is a country blessed by God in a great many ways. It is a large country, has a good climate, and is rich in agricultural land and minerals, especially gold and diamonds. But the country, which should have been a haven for all the peoples of Southern Africa, became instead a haven for a privileged white minority.

Many people tried in vain to change South Africa's iniquitous apartheid system. Finally Nelson Mandela appeared on the scene. He too tried to bring about reforms. But like the would-be reformers before him, he was rejected. Worse, he was hounded by the government, and ended up spending twenty-seven years in prison. However, he not only survived prison, but also came out of it with the respect of his enemies and of the entire world.

Furthermore, he came out without bitterness. In fact, he came out smiling, and immediately sought reconciliation with the leaders of the cruel regime that kept him in prison all those years. But even greater things were to follow. The man once rejected became the President of a new multi-racial South Africa. The stone which the builders rejected became the cornerstone of a new and better building.

Mandela's story is one of the greatest stories of our times. What makes it so great is the fact that in it good finally triumphs over evil. Make no mistake about it, what was done to Mandela was evil. He did not deserve to be treated like that. His only crime was to seek justice for his brothers and sisters. But in the end, thanks in large part to Mandela, good came out of this evil. A new, free society emerged.

Mandela's story helps us to understanding Jesus' parable of the vinedressers. God had bestowed on his people the sort of love and care that a dedicated vinedresser bestows on a vineyard. But the vineyard failed to produce the fruits of right living. He sent messenger after messenger to the tenants in the persons of the prophets. But far from listening to them, the tenants abused some of them and killed others. Finally he sent the son and heir – Jesus. But the tenants killed him in the hope of taking over the vineyard themselves.

What the tenants did was sinful and ugly. Most of the blame lay with the religious leaders, who had been given charge of the vineyard by God. Yet God did not abandon or destroy the vineyard. Instead, he handed it over to other tenants, who would produce the fruits. Jesus, the stone rejected by the builders (the religious leaders), became the cornerstone of a new building, the Church, which includes the Gentiles.

The parable shows us that there is only one way to overcome evil. Evil can be overcome only by good. What happens in the parable is evil. However, evil does not have the final say. In the end good triumphs, as in the case of the Mandela story.

No one can say that Jesus didn't live in the real world. He experienced its ugliness at first hand. But he didn't answer it with more ugliness. He triumphed over evil by good. He has become a model for all those who suffer unjustly in the cause of right.

And he looks to us his followers, the tenants of the new vineyard (the Church), to produce the fruits of justice, love and peace. It's a great privilege but a great challenge too.

With privilege comes responsibility

Peter and Anne raised four children but are now alone. They feel disappointed and sad. Anne tells us why.

'We did everything we could for those children. We wanted them to have the things we didn't have. Times were hard. Life was a constant struggle. Still, those children never lacked anything.

'Many's the night I didn't get a wink of sleep because of them. They had a lot of illnesses when they were young but, thank God, in time they grew out of them. Peter and I never went out. We saw others going abroad for their holidays, something we couldn't afford. But we gladly sacrificed these things for the sake of the children.

'We sent them to good schools. We taught them good values. We taught them their religion, and we tried to give them good example. And just look at how they have repaid us.

'John (the oldest) quit university and went into the pub business. He works hard, and by all accounts is doing well. But money has become his god. Though he sends us a couple of bottles at Christmas, we hardly ever see him.

'Anne, a teacher, married a fellow with a big job. They don't believe in having children. They rarely come to see us, though we get cards from them from exotic places such as the Costa de Sol and Hawaii.

'Peter has three children and seemed to be a happily married. But then he suddenly left his wife, and went to live with a younger woman. He never shows up.

'Paul, our baby, is still unmarried. He's touring the world like a hippie. Doesn't believe in working or settling down. Last time we heard from him he was somewhere in Australia.

'Of course, none of them darken the door of a Church. What more could we have done for them that we have not done?'

Today's readings seem to suggest that even God sometimes feels like this. The people of Israel had been treated in a privileged manner by God. But privilege brings responsibility.

God looked for peace from his people, and got war; for true worship, and got idolatry; for justice in their dealings with one another, and got injustice, corruption, and exploitation of the poor and the weak; for goodness, and got evil; for caring and sharing, and got greed and acquisitiveness; for temperance, and got excessive eating and drinking; for community, and got exclusiveness and snobbery; for humility, and got pride; for wise and godly living, and got a pagan lifestyle.

Yet God didn't give up on them. He sent messenger after messenger to them (the prophets). But far from listening to them, they abused some of them and killed others. God was disappointed in them, not for his own sake, but for their sake. They squandered the blessings he wanted them to enjoy. Sadly, the vineyard was destined to become a wilderness.

This to some extent is our story too. God wants us to make use of the gifts and opportunities he has given us so that we can grow as his children. But often we fail to respond to his love. And yet God doesn't write us off, but gives us chance after chance.

We fail not just as individuals but also as Church. The Christian community is the vineyard Christ planted and for which he gave his life. He looks to us, the tenants of his vineyard, to produce the fruits of justice, love, and peace. It's a great privilege but a great challenge too.

The way to peace

In our Second Reading, St Paul urges the Philippians not to be anxious. He tells them, 'There is no need to worry.' This might seem an unreal piece of advice. There is no way to avoid all worry. Good and sincere people are naturally worried about many things. It is part of the burden they carry precisely because they are people who care – care about loved ones, and many other things.

But Paul is not talking about normal concerns. He is talking about *anxiety*. Nothing is more debilitating or fruitless than anxiety. Of itself it does nothing to solve our problems. Rather, the opposite is the case. By dissipating our energy, anxiety weakens us, and makes it more difficult for us to find a solution to our problems.

The root of anxiety is lack of trust – lack of trust in oneself, in others, and especially in God. Hence, the first piece of advice Paul gives the Philippians is to pray. They must learn to commit their cares to the Lord. He says, 'If there is anything you need, pray for it.'

He is not suggesting that prayer should take the place of action.

Nor is he implying that their prayers will always be answered. What then does prayer do? Prayer implies a willingness to do what we can, and then to leave things in the hands of God. To accept what happens then as his will, even though we may not understand it.

Next Paul tells them to think positively. People who are over anxious tend to think very negatively. They imagine the worst scenario. This is disastrous. We must concentrate on the good, not on the bad.

Many people devour the newspapers every day. It's hard to read the newspapers these days without coming away depressed, so full are they of bad news. If we are into reading, then let us read something worthwhile, something that will inspire and encourage us.

Instead of filling our minds with all kinds of trash, Paul says, 'Fill your minds with everything that is true, everything that is noble, everything that is good and pure, everything that we love and honour, everything that is virtuous and worthy of praise.' The power of positive thinking is well known. We should try to fill our minds and nourish your hearts with wholesome things.

However, it is not just a question of thinking nice thoughts. We must endeavour to *do* these things. Thoughts alone will not suffice. We must pursue goodness in our actions. Paul says, 'Keep *doing* the things you have learned from me.'

In Jesus' parable of the vineyard a lot of ugly things happen. But evil does not have the last say. In the end good triumphs. This shows us that there is only one way to overcome evil, and that is with good. Jesus didn't answer evil with more evil. He triumphed over evil by good. If we sow good, cultivate good, we will reap good.

If we do what we can, and put our trust in God, then Paul assures us that the peace of God, which passes all understand, will guard our hearts and minds in Christ Jesus our Lord.

Peace comes, not from having an easy and tranquil life. We can have peace even in the midst of struggle and turmoil provided we are on the side of right. Then the God of peace will be with us.

TWENTY-EIGHTH SUNDAY OF THE YEAR
The wedding feast

Praying with the Word of God today

INTRODUCTION AND CONFITEOR

The Bible uses the image of a banquet in describing the blessings God wishes to bestow on his people, blessings that are now offered to us.

Let us call to mind our sins and infidelities, and open ourselves to receive the blessings that come from God. [Pause]

Lord Jesus, you bring pardon and peace to sinners. Lord, have mercy.

You bring light to those who live in darkness and in the shadow of death. Christ, have mercy.

You guide our feet into the way of peace. Lord, have mercy.

PRAYER OF THE FAITHFUL

Celebrant: Through Christ we enjoy the benefits of salvation. Let us pray that these benefits may be felt by all people, but especially by those in need.

Response: Lord, hear our prayer.

Reader(s): For the Church: that it may nourish the people of God with the bread of God's word in the Scriptures, and the bread of eternal life in the Eucharist. [Pause] Let us pray to the Lord.

For all government leaders: that they may spare no efforts to ensure that all people have enough to eat. [Pause] Let us pray to the Lord.

For all those who through poverty or oppression are locked out of life's banquet: that they too may know God's blessings. [Pause] Let us pray to the Lord.

For all gathered here: that we may experience a hunger and thirst for goodness of life. [Pause] Let us pray to the Lord.

For our deceased relatives and friends: that God may give them a place at the banquet of eternal life. [Pause] Let us pray to the Lord.

For our own special needs. [Longer pause] Let us pray to the Lord.

Celebrant: Heavenly Father, may we love you in all things and above all things, and reach the joy you have prepared for us, which is beyond all our imagining. We ask this through Christ our Lord.

OUR FATHER

God's kingdom is a kingdom of justice, love and peace. Let us pray for the coming of the kingdom as Jesus taught us.

REFLECTION

God is continually calling us
to a deeper and more authentic life here on earth,
and to eternal life in the hereafter.
God's call comes to us,
not so much as a voice in our ears,
as a tug at our hearts.
There is something missing in everybody's life.
However, a sense of something missing
is not a curse but a blessing.
It is God's ways of inviting us to his banquet.

FINAL BLESSING

May Christ, the Good Shepherd, guide you along the right path.

May he give you a sense of his comforting presence when you walk through the valley of darkness.

And when your earthly journey is over, may he lead you to the green pastures of eternal life.

Sharing the Word of God today

SCRIPTURE NOTE

First Reading (Is 25:6-10). This is one of the most universalist and 'ecumenical' passages in the Old Testament. Here Isaiah, the greatest of the messianic prophets, uses the image of a banquet to describe the blessings God will bestow, not only on Israel, but also on all nations. He talks, not about a plain meal, but about 'a banquet of rich food and fine wines'. Thus he underlines the generosity of God. He goes on to paint a picture of a world transformed, a world in which sorrow, suffering, and death will be no more. (Revelation 21:4 echoes the same hope.)

Gospel (Mt 22:1-14). Here we have the third of Matthew's three parables concerned with the judgement of Israel – the wedding feast. The parable echoes the messianic banquet of Isaiah above. It emphasises the negative response of those who were first invited, and how the invitation was then extended to all and sundry.

Matthew clearly means his readers to understand that he is describing God's dealings with the Jews, their disobedience to him, and the new covenant, which will include the Gentiles. The new covenant comes about through Jesus: through him all God's children are invited to the banquet feast of the kingdom.

In its original, simpler form, the parable made the point that those to whom the invitation was first sent (the Jews) rejected it, and their place has been taken by others (the Gentiles). The details about the sending of troops and the burning of the city were added later. They refer to the destruction of Jerusalem by the Romans in 70 AD, which was seen as a consequence of the refusal of the Jewish leaders to listen to Jesus.

The incident regarding the wedding garment seems to have belonged to a separate parable. Oriental courtesy demanded that any guest at a wedding banquet have the proper wedding garment, that is, clean and neat clothing. What we have here is an application of the original parable to the Christian community. Those Christians who are not worthy will suffer the same fate as those who formerly proved unworthy of the banquet.

Thus in none of these three parables is it simply a question of replacement of Jews by Gentiles; the issue for Matthew is the replacement of the unworthy in Judaism (especially the leaders) by a community of Jews and Gentiles who have come to believe in Jesus and have worthily responded to the demands of the kingdom.

Second Reading (Phil 4:12-14. 19-20). Writing from prison, Paul thanks the Philippians for the material support they have given him, and assures them that God will reward their generosity. But he goes on to say that while he is grateful for their kindness, he could survive without it because he has learned to cope with either abundance or poverty. Moreover, his real strength comes form the Lord.

The best is the enemy of the good

Jesus' story might seem a bit far-fetched. Who would be so crazy as to turn down an invitation to a royal wedding? But human beings are frail and foolish. There is a streak in us that not only refuses the good, but also can't even recognise it.

Tom was a farmer. One day he was doing his spring ploughing when the king's messenger appeared unexpectedly in his field. The messenger informed him that had been invited to the royal banquet.

On hearing this Tom began to glow like a full moon. In a flash, his humdrum life was transformed. 'When exactly is the banquet?' he asked.

'Tonight,' the messenger replied, adding, 'I'll be back in about an hour for your answer.' With that he departed.

The banquet was to be held that very night! This changed things. He looked back over the work he had done. It was going well. Then he looked ahead at what remained to be done. With luck he could finish it today. It would be a great relief to have it over with. Then he considered the oxen. He was still breaking them in. This was something that should not be interrupted.

At that moment he looked up and what did he see? He saw the royal messenger going into his neighbour's field. So *that* man was being invited too! Suppose, as was quite possible, he was placed next to him at table? That would be intolerable. All of a sudden the banquet began to lose some of its appeal.

Then there was the tedious business of getting washed and changed. And what clothes would he wear? Even his best suit was hardly good enough for a royal banquet, and he would hate to look shabby in the presence of the king and all the other guests.

Tom began to have second thoughts. Then third thoughts. 'Ah,' he sighed, 'if only the banquet was tomorrow night, and I had the ploughing done, I wouldn't think twice about accepting the invitation.'

By the time the messenger came back his mind was made up.

'Well,' said the messenger, 'are you going?'

'I have to finish this piece of ploughing,' Tom began. 'I have to finish breaking in the oxen. Besides, I ...' But the messenger was in a hurry and interrupted him: 'Just tell me whether it is yes or no.'

'I'm afraid it will have to be no,' said Tom. He was about to resume his litany of excuses, but the messenger was already out of earshot.

Notice that the things that kept Tom from accepting the invitation were not bad things, but perfectly reasonable things: the cares of work and life. But this is precisely what makes them so dangerous. We don't see them as posing a threat.

What is the banquet? The banquet stands for the fullness of life to which God is calling us. It is a call to intimacy with God, and to a deeper and more authentic personal life.

But it is also a call to community with others. The invitation challenges us to abandon our isolationism, our exclusivism, our self-sufficiency, and to be willing to share with others, to associate with others, and to collaborate with others.

Our banquets tend to be very exclusive – for a privileged few. God's banquet is for all, Jews and Gentiles, outcasts and sinners: 'Go to the crossroads and invite everyone you can find to the wedding.'

And, of course, in the final analysis, it is a call to eternal life in the hereafter. It is very easy for us to be so busy with the things of time that we forget the things of eternity.

The aim of the parable is not to consider how we will be punished if we don't heed God's invitation. Rather, it is to help us to see what we will miss if we do not heed God's invitation. Those who refused to come miss out on the joy of the wedding feast. Only God knows what is truly best for us.

Story

Excuses, excuses, excuses! We have excuses for not doing what we know we should do. And we have excuses for doing what we know we shouldn't do. Some of these excuses are reasonable, some shabby. But all are effective.

Once there was a tailor who mended the clothes of everybody in town, yet he himself went about with his coat in tatters. One day a friend said to him, 'It's a disgrace that you, a respectable tailor, should go around in a tattered coat. Shame on you.'

'But what can I do?' the tailor replied. 'I'm a poor man and I have to work all week long to make a living. Where am I going to find the time to mend my own clothes?'

'Look,' said the friend. 'Here's €20. Think of me as one of your customers. I'm paying you to mend your own coat.'

'I'll agree to that,' said the tailor as he took the money.

However, a week later the friend noticed that he was still dressed in his old tattered coat. Extremely annoyed, the friend said to him, 'Now there is no excuse for this. Didn't I give you €20 last week to mend your coat? Yet I can see that you never even touched it.'

'What can I do?' said the tailor apologetically. 'When I went home last week I examined my coat, and I realised that I'd be losing money on the job if I did it for €20.'

A man like that will always find an excuse.

Ways of responding

An invitation demands a response. Let us suppose that you are giving a party. When you have fixed the date, you draw up a list of the people you wish to invite. Then you send out the invitations with an *RSVP* emblazoned on them, and wait for the responses to come back. Basically you can expect three kinds of responses.

Some accept your invitation. Every acceptance makes you feel happy. Of course there can be degrees of acceptance. Some accept half-heartedly; they are coming only because they feel in some way obliged to come. But others accept with enthusiasm; they feel honoured and grateful for having been invited.

Others refuse your invitation. Every refusal disappoints you, perhaps even hurts you. There can also be degrees of refusal. In some cases it may that people would like to come but can't because they have a prior engagement on the date in question. But in other cases people are just not interested; it's not that they *can't* come, but that they *won't* come.

There is a third way of responding to the invitation – by not responding at all. Yes, that too is a response. You wait and wait for a reply but none comes. This is worst kind of response of all. It's worse than a refusal. When people refuse the invitation, you know where you stand with them. But here you don't. You are left wondering what's going on. Have you inadvertently done something to offend the invited ones? You don't know, and probably never will know. If you were to contact them, they would probably say, 'Oh, I meant to reply, but . . .' I meant to! What an empty feeling that leaves you with.

God doesn't compel us. God invites us. A command can't be so easily ignored, but an invitation can. Advertisers can't compel us to buy a certain product, but they resort to all kinds of gimmicks to try to persuade and cajole us into buying it. God doesn't act like that. God has too much respect for our freedom.

Often we don't know what we really want, or even what is good for us. What we are seeking, and what deep down we really value and desire, are not always the same thing. Perhaps we are so busy, our lives are so full, that even God has difficulty in breaking through to us.

What is God calling us to? God is calling us to a deeper and more authentic life here on earth. He is calling us into intimacy with himself. He is calling us into community with others. And at death he will call us into eternal life.

The greatest danger facing us is not that we might abandon God and turn to evil, but rather that we might just ignore his invitation. To ignore

God's invitation altogether is the worst form of refusal. It implies indifference. Indifferent people are the hardest to convert.

When we refuse God's invitation, it is not God who suffers. It is we who suffer. We miss out on the joy of the wedding feast.

A shocking parable?

The main thrust of the parable of the wedding feast is clear. It describes God's dealings with the Jews, their disobedience to him, and the new covenant, which will come about through Jesus and which will include the Gentiles.

However, Matthew version of the parable sounds quite shocking. It starts off very promisingly, with a king inviting guests to the wedding feast of his son. But it quickly turns ugly. The invited guests, instead of accepting the king's gracious invitation, turn on the king's servants and kill them. This rightly makes the king furious. But his reaction is way over the top – he dispatches his troops, who kill the murderers, and burn down their city.

By any reckoning, this is ugly stuff. It seems so alien to the mind of Jesus. What are we to make of it all? The allegorical elements in the story are no doubt additions, made by the evangelist or the Church to an earlier and more straightforward parable.

A simpler version of the parable is found in Luke's Gospel (14:15-24). It's about a man who invited people to a banquet. Once again those who were invited refused to come. One by one they began to make excuses. One had bought a piece of land, and had to go and look it over. Another had bought some oxen, and needed to try them out. Yet another has just got married, and so was unable to come. The king was angry at their refusal, but didn't retaliate. Instead, he sent out his servants to invite others to take their place.

This is all pretty straightforward. The banquet stands for the kingdom of God. The people who were first invited stand for the Jews. But since they refused their place would be given to the Gentiles.

In all probability, Luke's version is the original version. How do we account for Matthew's version? Matthew wrote his Gospel somewhere between 80 and 90 AD. By that time Jerusalem had been destroyed by the Roman army (in 70 AD). Hence, Matthew puts his own 'spin' on Luke's parable. He seems to suggest that the destruction of Jerusalem was a punishment for the rejection of Jesus by the Jews. This is highly problematic, because it portrays God as being very vindictive.

Jesus foresaw that Jerusalem would be destroyed. But he didn't suggest that this would happen as a punishment for his rejection by the Jews, but rather as a *consequence* of their failure to listen to him. With tears in his eyes, he said, 'If only you understood the message of peace. But, alas, it is hidden from your eyes. Of you there will not be left a stone upon a stone, everything will be destroyed' (Lk 21:41-44).

Jesus did not cause the destruction of Jerusalem. He wanted to prevent it. On another occasion he said, 'Jerusalem, Jerusalem, you that kill the prophets and stone those who are sent to you! How often have I longed to gather your children, as a hen gathers her brood under her wings, and you refused!' (Lk 13:34-35).

Christianity, by its very essence, is a message that can be accepted or rejected. At the heart of Christianity lies that terrible and mysterious possibility of rejection. That is a freedom which God has given us and will never take away from us. The acceptance of Christianity would be meaningless if rejection were not possible.

The aim of the parable is not to consider how we will be punished if we don't heed God's invitation. Rather, it is to help us to see what we will miss if we do not heed God's invitation. Those who refused to come missed out on the joy of the wedding feast. Only God knows what is truly best for us.

TWENTY-NINTH SUNDAY OF THE YEAR
God and Caesar

Praying with the Word of God today

INTRODUCTION AND CONFITEOR

Jesus says, 'Give to Caesar what belongs to Caesar, and to God what belongs to God.' We give something to God that we wouldn't give to any earthly ruler. That thing is worship.

It is precisely to worship God that we are gathered here. Let us reflect for a moment on the place God has in our lives. [Pause] Even though God is all-powerful, he exercises his power by showing mercy to sinners.

Lord Jesus, you are kind and full of compassion. Lord, have mercy.

You are slow to anger, abounding in love. Christ, have mercy.

You are faithful in all your words, and loving in all your deeds. Lord, have mercy.

PRAYER OF THE FAITHFUL

Celebrant: Let us pray that we may not be afraid to stand up and be counted in a world that often ignores the values of Christ.

Response: Lord, hear our prayer.

Reader(s): For Church leaders: that they may provide a voice for truth and justice in the world. [Pause] Let us pray to the Lord.

For temporal rulers: that God may guide their mind and hearts so that people everywhere may enjoy religious freedom, security and peace. [Pause] Let us pray to the Lord.

For those who are suffering in the cause of right: that they may have the strength to persevere. [Pause] Let us pray to the Lord.

For all gathered here: that we may honour God not only with our lips but also with our hearts. [Pause] Let us pray to the Lord.

For all the dead: that the Lord may gladden them with the light of his face. [Pause] Let us pray to the Lord.

For our own special needs. [Longer pause] Let us pray to the Lord.

Celebrant: Lord God, creator and ruler of all, to serve you is perfect freedom. Guide us in this present life, and lead us to that unfailing light in which you have your dwelling. We ask this through our Lord Jesus Christ, your Son, who lives and reigns with you and the Holy Spirit, one God, for ever and ever.

OUR FATHER

As Christians our first and deepest loyalty is to God. Let us pray To our heavenly Father in the words our Saviour gave us.

PRAYER/REFLECTION

We can't separate our faith from our actions,
or our belief from our occupations.
We can't spread our hours before us, saying,
'This is for God and this is for myself;
this is for my soul and this is for my body.'
Our daily life is our temple.
Lord, help us to live in such a way
that we may be good servants of the State
but your servants first.

FINAL BLESSING

May you walk without fault and act with justice.

May the words of your mouth, and the thoughts of your heart, win favour in the sight of God.

At when your earthly life is ended, may the Lord bless you with the vision of his glory.

Sharing the Word of God today

SCRIPTURE NOTE

First Reading (Is 45:1.4-6). In 546 BC Cyrus, king of Persia, launched a campaign against Babylonia. Having conquered Babylon, he allowed the Jews residing there to return to Jerusalem. No doubt he had his own reasons for doing so. Viewing the event from a religious point of view, Isaiah sees the return of the people from exile as a sign of God's love for his people, and of his lordship over all peoples. The lordship of God forms the link with the Gospel.

Gospel (Mt 22:15-21). Here we have the first of four clashes between Jesus and the various representatives of Judaism. The Pharisees (with the Herodians) confront Jesus about the tribute to Caesar.

The question put to him was a test question to see whether he would declare himself on the side of those who opposed paying taxes to the Romans (e.g. the Pharisees), or on the side of those who collaborated with the Romans (e.g. the Herodians).

If he said yes, he would lose the esteem of the people, and would be regarded as a traitor to the Jewish cause and the Jewish religion. (To a Jew, God was the only king; their nation was a theocracy). If he said no, he could be denounced as fomenting rebellion against Rome.

Jesus said that the money for the tax bore the emperor's portrait and name, and was therefore his; so it should be paid to him. But then he goes beyond the terms of the question, and demands that the Jews should also render to God the fruits, the just works, due to him. (We recall that in the parable of the vineyard the Jews were accused of not rendering to God the fruit that was his). They should worry less about what is due to Caesar and more about giving God his due.

Jesus does not give a detailed theory of church-state relations. How the two obligations are reconciled is not explained. Such an explanation would be useless when the audience is so insincere. Jesus recognises that the State (Caesar) has a role, but its power is limited and does not supplant God.

Second Reading (1 Thess 1:1-5). From this until the thirty-third Sunday inclusive, the Second Reading is taken from Paul's first letter to the Thessalonians. In the present extract we see Paul's esteem for the Christians at Thessalonika. They are always in his prayers, and he thanks God for the abounding faith, love and hope within the community.

Dual citizenship

The question as to whether or not it was lawful to pay taxes to Caesar was a very serious one, and it really put Jesus in a spot. If he said it was lawful, he would be regarded as a traitor to the Jewish cause and the Jewish religion. If he said it was unlawful, he could be denounced as fomenting rebellion against Rome.

Jesus replied: 'Give to Caesar what belongs to Caesar, and to God what belongs to God.' (For Caesar we can substitute the State.) This doesn't mean that there are some things that belong to Caesar and others that belong to God, as if reality were divisible into 'secular' and 'sacred'. It means that an obligation to Caesar stands under and is judged by a paramount obligation: to acknowledge the sovereignty of God.

Jesus was implying that there need not be conflict between the demands of the State and those of God. The State has a role, but its power is limited and does not supplant God. From this principle Christians deduced that they could accommodate loyalty to the State.

As Christians we have dual citizenship. We are citizens of the country in which we happen to be living or in which we were born. To it we owe many benefits. To its forces of law and order we owe the fact that we are able to live in peace and security. To its public services we owe transport, water, light, etc. To its social provisions we have access to education, medical care, and so on.

These benefits mean we are under obligation to the State. The legitimate State has rights, and Christians will respect those rights. We must respect its laws and rulers. We must be responsible citizens, and, as far as we are able, play our part in making the country a good place for all its citizens. Failure to be a good citizen is a failure in Christian duty. To cheat the State is to cheat one's fellow citizens, and to cheat one's fellow citizens is to cheat God.

But as Christians we are also citizens of the kingdom of God. To it we owe certain privileges, and to it we also have obligations. In most cases the two responsibilities do not clash. But at times they may. And when they do, Christians will spontaneously know which comes first.

Today the State is not so much against God as without God. It no longer bases its laws on God's laws. This can pose serious dilemmas for Christians – how to be a Christian in a secular world where the laws may often be unchristian.

When Jesus said, 'Give to Caesar what belongs to Caesar', his assumption was that Caesar's claim would be just. He wasn't giving Caesar a blank cheque. If it is a case of having to choose one against the other, the Christian has only one choice.

As Christians our first and deepest loyalty is to God. To God alone we render worship. In other things we gladly acknowledge and serve the secular powers, praying that they will rule wisely and justly.

Christians will strive to be good citizens of their country, and at the same time good citizens of the kingdom of God. They will fail neither in their duty to God nor to their fellow citizens. For a believer, in a sense everything is given to God, even what is given to Caesar.

The words of Thomas More should be an inspiration to us: 'I die the king's good servant, but God's first'. On the other hand, the words of Cardinal Wolsey (spoken on his death bed) should act as a warning to us: 'Would that I had served my God half as well as I served my king.'

The Christian and politics

The question posed to Jesus was an attempt to draw him into the world of politics. In our times politics has a bad name. Politicians are frequently caricatured and mocked. Hence, Christians tend to opt out of public life, and leave to others dangerous, daring, and responsible things such as politics, law-making, and business. But when they do this they are leaving these important things to others who may not be motivated by Christian values and principles.

Christians should not shirk public office. After all, it is an opportunity to serve their fellow men and women and thereby God. The Pharisees opted out of real life and kept themselves apart. The result was a vain religiosity that had little or nothing to do with life.

Dag Hammarskjold was Secretary General of the UN. When he died in a plane crash in central Africa in 1961 at the age of 56, the world lost a great servant of peace. He was that rare person for whom public service is not simply a career or a means of achieving power, but a religious vocation, a way of being faithful to God. He drew inspiration from the Old Testament prophets. He said, 'Indifference to evil is worse than evil itself, and in a free society, some are guilty, but all are responsible.'

Gandhi is another example of a deeply religious man who involved himself in politics. He said, 'I am in politics because I cannot separate life from belief. Because I believe in God I have to enter politics. Politics is my service of God.'

And Nelson Mandela is yet another example. Mandela tells how when he began to get interested in politics a friend tried to warn him off, saying, 'Politics brings out the worst in people. It is the source of trouble and corruption, and should be avoided at all costs.' Fortunately for South Africa and for the world, Mandela ignored his advice.

It's a great pity that politics is so lowly regarded. Politics plays a vital role in creating the kind of society in which we live. What greater vocation is there than to assume responsibility for national and international affairs – to work for peace and justice in the world, and for the betterment of human life for all. 'No life is more satisfactory than that of selfless service to your country or humanity' (Dag Hammarskjold).

But politics is not an easy profession, and the temptations are great. The chief temptation is to promote one's own good rather than the good of society. It's not easy for a Christian to be involved in politics and in business today. It means he or she is God's servant and Caesar's too.

Jesus' injunction: 'Give to Caesar what belong to Caesar, and to God what belongs to God' is only a principle. In practice it is not always easy to draw a clear line between the civil sphere and the religious sphere. We can't easily say this is for Caesar and that for God.

The lines of division are not clearly marked. The boundaries are often blurred and areas overlap. Of course, for a believer, in a sense everything is given to God, even what is given to Caesar. But if it is a question of having to choose one against the other, the Christian has only one choice.

What history shows unequivocally is that separation of Church and State is absolutely essential. However, when Jesus said, 'Give to Caesar what belong to Caesar, and to God what belongs to God,' his assumption was that Caesar's claim would be just. He was not giving a blank cheque to Caesar.

A true Christian is at one and the same time a good citizen of his country, and a good citizen of the kingdom of God. He will fail neither in his duty to God nor to his fellow men and women.

But as Christians, our first and deepest loyalty is to God. To God alone we render worship. In other things we gladly acknowledge and serve the secular powers, praying that they will rule wisely and justly.

Allegiance to God comes first

The most important part of a ship is the rudder. Without the rudder it could not be steered. It would simply run amuck. The most precious thing we possess is our conscience. Without a conscience we could not steer the barque of our lives towards the harbour of truth and right. As Christians God must always have the first claim on our conscience.

Franz Jaggerstatter was born in Austria and was brought up a Catholic. He was an unremarkable young man who had only an elementary education and who became a casual worker. There was nothing about him to suggest that he had in him the stuff of martyrs.

However, at some stage he suddenly matured. He became very responsible and began to take his religion seriously. He was not, however, fanatical about it. He married a girl by the name of Anna, and they had three children.

By this time the Second World War was raging. At 36, Franz was called up to serve in Hitler's army. But he refused to join up. This was tantamount to suicide. When friends tried to talk him into joining up, he said simply, 'I cannot join.'

'Why not?' they asked.

'Because I believe that this war is not a just war. Therefore, it would be wrong for me to join up. It would be against my conscience.'

'But many others have joined up. So why can't you?' they persisted.

'What others do is their business. I have to answer for my own conscience.'

'But where's your loyalty to your people, to your country, and to your flag?' they continued.

'I love my people, and I love my country. But there's a higher law – God's law. And God's law tells me that this war is wrong.'

Franz didn't have a death wish. He had a lot to live for. He was arrested and put in prison. There further efforts were made to get him to change his mind. Even his wife begged him to reconsider his decision. But all to no avail.

Franz was executed on August 9, 1943. He felt he was obeying the words of Christ: 'Give to Caesar what belongs to Caesar, and to God what belongs to God.' He was beatified by Pope Benedict XVI in 2007.

Today you could say that Caesar's place is taken by the secular State, which is not so much against God as without God. It no longer bases its law on God's laws. This can pose serious dilemmas for Christians, especially those in public office. They cannot impose their own moral values and beliefs on others, yet they must not take part in what, from a Christian viewpoint, is morally wrong.

Every Christian living in the modern world is faced with difficult decisions. There are many little 'Caesars' vying for a piece of our conscience. There is the party, the company, the club, and so on. Franz Jaggerstatter shows us that whatever else we might give to Caesar, we must not give him our conscience. Conscience is the divinist thing in us.

A true Christian is at one and the same time a good citizen of his country and of the kingdom of God. But his first and deepest loyalty is to God. To God alone we render worship. In other things we gladly acknowledge and serve the secular powers, praying that they will rule wisely and justly.

THIRTIETH SUNDAY OF THE YEAR
The two greatest commandments

Praying with the Word of God today

INTRODUCTION AND CONFITEOR

In today's Gospel Jesus tells us that the two greatest commandments are: love of God and love of neighbour. Here in a nutshell we have the whole teaching of the Bible.

The only real failure for a Christian is the failure to love. Let us reflect on this for a moment. [Pause]

Lord Jesus, you teach us how to love God with all our heart and all our soul. Lord, have mercy.

You teach us how to love our neighbour as ourselves. Christ, have mercy.

You teach us that these two commandments sum up the essence of religion. Lord, have mercy.

PRAYER OF THE FAITHFUL

Celebrant: As we bring our needs before God, we are mindful of the two great commandments of love, and of how much we need God's grace to be faithful to them.

Response: Lord, hear us in your love.

Reader(s): For Christians: that they may live out in their lives the two commandments of love. [Pause] Let us pray to the Lord.

For the world in which we live: that love and peace may prevail over hatred and violence. [Pause] Let us pray to the Lord.

For the poor and the needy: that through our love they may know that God cares about them. [Pause] Let us pray to the Lord.

For refugees, strangers and aliens: that they may find hospitality among us. [Pause] Let us pray to the Lord.

For this community: that our celebration of the Eucharist may deepen our love for God and for one another. [Pause] Let us pray to the Lord.

For our deceased relatives and friends: that the Lord may keep them safe in his love. [Pause] Let us pray to the Lord.

For our own special needs. [Longer pause] Let us pray to the Lord.

Celebrant: All-loving God, grant that we may make love the foundation of our lives. May our love for you express itself in our eagerness to do good to others. We ask this through Christ our Lord.

OUR FATHER

God is love, and anyone who lives in love lives in God. Let us pray to the God of love as Jesus taught us.

REFLECTION

To separate the two great commandments
goes clean contrary to the Gospel.
Yet unfortunately this often happens.
Those who have faith often have no love,
and those who love often have no faith.
Thus the Gospel has been torn in two.
Jesus spoke of two great commandments.
The first – that we should love God.

The second – that we should love our neighbour.
If we want the total Gospel we must have both.
He himself showed us how to do this.

PRAYER

Lord, open our hearts when they are closed,
soften them when they are hard,
warm them when they are cold,
fill them when they are empty,
heal them when they are wounded,
and mend them when they are broken,
so that we, your disciples, may bear the fruits of love.

FINAL BLESSING

May you be blessed with an unshakeable trust in God's love for you.
May the Lord, who conquered the evil one, keep you brave and strong.
May you be good witnesses for the Gospel by the love and joy you radiate.

Sharing the Word of God today

SCRIPTURE NOTE

First Reading (Ex 22:20-26). This reading comes from a section of Exodus known as the Covenant Code that lays down the conditions of the covenant on Israel's side. Here the Israelites are told that there must be no discrimination against, or exploitation of, the foreigner, the widow, the orphan, and the poor. These are the most vulnerable members of society.

The threat to kill them with the sword if they didn't abide by this is not to be taken literally. It is meant to emphasise how abominable it is to God to wrong the helpless.

Israel's God is a God who cares for the poor. To seek to be attached to God while remaining indifferent to one's fellows would be a contradiction in terms. This forms the link with the Gospel, where Jesus says that love of God and love of neighbour are intimately connected.

Gospel (Mt 22:34-40). Here we have the third of four clashes between Jesus and the various representatives of Judaism. A Pharisaic lawyer questions Jesus as to which commandment is the greatest.

By rabbinical count, the 'Law' consisted of some 613 commandments. The question as to which commandment was the greatest was one frequently discussed among the rabbis. Jesus was asked to name one, but responded by naming two. Both are found in the Old Testament: the first in Deut 6:4, the second in Lev 19:18.

What Jesus did was to put the two together, thus emphasising their essential relatedness. No rabbi had previously done this. The emphasis on love became for Christians the identifying characteristic of their religion.

Second Reading (1 Thess 1:5-10). Continuing his prayer of thanksgiving (see last Sunday), Paul reminds the Thessalonians of the joy with which they took to the Gospel. He says their conversion was so radical that it was widely spoken about and inspired many to follow their example.

The total Gospel

At the time of Jesus the Law consisted of some 613 commandments. What happened was that over time they surrounded the Ten Commandments with lots of other commandments, which became almost as important. 613 commandments is a lot of commandments. Many find 10 too many.

The question as to which commandment was the greatest was one that was frequently discussed among the rabbis. Jesus was asked to name one, but responded by naming two. Incidentally, both are found in the Old Testament; the first in Deuteronomy 6:4, the second in Leviticus 19:18.

What is new is that Jesus brought the two commandments together, and made them of equal importance. No rabbi had previously done this. Hence, we must not separate them. But in practice we often do – as the following story shows.

In the early centuries of Christianity thousands of people became monks, and went to live in the desert. In the desert they lived very strict lives: fasting, praying, and doing severe penances.

Once there was an abbot by the name of Moses who had a great reputation for holiness. Easter was approaching, so the monks met to see what they should do to prepare for it. They decided to fast the entire length of Holy Week. Having come to the decision, each monk went off to his cell, there to fast and pray.

However, about the middle of the week, two itinerant monks came to visit Abbot Moses. Seeing that they were starving, he cooked a little vegetable stew for them. To make them feel at ease he took a little of it himself.

The other monks saw the smoke rising from their abbot's cell. This could mean only one thing – he had lit a fire to cook some food, which meant he had broken the solemn fast. They were shocked. In a body they went to confront him.

Seeing judgement in their eyes, he asked, 'What crime have I committed that makes you look at me like this?'

'You have broken the solemn fast,' they answered.

'So I have,' he replied. 'I have broken the commandment of men, but in sharing my food with these brothers of ours, I have kept the commandment of God that we should love one another.'

On hearing this, the monks grew silent, and went away humbled but wiser.

There is a terrible sterility about the lives of those who claim to love God, but who dispense themselves from the obligation to love other people. Such people have at best got only half of the Gospel.

There are others who go to the opposite extreme. They exhaust themselves in working for a better world, but never think of God or pray to him. Even though the latter may be on firmer ground, they too have only half of the Gospel – the half believers sometimes throw away.

Christ showed us how to live the *total* Gospel, that is, how to love God and to love our neighbour as well. He didn't say they were the same thing, but that we can't have one without the other. We can see then why the emphasis on love became for Christians the identifying characteristic of their religion.

'If you have no love in your heart, you have the worst kind of heart trouble' (Bob Hope).

Love your neighbour as yourself

Jesus said that the two greatest commandments are: 'You must love the Lord your God ... and you must love your neighbour as yourself.' Undoubtedly it is the second commandment that causes us most trouble. Notice that Jesus says, 'You must love your neighbour *as yourself.'* Only when we love ourselves, will we be able to love other people as the Lord commanded.

Those who are filled with self-loathing and self-hatred are not going to be able to love others. They will project these feelings onto others. They will blame and castigate others for what they do not like in themselves.

An old man was sitting on a bench at the edge of town when a stranger approached. 'What are the people in this town like?' the stranger asked.

'What were they like in your last town?' replied the old man.

'They were kind and generous. They would do anything to help you if you were in trouble,' came the reply.

'Well, I think you will find them much the same in this town,' said the old man.

Some time later a second stranger approached the old man and asked the same question: 'What are the people in this town like?'

And the old man replied: 'What were they like in the town you have come from?'

'It was a terrible place,' came the answer. 'To tell you the truth, I was glad to get out of it. The people there were cruel and mean. They wouldn't lift a finger to help you if you were in trouble.'

'I'm afraid,' said the old man, 'you'll find them much the same in this town.'

The point of this little story is this. We see other people, not as *they* are, but as *we* are. A loving person lives in a loving world. A hostile person lives in a hostile world. Everyone you meet is your own mirror.

Those whose hearts are filled with goodness gaze upon the world and see what is good in humanity. Those who look upon the world with the eyes of a cynic find only the image of themselves. If we see people in a bad light, it is a sign that we are ill at ease with ourselves. A man who is not at peace with himself spreads a contagion of conflict around him.

Unless we love ourselves we cannot love others properly. There is an idea that love of self is wrong, even sinful. There is a form of self-love which is wrong. We call it selfishness or egoism. But there is a form of self-love which is healthy and good.

We can't offer warmth to others if our own fireplace is cold. We can only love with the amount of love that is in us. Whether we are conscious of it or not, we do love others precisely *as we love ourselves*.

It's very important, then to have a healthy love and respect for ourselves. This is where love starts, but of course it is not meant to end there. All true love of self overflows in the form of love of others and of God.

Remember that you were once strangers

We are often told to forget painful experiences. But how can we learn from them if we forget them? Memory of suffering can be used in a positive or negative way. It can be used to say, 'We know what suffering is like, and therefore we have no excuse for allowing it to be inflicted on others.' Or it can be used to say, 'We have suffered, therefore we have a right to inflict suffering.'

They say that compassion is not learned without suffering. Yet suffering doesn't always help people to grow in compassion. Suffering can harden people, so that they end up inflicting on others the cruelties inflicted on them. And so the cycle goes on.

The time of enslavement in Egypt was undoubtedly the darkest time in the history of God's people. It took them a long time to escape from there, and even longer to put it behind them. And yet they were told not to forget it but to remember it (First Reading). Why?

Because now things had changed for the better for them. They had a homeland of their own. They had a king of their own and an army of their own. However, there were many foreigners among them, as well as their own poor, especially orphans and widows. These people were very vulnerable.

The commandment to love one's neighbour occurs only once in the Hebrew Bible, and it referred only to one's fellow Israelites. But the commandment to love the stranger occurs 37 times – making it the most frequently cited moral injunction of ancient Judaism.

The Jews were reminded continually that they themselves were once strangers and exiles in Egypt, depending on the kindness of others. Now that they are settled, they have a duty to be kind to the stranger in their midst.

God commanded his people to remember so that history would not repeat itself. He wanted them never to forget the experience of being a minority without power in Egypt. They must not oppress the stranger, because they were once strangers themselves. They must plead the cause of the underprivileged, because they were once underprivileged themselves. Having felt the pain of injustice and oppression themselves, they must never inflict that pain on others.

Hermann Cohen believed that the biblical commandments protecting the stranger represent the beginning of true religion. He said, 'The stranger was to be protected, although he was not a member of one's family, clan, religion, community, or people. He was to be protected simply because he was a fellow human being.'

The saying of God, 'I will kill you by the sword,' sounds shocking. However, it is not to be taken literally. God does not act like this. What the prophet wants to convey is just how abominable it is in God's eyes when we mistreat anyone, especially the defenceless.

It's easy to forget where we have come from. There are signs that this is happening to American Catholics. Many of them seem to have forgotten that not so long ago they were strangers in a strange land, where they were subjected to economic and social discrimination. Increasingly they vote for candidates who spread rancour against the poor and the foreigner. In so doing they encourage people with twisted minds to take the next step – violent action against the stranger and outsider.

The health of a society can be measured by the way it treats such people. It's not good enough to give them charity. What they need is justice. If you say you love someone, then treat him justly. Charity is no substitute for real loving.

Story

There is a short but telling parable that goes like this.

First they came for the socialists, and I did not speak out – because I was not a socialist. Then they came for the trade unionists, and I did not speak out – because I was not a trade unionist. Then they came for the Jews, and I did not speak out – because I was not a Jew. Finally they came for me, and there was no one left to speak for me.

THIRTY-FIRST SUNDAY OF THE YEAR
The exposure of the scribes and Pharisees

Praying with the Word of God today

INTRODUCTION AND CONFITEOR

Jesus was very critical of the scribes and Pharisees. His chief criticism of them was: they didn't practise what they preached. Which of us can truthfully say that our deeds match our words? Do we not all fall short? [Pause]

Let us now confess our sins to God and to one another.

I confess to almighty God ...

PRAYER OF THE FAITHFUL

Celebrant: God listens to the prayers of the humble. Therefore, let us bring our needs before him with humility and trust.

Response: Lord, hear our prayer.

Reader(s): For the leaders of the Church: that they may practise in their own lives what they preach to others. [Pause] Let us pray to the Lord.

For all who hold public office: that they may not seek their own glory but to be of service to others. [Pause] Let us pray to the Lord.

For all those who are overburdened: that they may know God's strength in their weakness. [Pause] Let us pray to the Lord.

For all gathered here: that the practice of our religion may help us to grow in love and compassion. [Pause] Let us pray to the Lord.

For our departed relatives and friends: that the light of heaven may shine on them. [Pause] Let us pray to the Lord.

For our own special needs. [Longer pause] Let us pray to the Lord.

Celebrant: Lord, grant that what we have said with our lips, we may believe with our hearts, and practise with our lives. We make this prayer through Christ our Lord.

OUR FATHER

We have one Father, namely, the God who created us all. Let us pray to our heavenly Father as Jesus the beloved Son has taught us.

PRAYER/REFLECTION

The scribes and Pharisees were more concerned
with *appearing* good than with actually *being* good.
We don't have to put on an outward show,
or pretend to be what we are not.
All we have to do is to be true to what we are –

God's sons and daughters.
Lord, help us to shun all falsity and pretence,
and to live a life of genuine goodness.
Then our deeds will flow from what we are,
as naturally as good fruit from a good tree.

FINAL BLESSING

May your love not be mere words but something real and active.

May your lives bear witness to the faith that you have professed with your lips.

May the Lord confirm your hearts in holiness so that you may be blameless in his sight.

Sharing the Word of God today

SCRIPTURE NOTE

First Reading (Mal 1:14-2:2.8-10). The prophet attacks the laxity and carelessness that have set in regarding morality and worship. Here he specifically takes the priests to task, berating them for not living up to their calling.

Their calling was to mediate to the people God's word of love and reconciliation. Instead, by their lack of reverence for God's name, and by showing partiality in their administration, they have eroded faith and unity among God's people.

This prepares us for Jesus' criticism of the scribes and Pharisees, who occupied the chair of Moses.

Gospel (Mt 23:1-12). This is part of a lengthy denunciation of the Pharisees. What we have here is not an actual speech delivered by Jesus, but a compilation by the evangelist himself. We must keep the whole thing in proportion. Jesus denounced *some* Pharisees but took a favourable view of others.

Jesus begins by advising the people and his disciples to follow what they say, because of their historical authority. But on no account should they follow their example, because they don't practice what they preach.

They increase the duties of religion for others, but do not live what is at the heart of religion: love, compassion, and justice. They are ostentatious in the performance of religious practices, and look for honour and reward from people in the present rather than from God in the future. The person, who is a humble servant in the present, will be exalted by God in the age to come.

Matthew's fierce invectives against Pharisaic Judaism reflect a pastoral concern for his own church, which is in danger of repeating the mistakes of the Pharisees and so falling under the same judgement. Christian leaders are reluctant to let go of things such as ostentatious dress, places of honour, titles, and so on. With honours and titles come privileges. And privileges cause us to forget that we are supposed to be servants.

Second Reading (1 Thess 2:7-9.13). Paul is the antithesis of the priests condemned so vehemently by Malachi. He loved and cared for the Thessalonians like a mother. He might have lived on charity from them, but he didn't. He supported himself through work. He is grateful that his hard work bore fruit. The Thessalonians received the message, not as the fruit of human wisdom, but as the gift of God.

All words but no deeds

One of the greatest weaknesses of churches, parties, and individuals is the discrepancy between word and deed. This was the chief fault Jesus found with the Pharisees: 'They do not practise what they preach.'

They say that you should never recommend something unless you can provide a little sample of it. The rose is one of the most beautiful flowers of all. Once there was an expert on roses by the name of Damien. His fame had spread far and wide. Proof of this could be seen in the fact that he was in constant demand. He travelled the length and breadth of the country giving talks on roses and how to grow them. Thanks to his talks, many people filled their gardens with exquisite roses.

As I am keenly interested in roses, there was a time when I followed Damien around, lapping up every word that fell from his lips. One of the very first things I heard him say was, 'No garden can truly be called a garden if it does not possess at least one rose.' I also heard him say, 'If you wish to have good roses be prepared for a lot of hard work. If you are afraid of thorns then leave roses alone.'

One day I shook hands with him after one of his talks, congratulating him on the excellence of it. As I shook his hand I was acutely conscious that this was the hand of a master rose grower. Naturally I expected his hand to be hard and coarse. Yet to my surprise I found it to be soft and smooth. I looked at it. It didn't bear the slightest mark of a rose thorn.

The following evening I found out why those hands were so well preserved. I visited the expert in his own home. To my astonishment I found that his garden was in a state of total neglect. After that I lost faith in him as a teacher. I didn't, however, lose faith in the value of roses.

Sadly the master rose grower didn't practise what he preached. And he himself was the chief loser. His own garden, that little plot of ground which had been given to him alone to till, and which could have been filled with beautiful roses, was overgrown with weeds.

If we practise what we preach, if we live by our beliefs, we ourselves will be the first to benefit. Our lives will be the richer, and we will also be the happier for that. And when we speak about our beliefs, our words will carry more weight.

Love dies by words alone, but lives by deeds. What great prophets have *said* is forgotten, but what heroes and saints have *done* is still remembered.

There can be no happiness for us as long as the things we do are different from the things we believe in. On the other hand, when there is harmony between what we say and do, we are happy and at peace.

'Do not say things. What you *are* stands over you all the while and thunders so loudly that I cannot hear what you *say* to the contrary' (Ralph Waldo Emerson).

Story

Thomas Jefferson was the chief drafter of the American Declaration of Independence. One cannot but admire the brilliance and boldness of the words: 'All people are created equal, and have the right to life, liberty and the pursuit of happiness.'

Thomas Jefferson was also one of the signatories of the Declaration. It will come as a surprise then to learn that Jefferson and some of the other signatories were slave owners. It is one of the greatest ironies in history that they denied to millions of people in America the very freedoms they were demanding for themselves. This illustrates the immense disparity between human aspiration and human performance.

Looking into the mirror

There is a story about a Jewish man who survived the concentration camps. The night after his liberation, he went to stay in a nearby house. There he found about thirty other survivors gathered in one room. Seeing a mirror on the wall, he went over to it. He was anxious to see what he looked like. But in the mirror he saw the reflections of several of the other people as well. He couldn't tell which face belonged to him.

Only when he made faces and gestures was he able to distinguish himself from the group. And when he did distinguish his own face, he got a terrible shock – the person he saw in the mirror was one he had never seen before. He was so changed that the person in the mirror didn't bear any resemblance to the person he had seen before the war. A strange story, but a true one.

Christ's harshest words were directed, not at sinners, but at religious people such as the scribes and Pharisees. Right from the beginning of his ministry they had dogged him. He had been very patient with them. He had reasoned with them, but to no avail. Eventually he was forced to expose them.

How did he do this? In a manner of speaking, he did it by holding up a mirror in front of them so that for the first time in their lives they might be able to see their true image. It was an image that few of them would have recognised as their own. The picture he painted of them was not a pretty one.

What were the main faults he found in them? They didn't practise what they preached. They made things impossible for ordinary people by multiplying rules, and demanding exact observance of those rules, without offering the slightest help to those who found them burdensome. They sought their own honour, rather than the honour of God. And the most damning thing of all – they lacked charity and compassion in their dealings with others.

The scribes and Pharisees were not unique. For the most part they were good and sincere people. They could be any group of religious people any time and anywhere. The picture Christ painted of them was not a flattering one. But it is a mirror into which we too are invited to look. If we do look into this mirror, we will see our own face there, for we have some if not all of their faults.

Which of us can truthfully say that our deeds match our words?

Do we not sometimes consider ourselves better than others? Do we not lay down the law for others while excusing ourselves? Do we not demand sacrifices of others that we don't demand of ourselves? Do we not like to be noticed, and to take the best seat – if we can get it? Are we too not lacking in charity, compassion, and a spirit of service?

The real tragedy of the scribes and Pharisees wasn't the fact that they had faults, but that they were blind to those faults. Yet many of them were sincere and pious people. But what good is piety if it doesn't make us more humble, more loving, and more compassionate? Piety is no substitute for goodness.

Neglecting the interior

Today there is great emphasis on appearances. The image is everything. People put on a front, but deep down they are not like that at all. You can't go by appearances.

There is a castle that stands on an elevation overlooking beautiful woods and lakes. It dominates the surrounding countryside. Though it hasn't been lived in for the best part of a century, it still seems to be in good shape – from the outside at least. Not a stone appears to be missing. Its stout walls, turrets, towers, buttresses all are intact and give it an impressive appearance.

But just step inside the castle and you will see a completely different picture. Inside it is a complete shambles. There are heaps of fallen masonry and plaster everywhere. The main roof is missing and so are most of the ceilings and floors. Of course, there isn't a stick of furniture to be found in it. The big fireplaces are empty. The building is little more than a shell. How deceptive appearances can be.

So it was with the scribes and Pharisees. On the outside they appeared to be good and holy people. But inside they were anything but.

This is a danger that faces all of us. Each of us has two selves – an *outer* self and an *inner* self. To put it another way: each of us has a *public* self and a *private* self. The outer self is the shell; the inner self is the kernel. Frequently the nuts with the biggest shells are empty.

Why do we feel the need to pretend or to impress others? Because most of us get our self-worth from what others think of us. Hence, in our need for approval, acceptance, and status, we may promote the outer self at the expense of the inner self. But of what use is the appearance without the reality, the image without the substance?

We cannot achieve either happiness or holiness as long as we pretend to be what we are not. The moment we try to be what we are not, we become a fictitious personality, an unreal presence. Many religious people are not saints because they never succeed in being themselves.

When people concentrate on inner goodness they don't have to shout about it or even want to. They know with a quiet certainty that they have something that no one can take from them, something that makes them feel worthwhile, no matter what others may think of them. They have self-esteem and self-respect.

Christ was able to see beneath the appearances and behind the masks. He saw that beneath the pious exterior and the religious pomp and show, many of the scribes and Pharisees were hollow inside.

On the other hand, it gave him great joy when he found a genuine person – as was the case with Nathanael, whom he described as 'a true Israelite in whom there is no deceit' (Jn 1:47). He gladly put up with Peter because he knew that in spite of his obvious faults his heart was sound.

We don't have to put on an outward show, or pretend to be what we are not. All we have to do is try to be true to what we are – God's sons and daughters. 'Reputation is what people think of us. Character is what God and the angels think of us' (Thomas Paine).

In some so-called primitive societies outer beauty is believed to be the result of good inner moral character. There is an axiom: as in the inner, so in the outer. This means that if we take care of the inner self, the outer self will take care of itself.

THIRTY-SECOND SUNDAY OF THE YEAR
Parable of the lamps

Praying with the Word of God today

INTRODUCTION AND CONFITEOR

Every Christian is meant to be a bearer of the light of Christ to a darkened world. But sometimes, through a lack of prayer and watchfulness, we allow the precious light of Christ to grow dim. Let us turn to the Lord and ask for forgiveness. [Pause]

Lord Jesus, in a world darkened by unbelief, you help us to keep the lamp of faith burning brightly. Lord, have mercy.

In a world darkened by despair, you help us to keep the lamp of hope burning brightly. Christ, have mercy.

In a world darkened by indifference, you help us to keep the lamp of love burning brightly. Lord, have mercy.

PRAYER OF THE FAITHFUL

Celebrant: God raised Jesus from the dead that we might have a sure hope of an inheritance that will never fade. Let us pray to God as members of a hopeful people.

Response: Lord, hear our prayer.

Reader(s): For the Church: that through an effective preaching of the Gospel it may provide a lamp of hope for a world darkened by despair. [Pause] Let us pray to the Lord.

For political leaders: that they may be watchful and responsible, and so provide a lamp of peace for a world darkened by war. [Pause] Let us pray to the Lord.

For those who are grieving the loss of a loved one: that their faith may provide a beacon of hope for them. [Pause] Let us pray to the Lord.

For the members of this community: that through prayer and good works we may keep the lamp of our discipleship burning brightly. [Pause] Let us pray to the Lord.

For our departed loved ones: that the Lord may admit them to the wedding feast of heaven. [Pause] Let us pray to the Lord.

For our own special needs. [Longer pause] Let us pray to the Lord.

Celebrant: God of mercy, continue to pour out your love on us, so that we may travel in hope towards the wedding feast of your kingdom. We ask this through Christ our Lord.

The bridegroom said to the foolish bridesmaids,
'I tell you solemnly, I do not know you.'
How can we ensure that the Lord will recognise us
when we arrive at the door of the heavenly kingdom?
By keeping the lamp of love burning brightly.
And how do we do this?
Through a continuous input of small drops of oil.
What do these drops of oil consist of?
The small things of daily life,
the little deeds of kindness and of service.

FINAL BLESSING

May you go on growing in the knowledge and love of our Lord and
Saviour Jesus Christ.

May you await with unwavering hope the Lord's return in glory.

May the Lord keep you steadfast and without blame until the last day.

Sharing the Word of God today

SCRIPTURE NOTE

First Reading (Wis 6:12-16). Our reading sings the praise of wisdom, and
says that it can be found by those who seek it diligently. For Israel wisdom
meant an effective knowledge of God and a right relationship with God.

We see this wisdom exemplified in the five wise bridesmaids in the Gospel
parable. The consequences of not seeking this wisdom are seen in the sad
fate of the foolish bridesmaids.

Gospel (Mt 25:1-13). Today and for the next two Sundays the Gospel is
taken from Matthew's Eschatological Sermon (24:1-25:46) which deals
with the end times. The parable of the Ten Virgins stresses the need for
watchfulness.

To understand the parable we need a little background. In those days
when a couple married, they didn't go away for a honeymoon; they stayed
at home. For a week they kept open house. To the festivities of that week
their chosen friends were admitted. It was that joyous week that the foolish
virgins missed because they were unprepared.

Matthew and his community have come to accept that the parousia may
be delayed. The point of the parable is this: since the disciples do not know
the day nor the hour of the Lord's coming, they must be prepared so that
when he comes they can enter his kingdom. To be prepared means to be
a doer rather than a mere hearer of the word. It means living soberly in
the present with one's gaze directed towards the future.

Second Reading (1 Thess 4:13-18). (Longer form recommended.) In common with most, if not all, of the early Christians, Paul expected the second coming of Christ to happen soon. Here he consoles the Thessalonians who are worried about the fate of their loved ones who have died before the return of the Lord. He tells them that they are with the risen Lord, and that the living and the dead will be reunited at the final showing of the kingdom.

Waiting for the Beloved

One night a man dreamt that he was walking towards the gate of heaven. On the way he ran into some figures in the dark who were crying. 'Why are you crying?' he asked. 'We're crying because the Lord refused to admit us. He said he didn't know us,' they replied.

The man went on and arrived at the gate only to find it locked. So, with no little trepidation, he rang the bell. As he stood there waiting, he asked himself, 'I wonder will the Lord know *me*?' And a voice from inside him replied, 'Of course he'll know you! But that's not the question. The question is will he recognise you as a disciple of his?'

Yes, that indeed was the question. And he said to himself, 'I wonder what he is going to look for?' Then he thought of the parable of the lamps. The Lord would look for a lamp that was burning brightly. And so he asked himself, 'What have I done with my lamp?' He was relieved to discover that he still had it. But when he looked at it he found to his horror that it had gone out. However, at that moment he woke up to find that it was only a dream. What a relief!

Wouldn't it be terrible to arrive at heaven's door, and to have the Lord say to us, 'I do not know you.' And we find ourselves outside in the dark, while inside all is light and joy.

What lamp are we talking about? Essentially it is the lamp of love. Love, in order to be genuine, doesn't have to be extraordinary. What we need is to go on loving without getting tired or cynical.

How does a lamp burn? Through a continuous input of small drops of oil. If the drops of oil cease, the lamp will go out. What are these drops of oil? They are the small things of daily life: a smile, a handshake, a word of encouragement, a phone call, a card, an embrace, a kind greeting, a gesture of support, a moment of attention, a helping hand, a present, a financial contribution, a visit. These are the drops of love that keep our religious life burning like a lively flame.

Jesus shared our life, our loneliness, our anguish, and our death. He is not far away from us. He is very close to us. We can touch, serve, and love him every day of our lives. With the oil of prayer and good works we must keep the lamp of love burning, and he will recognise us as disciples of his.

We won't be judged on a momentary lapse, but on our life as a whole.

Since we do not know the day nor the hour of the Lord's coming, we must be prepared so that when he comes we can enter his kingdom. To be prepared means to be a doer rather than a mere hearer of the word.

All that Jesus says to us in this parable is meant as a warning. This warning is a sign of his love for us. It tells us that every moment should be beautiful. That the soul should always be ready for the coming of the Bridegroom, always waiting for the voice of the Beloved – waiting not in fear but in joyful hope.

A hopeful grieving

The Gospel is talking about rejoicing while the Second Reading is talking about grieving. But that's how it sometimes is in life. Today we may be attending a wedding, tomorrow a funeral.

The early Christians believed that Jesus would return soon and take them to heaven. This made it difficult for them to accept the death of some of their members before Jesus returned in glory.

That's the problem Paul is addressing in his letter to the Thessalonians. He tells them that as surely as God raised Jesus from the dead, Jesus will raise those who have died, and present them to God in the final showing of his kingdom.

But meanwhile they are grieving. What should be their attitude to grief? Paul doesn't tell them not to grieve. What he says is: 'Do not grieve like those *who have no hope.'*

Grief follows the loss of a loved one as surely and naturally as night follows day. Grief is not an easy thing to handle. It is one of the strongest emotions we will ever experience. Some have a problem about expressing grief, and may try to suppress it. To suppress grief is not a good idea; it can result in serious emotional problems. To grieve over the loss of a loved one is a good and necessary thing.

The way to deal with grief is not to run away from it, but to face it and work through it with as much courage and honesty as we can. Those who do this will emerge enriched as persons. Grief has a great purgative value. A great grief is a tremendous bonfire in which all the trash of life is consumed.

Faith should not be used as a barrier against grief. Even Christ grieved. He wept at the death of his friend, Lazarus. Faith doesn't do away with the necessity of grieving. What it does do is enable us to grieve *with hope.*

Faith is a wonderful comfort and support at a time of death. Paul says, 'We believe that Jesus Christ died and rose again, and that it will be the same for those who have died in Christ. Comfort one another with these thoughts.' To live fruitfully after the death of a loved one, people need to go through a period of grieving. But even though we may have tears in our eyes, we have hope in our hearts.

The wedding feast to which Jesus invites us will be all the more joyful for those who have walked through the dark valley of grief, and emerged with the lamp of love still burning brightly.

The lamp of wisdom

Wisdom is one of the great themes of the Bible. And it is easy to see why. Without wisdom we are like travellers in the dark. With wisdom we have a bright lamp for our steps. But wisdom, if acquired at all, is acquired slowly and often painfully. To meet someone who has gleaned wisdom along the path of life is a great joy, and a great inspiration.

Michael was a prisoner in his mid forties. When I met him he was serving a long sentence for a very serious crime. Though he looked serious, he was by no means dour or downcast. He came across as a reflective, intelligent man. He had already served eight years, and was hoping to be released in three or four years time.

When I had gained his confidence, I asked him, 'If on your arrival in prison, someone had offered you a drug that would have put you to sleep for the entire duration of your sentence, would you have taken it?'

'Would I have taken it? I would have asked for a double dose to make absolutely sure that I didn't wake up. But I wouldn't take it now,' he replied.

'Why not?' I asked.

'Because I've learned a lot about myself inside here,' he replied. 'And I've changed too. I'm now a wiser man.'

One can see why initially he would have taken the drug. He was embarrassed and ashamed at what he had done and wanted the ground to swallow him. But now he realised that to take the drug would have been to waste the whole experience. Like the foolish bridesmaids, he would have slept his life away. Sleep would have shortened his sentence and made it easier to bear. But he realised it was not something to be skimmed over lightly and painlessly. It had to be lived out slowly and deliberately, step by step, day by day.

It helped that Michael was a believer who attended church regularly. During all those dark years he never lost faith in God. He said, 'Without that faith I would have lost hope, and without hope I would have given up.'

Many prisoners squander their years in prison. They come out worse not better than they went in. There is no awareness, no reflection in their lives. Therefore, they learn nothing as they go along. By the grace of God, Michael had acquired wisdom.

Wisdom is the highest virtue. Through wisdom God communicates to us the meaning of life, and the grandeur of our destiny, which is to be with God. Unlike knowledge, which is acquired through hard work, wisdom is a gift of God and is found by those who seek it.

In Christ's story we are not talking about a momentary lapse of memory on the part of the foolish bridesmaids – forgetting to bring along extra oil for their lamps. What we are dealing with are two contrasting attitudes towards the wedding feast. For the wise maids, the wedding feast was the chance of a lifetime, a never-to-be-repeated opportunity to meet the bride-groom. For the foolish maids, it was more like a bit of a lark.

We can understand a prisoner wanting to sleep his life away, but not bridesmaids waiting for the bridegroom to come, so that they could ac-company him to the wedding feast. Since they didn't know exactly when he would come, they had to wait in readiness. Yet five of them couldn't do that and found themselves locked outside.

We are like those waiting bridesmaids. We are not dealing with a once-off wedding feast. We are dealing with something infinitely more precious – entrance into the kingdom of heaven. As a beacon guides a ship to port, this vision should guide our way on earth.

THIRTY-THIRD SUNDAY OF THE YEAR
The responsibility of talent

Praying with the Word of God today

INTRODUCTION AND CONFITEOR

God has given each of us particular talents. If used well, these talents will enrich our lives and the lives of others.

But which of us can say that we have made full use of the gifts God has given us? Have we not at times left them unused or even misused them? [Pause] Let us turn to the Lord who is generous with his forgiveness.

Lord Jesus, you are kind and full of compassion. Lord, have mercy.

You are slow to anger and abounding in love. Christ, have mercy.

You do not treat us according to our sins, or repay us according to our faults. Lord, have mercy.

PRAYER OF THE FAITHFUL

Celebrant: Let us pray that we may use well the talents God has given us, so that we may enrich our own lives and the lives of others.

Response: Lord, hear our prayer.

Reader(s): For the Church: that it may provide opportunities for its mem-bers to use the talents God has given them. [Pause] Let us pray to the Lord.

For all leaders: that they may appreciate the talents of those under them. [Pause] Let us pray to the Lord.

For all those who have buried their talents: that they may see the light before it is too late. [Pause] Let us pray to the Lord.

For all gathered here: that while we strive to develop our talents we may strive to develop our character at the same time. [Pause] Let us pray to the Lord.

For our loved ones who have died: that they may rest in the peace of God. [Pause] Let us pray to the Lord.

For our own special needs. [Longer pause] Let us pray to the Lord.

Celebrant: Heavenly Father, help us to use well the gifts of grace and nature that you have given us, so that one day we may merit to hear the words: 'Well done, good and faithful servant'. We ask this through Christ our Lord.

REFLECTION

I have not the fine audacity of men
Who have mastered the pen
Or the purse.
The complexes of many slaves are in my verse.
When I straighten my shoulders to look at the world boldly
I see talent coldly
Damning me to stooped attrition.
Mine was a beggar's mission
To dreams of beauty I should have been born blind.
I should have been content to walk behind
Watching the reflection of God's delight:
A second-hand teller of the story
A second-hand glory.
It was not right
That my mind should have echoed life's overtones
That I should have seen a flower
Petalled in mighty power.
Patrick Kavanagh

FINAL BLESSING

May you never forget that all talents are gifts from God.
May you use your talents to live an industrious and virtuous life.
May the Lord keep you steadfast and without blame until the last day.

Sharing the Word of God today

SCRIPTURE NOTE

First Reading (Prov 31:10-13.19-20.30-31). This is a poem in praise of the ideal wife. Even though it implies that a woman's place is in the home, nevertheless, it is a noble tribute to womanhood. By today's standards the woman would hardly be called a talented person. Yet she is held up as a model of someone who uses her talents to live an industrious and virtuous life.

Gospel (Mt 25:14-30). (Longer form recommended.) The parable of the talents is another extract from Matthew's Eschatological Sermon (24:1–25:46).

Matthew has accepted that the parousia would be delayed. Since the day of the Lord's coming is unknown, he stresses the necessity of being watchful. In the parable of the talents he spells out what this watchfulness consists in: it consists in carrying out the Lord's instructions to the best of one's God-given ability.

The first two servants are congratulated and rewarded for their enterprise and fidelity. Though their responsibility had been unequal, their reward is the same. What matters is not accomplishment, but wholehearted commitment. The third servant receives blame and condemnation – because he has done nothing. Instead of blaming himself, the servant blames his master, calling him 'a hard man'.

In the parable we are dealing with man's response to God's gift. Matthew seems to present God as a stern taskmaster. The parable is meant as a warning to the lazy and inactive disciple to shape up lest he lose everything. The warning is an expression of love and concern.

Second Reading (1 Thess 5:1-6). Paul had assured the Thessalonians of the certainty of Christ's coming. It seems that the community had speculated as to exactly when that would happen. Paul tells them that he himself doesn't know that. All he can tell them is that it will happen unexpectedly. He impresses on them the need to be always ready lest they be caught unawares.

What have I made of myself?

'You can be anything you want to be.' This is something one hears often in America. You might say that the American dream is built on it. It implies that you can achieve anything provided you work hard enough. It is meant to encourage the young to aim high.

You can be anything you want to be. It sounds great. But when you examine it, it doesn't stand up. You can't become a great singer if you haven't a note in your head. You can't become a great footballer if you can't tell your left foot from your right foot.

The mantra, 'You can be anything you want to be', is unrealistic and creates unrealistic expectations. A better message would be: 'You can be whatever your talents and abilities allow you to become.'

It is important to develop one's talents – as Jesus tells us in his parable. But there is something more important. It is possible to be very successful in one's career but leave one's personal life a long way behind. Indeed, success in one's career is often achieved at expense of one's personal life.

Picasso was a very successful artist but his personal life was a disaster, especially his relationships with women. If we over-achieve in one area, chances are that we will under-achieve in another.

It's sad to see a talent go to waste. But it's even sadder to see a person go to waste. Take the example of the footballer, George Best. He was admired for what he achieved with his talent, but pitied for what he did to himself. (He died prematurely of alcoholism).

When Jesus talks about talents, we must not think he means a musical talent or a footballing talent. Such talents are important, but are outrageously over-valued and over-rewarded. Ultimately the only thing that matters is what we make of ourselves.

Talent is important but character is even more important. Talent is formed in quiet; character in the midst of the world. Of what use is it to develop one's talent if one leaves one's character undeveloped? But when a person develops himself *and* his talent, a kind of wholeness results.

The woman we meet in the First Reading could hardly be described as being either successful or famous. Yet she is held up as a model. Why? Because of the kind of person she is – industrious, caring, wise, and virtuous. I'm sure she had her faults, but in the light of her goodness they were not worth mentioning.

She possessed something more valuable than wealth or beauty. She possessed a loving heart. She put her talents at the service of her family, her neighbours, and the poor. Hence, she has the respect of the entire community. Here is someone who has developed her talents *and* herself.

Life is God's gift to us. What we do with life is our gift to God.

Story

Once a reunion took place of the past pupils of a famous school run by a religious order. An elderly priest, who came back for the reunion, found himself surrounded by a host of former pupils. It was obvious from the way they flocked to him that he enjoyed great respect among them.

He received them with graciousness. Then, without the slightest prompting from him, they began to pour out their stories. One was an architect who had designed a number of public buildings. Another was a university professor who had written several learned books. Another was the head of a business company that had branches in over a dozen countries. Another was a highly successful farmer. Another was a Monsignor in the Church. Another was the principal of a very prestigious school. And so it went on.

The old priest listened with pleasure to the impressive litany of successes and achievements. There didn't seem to be any failures or losers among them, or if there were, they hadn't shown up at the reunion.

As they told their stories, the priest nodded his head and smiled. When they had finished, he complimented them on their achievements. Then, looking at them with affection, he said, 'And now, tell me what you have made of yourselves?'

'What do you mean?' they asked, puzzled.

'You have told me how you did in your careers. Now tell me how you have done in your personal lives?'

A long silence followed.

Wasted talent

Today's Gospel is about *stewardship*. Stewardship rests on the belief that everything we have is a gift from God, and we need to make a return to God for all he has given us.

There is no such thing as a born footballer. But Paul came very close to being an exception. He was a star footballer. Of course he had to work at it. But everybody agreed that he was *a natural*. He knew he was better than any of the kids around him.

It came as no surprise when at fifteen he was snapped up by a top professional club. He didn't have long to wait for his big chance. He had only just celebrated his sixteenth birthday when he found himself selected for the first team. He made an immediate impact. Almost overnight he shot from obscurity to fame.

From there on it was one success after another. Within two years he was the club's leading scorer. By now he was also playing for his country. Everywhere football was talked about his name was mentioned. To the fans he was a hero. To the media he was a celebrity.

He revelled in his success. A few years ago he was a poor kid playing in the back streets of a provincial town. Now he was rich and famous. He married a beautiful model, drove a Mercedes, and was the envy of every schoolboy who played football.

However, things soon started to go wrong. There were rumours that he was drinking heavily. The rumours proved to be well founded. His football began to suffer. His personal life began to disintegrate. His wife left him, claiming that he was selfish and immature.

Sadly, Paul's glittering career came to a premature end. And he was re-

membered as much for the manner in which he squandered a rare talent
as for what he achieved with it.

It is dangerous when a talent springs up overnight. Far better that it
should grow up by a slow natural process, like a seed grows into a tree.
When a talent grows up like that a kind of wholeness results.

Some people who start with great promise fail. Others who start with a
little talent succeed. Why is this? Because the qualities that help a person
to succeed are less those of talent than of *character* – faith, patience, readiness to learn, and ability to work hard. Many people are born with great
natural ability, but do not have the patience and self-discipline to build
on their endowment. Talent is a responsibility. In some cases it can be as
much a burden as a blessing.

Talented people can easily become inflated by their talent. They may
forget that all talents are gifts from God. We are merely the custodians of
those gifts.

Talent is important but character is even more important. Talent is
formed in quiet; character in the midst of the world. Of what use is it to
develop my talent if I leave myself undeveloped?

'Great talents are the most lovely and often the most dangerous fruits
on the tree of humanity. They hang upon the most slender twigs that are
easily snapped off' (Carl Jung).

Self-expression

It has been said that our true birthplace is the place in which we awaken
to our gifts and talents. Often it takes an outsider to recognise the talent.
Just as the sun helps to bring to birth the fragrant flowers that lie hidden
in the soil of the fields, so there are people who find their fulfilment in
helping to unfold the talents God has deposited in others.

The Russian writer, Fyodor Dostoevsky, was only 20 when he wrote his
first book, entitled *Poor Folk*. The foremost critic of the day was a man by
the name of Belinsky. When Belinsky read the manuscript of the young
Dostoevsky he said: 'You have a great gift. Take good care of this gift, and
you will become a great writer.' Dostoevsky was intoxicated by the words
of the famous critic. Many years later he wrote, 'That was the happiest moment of my life.' The recognition of Belinsky confirmed him in his belief
in his own talent. It did more. It launched him on his way. He spent the
rest of his life expressing himself through his writings.

One of our greatest needs is the need to express ourselves. 'There is
a great loneliness in almost everyone, a great hunger to express oneself'
(Kahlil Gibran). Unless we express ourselves we cannot realise or fulfil ourselves. Expression is as necessary for us as leaf and blossom are for a tree.

Expression is the opposite of repression. To *repress* is to bottle up, to stifle, to smother, to suppress. Repression inevitably gives rise to depression. To *express* is to articulate, to reveal, to bring out. Expression may involve pain but ultimately leads to joy.

To express oneself is the way to make oneself whole. How many of us could say that we have developed our full potential as human beings? Of course, there are many ways in which people can express themselves – art is only one of them.

Sadly, a lot of talent goes unexpressed. Often this is due to lack of opportunity. But sometimes people just drift through life. When talents go unexpressed, the possessors of the talents are the greatest losers. In the haunting words of G.K. Chesterton, 'they die with all the music inside them.'

It is by living that we discover our talents, and it is by using them that they grow. Every talent has to be developed. A lot of discipline, patience, and hard work are required if a talent is to bear its full fruit. We see this in the example of the first two servants in Jesus' story.

We see the opposite of it in the case of the third servant. It wasn't the harshness of his master that prevented him from using his talent – that was merely an excuse. Nor was it lack of opportunity. He himself was to blame, through a combination of laziness and cowardice.

We can't take any credit for a talent. It was a gift to us. So what have we to be proud of? Only the work we put into developing and using the talent. We must do the best we can to return our talent to God increased. If we do, we will have no regrets at the end.

Life is God's gift to us. What we do with life is our gift to God.

THIRTY-FOURTH SUNDAY OF THE YEAR: CHRIST THE KING
A kingdom of love and service

Praying with the Word of God today

INTRODUCTION AND CONFITEOR

Today we celebrate the kingship of Christ. Jesus is a strange kind of king. He came not to dominate but to liberate, not to rule but to serve.

We show loyalty to him, and help to spread his kingdom, by serving one another in love. Let us examine our lives on the quality of our service. [Pause]

Lord Jesus, you help us to serve with a humble heart. Lord, have mercy.
You help us to serve with a generous heart. Christ, have mercy.
You help us to serve with a joyful heart. Lord, have mercy.

PRAYER OF THE FAITHFUL

Celebrant: God has made Jesus head of the Church and ruler of all creation. Let us pray in his name for our own needs, the needs of the Church, and of the world.

Response: Your kingdom come.

Readers(s): For the Pope and the bishops: that they may give an example of humble and loving service of their brothers and sisters in the Church. [Pause] Let us pray to the Lord.

For temporal rulers: that as they may work to build the earthly city, they may not lose sight of the heavenly kingdom. [Pause] Let us pray to the Lord.

For the poor of the world: that they may experience the love of Christ through the care and concern of his followers. [Pause] Let us pray to the Lord.

For all gathered here: that the words of Jesus, 'Whatever you do to the least of my brothers, you do to me', may influence all our dealings with others. [Pause] Let us pray to the Lord.

For our deceased relatives and friends: that the Lord may bring them into the kingdom of his glory. [Pause] Let us pray to the Lord.

For our own special needs. [Longer pause] Let us pray to the Lord.

Celebrant: God of mercy, your Son so loved the world that he gave his life for our salvation. May we have the courage to live by that same love, so that we may share the joy of the kingdom, where he lives and reigns with you and the Holy Spirit, one God, for ever and ever.

OUR FATHER

God's kingdom is a kingdom of truth and life, holiness and grace, justice, love and peace. Let us pray for the coming of the kingdom as Jesus taught us.

SIGN OF PEACE

Lord Jesus Christ, you said to your apostles, 'The greatest among you is the one who serves.' Cleanse our hearts of selfishness, and give us a spirit of loving service, so that we may enjoy the peace and unity of your kingdom where you live for ever and ever.

PRAYER/REFLECTION

In the evening of our lives we will be examined on love.
Mother Teresa said:
'The biggest disease in the world today
is the feeling of being unwanted.
And the greatest evil in the world
is the terrible indifference towards one's neighbour.'

Lord, open our hearts when they are closed,
and warm them when they are cold,
so that we may produce the fruits of love,
and be found worthy of belonging to your kingdom.

FINAL BLESSING

May the Lord bless you with a noble and generous heart.
May he keep you joyful in his service.
And may he lead you through the darkness of this world to the radiant glory of his kingdom.

Sharing the Word of God today

SCRIPTURE NOTE

First Reading (Ezek 34:11-12.15-17). Ezekiel realised the importance of good leaders. Much of the misfortune that had befallen Israel had been due to bad leadership. So in the end God himself will assume the mantle of leadership. He will be a true shepherd who will bring together the scattered remnants of his flock. But even then the individual will be responsible for his own salvation, for God will still judge 'between sheep and sheep.' Ezekiel's prophecy found fulfilment in Jesus, 'the good shepherd'.

Gospel (Mt 25:31-46). Matthew's Eschatological Sermon (24:1-25:46) ends with the Last Judgement. The central point here is to show what the criterion of judgement will be. The judgement will be based on the treatment of deprived outcasts – a warning for the Church not to follow the world that pays more attention to the rich and the powerful.

Here Matthew portrays Christ as a stern King and Judge. But this image shouldn't be over-emphasised. Ezekiel (First Reading) has a gentler image – that of a good shepherd who cares for all the sheep in his flock, but shows particular care for the weak and wounded ones. This was the image Jesus himself used to describe his person and his mission. And his followers show that they truly belong to his kingdom by their care for 'the little ones'.

We don't know exactly how the last judgement will happen, but we do know what the followers of Jesus will be judged on. They will be judged on whether or not they rendered loving service to the poor. Care for one's neighbour is the core value of Christianity.

To be ready or watchful for the Lord's coming is to be able to recognise the Son of Man in all those in need, and to translate one's love into concrete works of mercy.

Second Reading (1 Cor 15:20-26.28). Here Paul looks to the parousia when all those in Christ will be raised. At the end of the world Christ will reign as universal King, having overcome all hostile forces, including death.

Serving the King

People's basic material needs have to be taken care of before any kind of higher life is possible. But in many countries these needs have been taken care of. Does this mean then that the words of Christ about feeding the hungry, clothing the naked, etc. are no longer relevant?

Mother Teresa said, 'What the poor need even more than food, clothes, and shelter, is to be wanted.' Hence, the words of Christ are as relevant today as ever. But we might put them as follows.

'I was hungry, not for food, but for a smile, and all I got from you was sour looks. I was hungry for a word of encouragement, but all you did was criticise me.

I was thirsty, not for drink, but for a word of recognition, but all you did was give out to me. I was thirsty for a sign of friendship, but you shunned me.

I was a stranger, and you refused to have anything to do with me. I was a neighbour, and you wouldn't allow me into your club because I wasn't in your class.

I was naked, not because I lacked clothes, but because I lacked self-worth, and you looked down on me. I was stripped of self- confidence, and you made me feel the chill wind of disapproval.

I was sick, not in body, but with doubt and worry, and you never even noticed. I was wounded by failure and disappointment, and you couldn't care less.

I was a prisoner, but not behind iron bars. I was a prisoner of loneliness, and you gave me the cold shoulder. I was a prisoner of guilt, and you could have set me free by forgiving me, but you let me languish there to punish me.

I was homeless, not for want of a home made of bricks and mortar, but for the want of sympathy and understanding, and you treated me as if I was a block of wood. I was homeless for want of love, and you locked me out of your heart.'

But then the king might say, 'I was hungry for a word of encouragement, and you praised me. I was hungry for a word of appreciation, and you thanked me.

I was thirsty for a word of recognition, and you took notice of me. I was thirsty for a sign of friendship, and you wrote me a letter.

I was a stranger, and you made me feel welcome. I was a young a person from a bad area, and you gave me a job.

I was naked for the want of self-esteem, and you covered me with self-worth. I was stripped of self-confidence, and you dressed me in the cloak of confidence.

I was sick with doubt and worry, and with your cheerful attitude you lightened my burden. I was in a pit of depression, and by your patient attitude you gave me hope.

I was a prisoner of loneliness, and through your friendship you released me. I was a prisoner of guilt, and through your forgiveness you set me free.

I was homeless for want of sympathy and understanding, and you listened to me. I was homeless from want of love, and you took me into your heart.'

There are lots of things we could do if we were more aware and more sensitive. It's not so much a question of giving *things,* but of giving of *ourselves* – of our time, our energy, and our love. Thus we will serve Christ and help to build his Kingdom.

In the evening of our lives we will be examined on love.

Messengers of the King

Oscar Wilde wrote a beautiful story called *The Happy Prince.* During his life on earth the prince had lived a very sheltered life. When he died the people erected a statue of him in the main square of the capital city. The statue was gilded all over with leaves of gold. It had two sapphires for eyes, and a large red ruby on the handle of the sword.

One cold evening, a little swallow, on its way south, landed at the base of the statue. As he was resting there a few drops fell on him. He looked up and saw that the Happy Prince was crying.

'Why are you crying?' the swallow asked.

'When I was alive I saw no suffering,' said the Prince. 'But from my perch up here I see that there is a lot of unhappiness in the world. I'd like to help but I can't because my feet are fastened to the pedestal. I need a messenger. Would you be my messenger?'

'But I have to go to Egypt,' the swallow answered.

'Please stay this night with me.'

'Very well, then. What can I do for you?'

'In a room there is a mother tending a sick child. She has no money to pay for a doctor. Take the ruby from my sword and give it to her.'

The swallow removed the ruby with his beak, and bore it away to the woman and she rejoiced. The doctor came and her child recovered. The swallow came back and slept soundly.

Next day the prince asked him to stay another night. Then he asked him to take out one of the sapphires, and give it to a little match girl down in the square. She had sold no matches that day and was afraid she would be beaten when she got home. Once again the swallow did as he was asked.

As he was running these errands of mercy, the swallow's own eyes were opened. He saw how much poverty and suffering there was in the city. Then he was glad to stay with the prince and be his messenger. One by one, at the Prince's urging, he stripped off the leaves of gold and gave them away to the poor and the needy.

Finally, he arrived back one evening. The night was very cold. Next morning the little swallow was found dead at the base of the statue. By now the statue was bare, having been stripped of all its ornaments. The prince had given away all his riches, but he could not have done so without his faithful messenger, the little swallow.

Christ, our King, gave himself away totally while he lived on earth. Even as he died, he was still giving to those who were receptive. And from his lofty perch in heaven he surveys the plight of God's children on earth. But his feet are fastened, his hands tied, and his tongue silent. He needs messengers. He needs us. He has no hands but ours, no feet but ours, no tongue but ours. And it is his riches, not our own, that we are called on to dispense – his love, his forgiveness, his mercy, his good news . . .

What is involved is helping in simple things, things that are available to everyone – giving a hungry person something to eat, or a thirsty person something to drink, welcoming a stranger, or visiting someone who is sick or in prison ...

To do things such as these one doesn't have to be either wealthy or talented. All one needs is a warm and willing heart. Every one can do something – yes, even a little 'swallow'.

Lord, if only we knew it was you

Nelson Mandela was still a young man when he became leader of the banned African National Congress (ANC). At a certain stage in the struggle he was forced to go underground. During that time he used many different disguises. In general he remained as unkempt as possible. He knew that by being so disguised he ran the risk of not being recognised even by his own. And this sometimes happened.

Once he was to attend a meeting in a distant part of Johannesburg. A priest had arranged with friends of his to put him up for the night. However, when Mandela arrived at the house, the elderly lady who answered the doorbell took one look at him and exclaimed, 'We don't want your kind here!' And she shut the door in his face. Later, when she found out who it was that she had turned away, she was horrified and said to him, 'If only I knew it was you, I'd have given you the best room in the house.'

Yet, in spite of his many disguises, there were friends who still managed to recognise Mandela. For instance, one day he was posing as a chauffeur in Johannesburg. Wearing a long dustcoat and cap, he was waiting on a corner to be picked up when he saw an African policeman striding deliberately towards him. He looked around to see if he had a place to run, but then the policeman smiled at him, surreptitiously gave him the thumbs-up

ANC salute, and was gone. Incidents like this happened many times, and Mandela was reassured to know that he had the loyalty of many Africans.

We could say that Jesus too goes about in many different disguises. We have no problem recognising him in church. But when we meet him out on the streets, where he is sometimes sunk in poverty and sorrow, we are reluctant even to bid him the time of day. Yet, the most distinctive mark of a Christian should be compassion for the poor and the marginalised.

'If only I had known it was you,' said the woman to Mandela. We hear the same words in today's Gospel: 'Lord, if only we had known it was you, we'd never have treated you like that.' But Jesus said that his disciples would be judged precisely by their response to such people – the poor, the lowly, and the unimportant.

It's easy to be kind to the important – there is or will be a return in some shape or form. But it's quite another matter to be kind to those from whom we can expect nothing in return, perhaps not even thanks.

The uncaring are full of excuses. The genuinely caring on the other hand are almost apologetic about their goodness: 'Lord, when did we see you hungry and feed you ..' They are embarrassed if you praise them. Charity is never so lovely as when it falls from people without their notice, as a leaf from a tree.

If we had before us those who have been a blessing to us, and could tell them how it came about, they would be amazed to learn what passed over from their life to ours.

In the judgement scene, people are condemned, not for sins of *commission,* but for sins of *omission.* We may think we are good simply because we don't do any harm to anyone. But what about the good we fail to do?

From a Christian point of view, there is only one real failure in life – failure to love. Let us not wait for big opportunities. Let us avail of the little opportunities that come our way every day – to be friendly, to be helpful, to be considerate, to be obliging ...

Thus we may be spared the ache of loneliness and sadness which good people often experience late in life at the realisation of having left undone what they ought to have done.

Stories

1. There was a queue of people outside the gates of heaven. Each person was asked the question: 'Why do you think you should be admitted?'

The first person in the queue, a very religious man, said, 'I studied the Bible every day.' 'Very good,' said the Lord. 'However, we'll have to carry out an investigation to see why you studied the Bible. So please step aside for a moment.'

The second was a very pious woman who said, 'Lord, I said my prayers every day without fail.' 'Very good,' the Lord answered. 'However, we'll have to see if your motives were pure. So step aside for a moment.'

Then an innkeeper approached. He just said, 'Lord, on earth I wasn't a very religious man, but my door was always open to the homeless, and I never refused food to anyone who was hungry.'

'Very good,' said the Lord. 'In your case no investigation is needed. Go right in.'

It has been said that if you do a good deed, but have an ulterior motive, it would be better not to do it at all. The only exception is charity. Even though it is not as good as doing it with a pure motive, it is still a good deed, and benefits the other person, no matter what the motive.

2. In the year 1880 in Paris a rather poorly dressed priest showed up at a presbytery looking for a night's lodgings. He had come all the way from Turin, in Italy, and was trying to raise funds to build a church. The visitor's name was John Bosco, but this meant nothing to the resident priest, so he put him in the attic. Many years later when John Bosco was declared a saint by the Church, the priest said, 'Had I known it was John Bosco, I would not have put him in the attic; I would have given him the best room in the house.'

We never know exactly who it is we are meeting in the person of our neighbour. But this is not important. What is important is that we see in that person a needy human being, and that we do our best to meet his need. For those with faith, behind every face, no matter how strange, the face of Christ lies hidden.

I commend you, my dear

nto the loving arms of Saint Anthony, and I ask
him to intercede on your behalf with almighty
God, and entrust you to your Creator.

May you rest in the arms of God the Father who
formed you from the dust of the earth.
May Christ who was crucified for you,
bring you freedom and peace.
May Christ who died for you
admit you into his garden of paradise.
May Christ, the true Shepherd,
embrace you as one of his flock.
May the Blessed Virgin Mary, the angels,
and all the saints welcome you now
that you have gone forth from this life.
May God forgive all your sins
and heal all of your brokenness.
May you see your Redeemer face to face
and enjoy the vision of God, forever.
Amen.

Messenger of Saint Anthony

Basilica del Santo - Via Orto Botanico, 11
I-35123 Padua, Italy - www.santantonio.org

Solemnities

ST PATRICK
17 March

Praying with the Word of God today

INTRODUCTION AND CONFITEOR

As we celebrate the feast of St Patrick, we draw inspiration from his holy life, and give thanks for the great gift he brought us – the gift of the faith.

In all his doubts and difficulties – and he had many – Patrick turned to God for help. Let us turn to God now for the help we need to live the faith that Patrick brought us. [Pause]

Lord Jesus, you keep us constant in prayer. Lord, have mercy.

You keep us active in good works. Christ, have mercy.

You keep us true to your teaching. Lord, have mercy.

PRAYER OF THE FAITHFUL

Celebrant: God showed his love for us by sending his servant Patrick to bring the Gospel to us. Let us pray that we may be worthy of the great gift we have been given.

Response: Lord, hear our prayer.

Reader(s): For all Christians: that the depth of their faith may be evident in the way they live. [Pause] Let us pray to the Lord.

For all who hold public office: that God may guide their minds and hearts so that all may live in true peace and freedom. [Pause] Let us pray to the Lord.

For the temporal and spiritual well being of our exiles. [Pause] Let us pray to the Lord.

For our missionaries, aid-workers, and peacekeepers: that God may sustain their courage and generosity. [Pause] Let us pray to the Lord.

For those who have come to Ireland from other countries: that they may experience true Christian kindness. [Pause] Let us pray to the Lord.

For those who passed on the faith to us, and who are now deceased: that God may bring them into the light no darkness can overpower. [Pause] Let us pray to the Lord.

Celebrant: God of love, may your strength uphold us, your light guide us, and your hand protect us, so that we may walk faithfully in the footsteps of your Son, who lives and reigns with you and the Holy Spirit, one God, for ever and ever.

PRAYER/REFLECTION

PRAYER/REFLECTION

In his *Confession* St Patrick says:

'I was like a stone lying in the mud, but God, in his mercy,

pulled me out and placed me at the very top of the wall.

In the course of a single day

I would say as many as a hundred prayers.

In preaching the Gospel to the Irish,

I endured many persecutions.'

Here we see Patrick's humility, his fidelity to daily prayer,

and his spirit of sacrifice.

Lord, grant that we may draw inspiration from Saint Patrick,

and experience joy in living the faith he brought to us.

BLESSING

May the road to God's Kingdom rise to meet you, and may the wind of God's grace be behind you.

May the sun of God's love shine warmly on you, and the rain of God's mercy fall softly on you.

And until we meet here again, may the Lord God hold you in the hollow of his hand.

Sharing the Word of God today

SCRIPTURE NOTE

First Reading (Sir 39:6-10). This is a poem in praise of the person who works diligently to acquire wisdom and is committed generously to sharing that wisdom. Hearing it read at Mass on St Patrick's Day brings to mind thoughts of Patrick's deep love of Scripture. This love is evident throughout his *Confessio* where all his observations echo the words and teachings of the Bible. This passage was clearly written by someone of great learning. Patrick, by contrast, described himself as unlettered. But, like Sirach, he was filled with the spirit of understanding and he could not keep silent on how the Lord had watched over him, giving him a great array of gifts. This poem speaks to us also of our appreciation of the man who was granted wisdom and who shared that wisdom.

Second Reading (2 Tim 4:1-8). There are scholarly disputes as to whether Paul himself write this letter or whether it comes from a disciple of Paul writing in his name. Whatever the outcome of these arguments, we have here a moving record of an ageing apostle saying farewell while giving advice and support to a younger disciple. In this, Paul is handing the torch of spreading the Gospel to the next generation.

Patrick too, towards the end of his life, wrote his *Confessio* to encourage those whom he had brought to faith and to explain his own motivation and inspirations. As in the text of St Paul, there is in Patrick's writing a strong sense of commitment to the future of the community and to ensuring that the faith is shared with the next generation in all its integrity.

Gospel (Mt 13:24-32). These two parables occur in the third of the five great discourses which shape the Gospel story as Matthew presents it to us. This discourse is made up a series of parables of the kingdom, and we hear and reflect on two of them today. These parables beautifully alert us to how the spread of the Kingdom of God is God's own doing. Those who minister so as to contribute to that growth need to be patient. This patience is not a matter of being passive, but involves acknowledging the reality of God's action. We must recognise that human interventions with apparently good intentions, such as cleaning away the weeds, may in fact damage God's work.

An inspiring story

There is something deeply moving about the story of Patrick. It's a story we can all draw encouragement from. He was born into a comfortable Christian family in Britain. Just before his 16th birthday he was snatched from his comfortable home by Irish raiders, and ended up minding sheep in the west of Ireland.

The experience might have destroyed him. Instead, it made him a deeper and stronger person. And, through the providence of God, great good came from it for the Irish people.

The experience might also have extinguished the spark of faith he received from his family. But what happen? It fanned that spark into a flame. Strange as it may seem, faith often thrives in adversity.

In his *Confession* Patrick tells us that when he was a boy at home God had seemed very far away. But now that he was away from home and feeling very lonely, God became a faithful friend to him. He discovered the joy of believing, the rapture of faith in God. And daily prayer became as important to him as daily bread.

After six years in captivity he escaped, and finally returned home. The experience of slavery left no obvious scars on him. He might have settled down to a comfortable life once more and forgotten the people who had imprisoned him. Instead, he felt called by God to return to Ireland, in order, as he tells us, 'to share with them the gift God gave me in the land of my captivity' – the gift of the Christian faith.

Patrick is a saint whose life story will always be relevant. His faithfulness to his vocation is an inspiration. He was a humble man, with a friendly personality, and a great capacity to forgive. He showed great courage in the face of all kinds of trials. And he had a great love for people.

Patrick was a living example of the Gospel he preached. His lifestyle, as well as his personal integrity, lent credence to his words. Little wonder that he made so many converts.

The faith as preached by Patrick was a positive, life-giving faith. It banished many fears. It brought something new and hopeful into people's lives. It was also a challenging faith that inspired sacrifice and service in those who embraced it.

Ireland is now a much more prosperous place than when Patrick lived here. We are in danger of abandoning the faith Patrick brought to us at such great personal cost. We must strive to ensure that this doesn't happen. Living it is the best way of preserving it, and it is also the best way of spreading it.

THE ASSUMPTION OF MARY: 15 AUGUST
God raises up the lowly

Praying with the Word of God today

INTRODUCTION AND CONFITEOR

Today we celebrate the fact that the humble, lowly Mary has been raised up to glory. It is fitting that she, who shared intimately in the joyful and sorrowful mysteries of Jesus' earthly life, should share his glory in heaven.

God wants us too to share in the glory of Jesus. Let us reflect for a moment on the glory to which we are called. [Pause]

Lord Jesus, you help us to walk without stumbling on the road to your kingdom. Lord, have mercy.

You prompt the love that shapes our witness to you. Christ, have mercy.

You keep alive our hopes of eternal glory. Lord, have mercy.

PRAYER OF THE FAITHFUL

Celebrant: Let us pray to God who comes to the help of his people, and never forgets his promises.

Response: Lord, hear our prayer.

Reader(s): For Christians: that Mary may inspire them to follow Christ with courage and generosity. [Pause] Let us pray to the Lord.

For the human family: that all of God's children may share in the fruits of Christ's redemption. [Pause] Let us pray to the Lord.

For the poor and the lowly: that they may be blessed with a sense of their great dignity as God's children. [Pause] Let us pray to the Lord.

For all gathered here: that we may learn from Mary how to serve God with a generous heart and a joyful spirit. [Pause] Let us pray to the Lord.

For our deceased relatives and friends: that God may lead them to the fullness of the resurrection and gladden them with the light of his face. [Pause] Let us pray to the Lord.

For our own special needs. [Longer Pause] Let us pray to the Lord.

Celebrant: God of love, you allow us to taste on earth the joys of the world to come. Turn us away from evil, and lead us to that unfailing light where you have your dwelling. We ask this through Christ our Lord.

OUR FATHER

As God's precious daughters and sons, we are destined to share Mary's glory in heaven. Let us pray to our heavenly Father in the words our Saviour gave us.

REFLECTION

Mary was a very humble person.
Humble people receive praise and honour
the way a clean window receives the light of the sun.
The brighter and more intense the light is,
the less you see of the glass.
Mary attributed everything to God:
'The Almighty has done great things for me; holy is his name.'
Mary will help us to be humble and trusting before God.
Then God will enrich us, and we too will sing his praises.

FINAL BLESSING

May Mary be a sign of hope and comfort for you on your pilgrimage to God's kingdom.

May you seek to do God's will as faithfully as Mary did.

May you rejoice in the mercy of God, and never tire of praising him.

Sharing the Word of God today

SCRIPTURE NOTE

VIGIL MASS

First Reading (1 Chron 15:3-4.15-16; 16:1-2). It's hard to exaggerate the importance of the ark for the Israelites. It contained among other things the two tablets on which were written the Ten Commandments. Carried around from place to place, it was seen as assuring God's presence with his people.

Mary is called the 'ark of the New Covenant' because she bore within her, not words etched in stone, but the living Word of God – Jesus.

Second Reading (1 Cor 15:54-57). Here Paul celebrates Christ's victory over death, a victory that he now shares with all believers. Mary is the first to share (body and soul) in his victory.

Gospel (Lk 11:27-28). We often hear it said, 'It's not *what* you are, but *who* you are that matters'. This is more or less what the woman in the crowd was saying about Mary. But Jesus turned it around. He said that Mary was blessed, not simply because she was his mother, but because she heard the word of God and did it. Which means she was doubly blessed. And we too will be blessed if, like Mary, we hear the word of God and do it.

DAY MASS

First Reading (Rev 11:19;12:1-6.10). The Book of Revelation describes the ultimate battle between God and evil, represented here by the dragon (the serpent of Genesis). The woman represents the Church, and the child represents Christ (the Messiah). Like the woman in the vision, the Church was undergoing suffering and persecution.

The dragon confronts the woman to devour her child. But the child is taken up to God – a reference to the ascension of Jesus. Jesus defeated the dragon and was exalted to God's right hand. The woman (the Church) flees to the desert to escape the persecution. There, like the Israelites of old, she is nourished by God. The final verse praises the triumph of God and Christ.

Even though the woman in the first place represents the Church, it can also be seen as representing Mary. As the mother of Jesus, she was at the heart of the battle between God and the powers of evil. Therefore, it is entirely fitting that (through her assumption) she should share in the spoils of victory. This is something all of us aspire to.

Second Reading (1 Cor 15:20-26). Paul portrays Jesus as the new Adam, who by his obedience to God restores for us the gifts lost by the disobedience of the old Adam. The Church sees Mary as the new Eve, who by her obedience to God undoes the harm done by the old Eve.

Gospel (Lk 1:39-56). The first part of this gospel (vv. 39-45) tells the story of the visitation of Mary to Elizabeth. This is an appendage to the two annunciation stories and brings together the mothers affected by them. Enlightened by the Holy Spirit, Elizabeth praises Mary, and hints at the uniqueness of the child she has conceived.

The second part (vv. 46-56) contains Mary's song of praise to God for his goodness to her and to his chosen people. The *Magnificat* is a mosaic of Old Testament themes. It echoes Hannah's canticle after the birth of her son, Samuel (1 Sam 2:1-11). But it also looks forward, echoing the Beatitudes as found in Luke 6:20-26. It is a joyful celebration of God's preference for the humble.

Reflecting on the Vigil Readings

(This homily is based directly on the vigil readings. It aims to show why these particular readings were chosen for this feast, and the relevance they have for our lives.)

First Reading. It's hard to exaggerate the importance of the ark for the Israelites. Built according to divine instructions, it contained among other things the two tablets on which were written the Ten Commandments. Carried around from place to place, it was seen as assuring God's presence with his people. When David established Jerusalem as the political capital of the united tribes, he built a tent for it there. Note the joy the ark causes, and the respect and reverence with which the people treat it.

Mary is called the 'ark of the New Covenant' because she bore within her, not words etched in stone, but the living Word of God – Jesus. Through her the Lord not only came among us, but also actually became one of us.

We also should have a sense of the presence of God with us and within us. St Paul tells us that our bodies are temples of the Holy Spirit. This should be a cause of great joy for us.

Second Reading. In this short but powerful text Paul celebrates Christ's victory over death. Like a snake that has lost its venom, death has lost its sting and cannot destroy us. It is sin that gives death its sting, because sin can cause eternal death. But Christ has defeated the power of sin, and so has taken the sting out of death.

It is a most appropriate text for this feast. Through his resurrection Christ overcame death, not just for himself, but also for all of us. Mary is the first one to share in Christ's victory. And she shares in it soul *and* body. We too hope to share in the fullness of Christ's victory over death.

Gospel. A woman in the crowd shouted out: 'Blessed is the womb that bore you and the breasts you sucked.' The woman was saying that the mother of Jesus was a very privileged and fortunate person simply because she was his physical mother.

But Jesus responded by saying that those who hear the word of God and keep it are even more fortunate. In saying this he wasn't putting down his mother. Quite the opposite. He was saying that she was in fact doubly blessed. She was blessed because she was his physical mother, and she was blessed because she met his criterion for true discipleship – she heard the word of God and acted on it.

And we too will be blessed if, like Mary, we hear the word of God and do it. Mary will help us to hear God's word and to do it. Then we will have a spiritual kinship with Jesus, which is closer and more important than a blood relationship. This new relationship does not abolish our family ties; it transcends them.

It's not the role that honours the person; it is the person that honours the role. People are not great because of the particular role (office, task) that they have been given to play. They can become great by the way they play that role.

Sharing his glory

Once the Comaches (native American tribe) were desperate for rain. For three days they prayed to the Great Spirit to send rain to restore life to their parched land. But no rain came. The children and the old people began to die.

Then the elders of the tribe went into the hills to listen to the wind that carried the voice of God. When they returned, they said to the people, 'The drought has been caused by our selfishness. For years we have taken from the earth but given nothing back. We must all make a burnt offering to God of our most valued possession. We must scatter the ashes over the land. Then the rain will come, and life will return to the earth.'

The people thanked God for the message. But when they went home and looked at their most valued possession they hesitated, and began to make excuses. Instead of sacrificing their most valued possession they sacrificed something else in its place.

Now there was a little girl by the name of Miriam who had a blue doll that she treasured above everything else. Since she was the last child left alive, she realise that a sacrifice was being asked of her too. So one night she crept out of the camp. Taking the doll with her together with a lighted stick, she made her way to the top of the hill.

There she set fire to the doll. With tears in her eyes she watched it turn into ashes. Then she gathered the ashes into her hand and threw them into the air so that the wind scattered them over the land. Then she fell asleep right there on the hilltop.

When she awoke next morning, she looked out over the land. As far as she could see, the ground was covered with blue flowers. The people were delighted when they saw what had happened. They got the message at once.

Ashamed at their selfishness, each got out the treasure they had been guarding so carefully, sacrificed it, and scattered the ashes over the land. Once again they began to pray to God, and this time God answered. Soon a gentle rain started to fall. On seeing it, they embraced little Miriam who had shamed them into doing what God had asked of them.

This delightful story helps us to understand the role of Mary, and to appreciate why the Church honours her on this day. It was through the sacrifice of her Son that God's forgiveness, peace, and love rained down on our earth and brought life to us. Mary played a vital role in that sacrifice.

She consented to bring him into the world. She loved him tenderly and valued him above every other possession. But when the salvation of her people demanded that she sacrifice him, she did so, even though sorrow pierced her heart like a sharp sword.

Today we honour her crowning in heaven, which means that she shares body and soul in the fullness of Christ's glory. It is a day for joy and celebration. She will shame us into being more generous in following her Son, and in sacrificing what we hold dear so as to bring life to others.

Mary is blessed because she is the mother of Jesus. But she is more blessed still because, like little Miriam, she heard the word of God and obeyed it. She will help us to obey that word too, and so follow Jesus along the road that leads to glory.

True self-esteem

Elizabeth said to Mary, 'Of all women you are the most blessed.' Great praise indeed. It might have gone to Mary's head. But what happened? She denied it? No. She accepted it graciously, but attributed everything to God: 'The Almighty has done great things for me. Holy is his name.'

We may have been taught that humility involves self-depreciation. Humility is the opposite of that. Humility is the grateful recognition of our goodness, but acknowledging the source of this goodness – God.

Today in psychology and in therapy great emphasis is placed on self-esteem. The unhappiest state of all is to have low self-esteem. And the happiest state of all is to have high self-esteem. The important thing, we are told, is to feel good about ourselves, to like ourselves, to be able to say 'I'm okay.'

This approach is good – up to a point. Self-esteem is a good thing. It is important to have a good self-image, but this self-image must be founded on truth, otherwise we are building on sand.

We have every reason to have high self-esteem. We are made in God's image, and God sustains and loves us as his children. Therefore, we have every right to feel good about ourselves. But, like Mary, we owe everything to God. Hence, we should make our own Mary's beautiful and joyful prayer: 'The Almighty has done great things for me. Holy is his name.'

However, this is not the whole truth about us. We also have a dark side. We mustn't be afraid to look at the dark side of ourselves. This dark side makes us prone to evil, and we need to be saved from it. Psychology won't save us. Only God can save us.

False self-esteem makes people preoccupied with themselves, and therefore makes them self-centred. True self-esteem on the other hand helps people to forget themselves, and makes them capable of reaching out to others. We see this realised in Mary.

After hearing the wonderful words of praise from Elizabeth, she might have gone back home immediately and basked in the sunshine of approval, expecting others to wait on her. Instead she stayed on with her aged relative for three months in order to help her through her pregnancy.

Today we celebrate the glorification of Mary. Since she shared the life, passion, and death of Jesus on earth, it is fitting that she should share his glory in heaven. But we mustn't think that everything was easy for her. The opposite would be nearer the truth. She too had to live her life in the darkness of faith. For her there were no short cuts. She had to hear the word of God and *do* it.

We are called to share in the glory of Jesus. Mary, who is our spiritual mother, will help us in moments of discouragement and failure. Just because she is in heaven doesn't mean that she can't help us on earth. It is precisely because of where she is now, with God, that she can help us.

ALL SAINTS
1 November

Praying with the Word of God today

INTRODUCTION AND CONFITEOR

Today we honour all the saints, but especially the unrecognised ones. When we look at the saints, we see the seeds of our own possibilities.

While the saints inspire us, they also frighten us a little because they remind us how much it costs to be what God wants us to be.

Let us call to mind the sins that hold us back from following in the footsteps of the saints. [Pause]

Lord Jesus, you inspire us by their heroic lives. Lord, have mercy.

You help us by their constant prayers. Christ, have mercy.

From their place in heaven they guide us still. Lord, have mercy.

PRAYER OF THE FAITHFUL

Celebrant: Let us pray to God for those qualities Jesus wants to see in his followers, qualities exemplified in the lives of the saints.

Response: Lord, hear our prayer.

Reader(s): For Christians: that the saints may inspire them to live by the values of the Gospel. [Pause] Let us pray to the Lord.

For all in positions of authority: that God may bless them with wisdom and integrity. [Pause] Let us pray to the Lord.

For the poor and the lowly: that they may know the blessedness of those who put their trust in God. [Pause] Let us pray to the Lord.

For those who are working for peace: that their efforts may bear fruit. [Pause] Let us pray to the Lord.

For those who suffer for doing what is right: that they may be brave and strong. [Pause] Let us pray to the Lord.

For all gathered here: that we may draw strength from the example of the heroes and saints who have gone before us. [Pause] Let us pray to the Lord.

For those who have died and whose lives have been an inspiration to us: that the Lord may reward them for their goodness. [Pause] Let us pray to the Lord.

For our own special needs. [Longer pause] Let us pray to the Lord.

Celebrant: God of mercy, you have given us a host of friends in heaven. Grant that we may follow their footsteps on earth and have fellowship with them in the joy of heaven. We make all our prayers through Christ our Lord.

OUR FATHER

We are God's chosen ones, holy and beloved. Let us pray to our heavenly Father as Jesus taught us.

REFLECTION

The beatitudes are the badges of a disciple of Jesus.
The things they stand for are very beautiful –
things such as peace, goodness, joy, love,
gentleness, compassion, mercy, and integrity.
A person who lives according to the beatitudes
is already living in the kingdom of heaven.
Eternal life will merely be the full blossoming
of a plant that is green with life.

FINAL BLESSING

May the Lord confirm your hearts in holiness so that you may be blameless in his sight.

May you live a life worthy of God, who is calling you to share the glory of his kingdom.

May you be inspired by the example of the saints, and supported by their prayers.

Sharing the Word of God today

SCRIPTURE NOTE

First Reading (Rev 7:2-4.9-14). Here we have a vision of the victorious followers of Christ rejoicing in his presence in the heavenly Kingdom. Pride of place goes to the martyrs. They receive immediately their white robes of victory; palm branches are a symbol of triumph and joy. But the martyrs stand for all faithful Christians.

It was visions such as this that inspired the saints. It should inspire us to follow in their footsteps in the hope of sharing the glory of the Lord.

Second Reading (1 Jn 3:1-3). In his love for us, God has made us his children, and destined us one day to see him as he is. We should live a life that is consistent with this great hope.

Gospel (Mt 5:1-12). The Sermon on the Mount contains the essence of Christ's teaching. The Beatitudes are the essence of that essence. They list the qualities Christ wishes to see in his followers, qualities that are exemplified in the lives of the saints.

The beatitudes are the badges of a disciple of Jesus. The things they stand for are very beautiful – things such as peace, goodness, joy, love, gentleness, compassion, mercy, integrity … A person who lives according to the beatitudes is already living in the kingdom of heaven. Eternal life will merely be the full blossoming of a plant that is green with life.

The Beatitudes

In the Beatitudes we see the qualities Jesus wishes to see in his disciples, qualities that are exemplified in the lives of the saints.

These qualities are a complete reversal of conventional standards and values. (Two voices could be used in presenting what follows).

The world says: Happy are you who put your trust in money. Be glad and rejoice when it is coming in fast. You'll be the envy of all.

Jesus says: Happy are you who put your trust in God. Remember that it's not the amount of money you possess that makes you rich, but what you are in the sight of God.

The world says: Happy are you who are hard and ruthless. People will be afraid of you, and you'll get results.

Jesus says: Happy are you who are gentle and kind, and who refuse to get on by trampling on others. Gentleness is a form of strength. There are many vital tasks which only gentleness can accomplish.

The world says: Happy are you who live it up. Remember you only live once. So let your hair down. You'll have great fun.

Jesus says: Happy are you who remember that the most valuable things in life have to be bought with pain and sacrifice. You who don't confuse real happiness with passing thrills. Even though you may sow in tears, you will sing when you reap.

The world says: Happy are you who hunger for power, status, and fame. You will always be in the limelight.

Jesus says: Happy are you who have standards and values, and who are prepared to live up to them. You who realise that to live rightly is what life is about. Those who rate this as important as eating and drinking will taste real happiness even here on earth.

The world says: Happy are you who show no tolerance to those who make mistakes, and no mercy to those who oppose you. You'll be the boss, and everybody will know it.

Jesus says: Happy are you who make allowance for the sins of others, and whose greatness lies in your ability to forgive. The sun of God's mercy will shine warmly on you.

The world says: Happy are you whose main concern is to have a clean skin, and who keep up to date with the latest style in clothes. You'll be really with it.

Jesus says: Happy are you whose main concern is to have a clean heart. It is from the heart that all our thoughts, words, and deeds flow. If the heart is clean, all that flows from it will be like water flowing from an unpolluted spring.

The world says: Happy are you troublemakers and warmongers. People will fear you, and you will get sensational headlines.

Jesus says: Happy are you peacemakers. You who spread understanding among people, who welcome the stranger, and who work for a just society. You are true children of God.

The world says: Happy are you who don't hesitate to lie, steal, and cheat, and who manage to get off scot-free. You'll have a great laugh over a pint with your cronies.

Jesus says: Happy are you who make a stand for what is right. If you suffer for your stand, the wounds you bear will be honourable wounds, and will mark you out as true disciples of mine. You will gain honour on earth and glory in heaven.

The Beatitudes are the standards by which we measure holiness. A person who lives according to the beatitudes is already living in the kingdom of heaven. Does one need to have all eight of them? I doubt if a single saint had them all. Only Jesus had them all. We don't have to have them all. Any one of them, lived to the full, will suffice.

How not to imitate the saints

Today in popular psychology (and indeed in spirituality) great emphasis is put on *finding* oneself. But there is something more important, namely, *being* oneself, or better, *becoming* oneself. Society is no help here. It encourages us in so many ways to act and look like someone else. (The following two stories address this issue. One of them is enough to use at a time.)

1. Simon was a young monk who wished to live a holy life. He decided to model himself on Francis of Assisi. He was deadly serious about it. He had only one goal in life – to turn himself into a copy of Saint Francis.

Years went by. There was no doubt but that outwardly at least he had made progress. His friends jokingly referred to him as a 'Saint Francis look-alike'. Yet he wasn't happy. In his unhappiness he went to consult an old monk by the name of Barnabas. Barnabas listened patiently as Simon poured out his story. When he had finished he said:

'Simon, you have chosen an excellent model. But a model is not a mould into which we pour ourselves. A model is a spur to help us to be true to what is within us, to what is given to us and only to us. Simon, you have been living outside yourself. You have been playing a part written for another.

'The most important task in life is to become ourselves. Unless we become ourselves, no growth, no happiness, no holiness is possible. But when we become ourselves, then everything about us becomes real and true. Francis of Assisi became a saint, not by becoming someone else, but by becoming his true and full self.

'Simon, when you come before the Lord on the day of judgement, he won't ask you, "Why didn't you become Francis of Assisi?" He will ask you, "Why didn't you become what Simon was intended to be?"'

2. When the legendary Bill Shankley retired as manager of Liverpool Football Club, Bob Paisley was appointed to succeed him. Realising that it would be a hard act to follow, the soft-spoken, retiring Paisley at first refused the job. However, after a lot of persuasion, he agreed to accept it.

It truly was an onerous job to take over from someone who was as successful as Bill Shankley. Liverpool not only prided itself on success on the football field, but on possessing a special approach off it. The manager, the players, and the ladies who made the tea – all felt part of a great family. That's how the Club was run.

Hence, there was enormous pressure on Paisley to be another Bill Shankley. But he resisted the temptation. Instead, he brought his own style to the job. He managed to continue the traditions of the Club, while remaining the unique individual he was. And he went on to become even more successful than Shankley.

When he retired he was asked what the key to his success was. He replied, 'There is no way you can imitate someone else and be great. You've got to be yourself.' Wise words.

Many religious people are not saints because they never succeed in being themselves. To be a saint one doesn't have to be an ascetic, or even serious and solemn. But one has to be oneself. Anyone who would lead a Christlike life must be entirely and absolutely himself.

Saints help us to do this, even the little ones. They cause the vision of a higher and purer life to rise up before us. They inspire us to try to win back our finer, kinder and healthier selves.

They provide us with a mirror. Looking at them, we see what we could be. In them we see human beings at their brightest and best. They are examples, teachers, friends, and advocates.

Each person is born in only one copy and when he/she dies no one can take his/her place. Whatever our path in life, what really matters is that we should be ourselves, our unique selves, but the best that we can be – the kind of people God intended us to be. This is the journey home.

Being the genuine article

Tropical woods such as mahogany and teak are very beautiful. They are beautiful as they are, that is, in their natural state. They should never be painted. It would be a sin to cover up their natural beauty. If anything is added it should serve one purpose and one purpose only – to bring out the natural beauty of the wood.

Yet sometimes one finds them painted, presumably with the aim of making them more attractive. Even when this is done tastefully and imaginatively, harm rather than good results. The finished object comes across as false, or at least unreal. And while it may be pretty, it is not authentic. Tropical woods are best left as they are. They are far more interesting and impressive in their natural state.

Beautiful wood is a gift from God. To paint over it is akin to desecration. The role of the cabinet-maker is to enhance the beauty inherent in the wood, not to obscure it with paint.

There is a tendency to do something similar with the saints. We tend to so polish up the image that their humanity disappears. They cease to be human beings. But if they cease to be human, they become unreal and unbelievable.

The saints didn't become saints by putting on a false or artificial self. To be a saint one doesn't have to be an ascetic, or even serious and solemn. But one has to be one's true self. The best way to imitate the saints is to be ourselves, our unique selves, but the best that we can be.

The role of spirituality is not to cover-up. Its purpose is to bring out what is inside us. Grace builds on nature. It doesn't destroy nature, but brings it to its fullest development.

When a person combines true religion and deep humanity, you have a powerful combination. It's like well-polished mahogany. Here you have true holiness. Such people are other Christs.

Even the little saints cause the vision of a higher and a purer life to rise up before us. They inspire us to try to win back our finer and kinder selves. They expand the possibilities of human love and courage.

Piety is no substitute for goodness. Perhaps there can be goodness without holiness. But I'm quite sure that there is no holiness without goodness. Since we are made in God's image, all of us have the capacity for goodness. The saints show us how to express this goodness.

Our real goal is not to strive for happiness but for goodness. If we strive for goodness, happiness will follow. There are good people who ache with loneliness and a feeling of sadness for having left undone what they ought to have done. This is the sadness we all feel at times – the sadness of not being saints.

The pedestal

One of the worst things we can do to someone is to place him/her on a pedestal. Let us listen to what it feels like to be on a pedestal.

I'm up here on this pedestal, not able to touch or be touched. I admit that in the beginning I liked it. It's nice to be noticed and regarded. It's certainly better than lying in some dark corner, forsaken and forgotten.

But gradually I came to dislike it. It's terrible to feel that you are always on display. People expect you to be perfect. You end up a prisoner of peoples' expectations.

Right now, I hate being up here. I'm obliged to behave in ways that are false. At times I feel like flinging myself from this pedestal. How wonderful it would be to experience even a moment's relief from the necessity of being perfect.

People who admire and praise me don't know me any better than those who despise and criticise me. I have enemies too, you know. Some of these are just envious of me. They think I'm having a wonderful time up here. Others say that it was I who put myself up here, because I felt superior and wanted to show off.

Being up here makes me vulnerable before my friends *and* my enemies, because my faults are on display as well as my virtues. Were I to fall off, my friends would be very disappointed. Some of them would never forgive me. As for my enemies, how they would rejoice to see me fall. The greater the fall, the happier they would be. I'm sick of it all. I just wish people would allow me to be myself.

There is a tendency to put the saints on such an exalted pedestal that we feel justified in excusing ourselves from imitating them. Biographers have tended to concentrate on the exemplary in their lives to the exclusion of anything approaching weakness or sin. But that is to remove their humanity. The tendency to idealise the saints leads to a distortion. 'You don't have to be an angel to be a saint' (Albert Schweitzer).

The saints were made of flesh and blood. They were human beings with human flaws. They were vulnerable to the same temptations as us. God did not spare them the bumps, bruises, and scars that mark all our lives. They were not perfect people. It's just that their over-all goodness overshadowed their sins and mistakes. They serve as models precisely because they were sinners like us. In them we see the triumph of grace over human weakness and sinfulness.

The Church holds them up as models, not merely to arouse our admiration for them, but for us to imitate them. Here lies the challenge. To look at the saints is to get a vision of what we ourselves might become. All we need is the will to walk in the light of what we have seen.

THE IMMACULATE CONCEPTION
8 December

Praying with the Word of God today

INTRODUCTION AND CONFITEOR

On this feast we celebrate the holiness of Mary. From the first moment of her existence, she walked in the light of God's grace.

We are called to walk in that same light. But our souls are darkened by original sin and personal sin. Let us call to mind the sins that darken our lives. [Pause] Let us turn to the Lord who is our light and our help.

Lord Jesus, you free us from the darkness of our sins. Lord, have mercy.

You help us to walk in the light of truth and goodness. Christ, have mercy.

You help us to live in the freedom of the children of God. Lord, have mercy.

PRAYER OF THE FAITHFUL

Celebrant: God's mercy reaches from age to age for those who revere him. Let us bring our needs before God with confidence, knowing that Mary is praying with us and for us.

Response: Lord, hear our prayer.

Reader(s): For Christians: that they may accept the word of God in faith, and obey it as Mary did. [Pause] Let us pray to the Lord.

For all who hold public office: that in a world darkened by pride and selfishness, they may set an example of humble and generous service. [Pause] Let us pray to the Lord.

For those who are suffering or grieving: that Mary, who stood at the foot of the cross as her Son died, may comfort and console them. [Pause] Let us pray to the Lord.

For all women: that the Church and society may give them their rightful place and role. [Pause] Let us pray to the Lord.

For our deceased relatives and friends: that they may dwell in the house of the Lord for ever. [Pause] Let us pray to the Lord.

For our own special needs. [Longer Pause] Let us pray to the Lord.

Celebrant: God our Father, in Mary you gave us an example to follow. Living in a sinful world, she shared the pain of the world but not its sin, and so became a worthy mother for your Son, who lives and reigns with you and the Holy Spirit, one God, for ever and ever.

OUR FATHER

God humbles the proud and exalts the humble. Let us pray to our heavenly Father in the words our Saviour gave us.

PRAYER/REFLECTION

Mary didn't live a sheltered life.
On the contrary, she travelled the path of human existence
with all its darkness and pain.
She is a model of faith and fidelity.
Her life was characterised by a loving service
of God and of neighbour.
Lord, help us to imitate the faith and love of Mary,
and guide us through the sorrows of this world
to the joys of the kingdom where you live and reign
for ever and ever.

FINAL BLESSING

May the faith and love of Mary inspire you to serve God more faithfully.

May the prayers of Mary bring you protection and enable you to do God's will with gladness.

And may the sorrows of Mary enable you to bear your own sorrows with courage and hope.

Sharing the Word of God today

SCRIPTURE NOTE

First Reading (Gen 3:9-15.20). This tells part of story of the fall of Adam and Eve. Their sin had very serious consequences. Firstly, it damaged their relationship with God. Before their sin they enjoyed a beautiful closeness to God. Afterwards they are trying to hide from God. Secondly, it damaged their relationship with one another. Before their sin they enjoyed harmony with one another. After it a breakdown occurs between them, and they start to blame one another for what happened.

But the story has a hopeful ending because it includes a promise of salvation. Mary had a major role to play in that salvation. That is why this reading is chosen for today's feast.

Second Reading (Eph 1:3-6.11-12). This reminds us that God, in his graciousness, has an eternal plan of salvation for humankind. In Christ we have become God's adopted children. As his children we are called to holiness. All holiness comes through Christ.

Gospel (Lk 1:26-38). God's promise of salvation was fulfilled in Jesus. By her 'yes' to God, Mary opened the way for the Saviour to come into the world. She is the new Eve. With her perfect obedience, she cancelled out the disobedience of the first Eve.

Mary keeps the vocation of holiness before us, and serves as a model for us. She is blessed, not simply because she was the mother of Jesus, but because she heard the word of God and did it. We too will be blessed if, like Mary, we hear the word of God and do it.

Reflecting on the Readings

(This homily is based directly on the readings. It aims to show why these particular readings were chosen for this feast, and the relevance they have for our lives.)

First Reading: This tells part of story of the fall of Adam and Eve, a story which deals with the origin and consequences of sin. God gave Adam and Eve the freedom to choose good or evil. But they chose evil. To choose evil is to abuse freedom. Sin consists in disobedience to God.

Their sin had very serious consequences. Firstly, it damaged their relationship with God. Before their sin they enjoyed a beautiful closeness to God. We have the image of them walking with God in the cool of the evening. But after their sin, that closeness is no more. Now they are trying to hide from God. Sin damages our relationship with God.

Secondly, sin damaged their relationship with one another. Before their sin they enjoyed harmony with one another. After it a breakdown occurs between them, and they start to blame one another for what happened. Sin damages our relationships too.

All of this came as a result of their sin, and as a punishment for it. But it wasn't God who punished them. They brought it on themselves. It is not God who changed but they. We are not punished *for* our sins, but *by* our sins.

And like children who have done wrong, Adam and Eve tried to hide rather than face the consequences of what they had done. But God came looking for them and confronted them about it. He did this out of love for them. God confronts us too when we do wrong through the still, small voice of conscience, or through the voice of others.

But the story has a hopeful ending because it includes a promise of salvation. And this is the main reason why this reading is used on this feast.

Second Reading: This reminds us that God, in his graciousness, has an eternal plan of salvation for humankind. Through Christ, God has adopted us as his children, and called us to holiness. This feast reminds us of that call.

Gospel: This shows that God's promise of salvation was fulfilled in Jesus. And Mary had a vital part to play in that. By her 'yes' to God, she opened the way for the God's Saviour to come into the world.

Christ is the new Adam. Unlike the first Adam, he obeyed God and conquered Satan. Through his death and resurrection he undid the first Adam's sin and its evil effects. In the Immaculate Conception, he conquered sin first of all in his own mother.

And Mary is the new Eve. With her perfect obedience, she cancelled out the disobedience of the first Eve, when she said, 'Let it be done to me according to your word.' In this way she became a model for believers. She is the 'handmaid of the Lord'. This is how she is portrayed in the Gospel.

In Christ we have become God's adopted children. As God's children we are called to holiness. All holiness comes through Christ.

Mary attained to holiness by obedience to God. She keeps the vocation of holiness before us, and serves as a model for us. She is blessed, not simply because she was the mother of Jesus, but because she heard the word of God and did it.

And we will be blessed too if, like Mary, we hear the word of God and do it. Mary will help us to do this. Then we too will be responding to the call of holiness.

Mary's sinlessness

The feast of the Immaculate Conception underlines the radical holiness of Mary. The angel Gabriel addressed her as 'full of grace'. Because she was chosen to become the mother of the Saviour, God enriched her with gifts appropriate for such a role. Right from the beginning of her existence she was free from any stain of original sin. She was the first one to receive the fruits of the redemption.

But Mary's Immaculate Conception does not remove her from us. The gift of freedom from original sin is a gift given to all disciples of Jesus in baptism. Through baptism *we* are delivered from original sin.

We believe that Mary was not only conceived free from original sin but that, by the grace of God, she remained free of every personal sin her whole life long. Now there is a suggestion that unless we know sin, we are not human. When someone falls you hear people say, 'Ah, sure he's only human.' Thus we use humanness as an excuse for laziness, carelessness, and selfishness.

The fact that Mary didn't sin does not imply any lack of humanness. Mary was wholly human. Sin is not an intrinsic ingredient of humanness. Quite the contrary. Sin is a fall from humanness. Sin is blindness, sin is ignorance, and sin is absence of love. Far from understanding more of human life because we sin, we understand less of it. Sin separates us from others, and imprisons us in our own selfishness.

Mary had the freedom to choose evil rather than good. It wasn't that she couldn't sin, but that she chose not to sin. But we might say, 'It was easy for Mary!' It wasn't easy for her. She too had to struggle to do the will of God. Mary's sinlessness does not remove her from us. In her sinlessness she is the image of what the Church desires to be, and what we should desire to be.

We must seek to be ever more free from evil and guilt. As we celebrate God's mercy towards her, we are strengthened in our personal hope to receive that same mercy which will also keep us free from sin.

Mary understands our struggles and our weakness. Every day we are faced with choices: to do good or to do evil. We have in us a strain of re-belliousness, of self-centredness, of shortsightedness, which causes us to make the wrong choices. But with the grace of God we can make the right choices. Even though there is no once- and-for-all victory over evil, every right choice makes the next right choice easier.

Images of Mary

Many people have a completely unreal image of Mary. It's as if she never got her hands dirty, never made mistakes, never experienced doubt or fear, never had to struggle against evil, and so on. Because of this we find it hard to see how she could serve as a model for us. Donald Nicholl would have included himself in this category until something happened to him.

Donald Nicholl was an English Catholic (a convert), and a very good one. He died of cancer in 1997. As a lecturer, he spent most of his life in universities. From 1981 to 1985 he was Rector of the Ecumenical Institute at Tantur, near Jerusalem. The experience of being in the Holy Land served as an eye-opener to him in many ways, but one in particular. It changed his image of Mary forever.

In his book, *The Testing of Hearts,* he tells us that prior to going to the Holy Land his image of Mary was derived from famous paintings, poems, and music. His image was that of 'some dreamy, ethereal young lady, un-touched by human toil'. But after meeting the peasant women of Galilee he formed a very different image of Mary.

He says: 'The image which now comes spontaneously to mind is of a woman with strong hands, sinewy through much work; of a face whose skin is rough from exposure to the sun and wind; of feet that are broad-spread through climbing the hills around Nazareth barefoot; but above all, of eyes that are steady, and a mouth that is firm, through enduring the sorrows of the refugee, the poor, and the oppressed.'

Mary didn't live a sheltered life. She was a woman of the world, and a strong woman. Strength is not the same as power. One could enjoy great power and yet be very weak. And one might have no power at all and yet be very strong.

Women at their best can be very caring and loyal. They have a different kind of strength to men. Their strength is less obvious, less showy, and is allied to apparent fragility. It is longer lasting. It is marked by grit, shrewdness, patience, courage, and steely determination. This kind of strength may often go unnoticed. Indeed, it may even be seen as weakness. But nothing could be further from the truth.

Mary possessed this kind of strength. Like most mothers, she had remarkable powers of endurance and survival, overcame disappointment and distress, was dogged but not insensitive, and seemed always capable of renewing herself, no matter what misfortune hit her.

We honour her sinlessness on this feast. But this must not be seen as something negative. It is something positive. Mary was a loving, caring and compassionate person. That is where her holiness lay. And that is where our holiness must lie too, because we too are called to holiness. There can be no holiness without goodness.

Mary is a model not just for mothers but also for all Christians. She understands all those who struggle with the demands of ordinary, decent, human living in a world that sometimes makes little sense. And she understands, and is especially supportive of, those who try to be faithful followers of her Son, Jesus.